PREFACE

    This verbatim transcription of the Minutes of the County Court of Pleas and Quarter Sessions of Gates County, from 1832 through 1836, was made from North Carolina State Archives Microfilm Reel C.041.30003, Gates County Court Minutes, 1827-1850.

    The original records of Gates County have fared far better than those of its parent counties of Chowan, Hertford and Perquimans. It was formed in 1779, and is bordered on the north by Nansemond County, now Independent City of Suffolk, Virginia. Prior to 1728, when William Byrd surveyed the line between North Carolina and Virginia, most of present-day Gates County lay in Nansemond County. That part of it was cut off to Chowan County at that time. All the land above Gatesville, and to the west of Bennett's Creek, was cut off to Hertford at its formation in 1759. Both Nansemond County, Virginia, and Hertford County, North Carolina, suffered devastating record losses on several occasions. Researchers are left with a 20-year gap in records between 1759 and 1779. Many families of both counties resided in Gates County, after its formation, where the records are well preserved.

    The minutes contain appointment of administrators, auditors of accounts, guardians, constables, patrolmen, overseers of the roads, sheriffs and justices of the peace. They record guardian returns, apprenticeship and bastardy bonds, jury lists, civil suits, orders for registration of bills and deeds of sale, probate of wills, allotments of dower and provisions for widows and families for one year after the death of the head of the household.

    For indexing purposes, each original page has been assigned a number, enclosed in brackets. Where the original page numbers exist, they are recorded to the right of the assigned number and are also underlined. Only odd pages are numbered in the first original book. Even-numbered pages are denoted by "<u>blank</u>" in this transcript.

    There were several clerks recording the minutes, at different times. Their styles and handwriting vary a great deal, which produced a number of "look-alike" letters and words. Some of the former are a=o; c=e; i=e; u=o; I=J; L=S; O=A; T=Y; Benton, or Winton, and David, or Daniel. Blended letters are "ar;" "un;" "on;" "om;" "or;" "ir;" and "iw."

    Punctuation was virtually non-existent and the quill pen touched the paper between words, giving the appearance of numerous periods within a sentence. They have been included in the transcription and may help the reader distinguish among the several different writers, but are not to be interpreted as punctuation.

    Marginal notations of """ and "issd" are typed in italics. They may appear more than once in any given entry, but all but the initial appearance have been omitted in the interest of continuity of the text. "/the/" denotes interlined words; "__est" denotes missing letters and "[?]" denotes doubt of accuracy. Spelling was not standardized and is so noted by underlining of stray letters, such as "audit<u>e</u>."

    Readers are strongly encouraged to consult the original documents in order to assess the accuracy of this transcript and form their own conclusions.

    All names are listed in the Name Index, including all spellings. Female names, as well as those of the decedents mentioned, are listed again in their own separate indexes. Females "of colour" are denoted by [C] after their names. The Miscellaneous Index includes various county officials, building and maintenance of the court house, diseases and newspapers. The location index includes all bridges, churches, ferries, mills, named roads, states, taverns, towns and watercourses.

    Blacks have been indexed under "Negroes," the term in use at the creation of these records. The single names are of slaves. "Of colour" may well indicate either Native-American heritage, or African-American. Many are noted to be "free," within the text.

CONTENTS

February Court 1832	1
May Court 1832	13
August Court 1832	21
November Court 1832	27
February Court 1833	32
May Court 1833	43
August Court 1833	50
November Court 1833	55
February Court 1834	62
May Court 1834	71
August Court 1834	78
November Court 1834	83
February Court 1835	89
May Court 1835	99
August Court 1835	105
November Court 1835	109
February Court 1836	114
May Court 1836	123
August Court 1836	132
November Court 1836	138
Decedent Index	145
Female Index	149
Name Index	153
Miscellaneous Index	173
Location Index	175

MINUTES OF COUNTY COURT OF PLEAS AND QUARTER SESSIONS

GATES COUNTY, NORTH CAROLINA

1832-1836

[1] 219 State of North Carolina.   February 20th. 1832.
At a Court of Pleas and Quarter Sessions, begun and held for the County of Gates at the Court House in Gatesville on the third monday of February in the Fifty sixth Year of our Independence, and in the year of our Lord One thousand Eight hundred and thirty two.
Present   Whitmell **STALLINGS** W^m. W. **COWPER** William **WALTON** Henry **GILLIAM** Esquires Justices

Grand Jury qualified at this Term to wit Lemuel **RIDDICK** Foreman Robert **WILSON**, Andrew **HARRELL**, Jethro **HARRELL** Reuben **PARKER**, Marmaduke **BAKER**, Lemuel **HOWELL**, Bryant **HARE**, Miles **BROWN**, Charles **WILLIAMS** Jeremiah **WHITE**, Joseph **HURDLE** of Abm. Joseph **HURDLE**, Jr., Abram **SPIVEY**, Jonas **HINTON**, Willis **BUNCH**

Pursuant to a Commission from Montfort **STOKES** Esqr. Governor for appointing Thomas **SAUNDERS**, Hardy D. **PARKER** and Richard **ODOM** Justices of the peace for this County, they came into Court and was duly Qualified for that Office by taking and subscribing the necessary Oaths prescribed by Law &c

[2] blank Ordered that administration upon the estate of Henry **PUGH** dec^d. be granted to William E. **PUGH** he giving a bond in the penalty of $6000 with John O. **HUNTER** Mills **ROBERTS**, Henry R. **PUGH**, John **MATTHEWS** and Willis **COWPER** Jr. securities

Ordered that Robert **ROGERS** have Letters of administration on the estate of Elizabeth **ROGERS** dec^d. and that he give bond for $5000—Levi **ROGERS** and John W. **ODOM** securities.

Ordered that Frederick **HINTON** Jr. be granted Letters of administration on the estate of Sarah **LEWIS** dec^d. and that he give bond for $500. Noah **HINTON** and John **ALPHIN** securities.

Ordered that Chitty **JONES** be appointed Guardian to Louisa **JONES** & Henry **JONES**, orphans of Henry **JONES** dec^d. and that she give bond for $3000 each William **LEE** and Dempsey S. **GOODMAN** securities Present in Court Whitmel **STALLINGS** Peter B. **MINTON** & Riddick **GATLING** Esquires Justices were present in Court & approved of the securities & concured in the appointment.

Ordered that Thomas **TWINE** be appointed guardian for Sophia **EASON** & Temble **EASON** orphans of Hardy **EASON** dec^d. and that he give bond for each $5000. Joseph **GORDON** & Tilly W. **CARR** securities Present in Court Whitmell **STALLINGS**, P. B. **MINTON**, W^m. W. **COWPER** Esquire Justices who approved of the securities & concured in the appointment.

Ordered that Humphrey **PARKER** be appointed Guardian for Christain **SMALL** orphan of Moses H. **SMALL** dec^d. and that he give bond for $150. Tilly W. **CARR** & John O. **HUNTER** offers themselves

1

February Court 1832

securities. Present in Court Peter B **MINTON** Whitmel **STALLINGS** & John **WILLY** Esquires Justices who approved of the securities & concurred in the appointment.

Ordered that John **ODOM** be appointed Guardian to Prissilla **ODOM** orphan of Benjamin **ODOM** deceased and that he give bond for $1000. Robert **ROGERS** and Levi **ROGERS** offered themselves securities. Present in Court Whitmel **STALLINGS**, Peter B. **MINTON**, Riddick **GATLING** Esquires Justices who approved of the securities & concurred in the appointment.

[3] 221 Ordered that Edwin **SMITH** be appointed Guardian to Henrietta **COPELAND** orphan of Henry **COPELAND** dec^d. and that he give bond for $3.000 Hardy **PARKER** & George **KITTRELL** offered themselves securities. Present in Court Peter B **MINTON**, Joseph **RIDDICK** W^m. W. **COWPER** and W^m. **WALTON** Esquires Justices who approved of the securities & concurred in the appointment.

Ordered that Mills **PILAND** be appointed Guardian [sic] Susan **PILAND**, John **PILAND** & Milly **PILAND** orphans of Elisha **PILAND** dec^d. and that he give bond for 500 dollars each. Dempsey **PARKER** & Willis **CROSS** offered themselves securities. Present in Court Peter B. **MINTON**, John **WILLY** and Whitmell **STALLINGS** Esquirs Justices who approved of the securities & concured in the appointment.

issd Ordered that Thomas **SAUNDERS**, William **PUGH** & Henry **GILLIAM** make a division among the heirs entitled to receive their portion of the am^t. lately recovered in the Supreme Court, in the case of John **SPEIGHT** adm^r. de bonis non of Henry **SPEIGHTS** [sic] against James **GATLING**s administrator.

issd. Ordered that Hillory **WILLY** John D. **PIPKIN** Dempsey S. **GOODMAN** & William **GOODMAN** make a division of the estate of Jonathan **ROGERS** dec^d. amongst the heirs at law & report.

issd. Ordered that Hillory **WILLY**, John D. **PIPKIN** Dempsey S. **GOODMAN** & William **GOODMAN** audite State & settle the estate of Elizabeth **ROGERS** dec^d. with Robert **ROGERS** her admr. & report

issd. Ordered that the same men make a division of said estate amongst the heirs at law agreeable to law &c

issd. Ordered that William **HARRELL** senr. Thomas B. **HUNTER**, John C. **GORDON** & David **PARKER** or any three of them audite State and Settle the estate of Hardy **EASON** dec^d. with Joseph **GORDON** admr and also the said men make a division of the personal & Perishable estate of said Hardy **EASON** deceased.

issd. Ordered that Jethro H **RIDDICK** Nathan **RIDDICK** Abel **ROGERON** [sic] & Whitmell **STALLINGS** or any three of them Audite State and settle the estate of Thomas **HOBBS** dec^d. with Amos **HOBBS** his Executor & Report to next Court.

Issd. Ordered that the above named men make a division of said estate amongst the Heirs at law.

issd Ordered that Elizabeth **BRISCO** be allowed One Black Poll in setling her Taxes which was charged to her through mistake.

issd. Ordered that Nathan **RIDDICK**, Joseph **RIDDICK** & Jethro H. **RIDDICK** audite State and Settle the estate of Henry **WALTON** deceased & Report to next term.

[4] blank Ordered that the Clerk issue an Execution against James D **WYNNS** for the Commissioners & surveyor fees in the Case of **WYNNS** against **VANN** including sheriffs fees.

issd. Ordered that Benjamin **SUMNER** be allowed forty dollars for his services as States attorney for the County of Gates.

Ordered that Isaiah **RIDDICK** be exempt from serving as a Juror for life.

Ordered that William W **POWELL** renew his Contables [sic] bond he Offers Abraham **MORGAN** sen^r.

February Court 1832

and John **WIGGINS** as his securities.

Ordered that Joseph **RIDDICK** streighten a piece of road on his own Land Called the **BRIGGS** place, and that he put said road in good order and deliver it to the Overseer of said road.

issd. Ordered that William **GOODMAN**, William **LEE**s & Frank **DUKE**s hands be given to W^m. **GOODMAN** to work the road from Piney Grove to Capt. **LEE**s Mill.

issd. Ordered that Robt. **SMITH** dec^d. hands return to Robert **ROGERS**es road leading from the va. line to Mrs **HARVEY**s mill

recorded The Last will and Testament of Robert **TAYLOR** dec^d. was exhibited into Court and was proved by the Oath of Simon **STALLINGS**, one of the subscribing witness [sic] thereto and Ordered to be recorded. The Executrix and Executor therein named, came into Court was duly qualified for that Office and prayed an Order for letters testamentary thereon.

recorded The Last will and Testament of Abraham **BEEMAN** dec^d. was exhibited into Court and was proved by the Oaths of W^m. L. **BOOTHE** and Mills **EURE** two of the subscribing witnesses thereto and Ordered to be recorded. The Executors therein appointed, Came into Court and was duly qualified for that Office and prayed an Order for letters testamentary thereon which was accordingly granted.

recorded The last will and Testament of Mathias **MORGAN** dec^d. was exhibited into and [sic] was proved by the Oath of William W. **RIDDICK** one of the subscribing witnesses thereto and Ordered to be recorded. The Executor therein therein [sic] appointed Came into Court and was duly qualified for that office and prayed an Order for letters testamentary thereon which was accordingly granted.

[5] 223 *recorded* The Last Will and testament of Milley **PILAND** dec^d. was exhibited into Court and was proved by the Oaths of Thomas **HOGGARD** and Wiley **CARTER** two of the subscribing witness [sic] thereto and Ordered to be recorded. Isaac **PILAND** the executor therein appointed was duly qualified for that Office-and prayed an Order for letters testamentary thereon which was granted.

" James **BOOTHE** Guardian to the Orphans of Benj^a **ODOM** dec^d. exhibited into Court his accounts with said Orphans on Oath &c.

" Exum **JENKINS** Guardian to the Orphans of Ira **ODOM** dec^d. exhibited into Court his accounts with said orphans on Oath &c.

" Thomas **TWINE** Guardian to Isaac **HUNTER** orphan of Isaac **HUNTER** dec^d. exhibited into Court his account with said Orphan on Oath &c.

" Hardy D. **PARKER** Guardian to the Orphans of James **WIGGINS** dec^d. exhibited into Court his accounts with said Orphans on Oath &c

" Jesse **PILAND** Guardian to James **PILAND** orphan of Jas. **PILAND** dec^d. exhibited into Court his account with said orphan on Oath &c

" Leve [sic] **ROGERS** Guardian to Mary **WILLIAMS** orphan of Halon **WILLIAMS** dec^d. exhibited into Court his account with said orphan on Oath &c.

" Timothy **HAYS** Guardian to Robt **PARKER** orphan of Jos **PARKER** dec^d. exhibited into Court his account with said Orphan on Oath

" Thomas **SAUNDERS** Guardian to Asa **ODOM** orphan of Asa **ODOM** dec^d. exhibited into Court his account with said Orphan on Oath.

" John D. **PIPKIN** Guardian to John B **GATLING**, Rich^d. B. **GATLING** and Martha B. **GATLING** orphans of Etheldred B **GATLING** dec^d. exhibited into Court his account with said orphans on Oath.

February Court 1832

" Willis **CROSS** Guardian to Margaret J. **CROSS** orphan of Taylor **CROSS** dec^d. exhibited into Court his account with said orphan on Oath &c

" George **COSTEN** Guardian to James **COSTEN** orphan of Jas **COSTEN** dec^d. exhibited into his [sic] Court his account with said orphan on Oath &c

" Joseph **FREEMAN** Guardian to David **FREEMAN** orphan exhibited into Court his account with said orphan on oath &c.

" William H. **GOODMAN** Guardian to John, Henry, Richard, Mariah and Penninah **GOODMAN** orphans of Lemuel **GOODMAN** dec^d. exhibited into Court his account with said orphan [sic] on Oath

" James **LASSITER** Guardian to the Orphans of Henry **LASSITER** dec^d. exhibited into Court his accounts with said orphans on Oath

" William **CLEAVES** Guardian to the orphans of Nathaniel **PRUDEN** dec^d. exhibited into Court his account with said orphans on oath.

" Jesse **SAVAGE** Guardian to his Children Mary & Benjamin **SAVAGE** orphans [sic] exhibited into Court his Guardian accounts with said orphans on Oath &c.

[6] blank " Elizabeth **RIDDICK** Guardian to Jane R. **RIDDICK** orphan of Micajah **RIDDICK** dec^d. exhibited her acct. with s^d orphan by W. F. **RIDDICK**

" Willis **BUNCH** Guardian to Nancy **HURDLE** orphan of Kadar **HURDLE** dec^d. exhibited into Court his account with said orphan on Oath &c.

" Andrew **MATTHEWS** Guardian to Kadar & Holloday **JONES** orphans exhibited into Court his accounts with said orphans &c

" William **GOODMAN** Guardian to Mary Jane B. **GATLING** and Harriet B. **GATLING** orphans of Etheldred B. **GATLING** decceased exhibited into Court his accounts with said orphans on oath.

" William **GOODMAN** guardian to Margaret **CROSS** orphan of Jno. **CROSS** dec^d. exhibited into his [sic] acct. with said orphan on oath &c

" Miles **HOWELL** guardian to the orphans of Elisha **CROSS** deceased exhibited into Court his accounts with said Orphans on oath.

" Edwin **SMITH** guardian to the orphans of Henry **COPELAND** dec^d. exhibited into [sic] his accounts with the Court on Oath &c

" John C. **GORDON** guardian to the Orphans of Moses H. **SMALL** dec^d. exhibited into Court his accounts with said orphans on oath.

" David L **MILTEAR** guardian to the Orphans of David **PARKER** dec^d. exhibited into Court his accounts with said orphans on Oath

" George **COSTEN** guardian to Mary Ann **RIDDICK** orphan of Jno. [?] **RIDDICK** dec^d. exhibited into Court his acc^t. with s^d. orphan on oath

" Whitmell **JONES** guardian to John, Joseph & Marmaduke **JONES** orphans exhibited into Court his account with s^d. orphans on oath.

" Inventory of the property of Elizabeth **ROGERS** dec^d. was exhibited into Court by Robert **ROGERS** her administrator on oath.

February Court 1832

" Account of sale of the perishable estate of Elizabeth ROGERS dec^d. was exhibited into Court by Robert ROGERS admr. on oath.

" Inventory of the property belonging to Robert SMITH dec^d. was exhibited into Court by Frances SMITH exetx on oath.

" Account of sale [sic] the perishable estate of Robert SMITH dec^d. was exhibited into Court by Frances SMITH exetx on oath.

" Account of sale of the property of Thomas GRANBERRY dec^d. was exhibited into Court by Jno. G. LILES admr. on oath.

Barnes GOODMAN, Dempsey KNIGHT, Jesse WIGGINS and James MORGAN Commissiners who were appointed to make a division of the negroes belonging to the estate of Charles E. SUMNER dec^d. made a report of their proceedings thereon &c.

Isaac PIPKIN, Hillory WILLY & William LEE the Commissioners who were appointed to make a division of the negroes belonging to the estate of Lem^l. GOODMAN made a report of their proceedings theron &c.

[7] 225 " George KITTRELL adm^r. of James WILLIAMS dec^d. exhibited his account Current with the estate of the dec^d. into Court &c.

" John G. LILES adm^r. of Thomas GRANBERRY dec^d. exhibited his account Current with the estate of the deceased into Court &c.

Deed of sale Willis F. RIDDICK trustee to James PRUDEN was in open Court proved by the Oath of David F. FELTON a witness thereto &c

Deed of sale Willis F. RIDDICK trustee to James PRUDEN was in open Court proved by the Oath of David F. FELTON a witness thereto &c

~~Deed~~ Bill of sale Willis F. RIDDICK trustee to James PRUDEN was in open Court proved by the Oath of David F. FELTON a witness thereto &c

Bill of sale Mary HUDGINS to Eli WORRELL was in open Court prov$\underline{d}$ by the Oath of Abram W. PARKER a witness thereto &c.

Deed of gift Abraham BEEMAN to Martha BEEMAN was in open Court proved by the Oath of Timothy WALTON a witness thereto.

Deed of Gift Abraham BEEMAN to Rachel BEEMAN was in open Court proved by the Oath of Timothy WALTON a witness thereto.

Deed of Gift Abraham BEEMAN to Nancy BEEMAN was in open Court proved by the Oath of Timothy WALTON a witness thereto.

Deed of Gift Abraham BEEMAN to Mildred BEEMAN was in open Court proved by the Oath of Timothy WALTON a witness thereto.

Deed of sale Isaac PIPKIN to Willis F. RIDDICK was in open Court proved by the Oath of William H. GOODMAN a witness thereto.

Deed of sale John LEWIS to James LASSITER was in open Court acknowledged in due form of law &c.

Deed of David BENTON to Rizeup RAWLS was in open Court acknowledged in due form of law &c.

February Court 1832

Deed of Gift James **BENTON** to Seth **BENTON** was in open Court proved by the Oath of James **MORGAN** a witness thereto &c.

Bill of sale Thomas D. **SPIVEY** to William **MOORE** was in open Court proved by the Oath of Riddick **TROTMAN** a witness thereto.

Deed of sale Frederick **HINTON** to James **COSTEN** was in open Court proved by the Oath of Ben. **BLANCHARD** a witness thereto.

Deed of sale Joseph **GORDON** to John **ALPHIN** was in open Court acknowledged in due form of law.

Bill of sale Penelope **CARTER** to James **CARTER** was in open Court proved by the Oath of James R. **RIDDICK** a witness thereto &c

Deed of sale George **COSTEN** to Frederick **HINTON** was in open Court proved by the Oath of Ben. **BLANCHARD** a witness thereto.

Deed of sale John **ARNOLD** to John P. **BENTON** was in open Court proved by the Oath of W^m. W. **POWELL** a witness thereto.

Deed of sale John **ARNOLD** to John P. **BENTON** was in open Court proved by the Oath of W^m. W. **POWELL** a witness thereto &c.

Bill of sale James **BENTON** Jr. & Seth **BENTON** Junr. to John P. **BENTON** for negroes was in open Court proved by the Oath of W^m. W **POWELL** a witness thereto.

[8] blank Deed of sale Richard H. **PARKER** to Robert **HILL** Jr. was in open Court acknowledged in due form of law.

Deed of [sic] Whitmell **HILL** to Richard H. **PARKER** was in open Court proved by the Oath of Riddick **HUNTER** [?] a witness thereto

Deed of sale Hillory **WILLY** to Jonathan **WILLIAMS** was in open Court proved by the Oath of John **WILLEY** a witness thereto.

Deed of sale Robert **ROGERS** Exor. &c. to Levi **ROGERS** was in open Court acknowledged in due form of law &c.

Deed of sale Levi **ROGERS** to Robert **ROGERS** was in open Court acknowledged in due form of law &c.

Deed in Trust John **CLEAVES** to James T. **FREEMAN** & Willis J. **RIDDICK** was in open Court proved by the Oath of John **WALTON** a witness thereto.

Deed of sale William **LEE** to Francis **DUKE** was in open Court acknowledged in due form of law.

Deed of sale Bernard **MARCH** to Francis **DUKE** was in open Court proved by the Oath of William **LEE** a witness thereto.

Deed of sale Reuben **HINTON** to Henry **PEARCE** was in open Court proved by the Oath of Ben **BLANCHARD** a witness thereto

Deed of sale Susannah **PILAND** to Exum **LEWIS** was in open Court proved by the Oath of W^m. W. **COWPER** a witness &c.

Ordered that the Clerk of this Court be allowed the sum of thirty one dollars & twenty cents his fees on sundry indictments tried in this Court and the defendents found not guilty as per account rendered & al-

February Court 1832

lowed and that the County Trustee pay the same &c.

Ordered that the Sheriff of this County be allowed the sum of Eighteen dollars & twenty cents for his fees on sundry Indictments tried in this Court and the defendents found not guilty as per account rendered and allowed and that the County Trustee pay the same &c.

Riddick **GATLING** John **WILLEY** John **SAUNDERS** & Dempsey S. **GOODMAN** four of the Commissioners who were appointed to make a division of the real Estate of Lewis **EURE** dec^d. made a report of their proceedings thereon which was Confirmed by the Court and ordered to be registered &c.

[9] 227 Tuesday morning Court met at 10 O.Clock
Present   Peter B. **MINTON** Joseph **RIDDICK** Whitmel **STALLINGS**} Esquires Justices}

Ordered that the State docket hereafter be taken up on Wednesday of each and every County Court and that all witnesses in and parties to State Cases appear on that day and not before, and that the clerk endorse on all Criminal process the day on which the attendence of parties & witnesses is required.

Ordered that Riddick **JONES** a Juror be fined the sum of two dollars for not attending as a Juror.

Ordered that Henry **GILLIAM** Esq be appointed Chairman of the Court

Ordered that letters of administration be granted to Joseph **GORDON** on the estate of Miles **BRINKLY** dec^d. and that he give bond for $3000 Kinchen **NORFLEET** & John R **NORFLEET** offered themselves securities.

Ordered that Joseph **GORDON** have letters of administration on the estate of James **GRANBERRY** dec^d. and that he give bond for $5000. Kinchen **NORFLEET** & John R **NORFLEET** offered themselves securities

On Motion, Ordered that Lassiter **RIDDICK** be appointed adm^r. de bonis non upon the estate of Christain [sic] **CROSS** dec^d. that he give bond & security for $1000. he gives for security John **GATLING** and James R. **RIDDICK**.

On motion Ordered that Abraham **RIDDICK** administer on the estate of Barsheba **FRANKLIN** and that he give bond for $50.0. [sic] with Kadar **ELLIS** & Jesse **MATTHIAS** for securities.

Ordered that Thomas B. **HUNTER** be appointed guardian to Isaac **HUNTER** orphan of Isaac **HUNTER** dec^d. & that he give bond for $10,000. Joseph **GORDON** & Isaac R. **HUNTER** securities. Present in Court Peter B. **MINTON** W^m. W. **COWPER**, W^m. **WALTON** Esquires Justices who approved of the securities & concurred in the appointment.

Ordered that Elijah **HARRELL** be appointed Guardian to Elisha **HARRELL** orphan of Elisha **HARRELL** dec^d. and that he give bond for $2,000. John **BEEMAN** & Eli **WORRELL** securites. Present in Court Riddick **GATLING**, W^m. W. **COWPER** John **WILLY** W^m. **WALTON** Esquires Justices who approved of the securities & concurred in the appointment.

Ordered that W^m. W. **COWPER** be appointed guardian to Uriah **BABB** orphan of Christoper [sic] **BABB** dec^d. & that he give bond for $1,000 Nathaniel **EURE** & Exum **LEWIS** securities. Present in Court John **WILLY**, Peter B. **MINTON** & W^m. **WALTON** Esquirs Justices who approved of the securites & concurred in the appointment.

[10] blank Ordered that Nathaniel **EURE** be appointed guardian to William **BABB** orphan of Christopher **BABB** dec^d. and that he give bond for $100. W^m. W. **COWPER** & Abram W. **PARKER** securities. Present in Court John **WILLY**, Peter B **MINTON** & William **WALTON** Esquirs Justices who approved of the securities & Concurred in the appointment.

February Court 1832

Ordered that William E. **PUGH** adm^r. of Henry **PUGH** give for security to his adm^n. Bond John **MATTHEWS** & Wills **COOPER** Jr. instead of W^m. **GOODMAN** & Dempsey **GOODMAN**

Orde<u>rd</u> that John **MATTHEWS** have Licen<u>c</u>e to retail Spirits by the small measures at his shop in Gatesville.

Ordered that Burwell **BROTHERS** have licence to retail Spirits by the small measure near Muddy Cross.

issd Ordered that Jesse M. **SAVAGE** be allowed the sum of Two dollars & that the County trustee pay the same.

issd Ordered that Henry **GILLIAM** Guardian to the Orphans of Jonas **FRANKLIN** sell a Certain negro boy named **HARRY** belonging to said heirs-on a credit of six months & report the same.

__*sd* Ordered that John R **GILLIAM** be appointed to Record all the old acct sales Guardian accts. Divisions & audited accounts which was omitted by the late Clerk Lawrence **BAKER** & that he be allowed the usual fee—to be recorded in bound Books with an Index.

Ordered that Dempsey **EURE** orphan child be bound to Barnabas **USHER** to learn the trade of a hatter.

issd. Ordered that John **WILLY** be permitted to turn a road running in front of his Gate that he put sad [sic] road in order & that the Overseer receive the same.

issd. Ordered that Tinson **EURE** be appointed Overseer of the road from Abm W. **PARKER** to Gatesville in the room of Nathaniel **HARRELL** re<u>s</u>gned

issd. Ordered that George W. **SMITH** be appointed overseer of the road in the room of Hardy D. **PARKER** resigned.

issd. Ordered that John **HOFFLER** Jr. be appointed overseer of the road in the room & stead of James C. **RIDDICK** resigned.

issd. Ordered that [Remainder of line is blank.] be appointed to lay off to Ann **GRANBERRY** widow of James **GRANBERRY** such part of the Crop stock & provisions of the estate of the deceased as they may Judge adequate and necessary for the support of the said widow and her family for one year agreeable to law &c.

issd. Ordered that [Remainder of line is blank.] be appointed to lay off to Mary **BRINKLY** widow of Miles **BRINKLY**

[11] 229 dec^d. such part of the Crop stock & provisions of the estate of the dec^d. as they may Judge adequate and necessary for the support of the said Widow and her family for one Year agreeable to law &c

Ordered that Henry **GILLIAM** be appointed guardian to Edward **WOOD**, James **WOOD** & W^m. **WOOD** orphans of Edward **WOOD** dec^d. & that he enter into Bond & security for $1,500. Peter B **MINTON** Riddick **GATLING** securities Present in Court P. B. **MINTON** R. **GATLING** W^m. W. **COWPER** Esquires Justices who approved of the securities and concurred in the appointment.

Ordered that William W. **COWPER** be appointed guardian to Selah **LEWIS** a Luntick [sic] that he give bond & security for $500. Exum **LEWIS** & John **LEWIS** securities. Present in Court Peter B. **MINTON** Riddick **GATTLING** [sic] & Wm **WALTON** Esquires Justices who approved of the securities & concurred in the appointment

Ordered that Jesse **BROWN** be appointed Guardian to Susan **BEEMAN** Orphan of Israel **BEEMAN** & that he enter into bond in the sum of five thousand dollars with John **BEEMAN** & Levi **BEEMAN** Securities. Present in Court Riddick **GATLING** W^m. W. **COWPER**, John **WILLY** & William **WALTON** Esquires Justices who approved of the securities & concurred in the appointment

February Court 1832

" Nathl. **EURE** guardian to James **BOGER** orphan of Jonathan **BOGE** [sic] dec^d. exhibited into Court his account with said orphan on Oath &c.

" Nathl **EURE** guardian to the orphans of Henry **SPEIGHTS** dec^d. exhibited into Court his accounts with said orphans on oath &c.

" James **COSTEN** guardian to his son & to James **COSTEN** orphan of Isaac **COSTEN** dec^d. exhibited into Court his accounts with said orphans on oath.

" Nathl. **EURE** guardian to William **BABB** orphan of Christopher **BABB** dec^d. exhibited into Court his account with said orphan on oath.

" Henry **BOND** guardian to James **BOND** orphan of Rich^d. **BOND** dec^d. exhibited into Court his accounts with said orphan on Oath.

" Exum **LEWIS** guardian to Celia **LEWIS** orphan exhibited into Court his account with said Orphan on Oath &c.

" Martha R. **SUMNER** guardian to the orphans of Chs E. **SUMNER** dec^d. exhibited into Court her accounts with said Orphans by the Oath of Riddick **GATLING** &c.

" Eli **WORRELL** guardian to William J **HUDGINS** orphan exhibited into Court his accounts with said orphan on Oath &c.

" Abraham W. **PARKER** guardian to W^m. **JOHNSON** orphan exhibited into Court his account wath [sic] said Orphan on oath &c.

" Nathan **NIXON** guardian to the orphans of Timothy **WALTON** dec^d exhibited into Court his accounts with said orphans on oath

" Jesse **BROWN** guardian to Louisa **BARNES** orphan exhibited into Court his acc^t. [sic] said orphan on oath.

[12] blank " Nathan **RIDDICK** guardian to Henry, Jesse & Mary **WALTON** orphans exhibited into Court his accounts with said orphans on oath.

" Nathan **RIDDICK** guardian to William & Sarah **BROWN** orphans exhibited into Court his accounts with said orphans on oath

" Nathan **RIDDICK** guardian to Drew **TROTMAN** & John **HUNTER** orphans &c exhibited into Court his accounts with said orphans on oath.

" Lemuel G. **DARDEN** guardian to Mary G. **CROSS** orphan of Abm **CROSS** dec^d. exhibited into Court his account with said orphan on oath.

Arthur **WILLIAMS** guardian to Mary **WILLIAM** [sic] orphan of Jonathan **WILLIAMS** dec^d. exhibited into Court his acct with said orphan on oath.

" James **SMITH** guardian to Edward **HARE** orphan of John **HARE** dec^d. exhibited into Court his acct with said orphan on Oath.

" Jethro H **RIDDICK** guardian to Calvin **BRINKLY** orphan of Elisha **BRINKLY** dec^d. exhibited into Court his acct. with said orphan on oath.

" William **HINTON** guardian [sic] Margaret A **BOND** orphan of Rich^d. **BOND** dec^d. exhibited into Court his acct. with said orphan on oath

February Court 1832

" William W. COWPER guardian to Uriah BABB orphan [sic] Christopher BABB dec^d. exhibited into Court his acc^t. with said orphan on oath.

" David PARKER guardian to John FELTON orphan exhibited into Court his account with said orphan on Oath &c

" Henry GILLIAM guardian to Joshua SKINNER orphan exhibited into Court his account with said orphan on oath.

" John WALTON guardian to Leah HINTON & to the orphans of Riddick TROTMAN dec^d. exhibited into Court his accts with orphans on oath.

" Willis J. RIDDICK guardian to the orphans of James HINTON decd exhibited into Court his accounts with said orphans on oath

" Thomas ROUNTREE guardian to Milly GREEN orphan of Aaron GREEN dec^d. exhibited into Court his acct with said orphan On Oath.

" Garrett HOFFLER guardian to the orphans of James HOFLER dec^d. exhibited into Court his accts with said orphans on oath

" Garrett HOFLER guardian to Nancy JORDON orphan of Armstead JORDON dec^d. exhibited into Court his acct. with said orphan on oath

" Inventory of the property belonging to the estate of Henry JONES dec^d. was exhibited into Court by W^m. LEE adm^r. on oath.

" Account of sale of the perishable estate of Henry JONES dec^d. was exhibited into Court by William LEE adm^r. on Oath.

" An additional account of sale of balance of the estate of Henry JONES dec^d. was exhibited into Court by W^m. LEE adm^r. on oath.

" Account of sale of the hire of negroes belonging to the estate of Henry JONES dec^d. was exhibited into Court by W^m. LEE adm^r. on oath.

" Inventory of the Estate of Hardy EASON dec^d. was exhibited into Court by Joseph GORDON adm^r. on oath.

[13] 231 " Inventory of the Estate of Thomas SPEIGHTS dec^d. was exhibited into Court by Henry SPEIGHTS adm^r. on Oath &c.

George COSTEN James COSTEN & Joseph GORDON three of the men who were appointed to make a division of the personal estate of Elisha HUNTER dec^d. made a report of their proceedings this Court &c

" Mills PILAND Guardian to the Orphans of Elisha PILAND dec^d. exhibited into Court his accounts with said orphans on Oath &c.

" Henry GILLIAM William E. PUGH and Thomas SAUNDERS three of the men who were appointed to make a division among the heirs entitled to receive their portion of the am^t. lately recovered in the Supreme Court in the Case John SPEIGHTS adm^r. de bonis non of Henry SPEIGHTS dec^d. made a report of their proceedings thereon.

Ordered that John WALTON & Henry GILLIAM Esqrs be appointed to take the private examination of Eliza H. RIDDICK wife of Willie RIDDICK relative to the sale of a tract of land & that a Commission accordingly issue &c.

February Court 1832

Deed of sale Willie **RIDDICK** & wife to John **ROBERTS** was in open Court proved by the Oath of John **WALTON** a witness thereto &c.

Deed of sale Henry W. **SKINNER** to the Trustees of Lebanon Church was in open Court acknowledged in due form of law

Deed of sale Henry W. **SKINNER** to Jesse **BROWN** was in open Court acknowledged in due form of law &c.

Deed of sale Henry W. **SKINNER** to Prior **SAVAGE** was in open Court acknowledged in due form of law &c

Bill of sale Marmaduke N. **ELLIS** to Kadar **ELLIS** was in open Court proved by the Oath of Joseph **GORDON** a witness thereto.

Deed of sale Marmaduke N. **ELLIS**, Kadar **ELLIS** & his wife Mary to Benjamin **BRINKLY** was in open Court proved by the Oath of Demsey **VANN** a witness

Deed of sale Marmaduke N. **ELLIS** to Kadar **ELLIS** & wife was in open Court proved by the Oath of Demsey **VANN** a witness thereto.

Deed of [sic] John B. **BAKER** to Abraham **MORGAN** was in open Court acknowledged in due form of law.

Deed of sale John **SAUNDERS** to Noah **ROUNTREE** was in open Court proved by the Oath of Timothy **WALTON** a witness thereto &c.

Deed of sale Timothy **WALTON** to Noah **ROUNTREE** was in open Court acknowledged in due form of law.

Deed of sale Sarah **PARKER** to John **MATTHEWS** was in open Court proved by the Oath of Riddick **MATTHEWS** a witness thereto.

Deed of sale Elisha **WALTON** to Reuben **HINTON**, was in open Court proved by the Oath of Henry **GILLIAM** a witness thereto.

[14] blank Wednesday morning Court met at 10. O.Clock
Present   Isaac R **HUNTER** John **WALTON** John B. **BAKER**} Esquires Justices

issd. Ordered that the Clerk of Gates County Court issue to Henderson **REED** a free man of Colour a native of this County a certificate of his freedom agreeable to law &c.

Ordered that the Sheriff summons a Jury to lay off and set a part to Rachel **MORGAN** one third part of the lands which her late husband Seth **MORGAN** died seized & possessed.

issd. Ordered that William L **BOOTHE**, John **BEEMAN**, James **CARTER** & Ethel^d. **CROSS** or any three of them audite & state the /accts/ of Abm W. **PARKER** adm^r. of Ebron **BRISCO** & that they make a report.

issd. Ordered that Reuben **FIELD** work on the road from the fork of the road at George **COSTEN** plantation to the Honey pott swamp

issd. Ordered that the County Trustee pay Jethro **WILLY** one dollar & Sixty cents for the cost accrueing in two warrants against David **ROOKS** for failing to work on the public road.

issd. Ordered that Lemuel **CLEAVES** be allowed the sum of two dollars & eighty cents for summonsing witnesses & carrying Danil [?] **MORGAN** to Jail & that the county Trustee pay the same.

February Court 1832

John **WALTON** John **ROBERTS** & John **HINTON** three of the men who were appointed to make a division of the personal estate of Richard **BOND** dec^d. made a report &c

" Account of the hire of the negroes belonging to the estate of Abram **CROSS** dec^d. was exhibited into Court by John R. **NORFLEET** administrator on Oath &c.

" Account of the hire of the negroes belonging to the estate of Abraham **CROSS** dec^d. was exhibited into Court by John R **NORFLEET** adm^r. on oath.

[15] 233 " James **BOOTHE** Guardian to Sally **POWELL** orphan exhibited into Court his guardian account with said Orphan on Oath &c.

" Mary **HUNTER** Guardian to Jacob B. **HUNTER** orphan of Isaac **HUNTER** dec^d. exhibited into Court her acct with said orphan by I. R. **HUNTER**.

" Isaac R. **HUNTER** guardian to the Orphans of Benjamin **BRIGGS** dec^d. exhibited into Court his accounts with said orphans on oath.

Deed of sale James R. **RIDDICK** shff to James A. **BALLARD** was in open Court acknowledged in due form of law.

Deed of sale Henry **GILLIAM** trustee to Thomas **SAUNDERS** was in open Court proved by the Oath of Jeptha **FOWLKES** a witness thereto &c.

" Benjamin **SUMNER** Exor. of Charles E. **SUMNER** dec^d. exhibited his account Current with the estate of the dec^d. into Court &c.

  Gates County Court. Feby. Term 1832.
   Ordered by the Court that Ben. **SUMNER** exor. of Charles E. **SUMNER** dec^d. be allowed 3 ¾ per cent on the foregoing disbursements and 4 percent on the above receipts.
       signed—Jno. B. **BAKER** Jno **WALTON** I. R. **HUNTER**

issd. " Ordered that the sheriff summon William **WALTON**, Benjamin **HAYS**, Frederick **HINTON** Jr. Paul **JONES**, Hardy **WILLIAMS**, Noah **ROUNTREE**, Levi **CREECY** John **WALTON** Esqr. Willis **CROSS** Exum **LEWIS** Thomas **ROUNTREE**, John C. **GORDON**, Dempsey **EURE**, Demsey **PARKER** of Jas. Timothy **HUNTER**, Dempsey **SPARKMAN**, William **LEE**, David **BENTON**, Jet **BENTON**, Charles **BRIGGS** John B. **BAKER**, John **WILLEY** Jesse **PILAND**, Riddick **MATTHEWS**, Jesse **HOBBS**, Levi **SUMNER** John **HARRELL** of Asa) Timothy **SPIVEY**, Joseph **RIDDICK** Esqr. Thomas **HOGGARD**, William W. **COWPER**, Peter B. **MINTON**, Henry **RIDDICK** of Ro. Prior **SAVAGE**, James **SUMNER** and Jordon **PARKER** personally to attend at the next Superior Court to be held for this County on the first monday after the fourth monday in march next then and there to serve as Jurors &c.

issd. Ordered that the Sheriff Summons Mills **SPARKMAN**, James **JONES** of Jas, William **SEARS**, Abraham **MORGAN** sen^r. Daniel **RIDDICK** of Isah. [sic] John O. **HUNTER**, Burrell **GRIFFITH**, Archibald **ELLIS**, William **HARRELL** S. Hall John **BRINKLY** William W. **STEDMAN** Edwin **CROSS** Nathaniel **EURE**, Daniel **WILLIAMS**, Benbury **WALTON**, Jesse **PARKER** William **PILAND**, Wiley **RIDDICK**, Abram **PARKER** C. H. John **HARE** John **HOFFLER** Jr. Levi **EURE** Jr. John **SPEIGHT** of Henry, Joseph **FREEMAN**, Isaac **PEARCE** Jr.. James **BOOTHE** C. House James **BRINKLY**

[16] blank Willis **HARRELL**, Humphrey **PARKER** and William A. **MATTHEWS** personally to attend at the next County Court to be held for this County on the third monday in May next then and there to serve as Jurors &c.

May Court 1832

State of North Carolina.   May the 21st. 1832.
At a Court of Pleas and Quarter sessions, begun and held for the County of Gates at the Court House in Gatesville, on the third monday of May in the Fifty sixth Year of our Independence and in the Year of our Lord One thousand Eight hundred and thirty two.
Present.   Henry **GILLIAM** Isaac R. **HUNTER** John D. **PIPKIN** Whitmell **STALLINGS** W^m. W. **COWPER**} Esquires Justices

issd. Ordered that Jethro **SUMNER** Jesse **WIGGINS** John **WIGGINS** & Dempsey **KNIGHT** or any three of them audite the accounts of James **MORGAN** adm^r. of John **HARE** dec^d. & report at the next Court &c.

Ordered that Thomas **HOGGARD** be appointed Guardian to Lavina **SMITH** orphan of Joseph **SMITH** dec^d. and the give [sic] bond in the sum of $350 and offers Willis **CROSS**, Jacob **ODOM** for the securities Present in Court W^m. W. **COWPER** Isaac R **HUNTER** Henry **GILLIAM**, W^m. L. **BOOTHE** & Jno. D. **PIPKIN** who approved of the securities & concurred in the appointment &c.

[17] 235 Ordered that William **BOND** be appointed Guardian to Nancy **BOND**, Noah **BOND** & Elizabeth **BOND** orphans of Rich^d. **BOND** dec^d. and that he enter into Bond in the sum of $200 Each & offers George **COSTEN** & Henry **COSTEN** for securities. Present in Court Joseph **RIDDICK**, H. **GILLIAM**, W^m. L. **BOOTHE** John C. **GORDON** & Isaac R. **HUNTER** Esquires Justices who approved of the Securities & concurred in the appointment.

Ordered that Jethro H. **RIDDICK** be appointed Constable for one year & that he enter into bond & security as the law directs.

Ordered that Miles **HOWELL** be appointed Constable and that he give bond and security as the law directs &c.

Ordered that Dempsey **SPARKMAN** be appointed a Constable in Capt Nathan **SMITH**s Captaincy or district & that he give bond and security as the law directs.

Ordered that Lemuel **CLEAVES** renew his Constable bond and that he give bond and security as the law directs.

Ordered that Henry **SPEIGHT** son of Noah **SPEIGHT** be bound an apprentice to John **ALPHIN** to learn the art of a Farmer

Ordered that Abraham **MORGAN** be discharged from serving as a Juror at this Term.

issd. Ordered that Ezekiel **LASSITER** be allowed one Dollar to be paid by the Treasurer.

Ordered that Henry **GILLIAM** receive a Licence to retail Spirits at his Bar at Gatesville &c.

Ordered that Jethro **WILLEY** be allowed Eighteen Dollars 37½ for services as Patrol. recinded

Ordered that Henry **WILLY** be allowed the sum of Seven Dollars 50pen [sic] for services as Patrol. recinded

issd. Ordered that the County Trustee refund to Mills & Josiah **RIDDICK** of Nansemond County va, the sum of Ten dollars & sixty cents for mistake in listing lands in this County

issd. Ordered that the Sheriff be allowed $1-96 cents in a settlement with the County Trustee for mistake in listing property

issd. Ordered that free Papers be granted to Joseph **BURKET** agreeable to an act of assembly in such cases made & provided.

May Court 1832

Ordered that Richard **ODOM** be appointed overseer of the road from **WOOD**s old field to Winton Cau<u>sw</u>ay in the room of Cyprian **CROSS** resigned &c.

[18] <u>blank</u> *recorded* The last will and Testament of Seth **BENTON** dec^d. was exhibited in open Court and proved by the oath of James **MORGAN** one of the subscribing witnesses thereto and ordered to be recorded. The Executors therein appointed Came into Court and was duly qualified for that Office and prayed an order for letters testamentary thereon which was accordingly granted &c.

recorded The last will and Testament of Micajah **RIDDICK** dec^d. was exhibited in open Court and proved by the Oath of James R. **RIDDICK** one of the subscribing witnesses thereto and ordered to be recorded. The Executor therein appointed Came into Court and was duly qualified for that Office and prayed an order for letters testamentary ther/e/on which was accordingly granted &c.

recorded The last will and Testament of Luke **HOLLOWELL** dec^d. was exhibited in open Court and proved by the Oaths of Willis **BUNCH** & Amos **HOBBS** two of the subscribing witnesses thereto, and ordered to be recorded. The executor therein appointed Came into Court and was duly qualified for that Office and prayed an order for letters testamentary thereon which was accordingly granted &c.

recorded The last will and Testament of William **KING** dec^d. was exhibited into Court and proved by the Oath of Amos **HOBBS** one of the subscribing witnesses thereto and ordered to be recorded. The Executor therein appointed Came into Court and was duly qualified for that Office and prayed an order for letters testamentary thereon which was accordingly granted &c.

" Inventory of the property of Robert **TAYLOR** dec^d. was exhibited into Court by Nathan **NIXON** & Fruzy **TAYLOR** Exor. & Exet^x. on oath

" Account of sale of the property of Robert **TAYLOR** dec^d. was exhibited into Court by Nathan **NIXON** & Fruzy **TAYLOR** Exo^r. & Exet^x. on oath

" Account of sale of the property of Abraham **BEEMAN** dec^d. was exhibited into Court by John & Levi **BEEMAN** Exors on oath

[19] <u>237</u> Deed of sale Rizop **RAWLS** to Noah **HARRELL** was in open Court acknowledged in due form of law &c

Deed of sale David **OUTLAW** to William W. **HAYS** was in open Court proved by the Oath of Robert **WILLIAMS** a witness thereto &c

Deed of sale Susan **WOLFREY** to John **WILLEY** was in open Court proved by the Oath of Lewis J. **HURDLE** a witness thereto &c

Deed of sale William D. **PRUDEN** to Elbert **RIDDICK** was in open Court acknowledged in due form of law &c.

Deed of sale George **COSTEN** to Thomas R. **COSTEN** was in open Court acknowledged in due form of law &c

Deed of sale Mary **BUTLER** to Gilbert G. **SAUNDERS** was in open Court proved by the Oath of H. H C **JONES** a witness thereto.

Deed of sale Elijah **HARE** Trustee to Gilbert G **SAUNDERS** was in open Court proved by the Oath of Myles **PARKER** a witness thereto

Deed of sale William **HOFFLER** to Henry **BOND** was in open Court proved by the Oath of Nathan **NIXON** a witness thereto &c

Deed of sale Milley **TOOLEY** to Jesse **MATHIAS** was in open Court proved by the Oath of Riddick

May Court 1832

JONES a witness thereto &c

Deed of sale Jethro EURE to Levi EURE was in open Court proved by the Oath of Samuel EURE a witness thereto &c

Deed of sale William GOODMAN to Benjamin EURE was in open Court acknowledged in due form of law &c

Deed of sale William GOODMAN [sic] Jethro TEABOUT was in open Court acknowledged in due form of Law &c

Marriage Contract from Arthur JNKINS [sic] to Ann GRANT was in open Court proved by the Oath of John WILLY a witness thereto

Deed of sale James BAKER sen[r]. to James BAKER Jr. was in open Court proved by the Oath of Jethro H. RIDDICK a witness thereto

Deed of sale John ODOM to Richard ALLSTIN was in open Court acknowledged in due form of law &c

Deed of Gift Mary MATTHEWS to Martha Jane MATTHEWS was in open Court proved by the Oath of Demsey KNIGHT a witness &c

Deed of sale Noah ROUNREE to John SAUNDERS was in open Court proved by the Oath of Nathan NIXON a witness thereto &c

Deed of Gift James WILLIAMS to Joshua ALLEN & wife was in open Court proved by the Oath of James R. RIDDICK a witness thereto.

Deed of sale Richard BOND to William BOND was in open Court acknowledged in due form of law &c

[20] blank Deed of sale John LANGSTON to Willoughby MANNING was in open Court acknowledged in due form of law &c

Deed of sale Lucy WALTON to William WALTON was in open Court proved by the Oath of A. BLANCHARD a witness thereto.

Deed of sale James GOODMAN & Benj[a]. RIDDICK to Nathan CULLINS was in open Court proved by the Oath of Kindred PARKER a witness &c

Lease from Martha S. MELVIN John LASSITER & wife, Joseph BROOKS & Margaret C. BROOKS to George BROOKS & wife was in open Court proved by the Oath of John WALTON a witness thereto.

Deed of Gift George BROOKS to Margaret C BROOKS was in open Court proved by the Oath of John WALTON a witness thereto.

Deed of Gift George BROOKS to Joseph BROOKS was in open Court proved by the Oath of John WALTON a witness thereto.

Deed of Gift George BROOKS to Ann E. LASSITER was in open Court proved by the Oath of John WALTON a witness thereto

Deed of Gift George BROOKS to Martha S. MELVIN was in open Court proved by the Oath of John WALTON a witness &c

Deed of sale Dempsey LANGSTON to John LANGSTON was in open Court acknowledged in due form of law.

May Court 1832

Deed of sale Mills **SPARKMAN** to David **UMPHLETT** was in open Court acknowledged in due form of law &c.

Deed of sale Cyprian R. **CROSS** to Ethel^d. **CROSS** was in open Court proved by the Oath of Thomas **SAUNDERS** a witness &c

Deed of sale Drew M. **SAUNDERS** to Jason **SAUNDERS** was in open Court proved by the Oath of John **SPAIGHT** a witness.

" Elizabeth **GRANBERRY** Guardian to the orphans of John **GRANBERRY** dec^d. exhibited into Court her acc^t. with s^d. orphans, by Wills **COWPER**

" Account of sale of the negroes belonging to the estate of Jonas **FRANKLIN** dec^d. was exhibited into Court by Daniel **FRANKLIN** executor on Oath &c.

[21] 239 Then the Court adjourned untill to morrow [sic] at 10.°Clock
Tuesday morning Court met
Present　　　John C. **GORDON**　William **GOODMAN**　Peter B. **MINTON**　John B. **BAKER**} Esquires Justices

Grand Jury qualified at this Term to wit Benbury **WALTON** Foreman). William **HARRELL**, Humphrey **PARKER**, Willis **HARRELL** Isaac **PEARCE**, James **BRINKLY** John **SPEIGHT** John O. **HUNTER** William A. **MATTHEWS**, James **JONES** of Jas. Edwin **CROSS**, Mills **SPARKMAN**, Daniel **RIDDICK**, Burrell **GRIFFITH** Levi **EURE**, Nathaniel C **EURE** Joseph **FREEMAN** and Daniel **WILLIAMS**

issd. Ordered that Jethro H. **RIDDICK** be allowed seven dollars & thirteen Cents for money improperly paid by him for Tax & that the County Trustee pay the Same.

issd. Ordered that a notice issue to John **JONES** Guardian to James **CROSS** Orphans to appear at next Court and renew his Guardian Bond

Ordered that Lassiter **RIDDICK** be appointed guardian to Mary Jane Boyt **GATLING** and he offers as security James R. **RIDDICK** & Henry **GILLIAM** he enters into for $3000. Present in Court John B. **BAKER**, Thomas **SAUNDERS**, Riddick **GATLING** & W^m. W. **COWPER** Esquires Justices who approved of the Securities and Concurred in the appointment &c

Ordered that Christian **GWINN** be appointed Guardian to her three children Thos. James & Edward **GWINN** & give bond for two hundred dollars, she offers Rich^d. H. **BALLARD** & Miles **BRIGGS** for securities Present in Court, Henry **GILLIAM** Jno C **GORDON**, Joseph **RIDDICK**, George **KITTRELL** Esquires Justices who approved of the securities & Concurred in the appointment.

Ordered that Dempsey S [?] **GOODMAN** be appointed Guardian to Louisa **JONES** & Henry **JONES** orphans of Henry **JONES** dec^d. he gives bond & security in the sum of $2.500 for Louisa & $1500 for Henry and offers for securitys [sic] Willis **CROSS** & William **LEE**. Present in Court Henry **GILLIAM**, John C. **GORDON** Joseph **RIDDICK** & George **KITTRELL** Esquires Justices who approved of the securities and Concurred in the appointment &c

[22] blank Ordered that the following magistrates take the list of Taxes for the ensueing year.
Honey Pot District—Thomas **SAUNDERS** Esq.　Capt. Nathan **SMITH**s—Rich^d. **ODOM** Esq.
Capt. **SAUNDERS**—Riddick **GATLING** Esq.　Capt. Willie **RIDDICK**'s—Hardy D. **PARKER** Esq.
Capt. **WIGGINS**—Isaac R. **HUNTER** Esq.　Capt. Bushrod **RIDDICK**—Whitmell **STALLINGS** Esq.
Capt. Jethro H. **RIDDICK**—Joseph **RIDDICK** Esq.

Ordered that the County Tax be laid for the year 1831 as follows to wit) twenty eight Cents on each poll and eight Cents on each Hundred dollars of the valuation of land in this County subject to Taxation.

May Court 1832

And that the Poor's tax for said year be laid as follows to wit fifty cents on each Poll & twelve & a half cents on each hundred dollars valuation of land, and that a tax be laid of twenty five cents on each Poll and five cents on each Hundred dollars of the valuation of land for the purpose of purchasing land and building a poor House in this County &c And also that a tax of ten cents be laid on each black poll in the County for the pupose [sic] of paying the Patrolls appointed by the severall Patrol Committees, and that the Sheriff collect the said taxes and account for them as the law directs &c

issd. Ordered that Henry **RIDDICK**, Hillory **WILLEY**, Riddick **GATLING** Dempsey **SPARKMAN**, Thomas **SAUNDERS** John **WALTON** and Joseph **GORDON** be appointed Commissions [sic] to Contract for a suitable piece of land, and the building of such buildings as may be necessary for the use of the poor of Gates County the purchase money to be paid in instalments of one and two year [sic] the land not to Cost over the sum of $__blank__.

Ordered that Isaac **PIPKIN**, Hardy D. **PARKER**, Walton **FREEMAN** Mills **EURE**, Henry **GILLIAM**, Joseph **RIDDICK** and Tilley W. **CARR** be appointed wardens of the Poor for the County of Gates for one year from this Court &c

issd. Ordered that John B. **BAKER**, John **WALTON** & Thomas **SAUNDERS** be appointed a committee to examine the Clerks offices of the Superior & County Court & that they report their proceedings to this Court at its next siting [sic] &c

[23] 241 *issd.* Ordered that John C. **GORDON**, Joseph **GORDON** & James **LASSITER** be appointed a Committee of finance & that they Report their proceedings to this Court.

issd. Ordered that the following persons be appointed inspectors at the ensueing elections at the following places (viz)

Gates Court House Joseph **RIDDICK** Jr Prior **SAVAGE** W^m. G. **DAUGHTRY** William **ELEY** Reuben **HINTON**
at **MINTON**s Timothy **WALTON** William **WALTON** Esqr. James T. **FREEMAN** James **BAKER** John **MITCHELL**
at John **MATTHEWS** Noah **HARRELL** William **CLEAVES** Richard **SMITH** John **FIGG** Thomas **SMITH**
at Dempsey **PARKER**'s Levi **EURE** Mills **EURE** Dempsey **SPARKMAN** Jacob **ODOM** Etheldred **CROSS**
at **HUNTER**'s mill Joseph **GORDON** William **HARRELL** Thomas **TWINE** Robert **HILL** James **COSTEN**
at William **GOODMAN**s store William **LEE** John **SAUNDERS** William **GOODMAN** Esqr. Joseph **FREEMAN** Francis **DUKE**
at the Folley John C. **GORDON** James **MORGAN** Dempsey **KNIGHT** Henry **RIDDICK** Jesse **WIGGINS**
at **HASLETT**'s shop Jesse **SAVAGE** Barnes **GOODMAN** Simon **WALTERS** Moore **SAVAGE** George W. **SMITH**

issd. Ordered that the House of Dempsey **PARKER** shall be substituted in lieu of the House of Etheldred **CROSS** to hold the next election for that district &c.

issd. Ordered that the Store House of William **GOODMAN** Jr. be substituted in leiu [sic] of the House of Isaac **PIPKIN** to hold the next election for that district

[24] blank Patroll Committee
Folley district John C **GORDON**, Tilly W. **CARR** Edward R. **HUNTER**
HUNTER's mill d^o James **LASSITER** Thomas **TWINE** George **COSTEN**
Bush **RIDDICK** d^o Jno. **ROBERTS** Will. **HINTON** John **HINTON**
L. **RIDDICK**'s d^o Jno. B. **BAKER**, Jesse **BROWN** Thos. **SAUNDERS**

May Court 1832

Nathan **SMITH**s d°· Mills **EURE** W^m. L. **BOOTHE** Dempsey **SPARKMAN**
Capt. **ODOM**'s d°· Isaac **PIPKIN** W^m. **GOODMAN** William **LEE**
W. **RIDDICK**'s d°· George **KITTRELL** Hardy D. **PARKER** Barnes **GOODMAN**

Ordered that the above be appointed as a Committee to appoint such number of Patrolls in their districts as they may think proper

On motion, Ordered that Henry **GILLIAM** administer upon the Estate of Peter **HARRELL** dec^d. and that he give bond with securities in the sum of one thousand five hundred dollars Lassiter **RIDDICK** & Jethro H. **RIDDICK** was offered as securities and was approved of by the Court &c.

On motion, Ordered that Nathan **RIDDICK** have the administration upon the estate of Jesse **WALTON** dec^d. he intering into bond in the penalty of $1000. with Jethro H. **RIDDICK** and Nathan **NIXON** securities who were approved of by the Court.

On motion, Ordered that Hance **HOFFLER** be appointed adm^r. upon the estate of Reuben **HINTON** Junr. dec^d. and that he give Bond & Security in the sum of $2.000. Willis J. **RIDDICK** and Jethro H. **RIDDICK** securities who were approved of by the Court &c

issd. Ordered that Henry **GILLIAM** be allowed the sum of sixty five dollars & forty eight /Cents/ for sundry fees on Indictments as per account rendered to Court. &c

issd. Ordered that Henry **GILLIAM** be allowed the sum of sixteen dollars for purchasing four large Blank Books for use of the Office and that the County Trustee pay the same &c

issd. Ordered that Henry **GILLIAM** be allowed the sum of twenty five dollars for sundry repairs on the Court House & bridge and for his services as Trustee of publick buildings for 10 years and that the County Trustee pay the same &c

issd. Ordered that Jethro **SUMNER** clerk of this Court be allowed for Extra Services $50. to be paid by the County Trustee.

issd. Ordered that James R. **RIDDICK** sheriff be allowed Fifty dollars for his extra services for the last year and that the County Trustee pay the same &c.

[25] 243 *issd.* Ordered that James R **RIDDICK** be allowed the sum of ninety eight Cents being the am^t. of the poll tax of James **MATTHEWS** & that he be allow^d. that am^t. in the settlement of his accts to prevent the sale of the land of said **MATTHEWS** he being a pauper, and that the County Trustee pay the same &c

issd. Ordered that Jethro H **RIDDICK** be allowed one dollar & sixty cents for two days attendance on the Jury this Term, and that the County Trustee pay the same &c

issd. Ordered that Jesse **BROWN** be allowed the sum of twelve dollars & Eighty nine cents for Jail fees as per account rendered to Court and allowed, and that the County Trustee pay the same

issd. Ordered that the County surveyor, survey one hundred & fifty acres land listed by **PINTARD** & sold for the Tax of 1829 for Isaac **LASSITER** & that the s^d. **LASSITER** or his representatives pay said expence of survey.

Ordered that William E. **PUGH** be permitted to build an offic_ on the south east of the public square in Gatesville & that he be permitted to remove the same whenever he pleases or when the Court shall direct him so to do &c

issd. Ordered that Jethro **WILLEY** be allowed the sum of Eighty cents cost of a warrant against James **WILLIAMS** for failing to /work/ the Public road, and that the County Trustee pay the same &c.

May Court 1832

Ordered that all orders made at this Term for the payment of Patrollers be recinded.

Ordered that Jethro **WILLEY**, James C. **RIDDICK**, John R **NORFLEET** Simmons **ROUNTREE** and James T. **FREEMAN** renew their Constable Bonds and that they enter bond & security as the law directs.

Ordered that Miles **BRIGGS** be appointed Constable in the Folley district in the room of Wm **COWPER** resigned, and that he give bond & security as the law directs &c

issd. Ordered that Willis **HARRELL** be appointed overseer upon the road leading from the Perquimans road near George **COSTEN** to the new road near Mrs Sarah **HARRELL**'s & that the hands living on said Road work on it &c

issd. Ordered that Abraham **SMITH** be appointed Overseer of the road from Richard **ODOM**s to the end of the Winton causway

[26] blank *issd.* Ordered that Henry **GILLIAM** Esqr Benbury **WALTON** Abram **PARKER** & Benjamin **HAYS** be appointed Commissioners to lay off & set apart one years /provision/ &c. for Mary **HINTON** widow of Reuben **HINTON** Jr. dec^d. agreeable to law &c

issd. Ordered that W^m. W. **COWPER** Esqr. W^m. L. **BOOTHE**, Exum **LEWIS** & Reuben **PILAND** be appointed Commissioners to lay off & set apart one years provision &c. for Mary **HARRELL** widow of Peter **HARRELL** dec^d. agreeable to law &c

issd. Ordered that the Sheriff summon a jury and go on the premises and then and there lay off to Mary **HARRELL** widow of Peter **HARRELL** dec^d. her dower in the land which her husband died seized & possessed agreeable to law &c

John & Hardy **JONES** }   May Term 1832.
    vs   }
Henry **JONES**' admr. }   Pet to account.

    This Cause coming on to be heard upon the petition of the plaintiff and the answer of the defendents and the report of the referee—The Court doth declare that Heny [sic] **JONES** the testator of the defendent doth owe to the petitioner Hardy **JONES** the sum of $80.46 and to the petitioner John **JONES** the sum of $94..53. It is therefore ordered, adjudged and decreed that the petitioner Hardy **JONES** recover of the defendant William **LEE** as adm^r. of Henry **JONES** dec^d. the sum of $80..46 to be paid out of the assets of the said Henry dec^d. in the hands of the said William to be administered. And it is further adjudged and decreed that the said John **JONES** recover of the said William **LEE** as the adm^r. of the said Henry dec^d. the sum of $94.53. to be paid out of the assets of the said Henry in the hands of the said William to be administered, and that execution issue accordingly. It is further Ordered that the referee be allowed the sum of $5. for his report, and that the said sum of $5. as well as the rest of the costs be paid in the following manner to wit) one half by the defendent William **LEE** and the other half by the petitioners equally.

[27] 245 Deed of sale Andrew **BAKER** to Burrell **BROTHERS** was in open Court proved by the Oath of Joseph **GORDON** a witness thereto &c

Deed of sale Thomas B. **HUNTER** to Thomas **RIDDICK** was in open Court proved by the Oath of W^m. L. **COWPER** a witness thereto

Deed of sale Ebenezar P. **AKERMAN** & wife to Exum **JENKINS** was in open Court proved by the Oath of Edward **HOWELL** a witness &c

Deed of sale James T. **FREEMAN** to David **OUTLAW** was in open Court proved by the Oath of Peter B. **MINTON** a witness thereto &c

Deed of sale Richard H. **BALLARD** to William W. **STEDMAN** was in open Court acknowledged in due

May Court 1832

form of law &c

Deed of sale Charles **WILLIAMS** to James R **RIDDICK** was in open Court proved by the Oath of John **WALTON** a witness &c

Deed of ~~sale~~ /Trust/ B. **BLANCHARD** & Judith **LEWIS**, to Riddick **BLANCHARD** was in open Court proved by the Oath of John **WALTON** a witness thereto &c.

The Commissioners appointed to make a division of the real estate of William **BROTHERS** dec^d. made a report of their proceedings thereon and the same was ordered to be registered.

" Jethro H **RIDDICK** Nathan **RIDDICK** & Joseph **RIDDICK** the men who were appointed to audite & state the accounts [sic] Whitmll **STALLINGS** adm^r. Henry **WALTON** dec^d. made a report of their proceeding

" Jethro H **RIDDICK** Nathan **RIDDICK** & Abel **ROGERSON** the men who were appointed to audite & state the accts. of Amos **HOBBS** adm^r. of Thomas **HOBBS** dec^d. made a report of their proceedings.

" Josiah **BRIGGS** adm^r. of Daniel **PEARCE** dec^d. exhibited his account current with the estate of the dec^d. into Court &c.

Nathan **RIDDICK** County Trustee returned his acc^t. for the year /1831/

" Inventory of the goods & chattles of Sally **LEWIS** dec^d. was exhibited into Court by Frederick **HINTON** admr. on oath.

" Account of sale of the perishable estate of Sally **LEWIS** dec^d. was exhibited into Court by Frederick **HINTON** adm^r. on oath.

" Account of sale of the property of Henry **PUGH** dec^d. was exhibited into Court by William E. **PUGH** adm^r. on oath.

[28] blank Then the Court adjourned untill to morrow at 10.°Clock
Wednesday morning Court met
Present Henry **GILLIAM** John D. **PIPKIN** Wm **GOODMAN** Joseph **RIDDICK**} Esquires Justices

Daniel **FRANKLIN**   }
    vs   }
Barsheba **FRANKLIN** et als} Pet to account
    This case Coming on to be heard upon the petition report and exhibits, the Court doth declare that the whole value of the personal estate of Jonas **FRANKLIN** dec^d. was $4089..83¼ of which Burwell the posthumus issue of the said Jonas was entitled to one eighth part (to wit) $511.23—the Court doth further declare that of the aforesaid sum of $4089.83¼ Jane **FRANKLIN** rec^d. $675.02—Eliza **FRANKLIN** $550.02—Daniel **FRANKLIN** $550.02—Owen **FRANKLIN** $525.02—Nathan **FRANKLIN** $675.02—Lucretia **FRANKLIN** $300.02—Benjamin **FRANKLIN** $525. and Barsheba **FRANKLIN** Widow) $275.02; it is therefore adjudged and decreed that the aforesaid Benjamin contribute $66—Jane $85. Eliza $69.—Daniel $69.—Owen $66—Nathan $85.—Lucretia $37.12 & Barsheba $34.11 to make up the aforesaid portion of $511.77 to which the said Burwell was entitled.

Ordered that Abraham W. **PARKER** have a Licence to retail spirits at his Bar—for one year.

issd. Ordered that John **WALKER** be permitted to sell Oysters & Cakes within the County of Gates for one year from this Term.

issd. Ordered that James M. **RIDDICK** the overseer of the road leading from **BENNETT**s Creek a cross the middle swamp towards the Court House make & keep up good & sufficient foot bridges over both

May Court 1832

said streams of water.

[29] 247 " Sidney HURDLE Guardian to the orphans of Henry HURDLE dec^d. exhibited into Court her acc^t with said orphans

" John MATTHEWS Guardian to the orphans of Jethro BENTON dec^d. exhibited into Court his acc^t with said orphans on oath &c

Deed of sale William G. DAUGHTRY to William ELEY was in open Court acknowledged in due form of law &c

Deed in Trust James WILLIAMS to James R. RIDDICK was in open Court [sic] Lassiter RIDDICK who swore to the hand writing of Wm W. RIDDICK, and James C. RIDDICK who swore to the hand writing of James WILLIAMS.

Ordered that James BENTON be appointed administrator de bonis non on the estate of Elisha BENTON dec^d. on giving bond in the sum of six hundred dollars with Riddick MATTHEWS and William BENTON securities and was approved of by the Court &c

issd. Oordered [sic] that the Sheriff Summons Whitmell HILL, David PARKER Elisha HUNTER, Charles JONES of Parker) Andrew BAKER Willis J. RIDDICK, William DAVIDSON, Isaac PIPKIN, James BOYCE Nathan WARD, Kindred PARKER, John SPARKMAN William HARRELL of s. H) William BLANCHARD sen^r., Josiah BRIGGS, John H. HASLETT Henry HAYS, James JONES, Jonathan WILLIAMS of sam^l. Edward BRIGGS, Jesse ARLINE Charles EASON, An^d. EASON Peter EURE Simon WALTERS, Benjamin BROWN, John BRADY Edward STALLINGS Henry GREEN, Mills ROBERTS, Kedar TAYLOR, Jacob OUTLAW W^m. PARKER, Barnes GOODMAN Rich^d. CURL & Joseph HURDLE Jr. personally to attend at the next County Court to be held for this County on the third monday in August next, then and there to serve as Jurors &c. Constables Jet. H. RIDDICK, D. SPARKMAN.

[30] blank State of North Carolina   August 20th. 1832.
    At a Court of Pleas and Quarter Sessions, begun and held for the County of Gates, at the Court House in Gatesville on the third monday of August in the Fifty seventh year of our Independence, and in the Year of our Lord One thousand Eight hundred and thirty two.
Present   Henry GILLIAM Isaac R. HUNTER John C. GORDON Peter B. MINTON} Esquires Justices

Ordered that Joseph RIDDICK of Thos) be permitted to streighten the road opposit [sic] his gate & put it in such order as may be satisfactory to the overseer, & that the overseer of said road receive the same.

Ordered that Henry ROBINS a Coloured boy son of Julia ROBINS be bound as an apprentice to Joseph RIDDICK to learn the the [sic] trade of a Farmer.

issd. Ordered that the Overseer of the road leading from Gatesville to MINGO's path keep up the bridge near John WALTON's being the one formerly kept by Benbury WALTON.

issd. Ordered that Thomas HURDLE be appointed overseer of the road leading from Warwick swamp to the snake branch in the room or sted [sic] of Frederick ROOKS resigned.

Ordered that John C. GORDON be appointed Guardian to Timothy LASSITER & Sarah Margaret LASSITER orphans of Henry LASSITER dec^d. he gives Noah HARRELL George COSTEN & Tilly W. CARR for securities. Present in Court Henry GILLIAM George KITTRELL John B. BAKER, Isaac R. HUNTER & W^m. GOODMAN Esquires Justices who approved of the securities & Concurred in the appointment

Ordered that Mills EURE be appointed Guardian to Louisa LEE, W^m. W. LEE & Step. LEE orphans of

August Court 1832

Step. **LEE**, that he give bond & security in the sum of $200. and offers Nathl. **EURE** & Demsey **SPARKMAN** as securities Present in Court H. **GILLIAM**, G. **KITTRELL**, I. R. **HUNTER** & Jno. **WALTON** Esqrs Justices who approved of the securites & concured in the appointmt.

Ordered that Martha S. **MELVIN** be appointed Guardian to Henry **MELVIN**, Mary Jane **MELVIN** & Sally Ann **MELVIN** orphans of Frederick H. **MELVIN** dec^d. and that she give bond for $100

[31] 249 and she offers as security Joseph **BROOKS** & Noah **HARRELL**. Present in Court George **KITTRELL**, Riddick **GATLING**, W^m. W. **COWPER** & John **WALTON** Esquires Justices who approved of the securities and concurred in the appointment &c.

The Inspectors of the several Elections held on the 9th. of this instant (August made their returns agreeable to law, and it appearing that James R. **RIDDICK** Esqr. was duly elected Sheriff of Gates County for the two succeeding years from this Court. -- It is there fore [sic] Ordered that the said James R. **RIDDICK** enter into bonds with security agreeable to the act of the General Assembly in such [sic] made and provided, at the same time Riddick **GATLING**, Henry **BOND**, Joseph **RIDDICK** of Thos) and John **ROBERTS** came into Court and offered themselves securities who were approved of by the Court, the Bonds was then executed and the said sheriff was qualified by taking & subscribing the Oaths prescribed by law. Present in Court John **WILLEY**, Henry **GILLIAM**, Isaac R **HUNTER**, Richard **ODOM** George **KITTRELL**, John **WALTON**, William **GOODMAN**, William L. **BOOTHE** John C. **GORDON**, William W. **COWPER**, William **WALTON** Whitmell **STALLINGS** Joseph **RIDDICK** & Hardy D. **PARKER** Esquires Justices &c.

recorded The last will and Testament of Thomas **ROUNTREE** dec^d. was exhibited into Court and was proved by the oath of John **WALTON** one of the subscribing witness [sic] thereto and ordered to be recorded. At the same time Seth Washington **ROUNTREE** the executor therein appointed came into Court and was duly qualifed for that office and prayed an order for letters testamentary thereon which was accordingly granted

" Inventory of the property of Barsheba **FRANKLIN** dec^d. was exhibited into Court by Abraham **RIDDICK** adm^r. on oath &c.

" Inventory of the property of William **KING** dec^d. was exhibited into Court by Amos **HOBBS** executor on oath &c

" Inventory & account of sales of the estate of Luke **HOLLOWEL** dec^d. was exhibited into Court [sic] William **BYRUM** exor. on oath &c.

" Account of sales of the property of Barsheba **FRANKLIN** dec^d. was exhibited into Court by Abraham **RIDDICK** adm^r. on oath

[32] blank " Account of sales of the property of Abner **PEARCE** dec^d. was exhibited into Court by Isaac R. **HUNTER** adm^r. on oath &c

" John C. **GORDON**, Edward R **HUNTER** & Richard H. **PARKER** three of the men who were appointed to audite & state the acct^s. of Isaac R **HUNTER** adm^r. of Abner **PEARCE** dec^d. made a report of their proceedings &c.

" Jethro **SUMNER**, John **WIGGINS** & Jesse **WIGGINS** three of the men who were appointed to audite & state the accts of James **MORGAN** adm^r. of John **HARE** dec^d. made a report of their proceedings &c.

" Peter B. **MINTON**, Jethro H. **RIDDICK** & Abel **ROGERSON** three of the men who were appointed to audite & state the accts of David **HOBBS** adm^r. of Josiah **OVERMAN** dec^d. made a report of their proceedings &c.

" Henry **GILLIAM** Guardian to Burwell **FRANKLIN** orphan exhibited into Court his guardian acc^t.

August Court 1832

with s^d orphan on oath.

Deed of sale James R **RIDDICK** shff. to Jonathan **WILLIAMS** was in open Court proved by the oath of Lassiter **RIDDICK** a witness.

Deed of sale Prudence **WILLIAMS** to Jethro **BARNES** was in open Court proved by the oath of John W. **ODOM** a witness &c

Deed of sale Richard **RIDDICK** & wife to W^m. H. **GOODMAN** was in open Court acknowledged in due form of law &c

Ordered that Henry **GILLIAM** & Isaac R **HUNTER** Esqrs take the private examination of Margaret **RIDDICK** wife of Richard **RIDDICK** in open Court touching her signature to a deed of sale to W^m. H. **GOODMAN** & report.

Deed of sale Elisha **WALTON** to Peter B. **MINTON** was in open Court proved by the oath of Abel **ROGERSON** a witness thereto

Deed of sale William W. **STEDMAN** to Andrew **MATTHEWS** was in open Court proved by the oath of Rich^d. H. **BALLARD** a witness

Deed in Trust Richd. H. **BALLARD** to James **MORGAN** was in open Court acknowledged in due form of law &c

Deed of sale Henry **RIDDICK** to Robert **RIDDICK** was in open Court acknowledged in due form of law &c

Receipt from Henry **RIDDICK** to Robert **RIDDICK** was in open Court acknowledged in due form of law &c

[33] 251 Deed of sale Joseph **GORDON** to Nathan **WARD** was in open Court proved by the Oath of Marmaduke **NORFLEET** a witness thereto

Deed of sale Willis J. **RIDDICK** to Lamuel **WARD** was in open Court proved by the Oath of John **WALTON** a witness thereto &c

Release from Marmaduke **BAKER** to Daniel **WILLIAMS** was in open Court proved by the oath of Henry G. **WILLIAMS** a witness

Deed of sale David **OUTLAW** to John **SAUNDERS** was in open Court proved by the Oath of Henry **BAGLEY** a witness thereto &c.

Deed of sale Elisha H. **BOND** to Isaac **PIPKIN** was in open Court proved by the oath of John **SAUNDERS** a witness thereto

Deed of sale Elisha **WALTON** to James **BAKER** was in open Court proved by the Oath of Wynns **BAKER** a witness thereto &c

Deed of sale Garrett **HOFFLER** to John **HINTON** [?]was in open Court proved by the Oath of James T. **FREEMAN** a witness thereto.

Deed of sale Richard **ODOM** to Demsey **PARKER** was in open Court acknowledged in due form of law &c

Deed of sale Kadar **GREEN** & wife to Benbury **WALTON** was in open Court proved by the Oath of Henry **BOND** a witness &c.

August Court 1832

Deed of sale Elizabeth LEE to Nathanel EURE was in open Court proved by the Oath of William LEE a witness &c

The Gentleman [sic] who was appointed to examine the Office of the County Court agreeable to an act of assembly passed in the year 1830 " Report that we have examined the Clerks Office, and found the Office properly kept, and the records of the same we find brought up to the time of the present order &c August 13th. 1832. Jno. B. BAKER T. SAUNDERS J. WALTON

" Wednesday morning the Court met Present Henry GILLIAM John B. BAKER Mills RIDDICK & Thomas SAUNDERS Esqrs Justices

Ordered that the County surveyor survey for Thomas SAUNDERS 44 acres of land which was listed by Benj^a BLANCHARD Junr. & sold for the Taxes of 1829. & purchased by said SAUNDERS to commence at any time he may think proper.

Ordered that the County surveyor survey for James BOOTH (Somerton 39) [sic] acres land listed in the name of Martha HORTON, & sold for the Taxes of 1829.

[34] blank Then the Court adjourned untill tomorrow 10. Oclock
Tuesday morning Court met
Present   William W. COWPER William GOODMAN Joseph RIDDICK W^m. L. BOOTHE} Esquires Justices

Grand Jury qualified at this term, to wit. Barnes GOODMAN Foreman) Charles EASON, David PARKER, Andrew EASON, John SPARKMAN, Andrew BAKER, Kindred PARKER Charles JONES of P. Henry HAYSE, Jesse ARLINE, Whitmell HILL, Willis J. RIDDICK Joseph HURDLE Jr. William HARRELL of S) W^m. BLANCHARD sen^r. Richard CURL, William PARKER & Peter EURE.

Petit Jury qualified at this term to wit John H. HASLETT Nathan WARD, Josiah BRIGGS, Simon WALTERS, Benjamin BROWN Henry GREEN, Riddick TROTMAN, William SEARS, Levi BEEMAN Riddick MATTHEWS, William GATLING & Demsey SPARKMAN

issd. Ordered that Isaac R HUNTER be appointed a Commissioner in the room of Henry RIDDICK to act with the others under an act of the Genl. assembly pass^d. for the purpose of building a poor house for the County of Gates &c

issd. Ordered that John WALTON Esqr. Willis J. RIDDICK, David PARKER & Henry BOND make a division of the real estate of Abner PEARCE dec^d. and that they make a report to next Court.

Ordered that Josiah BLANCHARD son of Will. BLANCHARD dec^d. be bound an apprentice to John WALTON to learn the art of farming business &c

Ordered that Hillory EASON son of W^m. EASON dec^d. be bound to Isaac PEARCE Jr. to learn the art [sic] the farming business.

Ordered that John POLSON a boy of Colour son of Ruth POLSON be bound to Abraham PARKER of Kedar) untill he is 21 years of age to learn the black smiths trade &c

issd. Ordered that Isaac PIPKIN be appointed overseer of the road from Isaac PIPKINs to WYNNs Ferry in the room of William GATLING resigned & that his own hands together with W^m. & Riddick GATLINGs hands work said road & that said road extend to the fork neare [?] where Robert SMITH formely [sic] lived.

[35] 253 *issd.* Ordered that Nathan CULLINS hands work on the road kept by Riddick TROTMAN as overseer.

August Court 1832

issd. Ordered that John **CLEAVES** be appointed overseer of the road leading from the fork of the main road near W^m. **HINTON**'s to the fork of the road near **PARKER**'s landing, and that he have the following hands to keep up the same (viz) Silas **SIMPSON** Isaac **PARKER**, Robert **PARKER** of Isaiah) [sic] Henry **LASSITER**, Mills **REED**, Elisha **ROOKS** Jesse **REED** & William **ROOKS** &c

" Inventory of the perishable estate of Micajah **RIDDICK** dec^d. was exhibited into Court by Lassiter **RIDDICK** Exor. on oath &c.

" Inventory of the perishable estate of Reuben **HINTON** Jr. dec^d. was exhibited into Court by Hance **HOFFLER** adm^r. on oath &c.

" Acc^t. sales & Inventory of the estate of James **GRANBERY** dec^d. was exhibited into Court by Joseph **GORDON** adm^r. on oath &c.

" Acc^t. sales & Inventory of the estate of Miles **BRINKLEY** dec^d. was exhibited into Court by Joseph **GORDON** adm^r. on oath &c

Deed of sale Henry W. **SKINNER** to Wright **HAYS** was in open Court acknowledged in due form of law &c.

Deed of sale Solomon **EASON** to Andrew **EASON** was in open Court proved by the Oath of Joseph **GORDON** a witness &c.

Deed of sale Solomon **EASON** to Reuben **EASON** was in open Court proved by the Oath of Joseph **GORDON** a witness &c.

Deed of sale James R. **RIDDICK** shff. to Peter B. **MINTON** was in open Court acknowledged in due form of law &c.

Deed of Mortgage Abraham **MORGAN** to Henry **GILLIAM** was in open Court proved by the Oath of John R. **GILLIAM** a witness &c

Deed of sale John A. **MARCH** & Jason **SAUNDERS** to Miles **PARKER** was in open Court proved by the Oath of Jethro **BARNES** a witness.

~~Deed~~ Bill of sale Etheldred **CROSS** to Thomas **SAUNDERS** was in open Court acknowledged in due form of law &c

Deed of sale John V. **SUMNER** shff to Timothy **WALTON** was in open Court proved by the oath of David **PARKER** a witness &c

Deed of Gift Sally **WILLIAMS** to her children Allen, Lavina, Martha & Robert **WILLIAMS** was in open Court proved by the oath of Jno. **WALTON** &c

Deed of sale Timothy **WALTON** to John **ALPHIN** was in open Court acknowledged in due form of law &c

[36] blank The commissioners who were appointed to make a division of certain lands lying in Gates County in the dismal swamp by the petitions of Willie M^C.**PHERSON** & others made a report of their proceedings thereon which was confirmed by the Court and ordered to be registered &c

" Richard **BRIGGS** guardian to Milicent **BRINKLEY** an orphan exhibited into Court his guardian account with s^d orphan on oath

Mary & Henry **WALTON** }	Pet. to sell negroes
to }	
The Court }	This cause coming on to be hear_ed_ upon the petition and evidence of-

August Court 1832

fered, it is ordered adjudged and decreed by the Court that Nathan **RIDDICK** after advertising at three or more public places in the said County for the space of thirty days the sale of the aforesaid negroes **ESTHER & MARTHA**, he proceed to sell the same at public sale to the highest bidder upon a credit of six months except so much as may be necessary to pay the costs of this petition and other Expences attending the said sale which am^o. he is to receive in Cash) he taking the bonds of the purchasers with good and sufficient security, and that he make a report of his proceedings at the next term of this Court.

issd. Ordered that the Sheriff summon Isaac R **HUNTER**, Blake **BRADY**, Jordon **PARKER**, Robert **WILSON**, Edwin **CROSS**, Exum **LEWIS** John **WILLEY** Joseph **GORDON**, Edward R **HUNTER** Demsey **SPARKMAN** Blake **BAKER**, John B. **BAKER** John H. **HASLETT** Willis J. **RIDDICK** William **BABB**, David **HOBBS** Amos **HOBBS**, John **WALTON**, Henry **GREEN**, Holloday **WALTON**, Demsey **EURE**, John O. **HUNTER**, Noah **HINTON**, Nathan **CULLINS**, Timothy **HUNTER**, Edwin **MATHIAS** Henry **HAYS**, Hardy **JONES** of H.) Daniel **WILLIAMS**, James **BOGER** David **BENTON**, Jesse **MATHIAS**, Hardy D. **PARKER**, Elisha **HUNTER** John **MITCHEL** & Miles **PARKER** of Amos.) personally to be and appear at the next Superior Court of law to be held for the County of Gates at the Court House in Gatesville on the first monday after the fourth monday of September next, then and there to serve as Jurors &c.

[37] 255 Ordered that the Sheriff summon Jonathan **WILLIAMS** of Jon^a.) Kader **RIDDICK**, James **GOODWIN**, Jesse **PARKER** [? blot] Prior **SAVAGE**, Isaac **PEARCE** Jr. Joseph **FREEMAN** Paul **JONES**, Jesse **PILAND**, Henry **BOND** Jasper **TROTMAN** Lem^l. **RIDDICK** Levi **CREECY**, John **SPEIGHT** of H. Levi **SUMNER**, Jethro **BLANCHARD**, John **SPARKMAN**, Timothy **SPIVEY** John **SANDERS**, Levi **ROGERS**, Job. R. **HALL**, Elisha **SMALL**, John **ROBERTS**, Jacob **POWELL**, Kinchen **HOWELL**, Willis **HARRELL**, Andrew **BAKER** William A. **MATTHEWS**, Jonas **HINTON**, James **BOOTHE**, C. H) Miles **BROWN**, Miles **PARKER**, William **BLANCHARD** sen^r. James **JONES**, Robert **HILL**, & Tilley W. **CARR** personally to attend at the next county Court to be held for the County of Gates at the Court House in Gatesville on the third monday in November next, then [sic] there to serve as Jurors &c.

issd. Ordered that the Sheriff be allowed in his settlement of the Taxes for the year 1831. with the Public Treasurer, County Trustee and wardens of the poor the Poll Tax on the following persons allowed by the Court as insolvents &c (to wit)

Charles **BAKER**	1	Robert **LEE**	1	Isaac **GREEN**	1
Henry H. **BENTON**	1	Peter **PILAND**	1	Wesley **PHELPS**	1
Nathaniel **DOUGHTIE**	1	John **POWELL**	1	Jeremiah **SMITH**	1
William **HUDGINS**	1	Nicholas **WADES**	1	James F. **SMALL**	1
JENKINS Isaac H	1	David **UMPHLET**	1	Thos. G. **COFFER**	1
Bryant **MATTHEWS**	1	Tulley **CALE**	1	Nathl. **GRIFFITH**	1
James **PERRY**	1	Thomas **JOHNSON**	1	Marmaduke **ELLIS**	1
David **ROOKS**	1	Charles **WILLIAMS**	2	Alfred **BALLARD**	2
Richard **RIDDICK**	4	James **WILLIAMS**	1	William **JONES** Jr.	1
Demsey **BOYT**	1	Jesse **WYOOT** [sic]	1	Timothy **WALTON** Jr.	2
Edwin **ELLIS**	1	Jacob K. **BUNCH**	1	Thomas **WALTON**	1
Rich^d. **CORNELIUS**	1	William **CLARK**	1	---	13
CORNELIUS Thomas	1	Charles **DELANY**	1	---	26
James **KING**	1	Moses **HOBBS**	1	---	24
James **WILLIAMS** Jr.	1	Isaac **LASSITER**	1	Total--	63
Levi **BRINKLEY**	1	James **LASSITER**	1		
Wiley **BROWN**	1	Thomas **MORGAN**	1		
Henry **EURE**	1	Robert **PARKER**	1		
John **FELTON**	1	James **POWELL**	1		
Samuel **GREEN**	1	Thomas **SPIVEY**	1		
Mills **HARRELL**	1	Thomas **BAGLEY**	1		
George **HARRELL** Jr.	1	Fred^k. **BLANCHARD**	1		

August Court 1832

Nehemiah **KING**   1   Demsey **BLANCHARD**   1
                    26   24

[38] blank   State of North Carolina   November 19th. 1832.

At a Court of Pleas and Quarter sessions, begun and held for the County of Gates, at the Court House in Gatesville on the third monday of November in the Fifty seventh year of our Independence, and in the year of our Lord one thousand eight hundred and thirty two &c.

Present   Henry **GILLIAM** John C. **GORDON** Richard **ODOM** Hardy D. **PARKER**} Esquires Justices

issd. Ordered that William **BOOTHE** Ethel^d. **CROSS** Mills **EURE** be appointed auditors to Settle the accounts of Jacob **ODOM** admr. of Monica **ODOM** dec^d. & that they make a report to next Court &c

Ordered that Abraham **RIDDICK** administer upon the estate of James **RIDDICK** son of Abm. that he enter into Bond & security in the sum of Five hundred dollars and offers Jesse **MATHIAS** & Riddick **JONES** as securities who [sic] approved of by the Court &c

On motion. Ordered that Jeptha **FOWLKES** be appointed adm^r. upon the Estate of Sophia **PARKER** & that he give bond & security in the sum of two hundred dollars & offers Henry **GILLIAM** for security who was approved of by the Court &c

Ordered that Reuben **HARRELL** be appointed Guardian to Daniel **PARKER** orphan of Abram **PARKER** dec^d. that he give Bond & security in the sum of Five hundred dollars and offers for security Jeptha **FOWLKES** and Edward R. **HUNTER** who was approved of by the Court & ~~concurred in the appointment~~

Present in Court Henry **GILLIAM**, John C. **GORDON** & Richard **ODOM** Esquires Justices &c

issd. Ordered that Jethro **BARNES** the County surveyor be appointed to procession the line dividing the lands of William **BABB** and Simon **WALTERS** and make a report of his proceedings at the next Court &c.

[39] 257 Ordered that Isaac **WILLIAMS** be appointed deputy Surveyor for the County of Gates and he be duly qualified for that office

Ordered that James **SAVAGE** be appointed [sic] to renew his Constable Bond, that he give Barnes **GOODMAN** & Jesse **SAVAGE** as securities

issd. Ordered that, that [sic] the Number of Elections now established be reduced to Three to say, Gatesville, Wm. H. **GOODMAN**'s & at Sunsbury & that the Sheriff hold said Elections as the law requires hereafter

issd. Ordered that James C. **RIDDICK** be allowed the sum of four dollars & eighty [sic] for sundry services & that the County Trustee pay the same &c

issd. Ordered that Nancy **RIDDICK** widow of James W. **RIDDICK** be discharged from any Extra Tax which she may have incurred from any neglect of listing as the law requires &c

issd. Ordered that Ephraim **BUNCH** be appointed overseer of the road in the room of Henry **SPIVEY** &c.

issd. Ordered that Adam **RABY** be appointed overseer of the road in the room of Job R. **HALL** resigned &c.

Ordered that John **WILLIAMS**, son of Enoch be bound as an apprentice to Richard **HAYS**, to learn the trade of Turning business

November Court 1832

" Hillory **WILLEY** William **GOODMAN** Dempsey **GOODMAN** & John D. **PIPKIN** the men who were appointed to audite & settle the estate of Jonathan **ROGERS** dec^d. made a report of their proceedings thereon &c

" Hillory **WILLEY**, John D. **PIPKIN** Dempsey **GOODMAN** & William **GOODMAN** the men who were appointed to audite & settle the Estate of Elizabeth **ROGERS** dec^d. made a report of their proceedings thereon &c.

recorded The last will and Testament of John **BEEMAN** dec^d. was Exhibited into Court and was proved by the oath of Jeptha **FOWLKES** one of the subscribing witnesses thereto and ordered to be recorded. At the same time Dempsey **SPARKMAN** & Levi **BEEMAN** the executors therein appointed Came into Court and was duly qualified for that office & prayed an order for letters testamentary thereon &c.

recorded The last will and Testament of Lewis **WALTERS** dec^d. was exhibited into Court and was proved by the oath of Elbert H. **RIDDICK** one of the subscribing witnesses thereto and ordered to be recorded. At the same time Richard **SMITH** the executor therein appointed came into Court and was duly qualified for that office and prayed an order for letters testamentary thereon &c.

[40] blank *recorded* The last will and Testament of George **KITTRELL** dec^d. was exhibited into Court and proved by the Oaths of Levi **ROGERS** & Dempsey **GOODMAN** two of the subscribing witnesses thereto and ordered to be recorded. And Milley **KITTRELL** the Executrix therein appointed came into Court and renounced her right of Executrixship [sic] to said will, and Daniel **WILLIAMS** the executor therein appointed Came into Court and was duly qualified for that Office and prayed an order for letters testamentary thereon which was accordingly granted &c

Inventory of the Perishable Estate of Thomas **ROUNTREE** dec^d. was exhibited into Court by Seth W. **ROUNTREE** adm^r. on oath &c

We the Subscribers being members of the County Court, do proteste [sic] against granting retail licence to any persons unless they shall be regular Tavern Keepers & prepared to entertain man & horse & that we will as members [sic] aforesaid Court oppose all such appointments this 19th. Novr. 1832. H. **GILLIAM** R. **GATLING** P. B. **MINTON** Jno C. **GORDON** Will. **GOODMAN** J. **RIDDICK** H. D. **PARKER** William **LEE** I. R. **HUNTER** Rich^d. **ODOM** W. **WALTON** J. **WALTON**

Bill of sale Nathan **WARD** to Timothy **PERRY** was in open Court acknowledged in due form of law &c.

Bill of sale Reuben **HINTON** to David **PARKER** was in open Court proved by the oath of Burwell **BROTHERS** a witness thereto &c

Bill of sale Hance **HOFLER** to David **PARKER** was in open Court proved by the Oath of Henry **GILLIAM** a witness thereto &c.

Bill of sale Elisha **WALTON** to Whit^l. **STALLINGS** was in open Court proved by the oath of Frederick **ROOKS** a witness thereto &c

Bill of sale William **SEARS** to Nancy **PARKER** was in open Court acknowledged in due form of law &c.

[41] 259 Deed of sale Jesse **MATHIAS** to John **TAYLOR** was in open Court acknowledged in due form of law &c.

Deed of sale Henry **HARE** to John **TAYLOR** was in open Court proved by the Oath of John **WIGGINS** a witness thereto &c.

Deed of sale John W. **ODOM** to James C. **SMITH** was in open Court acknowledged in due form of law &c.

November Court 1832

Deed of sale Thomas **TWINE** to Abel **ROGERSON** was in open Court acknowledged in due form of law &c.

Deed of sale Isaac K. **BUNCH** & wife to Willis **BUNCH** was in open Court proved by the Oath [sic] William **HURDLE** a witness &c

Deed of Sale Mary **HARRELL** to Abraham **PRUDEN** was in open Court proved by the Oath of Abraham W. **PARKER** a witness &c

Deed of sale Abel **ROGERSON** to W^m. E. **PUGH** & Henry R. **PUGH** was in open Court acknowledged in due form of law &c.

Deed in Trust Starkey **EURE** to D. **EURE** & James **EURE** was in open Court proved by the Oath of James **OUTLAW** a witness &c.

Deed of sale Isaac **LASSITER** to Starkey **EWER** [sic] was in open Court proved by the Oath of James **OUTLAW** a witness thereto &c.

Bill of sale **MORGAN & PARKER** to Abraham **MORGAN** was in open Court proved by the Oath of James **GOODMAN** a witness &c.

Deed of sale **MORGAN & PARKER** to Abraham **MORGAN** was in open Court proved by the Oath of James **GOODMAN** a witness &c.

Deed of sale H. H C **JONES** to Miles **HOWELL** was in open Court acknowledged in due form of law &c.

Deed of sale Kinchen **NORFLEET** to John **GRANBERRY** was in open Court acknowledged in due form of law &c.

Deed of sale Matilda **MELTEAR** to Walton **FREEMAN** was in open [sic] proved by the Oath of Miles **DAVIS** a witness thereto &c.

Deed of sale Joseph **GORDON** to James **BRINKLEY** was in open Court acknowledged in due form of law &c.

Deed of sale Henry W. **SKINNER** to John **MATTHEWS** was in open Court proved by the Oath of Wright **HAYES** a witness thereto &c

Deed of sale Robt. **PARKER** & wife & Frederick **MORRISS** to Timothy **WALTON** was in open Court acknowledged in due form of law &c.

Deed of sale John **RIDDICK** to John **GATLING** & George **COSTEN** was [sic] open Court acknowledged in due form of law &c.

Deed of Gift John **FREEMAN** sen^r. [sic] John **FREEMAN** Jr. was in open Court proved by the Oath of Francis **DUKE** a witness &c.

Deed of sale George **HARRELL** to Abraham **PRUDEN** was in open [sic] proved by the Oath of Abram W. **PARKER** a witness thereto &c

[42] blank Deed of sale Miles **PARKER** & wife & Thomas **SAUNDERS** to Robert R **SMITH** and Benjamin **SAUNDERS** was in open Court proved by the Oath of John **LANGSTON** a witness thereto &.

Deed of Sale Asa **HARRELL** to Nathaniel **HARRELL** was in open Court proved by the Oath of Reuben **HARRELL** a witness &c

November Court 1832

*Mildred **KITTRELL** widow of the late George **KITTRELL** decd. Came into /court/ and renounced her right of Executrixship to the said Will. and ordered that the same be entered on the minutes

Then the Court adjourned untill tomorrow 10. Oclock
Tuesday morning Court met.
Present			Henry **GILLIAM** Riddick **GATLING** John B. **BAKER**} Esquires Justices

Grand Jury qualified at this Term (to wit) John **ROBERTS** Forman Miles **BROWN**, Paul **JONES**, Levi **ROGERS**, Robert **HILL**, Jonathan **WILLIAMS**, Timothy **SPIVEY** W^m. A. **MATTHEWS**, Isaac **PEARCE** Jr. Andrew **BAKER** Jonas **HINTON**, Jesse **PILAND**, John **SAUNDERS**, Elisha **SMALL**, Jethro **BLANCHARD**, Willis **HARRELL**, Prior **SAVAGE** and Tilley W. **CARR**.

Ordered that a Sci Fa issue against Jethro **JENKINS** & his securities in favour of Nathl. **DOUGHTIE** & wife for an allowance for Bastardy &c.

On motion. Ordered that administration upon the estate of Nathaniel **MURPHEY** be granted to John W. **ODOM**, it is ordered that he enter into bond in the sum of $800 with Jethro **WILLEY** & Daniel **WILLIAMS** his securities.

Ordered that John **WALTON** be granted letters of administration on the estate of John **HARE** [?] dec^d. and that he give bond in the Sum of five hundred dollars with Timothy **WALTON** & Henry **BOND** as securities &c.

Ordered that Hardy D. **PARKER** be appointed guardian to W^m. **PARKER** orphan of Abram **PARKER** dec^d. and that he give bond and security in the sum of five hundred dollars with Barnes **GOODMAN** & Jesse **WIGGINS** as securities Present Court H. **GILLIAM** W^m. **LEE** & W^m. **GOODMAN** Esqrs. Justices who approved of the securities & Concurred &c

[43] 261 Ordered that Nathan **NIXON** be appointed guardian to Mary Ann & Joseph G. **WALTON** orphans of Timothy **WALTON** sen^r. dec^d. & that he give for [sic] thousand dollars each with Nathan **CULLINS** & Jethro H. **RIDDICK** as securities. Present in Court W^m. **LEE**, Will. **GOODMAN** & Hardy D. **PARKER** Esquires Justices who approved of the securities and concurred in the appointment &c

Ordered that Henry **GILLIAM** be appointed adm^r. upon the estate of Abraham **PARKER** dec^d. and enter into bond of $2.000. and offers James R. **RIDDICK** & Jethro H. **RIDDICK** as securities

issd. Ordered that Henry **GILLIAM** adm^r. of Abraham **PARKER** dec^d. sell two negroes belonging to s^d. dec^d. estate on a credit of Six or Nine months.

issd. Ordered that Riddick **GATLING** adm^r. of James W. **RIDDICK** dec^d. sell such part of the negroes belonging to s^d. Estate & that may be necessary to discharge the balance of the debts &c

Ordered that the Clerk issue a Certificate to Charles **JONES** a free man of Color Certifying his freedom upon the information of John C. **GORDON** Esqr. as the Law require. [sic]

issd. Ordered that Jesse **BROWN** be allowed Eleven dollars & 75/100 for medical services rendered by Dr. **FOWLKES** for negro **DICK** a Prisoner & for advertising the same with a negro **HARRY** also a prisoner.

issd. Ordered that David **PARKER** be allowed the sum of four dollars & eighty cents for six days attendance on the Grand Jury at Superior & November Courts 1832 & that the County Trustee pay the sam_

issd. Ordered that James **FIGG** be allowed the sum of one dollar and fifty cents for two days as witness in the Superior Court, State vs. James C **RIDDICK** & that the County Trustee pay the same

November Court 1832

issd. Ordered that Thomas **SAUNDERS** have a Licence to retail at his house in Gatesville for one year by the small measure.

issd. Ordered that Abraham **PRUDEN** be appointed overseer of the road leading from Sarum Creek landing to the white Oak Branch in the room of Thomas **HOGGARD** resigned.

" Inventory of the estate of John **HARE** dec^d. was exhibited into Court by John **WALTON** Special administrator on oath

" Account of sale [sic] the perishable estate of Reuben **HINTON** Jr. dec^d. was exhibited into Court by Hance **HOFLER** adm^r.

[44] blank Deed of sale James **BRINKLEY** to Nathan **RIDDICK** was in open Court proved by the Oath of Jethro H. **RIDDICK** a witness.

Deed of sale & Conveyance Lovey **BRADY** to W^m. **SEARS** was in open Court proved by the Oath of Blake **BRADY** a witness.

Deed of sale Abraham **RIDDICK** to James **MORGAN** was in open Court proved by the Oath of John **WIGGINS** a witness thereto.

Deed of sale Phereba **TROTMAN** to Riddick **TROTMAN** was in open Court proved by the Oath of Ezekiel **TROTMAN** a witness.

Deed in Trust Elisha H. **BOND** to John **WILLEY** was in open Court proved by the Oath of Jethro **WILLEY** a witness thereto.

Deed of sale James **POWELL** to William W. **STEDMAN** was in open Court proved by the Oath of Richard H. **BALLARD** a witness.

Power of attorney Levi W. **PARKER** to Randolph **SHERARD** was in open Court, and was ordered to be registered in the Registers Office in Gates County N. Carolina.

issd. Ordered that John C. **GORDON** Esq. Richard H. **BALLARD**, Humphrey **PARKER** Holloday **WALTON** and Jethro **BARNES** be appointed to make a division of the real estate of Abraham **BENTON** dec^d. among the heirs agreeably to law.

issd. Ordered that the Sheriff summon a jury and go on the premises and lay off to Wealthy **RIDDICK** widow of James **RIDDICK** dec^d. her dower in the lands which her late husband died seized and possessed agreeable to law &c.

issd. Ordered that John C. **GORDON** Esqr. Rich^d. H. **BALLARD**, Riddick **JONES** & John O. **HUNTER** be appointed to lay off and allot to Wealty **RIDDICK** widow of James **RIDDICK** dec^d. her years provision agreeably to law &c

issd. Ordered that Thomas **SAUNDERS** Esqr. W^m. G. **DAUGHTRY**, Prior **SAVAGE** & Jesse **BROWN** be appointed to lay off and allot to Martha **PARKER** Widow of Abram **PARKER** dec^d. her years provision agreeably to law &c.

issd. Ordered that Dempsey **SPARKMAN** Reuben **PILAND** Richd. **ODOM** John **RIDDICK** & Prior **SAVAGE** be appointed Commissioners with the County Surveyor to make a division of the real [sic] of Peter **HARRELL** dec^d. amongst his lawfull heirs agreeably to law &c.

[45] 263 *issd.* Ordered that the Sheriff summon Mills **SPARKMAN**, Willis **CROSS**, Andrew **HARRELL**, William **HARRELL** Senr. Daniel **RIDDICK** of Isaiah) Nathan **WARD**, James **MORGAN** David **PARKER** Jacob **ODOM** Edward **BRIGGS**, Humphrey **PARKER** sen^r. John **HINTON** Kedar

November Court 1832

TAYLOR, John MORRIS, John BRADY Willis RIDDICK of Isaiah) Richard SMITH, Shadrach PILAND Seth SPIVEY, Clement HILL Abraham SPIVEY, Jonathan WHITE David RIDDICK James C. RIDDICK Richard H. BALLARD, Moses SPIVEY, William PARKER James SUMNER Benjamin BROWN, Levi EURE, Nathaniel EURE, John BROWN of Willis) Andrew EASON, Rizup RAWLS, William. DAVIDSON and Jethro HARRELL SC. Hall) personally to attend at the next County Court to be held for the County of Gates at the Court House in Gatesville on the third monday in February next, then and there to serve as Jurors &c [Remainder of page is blank.]

[46] blank State of North Carolina February the 18th. 1833.
 At a Court of Pleas and Quarter Sessions, begun and held for the County of Gates, at the Court House in Gatesville on the third monday of February in the Fifty seventh year of our Independence, and in the year of our Lord One thousand eight hundred and thirty three.
Present Hardy D. PARKER Wm. W. COWPER Mills RIDDICK} Esquires Justices

On Motion. Ordered that John WIGGINS administer upon the estate of his deceased wife Prisscilla [sic] WIGGINS, he giving bond in the sum of $400. with Hardy PARKER and Barnes GOODMAN as securities.

On motion. Ordered that administration upon the estate of Frederick HINTON decd. be committed to Kedar FELTON, he giving Bond for $5000, with John FELTON and Noah HINTON as securities to the within Bond &c.

Ordered that Mills R. FIELDS be appointed administrator on the estate of Enos SCARBOROUGH decd. & that he give bond in the sum of one thousand dollars—Offers Robert ROGERS & Levi ROGERS as securities &c.

issd. Ordered that John WALTON, John HINTON Senr. Nathan NIXON & William HINTON be appointed to make a division of the estate of James HOFLER decd. among the heirs agreeable to law

issd. Ordered that William GOODMAN Esqr. Dempsey GOODMAN William LEE Joseph FREEMAN & John LANGSTON or any three of them Audite & state the accts of Dempsey LANGSTON admr. of Charity SPEIGHTS decd. & that they make a report &c.

issd. Ordered that John WALTON Esqr. James BOOTHE, Reuben HINTON and Benbury WALTON be appointed to audite & state the accounts of Frederick HINTON Jr. decd. admr. of Sarah LEWIS decd. and that they make a report &c.

Ordered that Thomas HOGGARD a regular Licenced minister of the Gospel, it is therefore ordered that he be exempt from military duty—working on the road &c.

Ordered that Henry GILLIAM & William LEE Esqr. be appointed to examine Lavina FIELDS, touching her signature to a deed of sale from herself & Mills R. FIELDS to Robert ROGERS &c

[47] 265 Ordered that Miles HOWELL renew his guardian bond to John, Alfred Benjamin & Sally CROSS orphans of Elisha CROSS decd. he offers John WILLEY & Nathaniel EURE as securities and was approved of by the Court Present in Court Wm. W. COWPER William LEE & John WILLY Esqrs. Justices.

issd. Ordered that Isaac HARRELL & Thomas COSTEN work upon the road leading from MINTONs store to old Town under John B. HARRELL as overseer.

issd. Ordered that Jethro TEBAULT [sic] be appointed overseer of the road from the fort Island to near where John BEEMAN formely [sic] lived.

issd. Ordered that Thomas HINTON be appointed overseer of the road in the room of Docton HAYS resigned.

February Court 1833

issd. Ordered that James **SMITH** be appointed overseer of the road in the room of John **LEWIS** Jr. resigned.

Ordered that William W. **POWELL** be permitted to renew his Constable Bond with John **WIGGINS** & Hardy D. **PARKER** as securities &c.

recorded The last Will and Testament of Judith **HARRELL** dec^d. was exhibited into Court and was proved by the Oaths of Mills **EURE** & Nathan **SMITH** two of the subscribing witnesses thereto and ordered to be recorded. At the same time the said Abraham **PARKER** the executor therein appointed Came into Court and was duly qualified for that office and prayed an order for letters testamentary thereon which was accordingly granted &c.

" Inventory of the Perishable estate of Frederick **HINTON** dec^d. was exhibited into Court by Kedar **HINTON** adm^r. on oath.

" Inventory of the property of Nathaniel **MURFREE**'s dec^d. was exhibited into Court by John W. **ODOM** adm^r. on oath

" Account of sale of the property of Lewis **WALTERS** dec^d. was exhibited into Court by Rich^d. **SMITH** exo^r. on oath.

" Account of sale of the property of Thomas **ROUNTREE** dec^d. was exhibited into Court by Amos **HOBBS** exo^r. on oath.

" William L. **BOOTHE** Mills **EURE** & Etheldred **CROSS** the men who were appointed to audite & state the accounts of Jacob **ODOM** adm^r. of Monica **ODOM** dec^d. made a report of their proceedings to this Court &c.

" Jeptha **FOWLKES** adm^r. of Sophia **PARKER** dec^d. returned an accoun_ with sd. estate into Court on oath.

[48] blank *issd.* Ordered that William **LEE**, William **GOODMAN**, Dempsey **GOODMAN** & Hillory **WILLEY** be appointed to auditie [sic] the accounts of Francis **SMITH** exec^r. of Robert **SMITH** dec^d. & that they make make [sic] a report of their proceedings to this Court at the next siting hereunto amuted [?]

issd. Ordered that the Sheriff summons a Jury to meet on the premises to lay off a road from **HARRELL**s meeting house in as direct Course as possiable to the end of Abraham **PARKER**s lane &c.

Dempsey **SPARKMAN**, Pryer **SAVAGE** & John **RIDDICK** the men who were appointed to make a division of the real estate of Peter **HARRELL** dec^d. made a report of their proceedings to this Court.

John **WALTON**, Henry **BOND**, Willis J. **RIDDICK** & David **PARKER** the men with the County surveyor who were appointed to make a division of the real estate of Abner **PEARCE** dec^d. made a report of their proceedings &c.

" Nathaniel **EURE** guardian to the orphans of Lewis **EURE** dec^d. exhibited into Court his acc^t. with sd. orphans on oath &c

" W^m. **CLEAVES** guardian to Lewis W. **PRUDEN** orphan, exhibited into Court his guardian acct. with s^d. orphan on oath &c.

" Hardy D. **PARKER** guardian to the orphans of James **WIGGINS** dec^d. exhibited into Court his acc^t. with s^d. orphans on oath.

" Exum **JENKINS** guardian to the orphans of Ira **ODOM** dec^d. exhibited into Court his guardian account with sd. orphans on oath &c

February Court 1833

" Henry **BOND** guardian to James **BOND** orphan of Rich^d. **BOND** dec^d. exhibited into Court his acc^t. with s^d. orphan on oath.

" Henry G. **WILLIAMS** guardian to Joseph **SPEIGHTS** orphan &c. exhibited into Court his guardian acc^t. with s^d. orphan on oath

" James **SMITH** guardian to Edward **HARE** ophan of John **HARE** dec^d. exhibited into Court his account into Court [sic] with sd. orphan on oath

" Whit^l. **JONES** guardian to Jos. John & Marmaduke **JONES** orphans exhibited into Court his guardian acc^t. with s^d. orphan [sic] on oath

" John W. **ODOM** guardian to Pricilla **ODOM** orphan of Ben. **ODOM** exhibited into Court his account with s^d. orphan on oath.

" John H. **HASLETT** guardian to Lewis & Sophia **HURDLE** orphans of Henry **HURDLE** dec^d. exhibited into Court his guardian account on oath &c.

[49] 267 " Levi **ROGERS** guardian to Mary **WILLIAMS** orphan of Halon **WILLIAMS** dec^d. exhibited his acc^t. with sd. orphan on oath into Court

" Leml. G. **DARDEN** guardian to Mary G. **CROSS** orphan of Abm. **CROSS** dec^d. exhibited his acc^t. with sd. orphan onto Court on oath.

" Jesse **SAVAGE** guardian to his children exhibited into Court his account into Court [sic] with said orphans [sic] on oath &c

" Nathl. **EURE** guardian to the orphans of Jonathan **BOYCE** dec^d. exhibited into Court his acc^t. with sd. orphans on oath &c

" Miles **HOWELL** guardian to the orphans of Elisha **CROSS** dec^d. exhibited into Court his account into Court [sic] with s^d. orphan on oath.

" William H. **GOODMAN** guardian to the orphans of Lem^l. **GOODMAN** dec^d. exhibited into Court his acc^t. with s^d. orphans on oath &c

" Arthur **WILLIAMS** guardian to Mary **WILLIAMS** orphan exhibited into Court his account with said orphan on oath &c.

" Nathl. **EURE** guardian to the orphans of Henry **SPEIGHTS** dec^d. exhibited into Court his accounts with s^d. orphans on oath.

" Edwin **SMITH** guardian to Henrietta **COPELAND** orphan of Heny **COPELAND** dec^d. exhibited into Court his acc^t. with s^d. ophan on oath

Deed of sale Charles **WALTERS** to Sinon **WALTERS** was in open Court acknowledged in due form of law and ordered to be registered

Deed of sale Thomas **CORNELIUS** to Nathl. **EURE** & Peter **EURE** was in open Court proved by the Oath of Benj^a. **SAUNDERS** a witness &c.

Deed of sale Robert **ROGERS** exo^r. to James **ROGERS** was in open Court acknowledged in due form of Law &c.

Deed of sale Simon **WALTERS** to John H. **HASLETT** was in open Court acknowledged in due form of law &c.

February Court 1833

Deed of sale Nathan HARRELL to Elizabeth HARRELL was in open Court proved by the Oath of Mills EURE a witness thereto &c.

Deed in trust Levi CREECY to Jethro WILLEY was in open Court proved by the Oath of Henry G. WILLIAMS a witness thereto &c.

Deed of sale James R. RIDDICK shff. to Pleasant TAYLOR was in open Court, acknowledged in due form of law &c.

Deed of sale Arthur WILLIAMS to Robert ROGERS was in open Court acknowledged in due form of law &c.

Deed of Sale Lucretia BEEMAN to John BEEMAN was in open Court proved by the Oath of W^m. L. BOOTHE a witness &c.

Deed of sale Levi BEEMAN and Dempsey SPARKMAN exor^s. of John BEEMAN dec^d. to Titus DARDEN & Clement ROCHELL, was in open Court, proved by the oath of Lawrence S. DAUGHTRY a witness thereto &c.

[50] blank Deed of Sale Mills R. FIELD & wife to Robert ROGERS was in open Court acknowledged in due form of law &c.

Deed of sale Charity WILLIAMS to W^m. CLEAVES was in open Court proved by the Oath of Lem^l. CLEAVES a witness thereto &c

Deed of sale James R RIDDICK to John LEWIS was in open Court acknowledged in due form of law &c.

Deed of sale John LEWIS to W^m. CLEAVES was in open Court acknowledged in due form of law &c.

issd. Ordered that the Clerk of this Court be allowed the sum of Fifty three dollars and sixty Cents for fees on sundry indictments wherein the State failed in the prosecution & for Calculating the Tax for the Sheriff to Collect—Stationary for the last year &c and that the County Trustee pay the same &c.

Pursuant to a commission from his Excellency David S. SWAIN Esquire Govenor &c. for appointing Barnes GOODMAN, Willis F. RIDDICK, Simon WALTERS Abraham W. PARKER and Henry COSTEN esquires Justices of the Peace for this County, they came into Court, and was duly qualified for that Office by taking & subscribing the Oaths prescribed by law &c.

Tuesday Morning Court met
Present   Henry GILLIAM Joseph RIDDICK Thomas SAUNDERS} Esquires Justices

Grand Jury qualified at this Term (to wit) Rizeup RAWLS Forman) Humphrey PARKER sen^r. Richard SMITH William PARKER John BRADY, Nathan WARD, Clement HILL, James C. RIDDICK Mills SPARKMAN, Levi EURE John MORRISS, Seth SPIVEY John HINTON, Nathaniel EURE, John BROWN of willis) Abram SPIVEY Shadrack PILAND & William HARRELL sen^r.

Ordered that Timothy SPEIGHTS a boy of Color be bound an apprentice to Abel ROGERSON to learn the trade of a farmer.

Ordered that Matthew JONES a free boy of Colour be bound an apprentice to John BENTON to learn the trade of a Farmer.

issd. Ordered that Benjamin SUMNER states attorney be allowed for his Services the sum of Forty dollars for the last year & that the County Trustee pay the same.

issd. Ordered that Hardy EASON be allowed the sum of one dollar & thirty three cents for a mistake in

February Court 1833

his tax list & that the County trustee pay the same

[51] 269 Ordered that John **WALTON** administer on the estate of Elisha **TROTMAN** dec^d. & that he give bond & security in the sum of one thousand dollars & offers for security Timothy **WALTON** & Benbury **WALTON** who was approved of by the Court.

issd. Ordered that Henry **GILLIAM**, William G. **DAUGHTRY**, Lawrence S. **DAUGHTRY**, Thomas **SAUNDERS** & Jesse **BROWN** or any three of them make a division of the estate of Elisha **TROTMAN** dec^d. among the heirs agreeably to law, & that they make a report of their [End of entry.]

issd. Ordered that William **HARRELL** sen^r. William **HARRELL** Junr. David **PARKER** & Willis F. **RIDDICK** divide the negroes belonging to the estate of Hardy **EASON** dec^d. among the heirs at law & that they make a report of their proceedings.

issd. Ordered that the above named men be appointed to Audite the accounts of Joseph **GORDON** adm^r. of Hardy **EASON** & divide the balance of the estate among the heirs & that they make a report of their proceedings.

issd. Ordered that the above named [sic] be appointed to audite the accounts of Joseph **GORDON** adm^r. of James **GRANBERY** dec^d. & that they make a report of their proceedings.

issd. Ordered that the above named men make a division of the estate of James **GRANBERY** & the negroes among the heirs agreeably to law & that they make a report of their proceedings

issd. Ordered that the same men audite & state the accts of Jos. **GORDON** adm^r. of Miles **BRINKLY** dec^d. & that they make a report.

issd. Ordered that the same men make a division of the estate of Miles **BRINKLY** dec^d. in the hands of Jos. **GORDON** adm^r.

issd. Ordered that Isaac R. **HUNTER**, Edward R. **HUNTER**, Noah **HARRELL** & Seth **MORGAN** make a division of the negroes belonging to Doct^r. Rich^d. B. **GREGORY** among the heirs - & that they make a report

Ordered that James **PRUDEN** be appointed guardian to Harriett B. **GATLING** orphan of E. B. **GATLING** dec^d. and that he give for /security/ Lassiter **RIDDICK** & Etheld **CROSS** in the sum three thousand dollars. Present in Court Mills **RIDDICK**, Henry **COSTEN** & Whit^l. **STALLINGS** Esquires Justices who approved of the securities &c.

Ordered that Dempsey **PARKER** be appointed guardian to Louisa **JONES** & Henry **JONES** orphans of Henry **JONES** dec^d. & that he give bond in the sum of five thousand dollars & offers Abraham W. **PARKER** & Nathaniel **EURE** as securities. Present in Court William W. **COWPER**, Henry **COSTEN** & Whitmell **STALLINGS** Esquirs Justices who approved of the securities.

[52] blank Ordered that Henry **GILLIAM** be appointed guardian to Nathan Owen, [sic] **WARD** son of Daniel **WARD**, and that he enter into bond for eight hundred dollars & gives for security Nathan **RIDDICK** & Nathan **WARD**. Present in Court W^m. W. **COWPER** Henry **COSTEN** & whitl. **STALLINGS** Esq^rs. Justices approved of securities

Ordered that James **BOOTHE** be appointed guardian to Sarah **HINTON** orphan of Fredk. **HINTON** Junr. dec^d. & that he give bond for three thousand dollars & offerrs Willis J. **RIDDICK** & W^m. **HINTON** as securities Present in Court Mills **RIDDICK**, Henry **COSTEN** & William **WALTON** Esqrs. Justices who approved of the securities.

Ordered that Wright **HAYS** be appointed adm^r. on the estate of William **BOND** dec^d. & that he enter into Bond & security in the sum of one thousand dollars offers Henry **GILLIAM** & John B. **HARRELL** as

February Court 1833

securities, who were approved by the Court.

Ordered that Thomas **SAUNDERS** be appointed guardian to Asa **ODOM** orphan of Asa **ODOM** dec^d. & that he give bond & security for five thousand dollars and gives Henry **GILLIAM** & Rich^d. **ODOM** securities Present in Court W^m. W. **COWPER**, Abm. W. **PARKER** & W^m. **WALTON** Esqrs Justices approved of the securities &c.

issd. Ordered that Joseph **GORDON**, Jos. **RIDDICK** & Jethro H. **RIDDICK** be appointed to audite & state the accts of Nathan **RIDDICK** adm^r. of Jesse **WALTON** dec^d. & that they make a report.

issd. Ordered that the same men be appointed to make a division of the estate of s^d. deceased.

issd. Ordered that Jonathan **WILLIAMS** Levi **ROGERS** Levi **CREECY** & W^m. **CROSS** be appointed Commissioners for the purpose of establishing the line between Henry **WILLEY** and George **KITTRELL** heirs &c

issd. Ordered that Daniel **WILLIAMS** be appointed Guardian ad litem to John **KITTRELL** orphan of George **KITTRELL** dec^d. to attend to the running the dividing line between s^d. orphan & Henry **WILLEY**

issd. Ordered that Henry **GILLIAM** be allowed the sum of ninety three dollars as per account rendered for services done for the County and that the County Trustee pay the same.

issd. Ordered that the Coroner be allow^d. twenty dollars for holding two inquests one over James **RIDDICK** dec^d. & the other over an infant name unknown & that the County Trustee pay the same

issd. Ordered that Mills **RIDDICK** transcribe and record all the papers not now recorded in the clerks office of the County of Gates & that he be allow^d. agreeably to an act of Assembly past [sic] at the last session of the State Legislature.

issd. Order^d. that Josiah **BRIGGS** be allow^d. the sum of one dollar & thirty three cents, a mistake in his tax list as guardian for Daniel **HURDLE** and that the County trustee pay the same.

[53] 271 Acc^t. of Straysers [sic] entered on the book Nov. 7th. 1831. up to the 18th. of February 1833 Fees $1.45 p^d.} Taken up by Jesse **HUDGINS** one brinded Cow, Posted and appraised to six dollars $6..00 Jesse **HUDGINS** ranger

issd. Ordered that Seth **BENTON** have leave to alter or turn the public road leading from **BENTON**s cross roads to the white marsh road a short distance commencing near the plantation whereon James **BENTON** sen^r. lives and running about six hundred yards, provided he straiten [sic] said new road & put it in good order as the law requires

issd. Ordered that John **MITCHELL**, Whitmell **STALLINGS**, Willis **BUNCH** & Abel **ROGERSON**, divide a certain tract of land owned by Hardy **EASON** dec^d. & Solomon **EASON** between the said Solomon **EASON** & the Heirs of Hardy **EASON** dec^d. and make a report.

issd. Ordered that John **SPEIGHTS** be appointed overseer of the road in Stead [sic] of Isaac **PIPKIN** who was appointed instead of William **GATLING** resigned & that said **SPEIGHTS** be authorized to take five hands from Isaac **PIPKIN** & attach to the road to which he is appointed overseer.

issd. Ordered that Jason **ROUNTREE** be appointed overseer of the road leading from **BARNES** Creek to the fork of the road at the dec^d. John **BEEMAN**'s in the room of Saml. **EURE** removed.

issd. Ordered that the hands of Thomas **COSTEN** & Isaac **HARRELL** work under Thomas **HURDLE** overseer of the road—also W^m. **MOORE**.

February Court 1833

issd. Ordered that Seth **SPIVEY**s hands and Nathl. **TAYLOR** work on the road under John **HARRELL** also—James **HOWARD**.

issd. Ordered that Willis **HAYS** be appointed overseer of the road in the room of John **HOFLER** Jr. resigned &c.

Ordered that William H. **SAVAGE** be appointed Constable in Capt. Nathan **SMITH**s Captaincy and that he enter into bond with Abram W. **PARKER** & Dempsey **PARKER** as securities.

Ordered that John D. **PIPKIN** & John **WILLEY** Esqrs. be appointed to take the private examination of Elizabeth **SMITH** wife of James C. **SMITH** of the State of Virginia at such time & place within the State of No. Carolina touching her signature to a deed of sale from said James C. **SMITH** & wife to James **BOOTHE** & that they make a report to this Court.

In obedience to an order of Court for the purpose of selling the negroes **ESTHER** & **MARTHA** to the highest bidders, when Jesse **CORNWELL** appeared and bid for negro **MARTHA** the sum of three Hundred and forty three 20/100 dollars which being the highest bid

[54] blank Offered for her she was accordingly knock [sic] off to him negro **ESTHER** was offered for the most that would be bid for her but no one being willing to give any thing for her she was knocked off to Henry **SPIVEY** at the sum of forty dollars, that being the least any one would take her for all of which is submitted Nathan **RIDDICK**

Deed of sale Walton **FREEMAN** to John **ROBERTS** was in open Court proved by the oath of John **WALTON** a witness thereto &c.

Deed of sale Samuel **BROWN** to John **ROBERTS** was in open Court proved by the Oath of James T. **FREEMAN** a witness thereto &c.

Deed of sale John V. **SUMNER** late shff to Milliam [sic] A. **MATTHEWS** was in open Court proved by the oath of John **MATTHEWS** a witness &c.

Deed of sale Reuben **HINTON** to George **FREEMAN** was in open Court proved by the oath of Henry **GILLIAM** a witness thereto &c.

Deed of sale Henry B. **LASSITER** to Clement **HILL** was in open Court proved by the oath of James **OUTLAW** a witness thereto &c.

Receipt from Milley **PILAND** to Isaac **PILAND** was in open Court proved by the oath of Thomas **HOGGARD** a witness thereto &c.

Deed of sale Dempsey **KNIGHT** & wife to James **BOOTHE** was in open Court proved by the oath of William **BOOTHE** a witness &c.

Deed of gift Mary **HUDGINS** to Solomon **ROUNTREE** was in open Court proved by the Oath of John R. **NORFLEET** a witness &c.

Deed of sale Sarah **BOND** to Steward **BOND** was in open Court proved by the oath of Benj^a. **BLANCHARD** a witness thereto &c.

Deed of sale James C. **SMITH** & wife to James **BOOTHE** was in open Court proved by the oath of James R. **RIDDICK** a witness thereto &c

Deed of sale David **OUTLAW** to Abel **ROGERSON** was in open Court proved by the oath of John **WALTON** a witness thereto &c.

February Court 1833

Deed of sale Elisha **ROBERSON** to Henry B. **LASSITER** was in open Court proved by the oath of John **WALTON** a witness thereto &c

Deed of sale Garrett **HOFLER** to Henry B. **LASSITER** was in open Court proved by the oath of John **WALTON** a witness thereto &c.

Deed of sale Henry B. **LASSITER** to Reuben **LASSITER** was in open Court proved by the oath of John **WALTON** a witness thereto &c.

Bill of sale Isaac **PILAND** to Thomas **SAUNDERS** was in open Court acknowledged in due form of law &c.

" Inventory of the estate of Jesse **WALTON** dec^d. was exhibited into Court by Nathan **RIDDICK** adm^r. on oath &c

" Inventory of the property of George **KITTRELL** dec^d. was exhibited in open Court by Daniel **WILLIAMS** executor on oath &c

" Account of sales of the property of George **KITTRELL** dec^d. was exhited [sic] in open Court by Daniel **WILLIAMS** executor on oath &c

[55] 273 " Account of sale of the property of James **RIDDICK** dec^d. was ex<u>h</u>bited in open Court by Abraham **RIDDICK** adm^r. on oath &c

" Account of sale of the property of John **BEEMAN** dec^d. was exhibited in open Court by Levi **BEEMAN** & Dempsey **SPARKMAN** exor^{ss}. [sic] on oath

" John **WALTON** guardian to Leah **HINTON** and Moses **TROTMAN** orphans &c exhibited in open Court his guardian acct. with s^d. orphans on oath

" Elijah **HARRELL** guardian to Elisha **HARRELL** orphan exhibited into Court his guardian account with said orphan on oath &c

" Whitmell **STALLINGS** guardian to the orphans of Chs. E. **SUMNER** dec^d. exhibited into Court his guardian account with said orphans on oath

" Whitmell **STALLINGS** guardian to the orphans of Henry **WALTON** dec^d. exhibited into Court his guardian acc^t. with said orphans on oath

" John D. **PIPKIN** guardian to Rich^d. B. **GATLING** orphan &c exhibited into Court his guardian acct. with said orphan on oath

" John D. **PIPKIN** guardian to John B. **GATLING** orphan &c exhibited into Court his guardian account with said orphan on oath &c

" Isaac R. **HUNTER** guardian to (he) orphans of Benj^a. **BRIGGS** dec^d. exhibited into Court his guardian acct. with s^d. orphans on oath

" Mary **HUNTER** guardian to Jacob B. **HUNTER** orphan &c. exhibited into Court her guardian acc^t. with s^d. orphan by the oath of I. R. **HUNTER**

" George **COSTEN** guardian to Mary Ann **RIDDICK** orphan &c exhibited into Court his guardian acct. with said orphan on oath.

" Thomas B. **HUNTER** guardian to Isaac **HUNTER** orphan, exhibited into Court his guardian acct. with said orphan on oath &c

February Court 1833

" John C. **GORDON** guardian to the orphans of Henry **LASSITER** dec^d. exhibited into Court his guardian acct. with said orphans on oath

" John C. **GORDON** guardian to Thomas A. **SMALL** orphan of M. H. **SMALL** dec^d. exhibited into Court his guardian acc^t. with said orphan on oath

" Humphrey **PARKER** guardian to Christain [sic] **SMALL** orphan &c exhibited into Court his guardian acc^t. with s^d. orphan on oath.

" Charles **EASON** guardian to Elizabeth & Lena **EASON** orphans &c exhibited into Court his guardian acct. with said orphans on oath

" David **PARKER** guardian to John **FELTON** orphan &c exhibited into Court his guardian account with said orphan on oath &c

" Thomas **SAUNDERS** guardian to Asa **ODOM** an orphan, exhibited into Court his guardian account with said orphan on Oath.

" Willis **BUNCH** guardian to Nancy **HURDLE** an orphan exhibited into Court his guardian account with said orphan on oath.

" Eli **WORRELL** guardian to W^m. J. **HUDGINS** an orphan Exhibited into Court his guardian account with said orphan on oath.

" James **BOOTHE** guardian to Sally **POWELL** an orphan exhibited into Court his guardian account with said orphan on oath.

[56] blank " Lassiter **RIDDICK** guardian to Mary Jane B. **GATLING** an orphan exhibited into Court his guardian acc^t. with s^d. orphan on oath

" David L. **MILTEAR** guardian to the orphans of David **PARKER** dec^d. exhibited into Court his guardian accounts with s^d. orphans on oath

" Abraham W. **PARKER** guardian to William **JOHNSON** orphan, exhibited into Court his guardian account with sd. orphan on oath.

" William W. **COWPER** guardian to Uriah **BABB** orphan exhibited into Court his guardian account with said orphan on oath.

" Mills **EURE** guardian to the orphans of Stephen **LEE** dec^d. exhibited into Court his guardian acc^t. with said orphans on oath.

" William **GOODMAN** guardian to Harriett B. **GATLING** orphan exhibited into Court his guardian account with said orphan on oath &c

" Andrew **MATTHEWS** guardian to Kedar & Holloday **JONES** orphans, exhibited into Court his guardian acct. with said orphans on oath

" Willis J. **RIDDICK** guardian to the orphans of James **HINTON** dec^d. exhibited into Court his guardian accounts with said orphans on oath.

" Jesse **BROWN** guardian to Susan J. **HILL** orphan exhibited into Court his guardian account with said orphan on oath &c

" Jesse **BROWN** guardian to Louisa **BARNES** orphan &c. exhibited into Court his guardian account with said orphan on oath.

February Court 1833

" William **COWPER** guardian to Celia **LEWIS** orphan exhibited into Court his guardian account with said orphan on oath &c.

" Nathan **RIDDICK** guardian to Henry, Jesse & Mary **WALTON** & to William **BROWN** & Sarah **BROWN** & to Drew **TROTMAN** orphans &c exhibited his guardian accts. with said orphans on oath &c

Wednesday morning Court met.
Present -- Henry **GILLIAM** W^m. L. **BOOTHE** W^m. W. **COWPER**} Esquires Justices

Ordered that Jethro **SUMNER** be appointed Guardian ad litem to the orphans of William **BOYCE** dec^d.

[57] 275 Ordered that Riddick **GATLING** be appointed guardian to Elizabeth and Mary **SUMNER** orphans of Charles E. **SUMNER** dec^d. and he give bond & security in the sum of four thousand dollars & offers James R. **RIDDICK** & John **GATLING** for securities. Present in Court Whit^l. **STALLINGS**, W^m. W. **COWPER**, & Joseph **RIDDICK** Esqrs. Justices who approved of the securities and concurred in the appointment.

Ordered that John G. **LILES** be appointed guardian to his daughter Margaret Ann **LILES** and that he give bond in the sum of One Hundred & twenty dollars with Andrew **HARRELL** and John **HOFLER** as securities. Present in Court W^m. W. **COWPER** Abram W. **PARKER** and Whitmell **STALLINGS** Esquires Justices who approved of the securities and Concurred in the appointment.

Ordered that Wright **HAYSE** be appointed Guardian to Robert **HARE** & Mary **HARE** orphans of John **HARE** dec^d. and he gave bond $500. each and Dempsey **SPARKMAN** & William E. **PUGH** offered themselves as securities. Present in Court W^m. W. **COWPER** William **WALTON** and W^m. L. **BOOTHE** Esquir<u>s</u> Justices who approved of the securities and concurred in the appointment &c.

Ordered that James **BOND** be appointed Constable in Capt. Bushrod **RIDDICK**s captaincy & that he give Bond and security with Henry **BOND** and John **BOND**—as securities.

Ordered that John **PARKER** be appointed Constable in Capt. Jason **SAUNDERS** Captaincy & that he give bond & security with Abram W. **PARKER** and Kindred **PARKER** as securities.

Ordered that Charles **JONES** a boy of Colour son of Elizabeth **JONES** be bound an apprentice to Henry **COSTEN** to learn the trade of a farmer

issd. Ordered that Simmonds **ROUNTREE** be allowed the sum of eight dollars & twenty cents for waiting on the Superior & County Court Jurors and that the County [sic] the same.

issd. Ordered that William L. **BOOTHE** be allow^d. the sum of One dollar & thirty three [sic] for one black poll tested & paid through mistake in 1831. and that the County Trustee pay the same &c.

issd. Ordered that Benbury **WALTON** keep up the bridge and dam a cross his mill pond below John **WALTON** Esqr. on the main road leading from Gatesville to Edenton and that his hands be Exempt from all other roads and all orders Compelling the Overseer to keep up this bridge and dam be re<u>c</u>inded.

issd. Ordered that the Workman under **STAFFORD** & **SAVAGE** with the firm also and Joseph J. **BARNES** hands work on the road under John **BROWN** overseer.

" Account of sale of the hire of negroes belonging to the estate of Henry **PUGH** dec^d. was exhibited into Court by W^m. **PUGH** adm^r. on oath

[58] blank " Jethro H. **RIDDICK** Guardian to Calvin **BRINKLY** orphan exhibited into Court his guardian account with said orphan on oath &c

" Mills **PILAND** guardian to the orphans of Elisha **PILAND** dec^d. exhibited into Court his guardian account with said orphans on oath &c

February Court 1833

" William E. **PUGH** guardian to the orphans of Henry **PUGH** dec^d. exhibited into Court his guardian account with said orphans on oath.

" Nathan **NIXON** guardian [sic] Joseph G. **WALTON** orphan exhibited into Court his guardian account with said orphan on oath.

" Nathan **NIXON** guardian [sic] Mary Ann **WALTON** orphan exhibited into Court his guardian account with said orphan on oath.

Deed of sale Jethro **SUMNER** & John **GATLING** to William G. **DAUGHTRY** was in open Court proved by the oath of John B. **BAKER** a witness &c

Deed of sale John **JONES** to James **WILLIAMS** sen^r. was in open Court acknowledged in due form of law &c.

Deed of sale Nathan **RIDDICK** to James R. **RIDDICK** was in open Court proved by the oath of Thomas S. **GARY** a witness.

Deed of sale Seth **TEABOUT** to William L. **BOOTHE** was in open Court proved by the oath of John **WILLEY** a witness &c.

Deed of sale William L. **BOOTHE** to William W. **COWPER** was in open Court, acknowledged in due form of law &c.

Deed of gift Milley **WILLIAMS** to her four daughters Mary **WILLIAMS** Nancy **PARKER**, Prissilla **PARKER** & Elizabeth **ROGERS** was in open Court proved by the Oath of Charles **VANN** a witness thereto.

Bill of Sale Simmonds **ROUNTREE** to Dempsey **PARKER** was in open Court proved by the Oath of W^m. E. **PUGH** a witness thereto &c

Pursuant to an order (hereunto annexed) of the County Court of Gates, State of North Carolina, to me the County surveyor directed for the purpose of processioning the lines dividing the lands of William **BABB** and Simon **WALTERS** as are therein specified beg leave to report) I met according to appointment, and the parties being present, proceeded to run the line not in dispute to a large pine stump in the parth [sic] leading from Simon **WALTERS** to the main road at the commencement of the line in dispute and there being fore warned by Simon **WALTERS** to proceed any farther, was forced to stop, which being the cause of not having discharged my duty is submitted to the Court. Given under my hand this thirteenth of February in the year of our Lord 1833. J. **BARNES** Co. Surv^r.

[59] 277 *issd.* William **BABB** vs Simon **WALTERS**} Order of Procession
In this case it appearing to the Court by the report of Jethro **BARNES** that he was forbidden to [sic] by Simon **WALTERS** to Complete the survey of the line between the said Simon and William **BABB**—it is ordered by the Court, that Hillory **WILLEY**, Jonathan **WILLIAMS** (of Jonathan) David **RIDDICK** Noah **HARRELL** and Kindred **PARKER** who with the said Jethro **BARNES** surveyor shall proceed to procession the lands of the said William and make a report of their proceedings to the next Term of this Court &c.

issd. Ordered that the sheriff summon Abner **EASON**, Whitl **SALLINGS** [sic] Mills **EURE** Esqr. Peter **EURE**, Abram W. **PARKER**, Jethro **HOWELL**, James **BRINKLY**, Riddick **GATLING**, William **HARRELL** of Saml. Jesse **SAVAGE** W^m. **WALTON**, George **COSTEN**, Nathan **RIDDICK**, James **COSTEN**, James **SMITH**, William **LEE**, Isaac **PIPKIN**, Dempsey **KNIGHT**, Barnes **GOODMAN**, W^m. W. **COWPER**, Henry **RIDDICK** of Robt.) Noah **ROUNTREE**, W^m. **GOODMAN** Esqr. Seth **BENTON**, William **WHITE**, Bushrod W. **RIDDICK**, Thomas **HOGGARD**, James **BAKER** Jr. Jethro H. **RIDDICK**, Henry G. **WILLIAMS** Benjamin **HAYS** James **GORDON**, Walton **FREEMAN** John **ALPHIN**, George W. **SMITH** & Rich^d. **ODOM** personally to attend at the next Superior Court of law to

February Court 1833

be held for this County on the first monday after the fourth monday in March next then and there to serve as Jurors &c.

issd. Ordered that the Sheriff summon Riddick **HUNTER**, James **WILLIAMS** of Demsey) Dempsey **PARKER** of Jas) William **PILAND**, Whit^l. **HILL**, James **CARTER**, Charles **EASON**, John **HINTON** Jr. Joseph **RIDDICK** of Thos.) William **MILLER** Archibald **ELLIS**, Charles **BRIGGS**, Reuben **HINTON** sen^r. James **JONES** of Jas), Elisha **UMPHLET** Briant **HARE** John **WORRELL**, Jesse **HARRELL**, Frederick **ROOKS**, Richard **CURL**, Abraham **MORGAN**, Bray **PARKER**, William **JONES**, Joseph **HURDLE** of Abm) James **BROWN** of James) Joseph T. **HURDLE**, W^m. **HINTON**, William **HARRELL** Jr. S.C.) Mills **ROBERTS**, Lemuel **HOWELL** Joshua **ALLEN**, Riddick **MATHEWS**, Miles **PARKER** Jr. Luke **GREEN**, John **LEWIS** Jr. & Luke **HOLLAND** personally to attend at the next County Court to be held for this County on the third monday in May next. then and there to serve as Jurors &c

[60] [blank] State of North Carolina   May the 20th. 1833.

At a Court of Pleas and Quarter sessions, begun and held for the County of Gates, at the Court House in Gatesville on the third monday of May in the Fifty seventh year of our Independence and in the year of our Lord, One thousand, eight hundred and thirty three.

Present   William **GOODMAN** Whit^l. **STALLINGS** Barnes **GOODMAN** John D. **PIPKIN** Joseph **RIDDICK**} Esquires Justices

Elizabeth **MATTHEWS** wife of John W. **MATTHEWS** dec^d. Came into Court and enters her dissent to the will of her husband.

issd. Garrett **HOFFLER** Guardian to Richard **BLANCHARD** and Isaac **BLANCHARD** of full age came into Court & prayed that the negroes given in the will of James **HOFFLER** dec^d. be divided according. [sic] Ordered that John **WALTON**, Nathan **NIXON** William **HINTON** & John **HINTON** divide said negroes and that they make a report of their proceedings.

Ordered that Archibald **ELLIS** be appointed adm^r. on the Estate of James **BRINKLEY** of David dec^d. and he enter into Bond for $500. Offers John O. **HUNTER** & Miles **BRIGGS** securi*tes*.

issd. Ordered that John O. **HUNTER**, Jesse **MATHIAS**, Riddick **JONES** Dempsey **VANN** & James **MORGAN** be appointed to lay off and allot to Levina **BRINKLEY** widow of James **BRINKLEY** dec^d. her years provision agreeably to law &c.

issd. Ordered that Hillory **WILLEY**, Joseph **RIDDICK** and Henry **GILLIAM** be appointed to Carry into effect, an order passed at the last May Court, to purchase land & Errect [sic] suffi*cent* buildings for the use of the parish of said County & that the Clerk issue the order passed at that time to this Committee

issd. Ordered that Jethro **GOODMAN** be appointed overseer of the New road, in the room of William **GOODMAN** Esqr.

issd. Ordered that Job R. **HALL** hands work on the road under Abraham **SMITH** also John **SPARKMANS** hands work under said overseer.

[61] 279 *issd.* Ordered that Isaac **PIPKIN**s hands & boys—**ELEY** & **ISAAC** belonging to Wm. **GOODMAN** Esqr. work upon the road under John **SPEIGHT** & that he keep the road also that Isaac **PIPKIN** kept

issd. Ordered that Willis **CROSS** be appointed overseer of the road from Jason **SAUNDERS** to said **CROSS**es & work same hands that David **CROSS** form*ely* worked.

issd. Ordered that John O. **HUNTER** be appointed overseer of the road in Stead of John **BRINKLEY** dec^d.

May Court 1833

issd. Ordered that John **BRADY** be appointed overseer of the road in the room or stead of John **SAUNDERS**.

Ordered that Miles **HOWELL** be allowed to renew his Constable bond & offers James **SAUNDERS** & Gilbert **SAUNDERS** securities

recorded The last will and testament of Benjamin **HAYS** dec^d. was exhibited into Court and proved by the Oath of John **WALTON** one of the subscribing witnesses thereto and ordered to be recorded. at the same time letters of administration with the will annexed was granted to Henry **GILLIAM** Ordered that he give bond & security in the sum of __[blank]__ dollars. The said administrator was duly qualified for that Office &c.

recorded The Last will and Testament of John W. **MATTHEWS** dec^d. was exhibited into Court, and proved by the Oath of Etheldred **MATTHEWS** one of the subscribing witnesses thereto.

Pursuant to an order of the County Court of Gates State of North Carolina, to us directed, we your Commissioners, with the surveyor have proceeded to establish the line between William **BABB** and Simon **WALTERS**—beg leave to report Commencing at a forked pine Corner of William **BABB** & Simon **WALTERS** thence down their line—thence beginning at a /oak/ post ~~Oak~~ of Simon **WALTERS** then S63° E. 4 poles 20 links to pine stump then S66° E. 10 po. 12 links to a post oak post of Wm. **BABB** and S. **WALTERS**, which being the point in dispute & agreeable to the best information that could be obtained is the true lines—all of which proceedings are submitted to the Court. Given under Our hands and seals this 10th. day of May 1833. H. **WILLEY** {seal} Noah **HARRELL** {seal} Kindred **PARKER** {seal} (J. **BARNES** Co.) [sic] Surv.)

[62] blank Pursuant to an order hereunto annexed of the County Court of Gates State of N°. Carolina to us directed, we your Commissioners with the County Surveyor have proceeded to establish the line between Henry **WILLEY** and George **KITTRELL**s heirs beg leave to report Commencing at a large pine Corner of Nisom **CUFF** and George **KITTRELL** heirs in H. **WILLEY**s line thence along s^d. line s 27°. E. 24 poles to a gum, thence s 76 W 36 poles to a sweet gum, then along a line of marked trees due west to a pine stump and sweet gum at the Edge of the low ground, then S 88° W 116 po. to the new road a pine and sassafras then along the edge of said road to a large pine standing on the edge of s^d. road making said lines plain and satisfactory. Given under our hands and seals the 20th. day of May 1833.
    All of which proceedings are submitted to the Court Jonathan **WILLIAMS** {seal} Levi **ROGERS** {seal} Levi **CREECY** {seal} Hardy **CROSS** {seal} William **CROSS** {seal}
J. **BARNES** Co. Suvr.

William W. **STEDMAN** Noah **HARRELL** & Robert **HILL** the men who were appointed to make a division of the negroes belonging [sic] the estate of Sophia **HUNTER** dec^d. made a report of their proceedings to this Court &c.

John C. **GORDON** Humphrey **PARKER** & Holloday **WALTON** with the County surveyor who were appointed to make a division of the real estate of Abraham **BENTON** dec^d. made a report of their proceedings to this Court &c.

" William **GOODMAN** Dempsey S. **GOODMAN** & William **LEE** the men who were appointed to audite & state the accts of Dempsey **LANGSTON** adm^r. of Charity **SPEIGHTS** dec^d. made a report of their proceedings &c.

" James **BOYCE** adm^r. of William **BOYCE** dec^d. returned an account current into Court.

" Isaac R. **HUNTER** adm^r. of Sophia C. **HUNTER** dec^d. returned an account Current with said estate into Court.

[63] 281 " Account of sale of the Property of William **KING** dec^d. was exhibited into Court by Jesse **HOBBS** executor on oath &c.

May Court 1833

" Joseph **FREEMAN** guardian to David **FREEMAN** orphan exhibited into Court his account with said orphan on oath &c

" Elizabeth **BROTHERS** guardian to Robert, James & Rich^d. **BROTHERS** orphans exhibited into Court her acc^t. with s^d. orphans by the Oath of Joseph **GORDON** &c.

" Elizabeth **GRANBERRY** guardian to John & George **GRANBERRY** orphans exhibited into Court [sic] by Jos. **GORDON** &c.

Deed of sale Francis **SMITH** & Jane **PARKER** to Jethro **BARNES** was in open Court proved by the Oath of Demsey **GOODMAN** a witnes [sic]

Deed of sale Isaac S. **HARRELL** to Holloday **WALTON** was in open Court acknowledged in due form of law.

Deed of sale Jethro **BARNES** & Prudence **WILLIAMS** to Francis **SMITH** was in open Court proved by the Oath of Edwin **CROSS** a witness

Release Robert **RIDDICK** sen^r. to Henry **RIDDICK** was in open Court acknowledged in due form &c.

Release Robert **RIDDICK** sen^r. to Henry **RIDDICK** was in open Court acknowledged in due form of law.

Deed of sale Mary **HARRELL** to Thomas **SMITH** was in open Court proved by the Oath of Abram W. **PARKER** a witness.

Deed of mortgage Nathan **HARRELL** to Elizabeth **HARRELL** was in open Court proved by the Oath of Henry **GILLIAM** a witness

Deed of sale Thomas **SMITH** to David **UMPHLET** was in open Court acknowledged in due form of law &c.

Deed of sale James **SAUNDERS** to Barnett **MARCH** was in open Court acknowledged in due form of law &c.

Deed of sale John **HOFLER** to James **EURE** was in open Court, acknowledged in due form of law &c.

Deed of sale James T. **FREEMAN** to John **HOFLER** was in open Court proved by the Oath of Reuben **LASSITER** a witness

Deed of sale Jesse **ARLINE** to James **ARLINE** was in open Court proved by the Oath of William K. **MOORE** a witness.

Deed of sale Simon **WALTERS** to William **BABB** was in open /Court/ acknowledged in due form of law &c.

Deed of sale William **BABB** to Simon **WALTERS** was in open Court acknowledged in due form of law &c.

[64] blank Deed of sale Arthur R **SMITH** & wife to William K **MOORE** was in open Court proved by the Oath of H. D. **PARKER** a witness.

Deed of sale Allen **SMITH** & wife to Isaac **PIPKIN** was in open Court proved by the Oath of Hardy D. **PARKER** a witness.

Deed of sale Allen **SMITH** & wife to Kindred **PARKER** was in [sic] Court proved by the Oath of John D. **PIPKIN** a witness &c.

May Court 1833

Deed of sale Abram & Seth **MORGAN** to Willis **COWPER** was in open Court proved by the Oath of John J. **GRANBERRY** a witness.

Deed of sale Jethro **BARNES** to William **LEE** was in open Court acknowledged in due form of law &c.

Deed of sale Whitmell **EASON** to John **FELTON** was in open Court proved by the Oath of Shadrack **FELTON** a witness thereto &c.

Deed of sale Job. R **HALL** to Lassiter **RIDDICK** was in open Court proved by the Oath of Wills **COWPER** a witness thereto &c.

Deed of sale James R **RIDDICK** to James **SMITH** was in open Court acknowledged in due form of law &c.

issd. Ordered that the following persons be appointed inspectors of the Poll at the ensueing Elections at the following places (viz
At Job. R. **HALL**s—Etheldred **CROSS** Richard **ODOM** Dempsey **SPARKMAN** Dempsey **PARKER** John **RIDDICK** James **CARTER** Mills **SPARKMAN** Mills **EURE** John **LEWIS**
At W^m. H. **GOODMAN**'s—William **LEE** William **GOODMAN** John **LANGSTON** Hardy **CROSS** Demsey **GOODMAN** Riddick **GATLING** John **SAUNDERS** William **GATLING** Joseph **FREEMAN** Francis **DUKE**
At John H. **HASLETT**s—Samuel **CROSS** Simon **WALTERS** George **SMITH** James **SAVAGE** Jesse **SAVAGE** William **MOORE** Barnes **GOODMAN** Henry G. **WILLIAMS** Levi **CREECY** Jonathan **WILLIAMS** of Jon.
At Folley—John C. **GORDON** James **MORGAN** Demsey **KNIGHT** James **BALLARD** Miles **BRIGGS** Henry **RIDDICK** Wills **COWPER** Seth R. **MORGAN** Jesse **WIGGINS** Tilley W. **CARR**

[65] 283 At **HUNTER**s Mill—John **GATLING** Henry **COSTEN** Thomas **TWINE** George **COSTEN** Jethro H. **RIDDICK** Thos. **RIDDICK** Nathan **RIDDICK** Daniel **RIDDICK** Joseph **RIDDICK** John **ALPHIN**
At **MINTON**s—John **MITCHELL** Bushrod **RIDDICK** Nathan **NIXON** William **WALTON** Jesse **KEE** Abel **ROGERSON** James **BOYCE** Walton **FREEMAN** Timothy **WALTON** James T. **FREEMAN**
At Gatesville—Jeptha **FOWLKES** William G. **DAUGHTRY** Jesse **BROWN** Prior **SAVAGE** Joseph P **BARNES** Joseph **RIDDICK** John R. **GILLIAM** William E. **PUGH** Edward S. **NEAL** William **CLEAVES**

Tuesday Morning Court met
Present   Henry **GILLIAM** John C. **GORDON** Joseph **RIDDICK** Demsey **KNIGHT**} Esquires Justices

issd. Ordered that the following Justices take the list of Taxes for the present year
In Capt. **SMITH**s Captaincy—Abram W. **PARKER** Capt. Jason **SAUNDERS**—John **WILLEY** **DOUGHTIE**s—Simon **WALTERS** **HOFFLER**s—Willis F. **RIDDICK** Jet. H **RIDDICK**s Henry **COSTEN** Bush. **RIDDICK**—William **WALTON** W^m. E. **PUGH**—Tho. **SAUNDERS**

[66] blank Grand Jury impanneled to wit John **HINTON** sr. forrman Elisha **UMPHLET**, Jesse **HARRELL**, Riddick **HUNTER**, William **PILAND**, James **WILLIAMS**, Luke **GREEN**, Lemuel **HOWELL**, Archibald **ELLIS**, Charles **BRIGGS**, Dempsey **PARKER** Joseph T. **HURDLE** William **JONES** William **MILLER**, Whitmell **HILL**, Richard **CURL** Joshua **ALLEN** and Charles **EASON**.

Ordered that Henry **GILLIAM** administer on the estate of Benjamin **HAYSE** dec^d. and that he give bond & security in the sum of four thousand dollars Jeptha **FOWLKES** & James R. **RIDDICK** securities who were approved by the Court.
 Ordered that Jeptha **FOWLKES** be appointed guardian to the heirs of Reuben **HINTON** dec^d. and that he

May Court 1833

give bond in the sum of five hundred dollars—Henry **GILLIAM** & William **ELLEY** [sic] for securities. Present in Court Mills **RIDDICK** W^m. W. **COWPER**, Henry **COSTEN**, A. W. **PARKER** Esqui<u>rs</u> Justices who approved of the securities.

Ordered that George **COSTEN** be appointed Guardian to Isaac **HUNTER** orphan of Isaac **HUNTER** dec^d. and that he give bond and security in the sum of twelve thousand dollars—James **COSTEN** & Isaac R. **HUNTER** securities Present in in [sic] Court W. **STALLINGS** Jos. **RIDDICK** W. W. **COWPER** Esqui<u>rs</u> Justices were present in Court, & approved of the securities.

issd. Ordered that John C. **GORDON** Tilley W. **CARR** & Tho. **TWINE** be appointed Commissioners to settle between Thomas B **HUNTER** former guardian to Isaac **HUNTER** & George **COSTEN** the present Guardian &c.

issd. Ordered that the Commissioners appointed for the purpose of Contracting for and Superintending the erection of a poor House have permission to dispose of the public land at the late Poor House upon the best terms that Can be obtained & make report of their proceedings

Ordered that Noah **HINTON** be appointed guardian to Elizabeth, Louisa, & John **LEWIS** orphans of John **LEWIS** dec^d. and that he give bond in the sum of $100. with Kedar **FELTON** and Joseph R. **BILLUPS** securities. Present in Court W. **STALLINGS**, Joseph **RIDDICK** William W. **COWPER** Esquires Justices who approved of the securities.

[67] 285 *issd.* Ordered that James **MORGAN**, Demsey **VANN**, John O. **HUNTER** Demsey **KNIGHT** be appointed to lay off and allot to Lavina **BRINKLY** widow of James **BRINKLY** dec^d. her years provision agreeably to law & that they make a report &c.

issd. Ordered that the County surveyor lay off for Edwin **CROSS** twenty four acres land bought for tax belonging to Elizabeth **SAUNDERS** dec^d. also Twenty four acres land bought in the same way belonging to Sarah **WATSON**-agreeable to law.

issd. Ordered that John C. **GORDON**, Tilley W. **CARR**, Isaac R **HUNTER** & Thomas **TWINE** be appointed with the County surveyor to make a division of the lands of James **COSTEN**, between the Heirs of said deceased agreeable to law &c.

issd. Ordered that Joseph **GORDON**, John C. **GORDON**, Joseph **RIDDICK** & Benjamin **BALLARD** make a division of the estate of Abram **HARRELL** dec^d. among the heirs—in the hands of Theophilus **HARRELL** and that they make a report &c.

issd. Ordered that Jesse **BROWN** be allow^d. the sum of Twelve dollars and ninety five cents for Jaol [sic] fees and that the County Trustee pay the same &c.

issd. Ordered that William W. **POWELL** be allowed the sum of two dollars and sixty seven cents & that the County Trustee pay. [sic]

issd. Ordered that Jethro **WILLEY** be allow^d. the sum of Four dollars for attending on the Jury at the Superior Court Spring Term and that the County Trustee pay the same &c

Ordered that ~~the~~ James R. **RIDDICK** be allowed the sum of Fifty dollars for his extra services & that the County pay.

Ordered that Lem^l. **CLEAVES** renew his Constable bond by giving as security Henry **GILLIAM** & James R. **RIDDICK**

Ordered that James T. **FREEMAN** renew his Constable bond & that bond & security [sic] William **HINTON** & Henry **BOND** securities.

Ordered that Miles **BRIGGS** renew his bond as Constable & gave for security Joseph **GORDON** &

May Court 1833

Richard H. **BALLARD**.

Ordered that James C. **RIDDICK** renew his Bond as Constable [sic] Lassiter **RIDDICK** & James R. **RIDDICK** for securities.

Ordered that Simmonds **ROUNTREE** renew his Constable Bond he gaves [sic] James R. **RIDDICK** & James **BROWN** as securities.

Ordered that Jethro **WILLEY** renew his Constable Bond with Henry **GILLIAM** & William **LEE** for securities.

Ordered that David **PARKER** renew his Constable Bond with Jeptha **FOWLKES** & Joseph **RIDDICK** for securities.

[68] blank Ordered that Jethro **SUMNER** clerk of this Court be allow^d. the sum of Fifty dollars for his extra services, and that the County Trustee pay the Same &c.

issd. Ordered that Archibald **ELLIS** be appointed overseer of the road leading from his house to the Oreapeak [sic] Swamp, in the room of Etheldred **MATTHEWS** removed.

Ordered that Lawrence S. **DAUGHTRY** have a licence to retail Spirits at his bar or Tavern in Gatesville for one year.

issd. Ordered that John **LOVETT** have a lincence [sic] to retail spirits by the small measure at [sic] house in Gatesville.

issd. Ordered that Abram W. **PARKER** have a licence to retail Spirits by the small measure, at his store.

Ordered that Isaac **WILLIAMS** be appointed County surveyor for this County, and that he gave bond & security as the law requires, with Jonathan **WILLIAMS** & Dempsey S. **GOODMAN** for securities &c.

" Inventory of the notes & accounts of Henry **PUGH** dec^d. exhibited into Court by William E. **PUGH** executor &c

" John **MATTHEWS** guardian to the orphans of Jethro **BENTON** dec^d. exhibited into Court his guardian account with s^d. orphans

" Theophilus **HARRELL** exo^r. of Abm. **HARRELL** dec^d. exhibited into Court an account Current with said estate &c.

Deed [sic] Mortgage Isaac F. **STAFFORD** to H. **GILLIAM**, J. **BOND** Jepha [sic] **FOWLKES** & L. S. **DAUGHTRY** was in open Court proved by J. R. **GILLIAM**

Deed of Gift John **HAYS** sen^r. to Joseph **HAYS** was in open Court proved by the oath of James R. **RIDDICK** a witness thereto.

Lease from Charles **POWELL** to John **POWELL** was in open Court proved by the Oath of William **MOORE** a witness thereto &c.

Deed of sale John **GATLING** to William **GATLING** was in open Court proved by the Oath of Riddick **GATLING** a witness &c

Deed of [sic] Thomas E. **RIDDICK** to John R. **NORFLEET** was in open Court proved by the Oath of Riddick **MATTHEWS** a witness

Deed of sale Abram **HARRELL** Trustee to Thos. **EASON** was in open Court proved by the Oath of Simmons H **JONES** a witness

May Court 1833

Deed of sale K. **NORFLEET** & Prior **SAVAGE** to Joseph **RIDDICK** of Tho. was in open Court proved by the oath of Henry **GILLIAM** a witness

Deed of sale Kinchen **NORFLEET** to Joseph **RIDDICK** was in open Court proved by the oath of Henry **GILLIAM** a witness.

[69] 287 Deed in trust Jacob **POWELL** to Henry **COSTEN** was in open Court proved by the Oath of W^m. W. **HALL** a witness thereto &c

Deed of sale John **NORFLEET** to William W. **POWELL** was in open Court proved by the Oath of William **HUDGINS** a witness

Bill of sale John **LEWIS** to John R. **NORFLEET** was in open Court proved by the Oath of Lem^l. **CLEAVES** a witness.

Receipt from James R. **RIDDICK** to William **GATLING** was in open Court acknowledged in due form of law &c.

Bill of sale Jethro **WILLEY** to James R. **RIDDICK** was in open Court acknowledged in due form of law &c.

Ordered that James **EASON** be bound an apprentice to Abel **ROGERSON** to learn the farming business.

Ordered that Abram **UMPHLET** a boy of Color be bound an apprentice to Demsey **PARKER** to learn the farming business

Ordered that Kedar & Holloday **JONES** be bound an [sic] apprentices to Andrew **MATTHEWS** to learn the farming business.

Ordered that William **RELPH** an orphan be bound to John O. **HUNTER** to learn the farming business.

Ordered that Willie **BROWN** an orphan be bound to William L. **BOOTHE** to learn the farming business.

Wednesday morning Court Met
Present—John **WALTON** Thomas **SAUNDERS** William L. **BOOTHE**} Esquires

" Inventory of the estate of William **BOND** dec^d. was exhibited into Court by Wright **HAYSE** adm^r. on oath.

Deed of sale from James A. **BALLARD** to Charles & Hardy **BRINKLY** was proved in open Court by the Oath of Benjamin **FRANKLIN** a subscribing witness thereto &c.

issd. Ordered that the Sheriff summon a jury and go on the premises and lay off to Martha **PARKER** widow of Abram **PARKER** dec^d. her dower in the lands which her late husband died seized and possessed, agreeable to law &c.

[70] blank *issd.* Ordered that the Sheriff summon Wills **COWPER** Jr. John **RIDDICK** of Tho. James **BOOTHE**, John **WIGGINS**, Isaac **HARRELL** Robert **ROGERS**, James **BOOTHE** near Som^t.) Isaac **WILLIAMS**, Reuben **PARKER**, Henry **WILLEY**, Wiley **RIDDICK** Charles **JONES** of P. Kinchen **NORFLEET**, Charles **WILLIAMS** Frederick **JONES**, Elijah **HARRELL**, Nathan **CULLINS**, William **RIDDICK**, Miles **BRIGGS**, John **SPEIGHT** of H. Demsey **HOBBS** Tilley W. **CARR**, Henry R. **PUGH**, Jesse M. **SAVAGE**, Marmaduke **NORFLEET**, Asa **HILL**, Levi **BEEMAN**, Abram **SMITH** John **HAYSE** and Dempsey S. **GOODMAN** personally attend at the next County Court to be held for this County on the third monday in August next, then and there to serve as Jurors &c.

Chitty **PARKER** & her husband D. **PARKER** }
vs.

May Court 1833

Henry JONES adm^r. } Decree

This cause coming ton [sic] to be heard upon the petition and report of the Jury, the Court doth declare that the said Chitty is not as comfortably provided under the will of her late husband Henry JONES as She would have been had the said Henry died intestate The Court doth therefore order adjudge and decree the said Chitty to have a tract of land of which the said Henry died seized caled [sic] the VALENTINE tract, during the term of her natural life, in full of her right of dower in the real estate of the said Henry. And the Court doth further adjudge and decree the said Chitty to be possessed absolutely of the following person [sic] property in full of her share and proportion of the personal estate of the said Henry (to wit) negro man DAVID, man ABRAM, woman AMY & old woman PLEASANT one Gray mare & gig & harness four cows & calves four ewes & lambs one feather bed & furniture, and that she pay to the administrator of the said Henry the sum of two hundred and twenty eight dollars as soon as the negroes shall be placed in the possession of the said Chitty & that each party pay one half of the Costs.

END OF BOOK

[71] At a County Court of pleas & q^r [sic] Sessions be gan [sic] & held for the County of Gates at the Court house in Gatesville on the 3^r. Monday in August AD 1833.
the 19th Said Month.

Present the Worshipfull Justices
Simon WALTERS. Thomas SAUNDERS. Barnes GOODMAN. William LEE. John D. PIPKIN Riddick GATLING. William GOODMAN. W^m. L. BOOTH. Mills RIDDICK. Hardy D. PARKER. Richard ODAM & Willis F. RIDDICK. at Which time appeared

" William W. STEADMON having been duly Elected as Clerk of the County Court of pleas & q^r Sessions for the County of Gates he gave Bond & Security as the Law requirs & took the Oath prescribed. by Law. at same time Henry GILLIAM appeard in Open Court & was appointed deputy Clk & took the Oath.

orderd [sic] that Robt. ROGERS a regular Juror be discharged.

Orderd that the county Trustee loand [sic] the Shff the Sum of Seven hundred & fifty Dollars out of the public Treasure & that he refund the same when Collected.

Orderd that Eliz^a. HAYS be appointed Guardian to her infant Child Caroline that she enter into Bond & Secuity [sic] in the sum $1000

Orderd that Henry T. WATHAN & Riddick SMITH be removed from the road under Thos HINTON as overseer to the road of Willis J. RIDDICK

" Orderd that the County Trustee pay Benj SUMNER former Solicitor Twenty Dollars for his half years sallerey.

" Orderd that Henry G. WILLIAMS be permitted to straighten the road by his plantation & that after putting the same in proper repaire deliver the same to the overseer.

Orderd that James SMITH (of Jos) Willis CROSS & Etheldred CROSS return the number of hands belonging to the several roads over which they Command at the next. Term

Orderd that Henry GILLIAM W^m. E. PUGH John D. PIPKIN Jno C. GORDON John WALTON. & Willis F RIDDICK be appointed to Examine the records &c of the County Court office & make report to this Court.

A deed of Sale from Demsey BOND to Jethro LASSITER was proved in Open Court & orderd to be registerd.

August Court 1833

~~Orderd~~ A Deed of Sale from James. R. **RIDDICK** to John **BENTON** Jun' was acknowledged in Open Court & orderd to be registered.

[72] Monday 19th. augt. 1833.

A Deed of Sale from Abraham **MORGAN** to Levin **HOFFLER** was proved in Open Court & orderd to be registerd

" Orderd that Edward **JONES** be appointed overseer of the road leading from the Watrey Swamp. to **HUNTER**s Mill.

On Motion orderd that Benj. **FRANKLIN** be appointed admr. upon the Estate of John **BRINKLEY** decd. that he enter into Bonds with Marmaduke **BROTHERS** & John **WIGGINS** Security in $2000.

Orderd that John D **PIPKIN** be appointed in the room of Hillory **WILLEY** Esqr. as one of the poore house Comittee

The Last will & Testament /of David **LEWIS**/ was exhibiteed in Open Court by David **CROSS** the Exor & was proved as the Law directs.

Orderd that Eliza. **TAYLOR** Daughter of Mary **TAYLOR** a Coloured Girl be bound as an apprentice to Timo. **WARD**

A Bill Sale [sic] from James R **RIDDICK** to Demsey **SPARKMAN** was provd in Open Court & orderd to be registered.

A Deed of Sale from James **LASSITER** to Demsey **PARKER** was proved in Open Court & orderd to be registered

A Bill of Sale from John **BEEMAN** to Elisha **HARRELL** Jur was proved in Open Court & orderd to be registerd.

James. R. **RIDDICK** appeeard [sic] in Open Court & produced his recepts from the public offices as the Law requires. orderd that he renew his Shff Bond

Orderd that Joseph **HURDLE** Jur be appointed Guardian to Mary & Caroline **SUTTON**s orphan [sic] of Geo **SUTTON** decd—that he enter into Bond with Kedar **FELTON**. Bushrod **RIDDICK** & Levi **SUMNER** Security for the Sum of $2.000.

James. R. **RIDDICK** Shff made the return of the number of retail & Merchants Licence & taxes Colleced [sic] from Itinerant stage players & others.

Orderd that Nathan **NIXON** be appointed admr. on the Estate of Mary **KING** that he give Bond & Security in $500.

Orderd that Thomas **SAUNDERS** Esqr be appointed Chairman of this Court.

Orderd that the following Taxes be laid & Collectd by the Shff
County Taxes. $ 20/100 on the poll. 6^{Cts} on the 100$ Valuation Land. parish Tax. 35^{Cts} on poll. & 10^{Cts} on Lands. poor house 20^{Cts} & 5^{Cts} on $100 Valuation Lands.

[73] Monday 19th. August 1833.

A Deed of Sale from Will W. **HAYS** to Thos **COSTON** was proved in Open Court & orderd to be registered.

A Deed in Trust from Easther **MITCHEL** to Wm. E. **PUGH** was proved in Open Court & orderd to be

August Court 1833

registerd.

A Deed of Sale from Peter. B. **MINTON** to I. S. **HARRELL** & Thos. R **COSTON** was proved in Open Court & orderd to be registered

A Deed of Sale from James **HOWARD** To **HARRELL** & **COSTON** was proved in Open Court & ordered to be registered.

A Deed of Sale from Eliz^a. **HAYS** to James **SMITH** was proved in Open Court & orderd to be registered.

A Deed of Sale from James **SMITH** to Eliz^a. **HAYS** was proved in Open Court & orderd to be registered.

A Deed of Sale from John **MATHEWS** to Pryor **SAVAGE** was proved in Open Court & orderd to be registered.

A Deed of Sale from Francis **ROGERS** & wife Elizabeth was [sic] to Timothy **HOWELL** was proved in Open Court & orderd to be registerd

" Orderd that William **LEE** & Willis F **RIDDICK** Esqr. be appointed to take the private Examination of Eliz^a. **ROGERS** wife of Francis **ROGERS**

The audited acct. of Jos **GORDON** adm^r. of Hardy **EASON** /dec^d/ was returned to Court & orderd to be recorded.

A Division of the Estate of Hardy **EASON** dec^d. was returned to Court & orderd to be recorded.

William E. **PUGH** was duly Elected County Solicitor

Tuesday morning Court met
Present W^m.. **GOODMAN** Joseph **RIDDICK** W^m. **LEE**} Esqrs

The Shff returned the following List of Jurors to Serve at this Term. (to Wit) Wills~~is CROSS~~ **COWPER** Jur John **RIDDICK** of Thos. James **BOOTH** (Somerton) Johm [sic] **WIGGINS**. Isaac **HARRELL**. James **BOOTH** (C^t. Isaac **WILLIAMS**. Rubin [sic] **PARKER**. Henry **WILLEY**. Willie **RIDDICK** Charles **JONES** of R Kinchen **NORFLEET**. Fre^d. **JONES**. Elijah **HARRELL** Nath. **CULLINS**. William **RIDDICK**. Miles **BRIGGS**. John **SPEIGHT** (of Henry) Demsey **HOBBS**. T. W. **CARR**. Henry. R. **PUGH**. Jesse. M. **SAVAGE** Marmaduke **NORFLEET**. Asa **HILL**. Levi **BEEMAN**. Abram **SMITH**. John **HAYS** & Demsey S. **GOODMAN**.

[74] The following persons drawn & Sworn as Grand Jurors.
Demsey S **GOODMAN** (foreman) James **BOOTH** (Somerton) Fre^d. **JONES** Wills~~is~~ **COWPER**. John **HAYS**. John **WIGGINS**. T. W. **CARR**. Ab **SMITH** Asa **HILL**. Charles **JONES** (of P. Elijah **HARRELL**. Henry **WILLEY**. Demsey **HOBBS**. Levi **BEEMAN**. Mar^k. **NORFLEET**. Rubin **PARKER**. Kinchen **NORFLEET** & John **RIDDICK** (of Thos.

Charles **BRIGGS** Wits. State vs Andrew **HARRELL** Call^d. out issue Sci fa

The following Jurors. Willie **RIDDICK** & Jno **SPEIGHT** original panel
M & C **WILLIAMS** by Their Gu^d. Nat **EURE** vs Mills **EURE** et als.} The following Jurors, Willie **RIDDICK**. John **SPEIGHT**. Rich^d.. **CURL**. Willis **CROSS**. Arch^d. **ELLIS**. John R **NORFLEET**. Thomas **RIDDICK** Riddick **JONES**. Jesse **MATHIAS** Demsey **VANN** & Britton **OBARR** being impannell^d. & Sworn find all the issues infavour [sic] of Pltff & asses [sic] the pltff damage to $61.90 penalty Bond $500 & Costs.

John A **ANDERSON** vs Elisha H **BOND** } Case
Henry **GILLIAM** Security in this Case Surrenderd the body of Def^d. Orderd that he be discharged from

August Court 1833

Said Bond

On Motion of W^m. E. **PUGH** Esqr Orderd that the Shff bring into Court the body of Lewis **CARTER**. to testify in his Case vs Jethro **WILLEY**

WYNNS & **JERNIGAN** vs Ira **CARTER**} Case. In this Case Nathl **EURE** Surrende_rd_ the body of the defendant. & the Said Ira **CARTER** was admitted to take the Oath prescribed by Law. & was orderd to be discharged

William **SPIVEY** vs Peter. B. **MINTON**} A. & B. The following Jurors. Willie **RIDDICK** Richard **CURL**. Willis **CROSS**. John **LEWIS** John R **NORFLEET**. Thomas **RIDDICK** Riddick **JONES**. Jesse **MATHIAS**. Demsey **VANN** Demsey **SPARKMAN** Britton O. **BARR** & Kin^d. **PARKER** being duly imp^d. & Sworn find all the issues infavour of pltff & asses his Damage to $60. & Cost. Wher_up_on the s^d. Defendant applied for & obta_in_d an appeal to the next Sup Court of Law & he enter_d_ into Bond with Henry **GILLIAM** & Jethro H. **RIDDICK** Security.

Orderd that Gideon **PHELPS** orphan of James **PHELPS** be bound as an apprentice to Geor [sic] **COSTON** to learn the business of farming

[75] Tuesday. 20th. aug^t. 1833.

Orderd that Edward **HOWELL** orphan of Lottey **HOWELL** be bound as an apprentice to Fre^d. **JONES** to learn the business of a Farmer.

Orderd that Emeline **LANG** a Girl of Colour orphan of Betsey **LANG** be bound as an apprentice to James **BOOTHE** (Somerton

Orderd that Thompson **PRICE** a free boy of Colour Child of Betsey **PRICE** & Alfred **PRICE** of the Same be bound to Lass [sic] **RIDDICK** to be farmer [sic]

Orderd that Elisha **REED** a Coloured boy Son of Sophia **REED** be bound to Will **HINTON**.

Orderd that Thomas **BUTLER** a free boy of Colour Son of Mary **BUTLER** be bound as an apprentice to Kind. **PARKER**

Orderd that Luke **BAGLEY** & John **BAGLEY** Children of Jacob D. **BAGLEY** be bound to John **WIGGINS**.

" Orderd that John **WALKER** a free man of Color from Suffolk V^a. be permitted to retail Oysters Cakes &c within the County of Gates for one year_e_ & that the Clk issue a Certificate

Jos. J. **BARNES** vs Ab. W. **PARKER**... N°. 2 on Trial Docket dismiss^d.

" Orderd that James R **RIDDICK** be allow^d. Ten Dollars for his trouble & expence in furnishing paper & Sumoning [sic] inspectors to attend & hold the Several Elections -- & that the County Trustee pay the same.

" Orderd that James R **RIDDICK** be allow^d. four Dollars for laying off a New road leading from **HARRELL**s Meeting house to Ab W. **PARKER**s lane & that the Cty. Trustee pay it

" Orderd that Thomas **HOGGARD** have leave to Move the road leading to Sarum Creek by his house not exceeding 90. feet. provided he put it in Good Order

" Orderd that John **SPEIGHT** be appointed overseer of the road leading from **WOOD**s Old field to the fork of the road where Philip **ROGERS** formerly lived & that he have the follo_w_ing hands to Work on said Road. Isaac **PIPKIN**'s hands Riddick **GATLING**s hands. William **GATLING's** hands Jainy [sic] **WILLIAMS** hands. Eff **LEWIS**. hands & 2 hands of William **GOODMAN**s Senr.

August Court 1833

Orderd that the present Clk issue an Execution at the instance **DAUGHTRY & WEBB**. Henry **BOND** real plf. vs John B. **BAKER**

[76] Tuesday 20th Aug'. 1833.

Orderd that the Clk issue a new Execution ag' Benj **BLANCHAD** infavor of Tim°. **WALTON**.

issd. Orderd that John **GWINN** be allow^d. One Dollar & 20/100 for provisions furnish^d. Jos. & Daniel **GWIN** while in the Juniper Swamp

Orderd that Wright **HAYS** be appointed Guardian to Nancy **BOND**. that he enter into Bonds in the sum of $200. with John **BOND** & Tim°. **HAYS** Security.

A Deed of Sale from Jas R **RIDDICK** to Jesse **PARKER** was ack^d. in Open Court & orderd to be registered.

A report of the road from **HARRELL**s. Meeting house to A. W. **PARKER**s lane was returned & orderd to be filed

An Inventory of the Estate of Jn°. **BEEMAN** was return^d. by the Exor & orderd to be recorded.

A Bill of Sale from William **GLOVER** to Benbury **WALTON** was ack^d. in Open Court & orderd to be registerd.

An Inventory of the Estate of James **BRINKLEY** dec^d. was returned by the adm^r.. & orderd to be recorded.

A Bill of Sale from Kedar **ELLIS** to Benj **BRINKLY** was proved in Open Court & orderd to be registerd.

A Deed of Gift from Ann **PARKER** to Louisa **PARKER** was proved in Open Court & orderd to be registered.

A Deed /in trust/ of Sale from Nathl. **WATKINS** to James **MORGAN** was proved in Open Court & orderd to be registered.

A Deed of Sale from Mary **PARKER** to Miles **PARKER** was proved in Open Court & orderd to be registered.

A Deed of Sale from James **DUKE** & wife Sophia ~~was proved~~ to John **SMALL** Senr. was proved in Open Court & orderd that Commission issue to take the private Examination of Sophia & orderd to be registered.

A Deed of Sale from John **EURE** Senr. to Mills **EURE** was proved in Open Court & orderd to be registered.

A Deed of Sale from Henry W. **SKINNER** to John S. **ROBERTS** was ack^d. in Open Court & orderd to be registered.

A Deed of Gift from Ann **PARKER** to Thursey **PARKER** and Margaret **PARKER** & others was proved in Open Court & ored [sic] to be registerd

A Deed of Sale from Robert **PARKER** to John **MATHEWS** was proved in Open Court & orderd to be registered.

A Bill of Sale from John **WORRELL** to Eli **WORRELL** was ack^d. in Open Court & orderd to be registered.

August Court 1833

[77] Tuesday 20th Augt. 1833.

A Deed of Sale from Edwd. R **HUNTER** to Marmaduke **NORFLEET** was proved in Open Court & orderd to be registered.

The last will & Testament of David **LEWIS** decd. was exhibited in Open Court & proved by the Oath of John B. **BAKER** one of the Subscribing witnesses therto & at the same time David C. **CROSS** the Executor therin named. Appeard & was quallified orderd that the same be recorded & letters Testamentry [sic] issue

State of No. Carolina}
Gates County.   } At a Court of pleas & qr. Sessions held for the County of Gates at the Court house in Gatesville on the 3rd. Monday of November 18th day 1833.
   Present   John C. **GORDON**. Hardy D **PARKER** Thomas **SAUNDERS** Barnes **GOODMAN**. Joseph **RIDDICK** & Willis F **RIDDICK** Esqrs.

Orderd that Hardy D **PARKER** be permitted to Streighten the road on his land so that the overseer will receive the Same

Orderd that Col Barnes **GOODMAN** recive from the Clk of this County Court the returns in his office of the Militia that Served in the late insurrection & that he recive the accot. for the Same from the County trustee & pay over the Same to the individuls

Orderd that Nathan **RIDDICK** renew his Bonds as County Trustee

issd. Orderd that Benjn. **FRANKLIN** admr of John **BRINKLY** decd. Sell two Certain Negros **JINNY** & **MOSES** to pay debts.

Orderd that Simon **WALTERS** be appointed admr on the Estate of Willey **JENKINS** decd. that he enter into bond & Security in $50.

Orderd that Simon **WALTERS** be appd. Guardian to the orphans of Willy [sic] **JENKINS** that he give bond & Security for $50.

Orderd that Thomas E **RIDDICK** be appointed Constable in the honey pot district that he give bond & Security.

issd. Orderd that John W **ODAM** be appointed overseer of the road leading from **KITTRELL**s Meeting house to the old road near Samuel **CROSS**es.

Orderd that the Clk of the County Court State the Sevral patrols roll returns & divide the funds Set a part between them & make report to next Court

Orderd that James M **SAVAGE** renew his Constable Bond.

Orderd that Richd. H **PARKER** admr with the will annexed of John W. **MATHEWS** & that he give bond & Security.

[78] Orderd that John C. **GORDON** adminster upon the Estate of James **GORDON** decd. that he give Bond & Security in the Sum of $15000

Court adjourned untill Tuesday morning

Tuesday morning court met.
Present { Wm. W. **COWPER** Whit. **STALLINS** [sic] & Thomas **SAUNDERS**} Esqrs

November Court 1833

issd. Orderd that W^m. L. **BOOTH** Jno. **RIDDICK** John **SAUNDERS** & Kindred **PARKER** be appointed to Set a part to Salley **JONES** Widow of James **JONES** dec^d. One years provision Out of the Crop Stock &c & report.

Orderd that John **EURE** be appointed adm^r on the Estate of John **EURE** Senr dec^d. that he give bound [sic] & Security in the Sum of $500. with Elisha **UMPHLET** & Charney **UMPHLET** Securities.

Orderd that Will. W. **COWPER** be appointed adm^r on the Estate of James **JONES** dec^d. that he enter into Bond in the Sum of $400—James **JONES** & William **SEARS** Securities—at the same time Salley **JONES** widow of Ja^s. **JONES** relinquished her right of admstration [sic]

issd. Orderd that Timothy **WALTON**. Henry **GILLIAM**. James **BOOTH** & Joseph **RIDDICK** Esqr. Lay off & Sett a part to Mary **HINTON** Widow of W^m. **HINTON** dec^d. out of the Crop Stock &c one years provision for Self & family & report to the Next Court.

issd. Orderd that Henry **BOND** & John **BOND** be appointed Admr^s. to the Estate of W^m. **HINTON** dec^d. that they enter into Bonds in the Sum of $20.000. with Henry **GILLIAM** & Tim^o. **WALTON** Securities.

issd. Orderd that the county Trustee pay W^m. **CLEAVES** one Dollar & fifty Cents

issd. Orderd that the County Trustee pay John S. **ROBERTS** Ten Dollars for a paper Case for the use of the Clks.

issd. Orderd that the County Trustee pay Jethro H. **RIDDICK** four Dollars for his attending as Constable at the Last Sup Court.

issd. Orderd that the County Trustee pay Lassiter **RIDDICK** Coroner the Sum of Ten Dollars for holding an inquest over Charles **BOGURE** & Ten Dollars for Same Services on the body of an infant of Helon **LEE**.

On Motion orderd that Henry **GILLIAM** admr on the Estate of James **LANDING** dec^d. an infant that he enter into Bond for $1000. with Jethro H **RIDDICK** & John **SAUNDERS** Securities.

issd. Orderd that Thomas **SAUNDERS** have a licence to retail Spirits by the Small measure at his house in Gatesville.

[79] Tuesday. 19th. Nov

Orderd that the Trustee of public buildings have locks put on the Jury rooms & that he render an act. [sic] for the Same & that he have the public bridges in Said County repaird.

On Motion of W^m. E. **PUGH** orderd that a Writ of Lunacey issue to the Shff to Examine Benjamin **HUNTER** & report to the next Term.

issd. Ordered that the County Trustee pay Simnons **ROUNTREE** the Sum of Twelve Dollars as Constable for attending the Court up to this day.

    Court adjourned untill Wednesday.
    Wednesday Court met. according to adjournment [sic]
Present {Thomas **SAUNDES** Mills **RIDDICK** Ab. W. **PARKER**} Esquires

Orderd that Jeptha **FOWLKS** adm^r upon the Estate of Richard **RAWLS** that he enter into Bonds in the Sum of Six hundred Dollars with Henry **GILLIAM** Security.

Caroline **HAYS** by her Guardian Eliz^a **HAYS** }
              vs   Petition } Granted
Henry **GILLIAM** adm^r. et. als   }

November Court 1833

Orderd that publication be made in the Edenton Misselany [sic] for the space of six weeks for Charles **WILLIAMS** and wife Margaret for them to appear plead answer or demur to the petition Otherwise Judg'. pro. Confe*so*. will be taken as to them.

Orderd that Henry **GILLIAM** Sell on a Credit of Six Months ~~all~~ the Negr*os* belonging to the Estate of Benj **HAYS** as mentioned to be Sold in the s^d. **HAYS** will.

The last will & Testament of Nathan **CULLINS** was Exibeted [sic] into Open Court & proved by the Oaths of Jno. T. **BENTON** and Henry **BAGLEY** two of the Subscribing witnesses theere to, [sic] at the Same time Whitm*il* **STALLINS** one of the Exors the*rin* named & appeard & qualified Orderd that the Same be recorded.

A Bill of Sale from Kedar **ELLIS** ~~was~~ to Benjn. **BRINKLEY** was prove*ed* in Open Court by the Oath of Jesse **MATHIAS** & ord*ed* to be registered.

A Deed of Sale from James R **RIDDICK** to Allen **SMITH** was proved in Open Court by the Oath of Joseph **RIDDICK** & orderd to be registerd.

[80] A Deed of Sale from Thomas **TWINE** to Henry **BOND** was ~~pro~~ ackg^d. in Open Court & orderd to be registered.

A Deed of Sale from John R **NORFLEET** & wife to Elisha **UMPHLET** was proved in Open Court by the Oath of Jno O **HUNTER** & orderd to be registered.

A Deed of Sale from William **BUSH** to Abraham **DAVIS** was proved in Open Court by the Oath of Henry R **PUGH** & orderd to be registered.

The report of Commissions [sic] appointed to Set a part one years provision to Lavinia **BRINKLEY** was returned to Court & filed

A Bill of Sale from Richard **BRIGGS** to Henry **BRIGGS** was proved in Open Court by W^m. W **STEADMAN** & orderd to be registerd

A Bill of Sale from James. R. **RIDDICK** to Christian **CULLINS** was proved in Open Court by Riddick **GATLING** & orderd to be registered.

A Deed of Sale from Jasper **TROTMON** to Jethro. H. **RIDDICK** was proved in Open Court by the Oath of Jason **RIDDICK** & orderd to be registered.

A Deed of Sale from John R. **NORFLEET** to John **FELTON** was ~~pro~~ ack^d. in Open Court & orderd to be registered.

A Deed of Sale from Thomas B. **HUNTER** to Thomas **TWINE** was ack^d. in Open Court & orderd to be registered.

A Deed of Sale from Treasey **WALTON** to William **BUSH** was proved in Open Court by the Oath of Jos **LILLEY** & orderd to be registered.

A Deed of Sale from John **ELLEN** to James **BOOTH** was proved in Open Court by the Oath of Allen **SMITH** & orderd to be registered

An acc^t. of the Sales of the Estate of John **BRINKLEY** dec^d. was retur^d. to Court by Benj. **FRANKLIN** adm^r. & orderd to be recorded.

An Inventory of the Estate of John **BRINKLEY** dec^d. was returned to Court by Benj. **FRANKLIN** admr & orderd to be recorded

November Court 1833

A Deed of Sale from Isaac P. **FREEMAN** to Miles **PARKER** was prov̲d in Open Court by the Oath of C. R. **KINNY** & orderd to be registerd

An acct of Sales & inventory of the Estate of Mary **KING**. dec^d. was returned to Court by Nathan **NIXON** adm^r. & orderd to be recorded

A Deed of Sale from James **BAKER** Senr. to James **BAKER** Jur. was proved in Open Court by the Oath of Abel **ROGERSON** & orderd to be registerd

A Deed of Sale from Riddick **GATLING** to John **LEE** was provd in Open Court by the Oath of John **SPARKMAN** & orderd to be registerd

A Deed of Sale from Amos **HOBBS** to Guy **HOBBS** was proved in Open Court by the Oath of Jos **HURDLE** & orderd to be registered.

[81] Wednesday

A Deed of Sale from Will **GOODMAN** to Jethro **HARRELL** was ack^d. in Open Court & orderd to be registered.

A Deed of Sale from Will **GOODMAN** to Jason **ROUNTREE** was ack^d. in Open Court & orderd to be registerd.

A Deed of Sale from Will **GOODMAN** to Lewis **GREEN** was ack^d. in Open Court & orderd to be registered.

A Deed of Sale from John **BENTON** to Jesse **BENTON** was ack^d. in Open Court & orderd to be registered.

A Deed of Sale from William **GOODMAN** to John **ROUNTREE** was ack^d.g [sic] in Open Court & orderd to be registered.

A Deed of ~~Sale~~ /Trust/ from William **DAVIDSON** to Hardy **CROSS** was ack^d. by Edwin **SMITH** & Hardy **CROSS** & the signature of William **DAVIDSON** was proved in Open Court by the oath of Saml. **CROSS** & orderd to be registd [sic]

A report of one years provision set a part to Louisa **BRINKLEY** was returned to Court & orderd to be filed.

A Deed of Sale from James H. **PILAND** to Jesse **PILAND** was proved in Open Court by the Oath of Thos **HOGARD** [sic] & orderd to be registerd

A Deed of Sale from Abraham **RIDDICK** to Kadar **ELLIS** was proved in Open Court by the Oath of Riddick **JONES** & orderd to be registrd

A Deed of Sale from Kedar **ELLIS** to Riddick **JONES** was proved in Open Court by the Oath of Benj **FRANKLIN** & orderd to be registrd

A Deed of Sale from Isaac **PILAND** to Rubin **PILAND** was proved in open Court by the Oath of Thos. **HOGARD** & orderd to be registered.

An acc^t. of Sales of the Estate of John **EURE** dec^d was returnd to Court by John **EURE** admr & orderd to be recorded.

An audited acct. of Fred. **HINTON** as trustee to the Estate of Salley **LEWIS** dec^d. was returnd to Court & orderd to be recorded

November Court 1833

A Deed of Sale from John **WORRELL** to Eli **WORRELL** was proved in Open court by the Oath of Simmons **ROUNTREE** & orderd to be registrd

The Shff returnd the following persons to Serve as Jurors to this Court Saml **HARRELL** (of Josiah) David F. **FELTON**. Will **SEARS** Ezekiel **JONES**. Saml **EURE** (of Mills) Aaron **PIERCE**. John. D. **HOFFLER** John **HOFFLER** Ju^r. James **WILLIAMS** Ju^r David **UMPHLET** John **MATHEWS** Benj **SAUNDERS**. Marmaduke **BAKER**. Jesse **ARLINE** Benj **EURE**. John **PARKER** (of R. Rubin **EASON**. Edward **BRIGGS** Guy **HOBBS**. Bray **PARKER**. James **SAUNDERS**. William **WHITE** Jesse **HOBBS**. William **HARRELL** Ju^r. Jacob **ODOM**. Ephraim **BUNCH**. Jesse **PARKER**. Riddick **MATHEWS**. Henry **HAYS**. Abr. **MORGAN** Senr. Miles **BROWN**. Riddick **HUNTER**. Rob. **HILL** & Whit **HILL**

[82] The following persons was drawn Sworn & Charged as Grand Jurors to this Term. David F. **FELTON**. John **HOFFLER**. Jesse **PARKER** Saml. **HARRELL**. Bray **PARKER**. William **SEARS**. Riddick **MATHEWS** Edward **BRIGGS** Arone [?] **PIERCE**. Ezekiel **JONES**. Henry **HAYS**. Benj. **SAUNDERS**. Riddick **HUNTER**. David **UMPHLET**. Marmaduke **BAKER** William **HARRELL** Senr. Guy **HOBBS**. & James **WILLIAMS**.

Governor to the use of John **WIGGINS** adm^r.}
ag^t. Jesse **MATHIAS** & Riddick **JONES**… } By the Court. orderd that the report in this Case be Confirm^d. for the Sum of ninty five Dollars & 21/100. let the Clk be allow^d. .5$. [sic] for report. one half to be paid by Each party. Jury imp^d. & Sworn find all the issues infavour of pltff. & asses the pltffs damage to $95.21. for Conditions broken. by the Court. Judg^t. accordingly.

Jos. J. **BARNES** }
    vs   Qui, tam }
Abraham W **PARKER**.} The following Jurors. John **HOFFLER**. John **BRADY**. Willis **CROSS** Riddick **HAYS**. Benj. **EURE**. Jesse **HOBBS**. Ephram **BUNCH**. James **SAUNDERS** Rubin **EASON**. Andrew **HARRELL**. Jos **FREEMAN** & Charny **UMPHLET** being duly Sworn & impannell^d. find all the issues infavour of the defendant.

William E. **PUGH** Exor }
    vs   }
John B. **BAKER**. } The following Jurors. Whitmil **HILL** Robert **HILL** Jur. Ephram **BUNCH**. James **SAUNDERS**. Jesse **HOBBS**. Isaac **SPEIGHT**. Richard **CURL**. Charny **UMPHLET** Rubin **EASON**. Isaac **BLANCHARD**. Jno R **NORFLEET**. & John **SPARKMAN** being duly Sworn & impannell^d. find all the issues infavour of the pltff & asses his damage to 6^d.

Nathan **RIDDICK** Exor }
    vs   }
Thomas **THOMPSON** } By the Court thure is such a record Same Jurey being Sworn & impannel^d. Say therir [sic] is no pay^t. Value of form Judg^t. $135.80. & asses pltffs damage by way of intes. to $53.83. Jugt. accordingl^{e}y for $189.63. & for Cost former Suite.

Lewis **CARTER** }
    vs   }
Jethro **WILLEY**.} Same Jury. find all the issues infavor of Pltff & asses pltffs damage to $2.

[83] Thursday

Edward S. **NEAL** }
    vs.   }
Margaret **HOSKINS**} Same Jurors Sworn & impanell^d. find infavour of pltff & asses his damg [sic] to $22.. whereupon the defendant prayed an appeal to the Sup Court. & gave Bond with John R **NORFLEET** & Henry **GILLIAM** Securities.

November Court 1833

William B. **WYNNS** }
    vs. } Attacht.
James R **CREECY** } upon looking into the answers of Isaac **PIPKIN**. John D **PIPKIN**. John **LOVET**. it is Considerd by the Court that the pltff recover Judg^t. of Isaac **PIPKIN** for $16.28 & from John **LOVET**. $325.35 & from John. D. **PIPKIN** $104.40 looking into the answer of Mills **ROBERTS** it is Considerd that the pltff have Judg^t. for $88. & that the pltff have Execution according to Law

Charney **UMPHLET** et als}
    vs }
David **UMPHLET** et als. } Is the paper Writing now offerd for probate the Last will & Testament of W^m. **UMPHLET**. Rept issue
The following Jurors, John R. **NORFLEET**. Whit **HILL**. Robt. **HILL** Ju^r. Benj **EURE**. Isaac **BLANCHARD**. Elisha. H. **BOND** Kindred **PARKER** Rubin **EASON**. Ephram **BUNCH**. Isaac **SPEIGHT**. James **SAUNDERS**. Jethro **WILLEY**. being Sworn & impannll^d. Say that the paper writing offered for probate is the last will & Testament of William **UMPHLET**. Orderd by the Court that the will be admitted to probate . Wherupon Elisha **UMPHLET** & Charney **UMPHLET** the two Exors therin named qualified as the Law directs orderd that said will be recorded.

Mary M. **CROSS** Jos. I. **BARNES** & wife Louisa. Mary G. **CROSS** by Lem^l. G. **DARDEN** her Guardian
    vs
John R. **NORFLEET**. adm^r. Ab **CROSS** & Cyprian **CROSS**.
This case coming on to be heard on the petition answer report of the Clk the depositions & exhibits filed in the Cause & now at this Term the Cause being set for hearing by Consent & Coming on to be heard at this time by Consent. it is ordered that the report be Confirm^d. & it appearing by the report. that the amount of the Estate of the testator provided for the

[84] payment of debts by the will including interest [?] & Comissions up to this time is $6177.73 & the amt of all the debts & Comissions with intest up to this time is $8163.46 & that the defficiency of the fund to pay debts was $2317 & that the Spicifice legacies to the different Legatees are bound to pay Said Sum. & that the whole Valuation of Said Spicifice Legacy is $8776.05. & that the Spicific Legacy of Mary M **CROSS** is Chargable with $4~~6~~76.67. & that the defendant **NORFLEET**. as Adm^r Sold of her legacy to the Value of $532.19. & the Spicific Legacy of Cyprian **CROSS** is Chargeable with $603.80 & that the def^d. [sic] **NORFLEET** adm^r. has Sold of his Spicific Legacy the Value of $213. 8. [sic] that Jno **NORFLEET** & wife Harrietts Legacy in like manner is Chargeable with $3~~3~~66.65 & has paid $418. & of Mary G **CROSS** is Chargeable with $560.85 & ~~of the~~ ~~Jos~~ defendant **NORFLEET** has Sold of her Legacey $697.34 and of Jos. J. **BARNES** & wife Louisa is Chargeable with $334.47 & the defendant **NORFLEET** has Sold of the Same to the Value of $457.89 and it appearing by Said report there is now due in the whole to the Complainants & to Jno **NORFLEET** & wife the sum of $642.29. & that there is of Said Sum due to Mary M. **CROSS** $123.52 to Mary G. **CROSS** $222. to Jos. J. **BARNES** & wife $165. & there is due to **NORFLEET** & wife $132.35. and that of $642.89 aforsaid there is $344. the excess of Contribution made to pay the difficiecy [sic] of the fund provided to pay debts. arising from all the spicific legaties [sic]. that have been sold & Converted into money by the defendant. **NORFLEET**. & that there is ~~due~~ $390..92 due from the defendant. for the Contributory Share of Cyprian **CROSS**. to be paid Out of his Spicfic legacey. of Slaves which or a part of them is Still in the possession of the defendant **NORFLEET**. as the adm^r of Abraham **CROSS** whereupon it is Considered that Mary M **CROSS**. recover of the defend amt. [sic] $123.52 Mary G. **CROSS** recover $222. that Jos J **BARNES** & wife recover $165. & that the defend ant **NORFLEET** & wife are entitled. to recover [?] & retain. for their Share $132.35. & that the Sum of $390.72. be paid Out of the Spicific Legacy of Cyprain **CROSS**. and that the defendant. Jno. R. **NORFLEET** as Adm^r. of Abram **CROSS** be directed to sell so much of the said Spicific legacy of Cypran **CROSS** as shall make the aforsaid sum of $390.72 & intes^t. & that he apply the same in Satisfaction of said Sum recovered ~~against~~ /by/ the Complainants as aforsaid & as is found due said **NORFLEET**. & wife. And it further

[85] appearing by the report that the defen^d. **NORFLEET** as admr of A. **CROSS** recover [?] for & on

November Court 1833

Two & a half shares of the dividend of the Winton Ferry Company after the death of Ab **CROSS**. & in the year of 1831. the Sum of $29. including inters^t. up to this time & by the will of the testator Said Sum to [sic] bequeathed to the Testators Children equally. It is therefore Considered that the Complinnants. Jos J. **BARNES** & wife & Mary G. **CROSS** by Lem^l. G. **DARDEN** recover Each one fourth part of Said sum say $7.25 & by consent of the Said ad$\underline{mi}$strator. & of Mary G. **CROSS** by her Guardian it is Considered that. the said Mary G **CROSS**. recover of the defendant. **NORFLEET**. $3.64 it being for rent of Land devised to said Mary by Abram **CROSS** & for the year of 1830. which was rec^d by Said **NORFLEET**. And it appearing that the $\underline{n}$egros by the will of the testator bequeathed to Mairy [sic] G. **CROSS** widow Still unsold & in the possession of the defendant. but hired out untill 1st. of Jan^{ry}. next are **GILES** & Woman **FANNY** & of Mary. G. **CROSS**. in like manner. remaining as aforsaid negro man **JERRY MILLS TEMPE MILEY** & increase. since the death of the testator & those also bequeathed by the testator. and of Jos. J. **BARNES** & wife in like manner. negros **ISAAC** (Call^d **BUNGER**) **PENNINAH**. **RACHEL** & Child **MARY**. It is Considered by the Court. that the Compl^{ts} recover each according to their shares the above distributed negros to be deliver$\underline{d}$ up by the defendant **NORFLEET**. on or before the 1st. day of Jan^{ry}. next 1834. It is considered that the Clk be allow^d. $50. for his report. & that the Cost of suite [sic] be paid Equally by Each of the Complaints [sic] & Cost of the defendant. including $10. fee paid Defend^{ts} attorney. And it is Considered that the Complainants on the receipt of the several sums. decree$\underline{e}$d therein & of the Slaves decreed to be paid & delivered to the Complainants that they give refunding Bonds according to Law.

And now a Certain Marriage ~~Contract~~ Settlmet [sic]. & Couvergance [?] from Louisa **CROSS** to Henry **GILLIAM** $\underline{b}$aring date __[blank]__ & proved & recorded.. At __[blank]__ Term __[blank]__ at Gates County Court. being look^d into & Examined & it appearing thereby that Henry **GILLIAM** is authorized to recover what ever ~~Lovina~~ [?] /Louisia/ was entitled to from the will of her father

[86] & now in Open Court. & by Consent of all parties. & all forms being waved, [waived?] said Henry **GILLIAM** is made a party pltff and it is order$\underline{d}$ & decreed that the sum of monies orderd & decreed to be paid **BARNES** & wife, & the slaves reco$\underline{v}$red by **BARNES** & wife, be paid & rec^d. by said **GILLIAM** in trust & for the benefit of said Louisa. & according to the tennor [sic] of said marriage Contract. & sett$\underline{lm}$ent. Its. orderd and decreed accordingly. Henry **GILLIAM** acknowledges the receipt of $79.82 paid by said **NORFLEET**. to Jos. J. **BARNES**. &. wife in part payment of the recovery as aforsaid

It is further Considered that in as much as there is money due the adm^r.. of Ab **CROSS**. from John **VANN**. Surviving partner for Juniper timber. Sold to **WESTON**. **HERON** & Co & others. by said **VANN** & **CROSS** in the life time of said Ab **CROSS**. It is by Consent of parties agreed that this decree is not to Conclude the parties. touching. said mone$\underline{ey}$s. but is to remain Open for sett$\underline{lm}$ent for the same. & when rec^d. by **NORFLEET** he is to account for the same to those entitled by the will of Ab **CROSS**.

Mills. R **FIELDS** }
vs }
George **KITTRELL**s Exor } Court of pleas & qr Sessions Nov Term 1833

This Case Coming on to be heard. upon the bill and answer & Exhibits in the Case it is orderd adjudged & d$\underline{e}$reed that the said Mills. R. **FIELDS** admr. as aforsaid recover from the said Daniel **WILLIAMS** Exor as aforsaid the sum of $143.50 with intes^t from aug^t Term on one hundred Dollars untill paid.

Lavinia **SMITH** by her Gu^d Thos. **HOGGARD**}
vs }
Joseph **SMITH**s Exor } Report made & Confirmed Cause set for hearing to be heard immedia$\underline{tl}$y. This Cause Coming on to be heard upon the petition. answer report & Testimony. offerd. it is orderd adjudged & decreed that the petitioner recover of the defendant $146.60 to be paid out of the assets of Joseph **SMITH** in the hands of his Exor. Nathan.^{1} to be administerd with intes on $84. & that he also. deliver to the petitioners Gua^d. Thos **HOGARD** [sic] the bed & furniture bequeathed in the will of Joseph **SMITH**

---

^{1} "Nathan" is Nathan **SMITH**, one of the sons in Joseph **SMITH**'s will. *Gates County, North Carolina Wills 1807-1838, Volume II*, Sandra L. Almasy, c. 1985, p. 127—Will Book 2, pp. 282-283.

November Court 1833

to the petitioner It is further orderd that the petitioner recover all Costs except. the Cost of the report. which is

[87] which is allowed at $5. one half of which is to be paid by Each party. Orderd that Execution issue accordingly.

State of N°. Carolina}
    Gates County} November County Court 1833.
    Benj **SUMNER**. brot. into Court a paper writing as the will of Jethro **SUMNER** wherupon Barnes **GOODMAN**. was offerd as a witness who being duly Sworn. made Oath that the paper writing offerd by Benj **SUMNER**. for probate as the last will of Jethro **SUMNER** is all in the proper hand writing of Jethro **SUMNER**. and duly Subscribed by Said Jethro **SUMNER**. in his own proper hand writing. & that the Said paper writing was found in his presence in the writing desk of Said Jethro **SUMNER**. wherin he Kept. his Valuable papers & in which many Valuable papers was found at the time of the finding of the aforsaid paper writing. wherupon James. R. **RIDDICK** Henry **GILLIAM** & Will W. **STEDMAN** was duly Sworn. & they & Each of them made Oath that they were well acquainted with Jethro **SUMNER**s hand writing & that the whole of the paper writing now offered for probate by Benj. **SUMNER**. as the last Will & Testament of said Jethro **SUMNER** is in the proper hand Writing. of Said Jethro **SUMNER**. Ordered that the said will of Jethro **SUMNER** be admitted to probate & that the same be recorded and that Letters Testamentry issue to Benj **SUMNER** the Exor. of Jethro **SUMNER** & at the Same time Benjn. **SUMNER** was qualified as Exor to Said will in due form of Law.

[88] State of N°. Carolina}
    Gates County   } At a County Court. began & held for Gates County at Gatesville on 3rd. monday of Feb^{ry}. 17th day 1834
    Present. Thomas **SAUNDERS**. Whit **STALLINS** & Hardy D **PARKER**

Orderd that. William **UMPHLET** be appointed Overseer of the road leading from the White Oak to Ethel^d. **CROSS**es. in place [sic] James **SMITH**

Orderd that admistration [sic] upon the Estate of Thomas **JOHNSON** dec^d be Granted to Simmonds **ROUNTREE** & he entered into bond & Secuity

Orderd that Jacob **CULLINS** be appointed Guardian to Nathan **CULLINS** his Child & he enterd into Bond & Secuity. with H. **GILLIAM**. & Whit **STALLINS**.

The Guardian accts of Andrew **MATHEWS** to Hollady [sic] & Kedar **JONES** Orphans was Exhibited into Open Court & orderd to be recorded

The Guardian acct. of Edwin **SMITH** with Henrietta **COPELAND** was Exhibited into Open Court & orderd to be recorded.

The Guardian acct^s. of Mills **EURE** with Eliz^a.. William & Stephen **LEE** was Exhibited into Open Court & orderd to be recorded.

The Guardian acct. of David **PARKER** with John **FELTON** was Exhibited into Open Court & orded to be recorded.

The Guardian acc^{ts}. of Jesse **SAVAGE** with Mary & Jesse **SAVAGE** his Children was Exhibited into Open Court & orderd to be recorded.

The Guardian acct^s of James **BOOTH** with Sarah **POWELL** & Sarah **HINTON** was Exhibited into Open Court. & orded to be recorded

The Guardian acct^s. of William E. **PUGH** with Rebeca Josiah & Nathaniel **PUGH** was Exhibited into Open Court & orderd to be recorded

February Court 1834

An Inventory of the Estate of John W **MATHEWS** was Exhibited into Open Court by Rich^d. H. **PARKER** & orderd to be recorded.

An acct. Sales of the Estate of Thomas **JOHNSON** dec^d. was Exhibited into Open Court by Simmons **ROUNTREE** adm^r. & orderd to be recorded

The Guardian acct of Henry G. **WILLIAMS** with Joseph **SPEIGHT**. was Exhibited into Open Court & orded to be recorded

The Guardian acct^s of William /H./ **GOODMAN** with Henry **GOODMAN** Penninah **GOODMAN** Mariah **GOODMAN** John **GOODMAN** & Richard **GOODMAN** was Exhibited into Open Court & orderd to be recorded

The Guardian acct^s of Hardy D **PARKER** with. Jesse. Marthal and Elizabeth **WIGGINS**. orphans was Exhibited & orded to be recorded

The Last Will & Testament of Mary **HARRELL** was Exhibited into Open Court & proved by the Oaths of Thomas **HOGARD** and Willie **CARTER**. at the Same time Ab **PRUDEN** the Executor therin name^d Qualified.

[89] Monday. 17th Feb^ry. 1834

issd. Orderd that. William **SAVAGE** be appointed Overseer of the road leading from Sarum Creek landing to the White Oak branch in room Ab **PRUDEN** resigned

A Report of Commissions appt^d to lay off to Salley **JONES** widow of James **JONES** a years provision was returned to Court.

A Deed of Sale from Thomas **SAUNDERS** & his wife Sarah **SAUNDERS** was proved in Open Court by the Oaths of Edwd. **HOWELL** & John A. **MARCH** & orderd to be registerd.

The Court adjurnd [sic] untill Tuesday morning 10. Oclock.

Tuesday morning Court. met. accoding to adjournmt.
Present Thos. **SAUNDERS**. Whit **STALLINS**. W^m. W. **COWPER**

The Guardian acc^t. of Exum **JENKINS** with Ira **ODOM** was Exhibited into Open Court & orderd to be recorded.

A Deed of Sale from Leven **CUFF** to Miles **PARKER** was proved in Open Court by the Oath of Jethro **WILLEY** & orderd to be registerd.

The Guardian acc^ts of David **MELTEAR** with Partheana **PARKER** & Kiddy **PARKER** orphans was Exhibited into Open Court & orderd to be recorded

A Deed /bill/ of Sale from Andrew **BAKER** to James **BAKER** was proved in open Court by the Oath of Daniel **HOBBS** & orded to be registerd.

The Guardian acc^t of Miles **HOWELL** with John. Albert. Sally and Benj **CROSS** orphans was returned to Court & orderd to be recorded

The Guardian acc^t. of James **SMITH** with Edward **HARE** orphans was returned to Court & orderd to be recorded.

A deed of Gift from Sidney **HURDLE** to Sophia. A. **HURDLE** was proved in Open Court by Lewis. J. **HURDLE** & orderd to be registerd

February Court 1834

A Bill of Sale from Andrew **BAKER** to James **BAKER** was provd in Open Court by the Oath of Daniel **HOBBS** & orderd to be registerd

The Guardian acc^t. of Willis **BUMCH** with Nancy **HURDLE** was returnd to Court & orderd to be recorded.

issd. Orderd that James **SAVAGE** be allow^d. three Dollars & 20/100 for sundry Costs.

The Guardian acct of Elijah **HARRELL** with Elisha **HARRELL** orphan was returned to Court & orderd to be recorded

issd. Orderd that Levan [?] **HOFFLER** be appointed Overseer of the road that Walton **FREEMAN** has been leading from the fork of the road at Thomas **WALTON**s. plan [sic] & leads to the **MINGO** path near J. W. **RIDDICK**s

A Deed of Sale from Hardy **WILLIAMS** to Moses D **HAIRE** was proved in Open Court by the Oath Nathl **DAUGHTY** & orded to be registerd.

[90] Tuesday. 18th. Feb^{ry} 1834

An Inventory of the Estate of Will **HINTON** dec^d. was returnd to Court by the admstrators [sic] & orderd to be recorded.

A Deed of Sale from Alexander **FREEMAN**. to James. T. **FREEMAN** was proved in Open Court by the Oath of Jno. **ROBERTS** & orderd to be registerd.

The Guardian acc^t. of John. C. **GORDON** with Thos **SMALL** orphan was returned to Court & orderd to be recorded.

Humphry **PARKER**s Guardian acc^t. with Christian E **SMALL** was returned to Court & orderd to be recordeed [sic]

A Deed of Sale from Jacob P **JONES** to Humphrey **PARKER** was proved in Open Court by the Oath of Joshua **JONES** & orderd to be registerd

John D **PIPKIN**s Guardian acct with Jno B **GATLING** & Rich^d. B **GATLING** orphs [sic] was returned to Court & orderd to be recorded.

Th Daniel **HURDLE**s Guardian acc^t. with Josiah **BRIGGS** orphan was returned to Court & orderd to be recorded.

issd. Orderd that Guy **HOBBS** be appointed Overseer of the road in room of Ephram **BUNCH** resigned.

issd. Orderd that Abraham **SPIVEY** be appointed overseer of the road leading from Warrick Swamp. to the Snake branch in the room of Thos. **HURDLE**

A Deed of Sale from Kedar **ELLIS** to Jesse **MATHIAS** was proved in Open Court by the Oath of Demsey **VANN** & orderd to be recorded.

An acc^t. Sales & inventory of the Estate of James **JONES** dec^d. was returnd to Court by W^m W **COWPER** adm^r & orderd to be recorded.

Lem^{el}. G **DARDEN**s Guardian acc^t with Mary G **CROSS** was returnd to Court & orderd to be recorded

An Inventory of the Estate of James **GORDON** was returnd to Court & orderd to be recorded. by Jno C **GORDON** adm^r.

February Court 1834

Orderd that Jn° C **GORDON** be allow^d. two Dollars for Examining Clks office

The last will & Testament. of Garret. **HOFFLER** dec^d.. was proved in open Court by the Oath of Jno B **BAKER** a Subscribing witness & at the Same time Rubin **LASSITER** the Exor therin named appeard & qualified thereto

issd. Orderd that Jno. C. **GORDON** & Benj. B. **BALLARD** Esqr take the private Examination of Sophia **DUKE** wife of James **DUKE** to a deed give [sic] Jno **SMALL**

issd. Orderd that Willis F. **RIDDICK** be allow^d. two Dollars as a Comitte [sic] in Examing Clks office

Arthur **WILLIAMS** Guardian acc^t. with Mary **WILLIAMS** orphan was returnd to Court & orded to be recorded.

A Deed of Sale from Wm. K **MOORE** to Jonathan **WILLIAMS** was provd in Open Court by the Oath of Levi **ROGERS** & orderd to be registerd.

[91] Tuesday. 18th. Feb^ry. 1834

Lavinia **FIELDS** widow of Mills. R. **FIELDS** Came into Open Court & enterd her dcent [sic] to the will of Mills R **FIELDS** dec^d.
Whereupon it is Considered by the Court that the Shff Summons a Jury to asertain whuther ~~She~~ the Said Lavinia **FIELDS** is as well provided for by the will of Said Mills. R. **FIELDS** as to the reality as She would be by Law. also to enquire whuther the Said Lavinia is as well provided for by the Said Will. as to personal as She would be by Law. & if the Said Jury Shall be of Opinion that she is not as well provided for by the Said will as he [sic] would be by Law. they Shall further more proceed to lay off her dower in the Lands of the Said **FIELDS**. & Also to allott & asses her Share of the personality. of Said Mills. R. **FIELDS** Estate. & make a report thereof to this Court.
Orderd that. Notice issue to the heirs of Mills. R. **FIELDS** & to his Exor. to attend & Object if they think proper.

An Inventory of the Estate of Jethro **SUMNER** was returned to Court by the Exor & orderd to be recorded.

The last will & Testament of Abraham **PIERCE** was Exhibited into Open Court by Jos **RIDDICK** the Excutor [sic] therin name^d. & proved by the Oath of Andrew **BRIGGS** a witness thereto & at Same time the said Exor qualified as the Law directs.

An Inventory of the Estate of Nathan **CULLINS** dec^d.. was returned to Court by Whit **STALLINS** Exor & orderd to be recorded.

An acct. Sales of the Estate of Nathan **CULLINS** was returned to Court by the Exor & orderd to be recorded.

A deed of Sale from Abraham **SPIVEY** to Thomas **TWINE** was proved in Open Court by the Oath of I. S. **HARRELL** & orderd to be recorded

A Deed of Sale from Jn°. O. **HUNTER**. to. Ed. R. **HUNTER** was ackg [sic] in Open Court & orderd to be registered.

James **PRUDEN**s Guardian acc^t. with Harriet. B **GATLING** orphan was returnd to Court & orderd to be recorded.

Eliz^a. **GRANBERY** Guardian acc^t. with George & James **GRANBERY** was returnd to Court & orderd to be recorded.

Thos **HOGARD**s Guardian acc^t. with Lavinia **SMITH** Orphan was returned to Court & orderd to be re-

February Court 1834

corded.

Lassiter **RIDDICK**s Guardian acc^t. with Mary. J. B. **GATLING** orphan was returnd to Court & orded to be recorded.

Thos **SAUNDERS** Gu^d. acct with Asa **ODAM** was returnd and orderd to be recorded.

[92] Tuesday. 18th. Feb^{ry}. 1834

issd. Orderd that Thomas **TWINE** be app^d. overseer of the road leading from **HUNTER**s Mill. to the long Cosway [sic] in room Henry **COSTEN** resignd

Exum **JENKINS** Gu^d. acc^t. with Sophia Ann **ODAM**. orphan was returnd to Court. & orderd to be recorded.

The Audited acc^t. of Nathan **RIDDICK** adm^r of Jesse **WALTON** & division of the Same was returned to Court & orderd to be recorded.

An Inventory. of the Estate of Jesse **WALTON** was returned to Court & orderd to be recorded. & acc^t. Sales of the Same.

A Deed in trust from Henry **SPIVEEY**. to Jet. H. **RIDDICK** was proved in Open Court by the Oath of Jos **RIDDICK** & orderd to be regis^{td}.

issd. Orderd that the County trustee pay Nathl. **EURE** one Dollar & 55/100 for Error in listing lands twicce in one yeare

Joseph **FREEMAN**s Gu^d. acc^t. with David **FREEMAN** a lunatic was returnd to Court & orderd. to be recorded.

An act. [sic] Sale & Inventory of Ab **PIERCE** dec^d. was returnd in Open Court. & orderd to be recorded.

A Deed of Sale from Thomas **SAUNDERS** & wife to Exum **JINKINS** was proved in Open Court by the Oath of Ed **HOWELL** & Jno A. **MARCH** whereupon Comission iss^d.

Abraham W. **PARKER**^{s}. Guardian acc^t with Will **JOHNSON** was returned to Court & orderd to be recorded

I. R. **HUNTER**^{s}. Guardian acc^t. with Mary & Julian **BRIGGS** orphans was returnd to Court & orderd to be recorded

An ac^t. Sales of Negros Sold belonging to the Estate of Jno **BRINKLY** de^d. [sic] by the adm^r. was returnd. to Court & orderd to be recorded.

Jno. C **GORDON** Guardian accts with Sarah M. & Timothy **LASITER** orphans was returnd to Court & orderd to be recorded

A Deed of Gift from Ann **BOND** to Eliz^a. **BOND** was proved in Open Court by the Oath of Easton **BLACHARD** & orderd to be registerd

Jesse **BROWN** Guardian acct. with Susan **HILL** was returnd to Court & orderd to be recorded

A Deed of Sale from Benj **BRINKLEY** & wife to Jesse **MATHIAS** was proved in open Court by the Oath of Demcy **VANN** & orded to be registrd

A Deed of Sale from James **SUMN** [sic] to Harrison **HARE** was ~~pre~~ ack^d. in Open Court & orderd to be registerd.

February Court 1834

issd. Orderd that Arthur **BURK** receiv a Certificate of his freedom

A Deed of Sale from Edwin **SMITH** to James **SUMN** was ack^d. in Open Court & orderd to be registerd.

[93] Tuesday. 18th. Feb^{ry}. 1834

Whit **STALLINS**s Guardian acct. with Willis Daniel and Asa **WALTON**s orphans was returnd to Court & orderd to be recorded.

A Bill of Sale from Humphry **PARKER** to Miles **PARKER** was ~~proved~~ /ack^d./ in Open Court ~~by the Oath~~ of & orderd to be ~~recorded~~. registerd

A Bill of Sale from Abraham **PARKER** to Miles [?] **PARKER** was proved in Open Court by the Oath of Hump. **PARKER** & orderd to be registerd

Orderd that Jno ~~W~~ F **PARKER** renew his Constable Bond with Kindred **PARKER** & W^m. W. **COWPER** Security

An acct of the hire Negros & rent lands belonging to the Estate of Jno **BEEMAN** dec^d. was returnd to Court & orderd to be recorded.

Mary **HUNTER**s Guardian acct. with Benj **HUNTER** orphan was returnd to Court & orderd to be recorded.

John W. **ODAM** Guardian acct with Prissilla **ODAM** Orphan was returnd to Court & orderd to be recorded.

A Deed of Sale from Jesse **MATHIAS** ~~& wife~~ to Benjamin **BRINKLY** was proved in Open Court by Dem$\underline{c}$ey **VANN** & orderd to be reg^d.

A Deed of Sale from James & Mary **EURE** to Martha **TAYLOR** was proved in Open Court by the Oath of Peter **PILAND** & orderd to be registerd

A Deed of Sale from John **SPARKMAN** to Riddick **GATLING** was ack^d. in Open Court & orderd to be registered

Mills **PILAND**^{s} Guardian accts with Susan. John. & Milly **PILAND** was returned to Court & orderd to be recorded.

Nathan **RIDDICK** Gu^d. acct. with Drew **TROTMAN** was returnd to Court & orderd to be recorded.

Nathan **RIDDICK** with [sic] acc^t. William **BROWN** orphan was returnd to Court & orderd to be recorded.

Nathan **RIDDICK** acc^t with Sarah **BROWN** orphan was returnd to Court & orderd to be recorded

Nathan **RIDDICK** Gu^d. acc^t. with Mary **WALTON** Orphan was returnd to Court & orderd to be recorded.

Nathan **RIDDICK** Gu^d. acc^t. with Henry **WALTON** orphan was returnd to Court & orderd to be recorded.

William **CLEAVES** Guardian acc^t with Lewis. W. **PRUDEN** orphan was returnd & orderd to be recorded.

The Last will & Testament of Mills R **FIELDS** was produced in Open Court & the Execution thereof duly proved by the Oath of Jonathan **WILLIAMS** one of the Subscribing witnesses thereto Isaac **WIL-**

February Court 1834

LIAMS one of the Exors therin named not appearing to qualify to the s^d. Will. & Levi **ROGERS** the other Exor. being in Court. & signifying his willingness to Qualify

[94] Tuesday. 18th Feb^{ry}. 1834

to the Said Will as the Exor there of Whereupon it is orderd that the Said Levi **ROGERS** be admitted to the usual Oaths of an Exor. and that letters Testamentry issue to him. all of which was accordingly in due form of law it is ordered that Said will be recorded

issd. Orderd that Lassiter **RIDDICK** be apptd overseer of the road in room of Adam **RABEY** resigned. Orderd that Isaac **PIPKIN** Jos **GORDON** & Henry **GILLIAM** be appointed to make an Estimate & draw a drf^t. [sic] for a Court house & report.

James **COSTON** in acct with James K. **COSTON** orphan ~~orderd~~ was returned to court & ordered to be recorded.

issd. Ordered that Mary **CUTLER** [?] be allowed fifty dollars pr year for Keeping Celia **LEWIS** to be paid by her guardian

Eli **WORRELL** Guardian acct with. William J. **HUDGINS** orphan was returd [sic] to Court & orderd to be recorded

An Inventory of the Estate of Wm. **MUPHREY** [sic] was returnd to Court by the Executor & orderd to be recorded

John H **HASLETT**^{s} Guardian acct. with Lewis & Sophia **HURDLE** was returnd to Court. & orderd to be recorded.

A Deed of Sale from Exum **LEWIS** to Will. W. **COWPER** was proved in Open Court by the Oath of Peter **PILAND** & orderd to be registerd

A Deed of Sale from Miles **PARKER** to Henry **CARTER** was ack^d. in Open Court & orderd to be registerd

issd. Orderd that Jesse **BROWN** be allow^d Thirteen Dollars & 15/100 for sundry prison fees of **CARTER** & **BENTON** & the County trustee pay the Same

John **WIGGINS**s Guardian acct with Prissilla ~~B~~ **WIGGINS** was returnd to court & orderd to be recorded.

  Court adjournd untill Wednesday
    Wednesday Court met according to adjoumnt [sic]
  Present. Richard **ODAM** John **WILLEY** Joseph **RIDDICK** & W. W. **COWPER**

issd. Orderd that Ezekiel **LASSITER** be appt^d. Overseer on the road leading from Ab. W. **PARKER**s to Gatesville.

issd. Ord^{ed} that. Joseph **RIDDICK** Esqr William **HARRELL** W^m. **HARRELL** Jur & Jethro H **RIDDICK** lay off & Set a part to Charlott **GREEN** wife of Henry **GREEN** dec^d. One years provision & make report.

issd. Orderd that W. W. **WIGGINS** & David O **DUKE** have a retail Licens [sic] to retail Spirits at their Shop.

Orderd that Jos **GORDON** adm^r upon the Estate of Jos **SMALL** that he enter into Bond in $1000. with Kinchen **NORFLEET** & Jno R **NORFLEET** Securties

February Court 1834

[95] Wednesday. 19th Feb^ry 1834

Orderd that Jos **GORDON** admr upon Henry **GREEN**s Estate & enter into Bonds for $1020. with Kinchen & Jn° R **NORFLEET** Security.

Orderd that David **PARKER** be permitted to renew his Constable Bond with Henry **GILLIAM** & James **BAKER** securities.

Orderd that William **POWELL** be permitted to renew his Constable Bond with John **WIGGINS** & Benj. **FRANKLIN** Securities.

issd. Orderd that the County trustee pay Ja^s. S. **JONES** Esqr the Sum of Eight Dollars for Services.

A Division of the Negros of Fre^d. **HINTON** dec^d. was returnd. to Court & orderd to be filed

John **WALTON**s Gu^d. acct. with Leah **HINTON** & Moses **TROTMAN** orphans was returnd to Court & orderd to be recorded

Orderd that Elisha **REED** a Coloured boy be bound to Willis. J. **RIDDICK** that he enter into Bond also as the Law directs

issd. Orderd that Henry **GILLIAM** Thomas **SAUNDERS** Jesse **BROWN** & W^m. G. **DAUGHTRY** or any three audite & State the accts of W^m. **BOND** former Gu^d. to Nancy **BOND** ~~with her~~ & make report.

George **COSTON** Gu^d. acc^t. with Isaac R **HUNTER** orphan was returnd to this Court & orderd to be recorded. & Mary A **RIDDICK**s also.

issd. Orderd that the County Trustee pay Henry **GILLIAM** fourteen Dollars for Sundry Services &c
Also as Clk Sup. Court orderd that the County trustee pay him the Sum Twenty three Dollars & 59/100 for Sundy [sic] Costs

W^m. W. **COWPER** Guardian acc^t with Celia **LEWIS** orphan was returnd to Court & orderd to be recorded.

An Inventory & acc^t. Sales of the Estate of Theo^s. **HARRELL** decd was return^d. to Court by the adm^r. & orderd to be recorded.

Nathaniel **EURE**s. Gu^d. acct. with Henry **EURE** Mary. A. **EURE** Mills **EURE** Cordey **WILLIAMS** Mary **WILLIAMS**. Susan A. **SPEIGHT** Sophia **SPEIGHT** & William **BABB**. orphans was retu^d. to Court & orderd to be recoded [sic]

W^m. W. **COWPER** Guardian acc^t with Uriah **BABB** orphan was returned to Court & orderd to be recorded.

Orderd that John **TAYLOR** a free Mulatto boy Son Eliz^a. **TAYLOR** be bound as an apprentice to John **KING**.

Ord^ed that John **LEWIS** be appointed Constable in Captain **SMITH**s district that he enter into Bonds with Jn° **WILLEY** Exum **LEWIS** S^ty..

issd. Orderd that Lassiter **RIDDICK** Coroner be allow^d. the Sum of Forty Dollars for the following inquests. Mary **DILDY** Absolom **LASSITER** Theo^s. **HARRELL** & Negro **SAM** belonging to David **RIDDICK**.

[96] Wednesday. 19th Feb^ry. 1834

issd. Orderd that Mills **EURE** be appointed Overseer of the road leading from **BARNES**^s. Creek to the

February Court 1834

fork of the road at Jno **BEEMAN** dec^d in the room of Jason **ROUNTREE** resigned.

Riddick **GATLING** Guardian to Eliza. & Mary **SUMNER** orphans returnd his accts. to Court. orderd the Same be recorded.

Willis J. **RIDDICK** Guardian to the orphans of James **HINTON** dec^d. returned his accts to Court orderd the Same be recorded.

Nathan **NIXON** Guardian to Joseph G. **WALTON** orphan returnd his acct to Court & orderd to be recorded.

Nathan **NIXON** Guardian to Mary Ann **WALTON** orphan returd his acct to Court & orderd to be recorded.

issd. Orderd that Thomas **RIDDICK** be appointed overseer of the road in room of George **COSTON** resigned.

Hardy H. C. **JONES** et als } Reffer^d. report made & Confirm^d.
vs }
William **LEE** admr Henry **JONES** } This Cause Coming on to be heard upon the report of the reffere [sic] & the pleadings it is orderd adjudged & decreed that all the Costs of this Suite be paid Out of the bals. reported by the reffere including the defendants att^{oy}. fee of $10—It is further adjudged that the defendant owes the plantiffs the Sum of $236.17½. which it is orderd adjudged & decreed that the plantiff^s recover of the defendant. deducting therefrom the Cost of the Suite & attoy. fee as aforsaid. It is further orderd and decreed that the defendant pay over to the plantiffs Such Bonds as are payable to him as the admistrator [sic] of Henry **JONES** dec^d. in discharge of the recovery effected in this Suite. as shall be pronounced by the refferee to be Good & well Served. It is further ordered & decreed that the refferee be allowd $20. to be taxed in the Bill of Cost & paid out of Said Judg^t.

Mills **ROBERTS** }
vs }
John **HINTON** } Genl. issue pay^t. & Set off Rep. &. Issue
The following Jurors Moses **SPIVEY**. Demsey **PARKER** David **UMPHLET**. Willis J. **RIDDICK**. James **FIGG** Prior **SAVAGE** John **SAUNDERS**. James **BOOTH**. Henry G. **WILLIAMS**. William **SEARS**. Exum **LEWIS** & John **LEWIS** being Sworn & immpanelld. [sic] find all the issues infavour of the defendant. Whereupon the Plantiff pray^d. for & Obtained an appeal to the Sup Court & he enterd into Bond & Security as the Law requires.

[97] Luke **GREEN** }
vs }
John **HOFFLER** et als } The following Jurors. Wills **COWPER** James **BAKER** Miles **GATLING** Thos. **COSTON**. Kindred **PARKER** David **HOBBS**. John **HINTON**. Burwell **BROTHERS**. Marmaduke **NORFLEET** Joseph **HURDLE** James **BRINKLY** & Henry **HAYS** being Sworn & impanel^d. find all the issues infavour of the plantiff & asses his damage $7. & Costs

Lawrence S. **DAUGHTRY** }
vs } Genl. issue pay^t & Sett off
James. R. **RIDDICK** } The Same Jurors as in the above Case Except Henry **HAYS**. in his room John **HOFFLER**. being Sworn & impannell^d. find all the issues infavour of the plantiff & asses his damage to $100. & defendant app^l. to Sup Court

Burwell **BROTHERS** }
vs }
Fre^d. **JONES** } The following Jurors. Wills **COWPER** Moses **SPIVEY** James **BAKER** Ju^r. Miles **GATLING**. Thos. **ASTON** [sic]. Kindred **PARKER** David **HOBBS**. John **HINTON** John **HOF-**

February Court 1834

FLER Marmaduke NORFLEET. James BRINKLY & Henry HAYS (Non Suite)
Test   Wm W. STEDMAN Clk
By
H GILLIAM D. C

[Remainder of page is blank.]

[98] State of No. Carolina}
        Gates County.} At a Court of pleas & q^r. Sessions began & held for the County of Gates at the Court House in Gatesville 3rd Monday of May 19th day 1834.
    Present. Jn°. C. GORDON. Hardy D. PARKER & Barnes GOODMAN Esquires

A Division of the Lands of James JONES de^d. was return^d & orderd to be registed

A Deed of Sale from Cyphan [sic] CROSS. to John VANN was ~~proved~~ /ack^d./ in Open Court by ~~the Oath~~ S^d CROSS & orderd to be registered.

A deed of Sale from Nathan WARD to William HOBBS was proved in Open Court by the Oath of Guy HOBBS & ord$\underline{ed}$ to be registered

A deed of Sale from Jesse HARRELL to James HARRELL was proved in Open Court by the Oath of Ab. W. PARKER & orderd to be regis$\underline{ter}$d.

A Bill of Sale from Mary TAYLOR to Nathl. TAYLOR was proved in Open Court by the Oath of Wes$\underline{tl}$y SPIVEY & orderd to be registerd

A Deed of Sale from Jesse SAVAGE to James SAVAGE was proved in Open Court by the Oath of Jesse M SAVAGE & orderd to be registerd

An acct Sales of the Estate of Garrot HOFFLER was Exhibited into Open Court by the Exor & orderd to be recorded

An Inventory of the Estate of Mills. R. FIELDS was Exhibited into Open Court by the Exor & orderd to be recorded.

A Deed of Sale from W^m E PUGH C. & M. to Ezekiel TROTMON was ack^d. in open Court & orderd to be registerd

" Orderd that Lassiter RIDDICK DShff [sic] be allowed in the Collection of his part the public Taxes 52 poll of insolvent Taxables.

issd. Orderd that the Shff be allow^d. the Sum of $21.79. in his Settlement with the County Trustee for Sundry Taxes listed in two districts

A Deed of Sale from Demsey PARKER to Daniel CUFF was ack^d.g [sic] in Open Court & orderd to be registerd.

An acct. Sales of the Estate of Mills R FIELDS was Exhibited into Open Court by the Exor & orderd to be recorded.

issd. Orderd that the County Trustee pay Henry GILLIAM Clk Sup. Court. the Sum of Seventy one Dollars & 42/100 for Sundry bill Costs

issd. Orderd that the County Trustee pay Wm STEDMAN Clk County Court Fifty four Dollars for Sundry bills Costs filed.

issd. Orderd that the County Trustee pay W^m. W. STEDMAN Clk of this Court. Seventy Dollars for Extra Services & Stationary.

" Orderd that Daniel WILLIAMS Exor. of George KITTRELL Sell a Negro for the purpose of paying

May Court 1834

debts on a Credit of Six Months.

Orderd that Thos. B. **HUNTER** be appointed Gud. to his Children Sarah Ann **HUNTER** & Thos. J. **HUNTER** that he enter into bond & Security for $2000

[99] Monday. 19th. May.

" Orderd that John. O. **HUNTER** James **BALLARD** James **MORGAN** & [sic] Audite & Settle the acct^s of Ab **RIDDICK** adm^r of James **RIDDICK** dec^d. & report to Next Term

" Orderd that the Same persons Settle the acct^s of Ab. **RIDDICK** adm^r of Barshaba **FRANKLIN** & make report.

" Orderd that Isaac R. **HUNTER** be appointed adm^r on the Estate of Ailsey **BRIGGS** that he give Bond & Security in the Sum of $150.

" Orderd that Jno C **GORDON** Edwd. **BRIGGS** & Wills **COWPER** audite & Settle the acct of Isaac R **HUNTER** adm^r of Ailsey **BRIGGS** de^d & report.

Orderd that Jethro **WILLEY** renew his Constable Bond.

" Orderd that Etheldred **CROSS**s hands work on the road from Rich^d. **ODAM**s to Winton Ferrey Causeway also John **UMPHLET**. Rich^d. **CURL** & Bray **PARKER**s. under the present Overseer.

issd. Orderd that the County Surveyor. Survey. Lay. off & Set a part to John **WILLIAMS** ~~Twenty five~~ /fifteen/ acres Lands of Monica **CROSS** which was Sold for Taxes

issd. Orderd that the County Surveyor Lay off & Set a part to Edwin **CROSS** twenty five acres land belonging to Sarah **WALTON** & Sold for the Taxes.

issd. Orderd that Ab W **PARKER** have a retail licence to retail$\underline{s}$ Spirits at his Store.

" Orderd that W^m. **POWELL** be appointed Overseer of the road in the room of John **WIGGINS** resigned

" Orderd that Seth W. **ROUNTREE** be appointed Gud. to Balinda & Matilda **BAGLEY** orphans of Trotmon **BAGLEY** that he enter into Bond & Secuity in the Sum of $200. Each

" Orderd that the County Surveyor lay off & Set a part to John **ODAM** Thirty acres land belonging to Martha **HORTON** [?] & Sold for Taxes.

" Orderd that the Shff Summons a Jury to Lay off to the Widow of Benj **BRIGGS**. a dower in the Lands of Said **BRIGGS**.

" Orderd that Jethro H **RIDDICK** renew his Constable Bond.

" Orderd that John **WALTON**. Benbury **WALTON**. Whit **STALLINS** & Nathan **NIXON** Divide the Estate of Thos **ROUNTREE** among$\underline{s}$ his heirs

" Orderd that Lem^l **CLEAVES** renew his Constable Bond.

" Orderd the Eli **WORRELL** be appointed Overseer of the road in the room of Levi **BEEMAN** resignd.

" Orderd that John **WALTON** Benbury **WALTON** Whit **STALLINS** & Nathan **NIXON** audite the acct^s. of Seth W **ROUNTREE** ~~admr~~ Exor of Thos **ROUNTREE** dec^d.

[100] Monday 19th May 1834

May Court 1834

A Deed of Sale from Demcy **FLOOD** & Mary **FLOOD** to Abraham **PRUDEN** was proved in Open Court by Thos **HOGGARD** & orderd to be registerd

" Orderd that Samuel **HARRELL** /Senr./ be appointed Overseer of the road leading from **WYNNS** Ferrey to the fork [sic] road neare Richd. **ODAM** in room [sic] E. **CROSS**

A Deed of Sale from Jesse **HOBBS** to William **HOBBS** was proved in Open Court by the Oath of James **BOYCE** [?] & orderd to be registerd.

" Orderd that the County Surveyor Lay off to Wm **HUDGINS** Forty nine acres Land. belonging to Saml. **MORGAN** & Sold for Taxes.

" Orderd that Miles **HOWELL** renew his Constable Bond.

A Deed of Sale from John **CUFF** to Nancy **EADERS** was ack^d.g in Open Court & orderd to be registerd.

" Orderd that Riddick **MATHEWS** have a licence to retail Spirits in the house at Gatesville formerly Occupied by John **MATHEWS**.

" Orderd that the County Surveyor lay off to Law. S. **DAUGHTRY** forty nine acres Land Listed by Demsy **EURE** & Sold for the Taxes of 1831.

" Orderd that the County Surveyor lay off to Law. S. **DAUGHTRY** thirty four acres Land listed by Saml **MORGAN** & Sold for the Tax of 1831.

" Orderd that the County Surveyor lay off to Law. S. **DAUGHTRY** nine & one half acres listed by Mason **BUTLER** & Sold for the Taxes of 1831.

" Orderd that John **LOVET** have a licens to retaile Spirits in his Store

A deed of Sale from John **MATHEWS** to Robt. **PARKER** was proved in Open Court by the Oath of H **GILLIAM** & orderd to be registerd

A Deed of Sale from Edward **HOBBS** Henry **STALLINS** & Peggy **STALLINS** was proved in Orpen [sic] Court by John **MITCHEL** & orderd to be registerd

" Orderd that Daniel **WILLIAMS** be appointed Gud. to Leml. K **FIELDS** orphan of Mills R **FIELDS** that he enter into Bond & Secuty for $4,000

Orderd that the following persons. T. W. **CARR**. Hardy. D. **PARKER**. Riddick **GATLING** Demcy **SPARKMAN** Tim^o. **WALTON**. Jos **RIDDICK** & Henry **GILLIAM** be appointed Wardens of the poore for the present yeare

" Orderd that the following persons be appointd inspectors of the Elections, Folly district. John C **GORDON**. Demcy **KNIGHT**. James **MORGAN** Wills **COWPER** & Jesse **WIGGINS**.
HUNTERs Mill, Joseph **GORDON**. Henry **COSTON**. George **COSTON**. J. H **RIDDICK** & Wm **HARRELL** Senr.
HARRELL & **COSTONs**, John **MITCHEL**. James T. **FREEMAN**. Nathan **NIXON**. Henry **BOND** & W^m. **WALTON**
Gatesville, W^m. G. **DAUGHTRY**. Jos **RIDDICK**. Rubin **HINTON**. Jesse **BROWN** &. Pryer **SAVAGE**
Demcy **PARKERs**, Mills **EURE**. Demcy **SPARKMAN** Ab. W. **PARKER** & Thomas **HOGGARD**.
at: W^m. H **GOODMANs**, W^m. **GOODMAN** Esqr. W^m. **LEE**. Demsey **GOODMAN**. John **SAUNDERS** & Jno **LANGSTON**
at: John H **HASLETTs**, Barnes **GOODMAN**. Simon **WALTERS**. Jesse **SAVAGE** Senr. W^m. K **MOORE**. & Geor. [?] W. **SMITH**

[101] Monday. 19th. May

May Court 1834

" Orderd that the following Justices be appointed to take the list Taxes & Taxables for the present yeare. in **HUNTER**s Mill district Henry **COSTON**. in Folley district. Willis F. **RIDDICK** in Bushrod **RIDDICK** district. John **WALTON**. in Honey pot district. The⁵. SAUNDERS /W^m. W. **COWPER**/ in W^m L **BOOTH**s. district. Will L **BOOTH** in Jason **SAUNDERS** district W^m. W. COWPER /John **WILLEY**/ in Captantain [sic] **DAUGHTERY**s district Henry **WILLEY**. Esq^urs.

Orderd that the Shff Collect the following Taxes for the yeare 1833. For the Court house Taxes. fifty Cents to the poll & 20 ^{Cts} on the 100$ Valuation Lands. for County Tax. fifteen Cents in poll & 6 ^{Cts}. on $100 lands. for parish Tax. 35/100 on poll & 8 ^{Cts} on $100 Land State Tax 20 ^{Cts} on poll & 6 ^{Cts} on $100. Valuation Lands

An acct. of the Sales of the Lands of Willis **JINKINS** dec^d. was Exhibited into Open Court by Simon **WALTERS** Gu^d & orded to be recorded

A Deed of Sale from John & Elizabeth **COFFIELD** to James **BOYCE** was proved in Open Court by Amos **HOBBS** & orderd to be registerd

A Deed of Sale from Mourning **WILLIAMS** to Henry. G. **WILLIAMS** was proved in Open Court by Levi **ROGERS** & orderd to be registerd

A Deed of Sale from James & Benjn. **SAUNDERS** to Willis **CROSS** was proved in Open Court by Miles **HOWELL** & orderd to be registerd.

A Deed of Sale from Jason & Gilbert G. **SAUNDERS** to Willis **CROSS** was proved in Open Court by Miles **HOWELL** & orderd to be registerd

A Deed of Sale from Jesse **SAVAGE** to Jesse M **SAVAGE** was ack^d. in Open Cout & orderd to be registerd.

An acct. Sales of the Estate of Mary **HARRELL** dec^d. was Exhibited into Open Court & orderd to be registerd.

A deed of Sale from Margaret **PARKER** To John **MATHEWS** was proved in Open Court by James **SMITH** & ordered to be registerd.

Orderd that Jethro **REED** & Augustus **REED** free boys of Color & Child___ of Mills **REED** be bound as apprentices to Jn°. D. **PIPKIN**

issd. Orderd that the County Trustee pay unto James R **RIDDICK** Shff Fifty Dollars for Extra Services.

A deed Sale of Sale [sic] from Andrew **EASON** & wife to Riddick **TROTMON** was proved in Open Court by Jos **RIDDICK** & orderd to be registred

A deed of Sale from Absalom **BLANCHARD** to Miles M [?] **DAVIS** was proved in Open Court by Wm **BLANCHARD** & orderd to be register [sic]

" Orderd that Levi **ROGERS** be appointed adm^r on the Estate of Enos **SCARBOROUGH** & give bond & Security for $400.

[102] Gatesville Monday 19th May

" Orderd that Nathan **NIXON** be appointed Overseer of the road leading from **POWELL**s Shop to the fork of the road near Rubin **HINTON**s in room of Garret **HOFFLER** dec^d.

Orderd that Lassiter **RIDDICK** Coroner be allow^d. Ten Dollars for holding an inquest on the body of a free boy. Hillery **WEAVER**

May Court 1834

" Orderd that James. T. **FREEMAN** renew his Constable Bond.

" Orderd that the County trustee pay James. R. **RIDDICK** Shff the Sum of Six hundred & Ninty Nine Dollars for building the poore house according to Contract with Commissions.

         & the Court adjorned until Tuesday morning
Tuesday Morning Court Met at. 10.Oclock

The Shff return^d the following persons to Serve as Jurors to this Term. Jesse **HARRELL**. Fre^d **ROOKS**. John **SPARKMAN**. Jacob **POWELL**. Robt. **WILSON**. Wm **PARKER**. Tim^o. **HUNTER**. James **SUMNER** Noah **HINTON** Wm **DAVIDSON**. Jesse **MATHIAS**. Demsy **PARKER** Rich^d. **CURL**. John **HINTON** Jur. Amos **HOBBS**. James **GOODWIN** Miles **PARKER** (of Moses) Jethro **HARRELL**. Levi **EURE** Jur. Isaac **PIERCE** Blake **BAKER**. James **COSTON**. David **HOBBS**. Charles **BRIGGS**. Joseph **HURDLE**. Jeremiah **WHITE**. Robt. **ROGERS**. Shadrick **PILAND** John **MORRIS**. Kinchen **HOWELL**. Arch^d. **ELLIS**. John **WORRELL**. Kedar **RIDDICK**. Briant **HARE**. & Blake **BRADY**.

At Same time the following persons was drawn & Charged to Serve as Grand Jurors. Ja^s. **COSTON** (forman) John **WORRELL** Briant **HARE** Rich^d. **CURL** Jasper **HARRELL**. Fre^d. **ROOKS**. Jeremiah **WHITE**. John **MORRIS**. James **GOODWIN** Shad. **PILAND**. Isaac **PIERCE** Robt. **WILSON**. Miles **PARKER**. James **SUMNER** Blake **BRADY**. Demsey **PARKER**. John **HINTON** & Arch^d. **ELLIS**

John **SPARKMAN**. Chas. **BRIGGS** & Kinchen **HOWELL** absent jurors Issue Sci fa.

Ab. W. **PARKER** }
    vs   }
Jos J **BARNES** & H. **GILLIAM** } The following Jurors Ed. **BRIGGS**. Pryer **SAVAGE**. Seth R. **MORGAN**. Tim^o. **HUNTER**. Noah **HINTON**. Jethro **BLANCHARD**. David **HOBBS**. James **BAKER**. Willis **HARRELL**. James **FIGG**. John **LEWIS** & Jesse **WIGGINS** being Sworn & impanell^d. find all the issues infavour pltff & asses his damage to 6^d. by the Court Judgt. for $232. to be dish^d. with pay^t. 6^d. & Cost. Ab W **PARKER** pltff in this Case being disatisfied with the Judgt. prayed for an appeal to Sup Court which was Granted & he gave Bond with Kin^d. **PARKER** & John **LEWIS** __[blank]__ Secuity.

[103] Tuesday. 20th. May 1834.

John A. **ROBERTS**}
    vs   }
Ab **MORGAN**. } The following Jurors. Tim^o. **HUNTER**. Burwell **BROTHERS**. Ed **BRIGGS**. Seth. W. **ROUNTREE**. David **HOBBS**. Ezekiel **JONES** Robt. **HAYS**. Nathan **NIXON** Ethel^d. **CROSS**. Jesse **HUDGINS** Noah **ROUNTREE**. &. John **HOFFLER** being duly Sworn & impd. find all the issues infavour of Pltff amt debt $1143. with intes from 27th. Jan^{ry}. 1834.

Pryor **SAVAGE** }
    vs   }
Asa **HILL** } The following Jurors. John **LEWIS** Nathan **NIXON** Burwell **BROTHERS**. Robt. **HAYS**. Seth W. **ROUNTREE**. David **HOBBS**. Noah **HINTON**. Tim^o. **HUNTER**. Ed **BRIGGS**. John **HOFFLER**. Noah **ROUNTREE**. Ethel^d. **CROSS**. being Sworn & imp^d. find all the issues infavor pltff & asses his damage to $10. Orded that the pltff pay all the Costs in this Suite

Govr to the use
Lavinia **BRINKLY** }
    vs   }
Riddick **JONES** et als. } The following Jurors Jethro **WILLEY** Jn^s. **NORFLEET**. John **MATHEWS**. Prior **SAVAGE**. James **BOOTH**. Jethro **BLANHD**. [sic] John **HOFFLER**. James **FIGG**. Ezekiel **JONES** Zac **HAYS**. Elisha **HAYS**. & Seth R. **MORGAN**. being Sworn & imp^d. find all the issues infav [sic] pltff & asses pltffs damage to $97.96 for Con^d. [?] broken By the Court Judg^t for $1100. to be dish^d. by pay^t. of $97.96. orded that the Clk be alo^d 2.50 to [?] to be p^d by Each party.

May Court 1834

In the Case upon the trial docket at this Term of Anthony MATHEWS ag^t. Benjn. WILLIAMS it is orderd by the Court that the Clk Surrender to Anthony MATHEWS all the papers in the Suite.

Upon Evidence offerd orderd that the Clk issue to Sally BLANCHARD a free woman of Colour a Certificate of her freedom.

" Orderd that John WALTON. D. PARKER Jethro. H. RIDDICK & Henry GILLIAM audite & Settle the accts of Hanse HOFFLER adm^r of Rubin HINTON dec^d & report.

" Orderd that Jethro. H. RIDDICK be allow^d. Fourteen Dollars & 40/100 for his attendance as Constable. at aug^t. Octr. Nov^r & Feb^{ry}. Terms

" Orderd that Henry COSTON be appointed Gu^d. to Noah BOND Eliz^a. BOND & Nancy BOND orphans of Rich^d. BOND that he enter into Bond with George COSTON & John GATLING Security.

" Orderd that Charles EASON be appointed overseer of the road in the room of John HOFFLER resigned

[104] Tuesday. 20th. May 1834.

Orderd that Letters of adm^r be Granted to Levi BEEMAN upon the Estate of Walton FREEMAN dec^d. that he enter into Bonds for $5000. with Henry GILLIAM & Demsey SPARKMAN Securities.

Orderd that Lassiter RIDDICK be allow^d. the Sum of Ten Dollars & 40/100 for insolvents paid to the Treasurer of No. Carolina.

A Report of the Jury Summon [sic] to Lay off to Lavina FIELDS her dower was ret^d.

The Guardian accts of John MATHEWS to Margaret & Eliz^a. BENTON was retur^d. to Court & orderd to be recorded.

The Guardian accts of Demsey PARKER with Louisa & Henry JONES was retr^d. to Court & orderd to be recorded.

A Deed of Sale from John ROBERTS to Benbury WALTON /& Co/ was proved in Open Court by the Oath of Law. S. DAUGHTRY & orderd to be registerd

The Last Will & Testamnt. [sic] of James PHELPS dec^d. was Exhibited into Open Court by George COSTON the Exor thein name^d & proved by the Oath of Jonathan LASSITER & at Same time the Exor thein named qualified agreeable to Law.

A Deed of Sale from John MATHEWS to Henry GILLIAM. Joseph RIDDICK & John D. PIPKIN Commissioners was proved in Open Court by the Oath of Jethro H. RIDDICK & orderd to be registerd.

A Deed of Sale from John SPARKMAN to Demsey PARKER was proved in Open Court by the Oath of W^m.. L. BOOTH & orderd to be registerd.

A Bill of Sale from Job R HALL was p to John ROBERTS was proved in Open Court by the Oath of John. B. BAKER & orderd to be registerd

A Bill of Sale from Walton FREEMAN to Jethro H RIDDICK was proved in Open Court by the Oath of Burwell BROTHERS & orderd to be registerd.

A Deed of Sale from Jos GORDON to Andrew HARRELL was proved in Open Court by the Oath of Willis W HARRELL & orderd to be registered.

A Deed in trust from Andrew R HARRELL to Jos GORDON was proved in Open Court by the Oath of

May Court 1834

Willis. R. **HARREL** [sic] & orderd to be registerd

A Bill of Sale from Simmonds **ROUNTREE** to Ab. W. **PARKER** was proved in Open Court by the Oath of Thomas **SAUNDERS** & orderd to be registerd.

A Deed of Sale from Zach **HAYS** & wife ~~was~~ to Robert **HAYS** was ~~proved~~ /ack^d./ in Open Court by the ~~Oath of~~ s^d parties & orderd to be registerd.

A Deed of Sale from Wm. **OVER__**[2] ata [sic] to Jos **RIDDICK** was proved in Open Court by the Oath of Jethro H **RIDDICK** & ord_ed_ to be registerd

Orderd that Ed **BRIGGS** be appointed Gu^d. to Ann E. **MANSARD** & Janet M. **MANSARD**. that he enter into Bonds with Richard H **PARKER** & John **WALTON** Security in the Sum of $10,000.

" Orderd that William **SEARS** be allowd. Fourteen Dollars & 25/100 for repairing the Bridge a Cross Mrs **HARVEY**s Mill Race.

[105] Wednesday 21st. May. Court met.

Orderd that James **BOOTH** be appointed Gu^d. to Robert **HARE**. William **HARE**. & Mary **HARE** orphans of John **HARE** that he give bonds with Henery **GILLIAM** & John **WALTON** Securities for $2.000.

" Orderd that James C. **RIDDICK** renew his Constable Bonds with James R **RIDDICK** & Lassiter **RIDDICK** Securities.

Orderd that Jethro. H. **RIDDICK** be allow^d. 365 insolvents in the districts that he Collects from.

" Orderd that Isaac R **HUNTER**. Noah **HARRELL**. Wills **COWPER** and John C **GORDON** audite & State the accts. of Levi **BEEMAN** Exor A. **BEEMAN** decd

An acct of Nathan **RIDDICK** as County Trustee was returnd to Court & orderd to be rec^d. & filed.

John **WALTON** Public Register renewed his Bond as the Law requires

In the Matter of Walton **FREEMAN**s will. it was orderd that. Demsey **SPARKMAN** be appointed Gu^d. to defend the rights of Tim^o. **FREEMAN**. Lovonya [?] **FREEMAN**. Richard B. **FREEMAN** & Walton **FREEMAN** infant heirs of Walton. **FREEMAN** dec^d. & the said Demsey **SPARKMAN** Consented [?] into Open Court & accpts notice to prove the will of S^d. Walton **FREEMAN** & Levi **BEEMAN** accepts Service of notice for Millicent **FREEMAN**. widow of S^d. Walton **FREEMAN**. Whereupon a Jury to wit, John **MATHEWS** Pryer **SAVAGE**. John **BROWN**. Seth R **MORGAN**. James **BOOTH**. James **BROWN** Jos. C. **RIDDICK** John **PARKER** Elijah **HARRELL**. Bray **EURE**. James T **FREEMAN** & Isaac **WILLIAMS** being Sworn & imp^d. Say that the Non Cupided [sic] will of Walton **FREEMAN** is not his will.

" Caroline **HAYS** by her next friend }
      vs   }
H **GILLIAM** admr et. als.   } This Cause Coming on to be heard upon the petition it is orderd that. by the Court. that a refference of the Case be made as to ~~W~~ Henery **GILLIAM** to make a report to the next Court the Value of the personal Estate. of Benj **HAYS** dec^d. deducting the amt of debts due from Said Estate. & also the respective Value of the Legacies & the Value of the residuence [?] of the Estate. It is further orderd that Thomas **SAUNDERS**. John **WALTON**. Prior **SAVAGE** W^m G **DAUGHTRY** & James **BOOTH**. be appointed Commissioners who or any three of them with the County Surveyor. Shall

---

[2] This name is "OVERMAN," as written in Gates County Deed Book 15:88. C.041.40007, Gates County Real Estate Conveyances 1829-1836, Vol: 14,15

May Court 1834

Lay off to the petitioner so much of the Lands of Benjn **HAYS** dec^d. as would have decended to her had no will been made & Shall also return a Corret [sic] Valuation of the Said Lands divided to Each ~~heir~~ devisee & the Value of the lands taken from devisees by the partition of the partition [sic]

[106] At a Court held for the County of Gates at the Court house in Gatesville on the 15th day August 1834. It is ord^{ed} to be Certified. that it Appears to the Court. by Satisfactory Evidence that James **WALLACE** who was a Lieutenant in the North Carolina line in the revolutionary ~~Service~~ War died intestate & that Miles **WALLACE** Sarah **WALLACE** Penina **WALLACE**. Warren **HARRELL**. Thomas **JONES**. & Wright **HOWELL** in right of his Wife Polly are his Onley heires. at Law.
    Test Will W. **STEDMAN** Clk By H. **GILLIAM** DC

At a County Court of pleas & qr Sessions began & held for the County of Gates at the Court House in Gatesville on the 3rd Monday in August 18th day 1834
Present Jos. **RIDDICK**. Jno. C. **GORDON** Richd **ODOM** Henry **WILLEY** & William **LEE** Esqui^{rs}

It appearing to the Court that James. R. **RIDDICK** has been duly elected Shff of Gates County. he Came into Court & offered John **GATLING**. Jos **RIDDICK**. Lassiter **RIDDICK** & Henry **BOND**. as his Securities who was accpted by the Court.

A Deed of Sale from Robert **HAYS** & wife Nancy was ack^d. in Open Court. & orderd to be registerd

The Last will & Testament of David **HOBBS** was proved in Open Court by the Oath of Henry **SPIVEY** one of the Subscribing Witnesses & at Same time appeard Daniel **HOBBS** the Exor therein Nam^d. & qualified agreeable to Law.

A Deed of Sale from Mary **EURE** & Others to John **MORRIS** was provd in Open Court by the Oath Ja^s T **FREEMAN** & orded to be registed

" Orderd that James **CARTERE** be appointed Overseer of the road leading from the late residence of John **BEEMAN** to the Cow pen Swamp.

Orderd that Jethro **HARRELL** be appointed Gu^d. to John. Richard & Lavinia **BRISCO** orphans of Ebon **BRISCO** dec^d. & that he enter into Bonds $400 with Ab W **PARKER** & Elisha **HARRELL** Securities

A Deed of Sale from James R **RIDDICK** Shff to John **ODAM** was ak^d. [sic] in Open Court & orderd to be registerd.

A Deed of Sale from James R **RIDDICK** Shff to Jonathan **WILLIAMS** was ack^d. in Open Court & orderd to be registerd.

[107] 18th Augt. 1834

A Deed of Sale from Robt. **SMITH** & Benj **SAUNDERS** to Hiram **LUMIS** [sic] was ack^d. in Open Court & orderd to be registerd.

A Deed of Sale from Kedar **ELLIS** to Riddick **JONES** was proved in Open court by the Oath of Miles **BRIGGS** & orderd to be registerd

A Deed of Trust from William **ARNOLD** to James **M__GAN** was proved in Open Court by John **WIGGINS** & orderd to be registerd

A Deed of Sale from John **POWELL** to James **POWELL** was proved in Open Court by the Oath of Daniel **POWELL** & orderd to be registerd.

A Deed of Sale from Kedar **ELLIS** to Riddick **JONES** was proved in Open Court by the Oath of Riddick **JONES** & orderd to be registerd

August Court 1834

An audited acct. of Nathan **NIXON** Exor of Robert **TAYLOR** dec^d. was Exhibited in Open Court & orderd to be recorded

Orderd that John C. **GORDON** adm^r on the Estate of Chas. **BRIGGS** de^d. that he give bond & Securitey in the Sum of $500—with T. W. **CARR** & Isaac. R. **HUNTER**.

issd. Orderd that the County Trustee pay Lem^l. G. **DARDEN** 80/100 for an error in Taxes.

issd. Orderd that Whit **STALLINS**. Nathan **RIDDICK**. Jethro. H. **RIDDICK** & James **BOYCE** Audite the Acct^s. of Wm **BIRAM** Exor of Luke **HOLLOWELL**

" Orderd that Richard **CURL** be appointed Overseer of the road from the White Oak to Ethel^d. **CROSS**es & that the usual hands work S^d. road

A Bill of Sale from Law S. **DAUGHTRY** to Seth. R. **MORGAN** was proved in Open Court by the Oath H. **GILLIAM** & orderd to be reg^d.

An acct. Sales of the Estate of Walton **FREEMAN** dec^d. was retu^d. to Court by Levi **BEEMAN** & orderd to be recorded.

A Lease from Jethro H **RIDDICK** to Jasper **TROTMAN** was proved in Open Court by the Oath of H **GILLIAM** & orderd to be registerd

The audited acct of Hanse **HOFFLER** admr. of Rubin **HINTON** dec^d. was Exhibited into Open Court & orderd to be recorded.

A Deed of Sale from Elisha **HUMPHLET** to W^m. H. **SAVAGE** was proved in Open Court by the Oath of Thos. **HOGARD** & orderd to be regis^d.

Orderd that James T **FREEMAN** be appointed Gu^d. to Edward David & Robert **TAYLOR**. that he give Willis. J. **RIDDICK** & Seth W. **ROUNTREE** as Security in a bond of $1500.

A Bill of Sale from Ab **MORGAN** & Henry **GILLIAM** to David F **FELTON** was ack^d in Open Court & orderd to be registerd

Orderd that the County Trustee pay John H **HASLET** two Dollars an Error in Taxes.

[108] 18th Augt. 1834

Orderd that a Dedimus Potestatum issue to Barnes **GOODMAN** Esqr one of the Justices of the Court to take the probate of a bill Sale from Mary **DARDEN** & James **GRIFFIN** to Col Jethro **SUMNER** & report the Same to Court.

Orderd that Fruzy **TAYLOR** be appointed Gu^d. to her daughter Mary **TAYLOR** that She enter into Bonds with Whit **STALLINS** & Hanse **HOFFLER** Secutey [sic] for $250.

" Orderd that Cap John **SPEIGHT** be appointed Overseer of the road in Stead of John **BRADY**.

A Deed of Sale from Henry **HARE** to Miles **PARKER** was ~~proved~~ /ack^d./ in Open Court ~~by the Oath~~. & orderd to be registered.

   Court adjourned to Tuesday Morning
  Tuesday Morning Court Met according to adjournment
  Present. W^m. W. **COWPER** Demsey **KNIGHT** & Ab W **PARKER** Esqui**rs**

A Deed in Trust from Joseph T. **HURDLE** to Jethro H. **RIDDICK** was proved in Open Court by the Oath of Jos. **RIDDICK** & orderd to be registerd

August Court 1834

A Deed of Sale from Kedar BRIGGS to Miles BRIGGS was proved in Open Court by the Oath of Rich[d] H BALLARD & orderd to be registerd

A Bill [sic] Sale from W[m]. HOFFLER to John ROBERTS was proved in Open Court by the Oath of James BOND & orderd to be registered.

A Bill of Sale from James BOND to Job R HALL was proved in Open Court by the Oath of Henry GILLIAM & orderd to be registerd

A Deed of Gift from Kedar BALLARD to Mary Jane BALLARD was proved in Open Court by the Oath of T. W. CARR & orderd to be registerd

A Bill of Sale from John B BAKER to Job R HALL was acknow[lgd]. in Open Court & orderd to be registered.

A Deed of Sale from Samel [sic] BROWN to Westly. W. SPEIGHT was proved in Open Court by the Oath of Henry HOFFLER & orderd to be registerd

The Last Will & Testament of Solomon EASON was proved in Open Court by the Oaths of Charlott EASON & Senah EASON the two Subscribing witnesses & at the Same time Abner EASON the Exor. therin named appeard & qualified as the Law requirs orderd that the Same be recorded.

A Deed of Gift from Isaiah RIDDICK to William RIDDICK was proved in Open Court by the Oath of Jos RIDDICK & orderd to be registerd

" Orderd that Abel ROGERSON W[m]. W. COWPER. W[m]. CLEAVES & Exum LEWIS be appointed to Lay of [sic] to the Widow of Walton FREEMAN decd. & family one years allowance.

[109] Tuesday 19th Auguest 1834.

" Orderd that the County Trustee pay Barnes GOODMAN Esqr Forty five Dollars /88/100/ for his Servics in Settling with the Militia of Gates County

issd. Orderd that the County trustee pay William E PUGH County Solisitor for his Servics to this Term Fifty Dollars.

Orderd that Letters admr of debonas non be Granted to Whit STALLINS upon the Estate of W[m] BLANCHARD dec[d]. that he give bond & Security in the Sum of $1000. Jas. T FREEMAN & Abner EASON securities

A Bill of Sale from John WALTON Trustee to Jethro WILLEY was proved in Open Court by the Oath of H GILLIAM & orderd to be registerd.

A Bill of Sale from Jas. R. RIDDICK Shff to Jethro WILLY was provd in Open Court by the Oath of H GILLIAM & orderd to be registerd

Ordered that the county Trustee pay Jethro H RIDDICK which /85/ that he paid into the public Treasurey for one Stud horse.

A Deed of Sale from John GATLING to W[m]. H. DAUGHTRY was proved in Open Court by the Oath of Robt. RIDDICK & orderd to be registerd.

The following persons was drawn & Sworn as Grand Jurors to this Term (To wit) T. W. CARR (foreman.) Marmaduke NORFLEET. Tim[o]. SPIVEY Geor [sic] COSTON. Ab SPIVEY. Noah ROUNTREE. Jas BROWN of Jas. Jetho [sic] BLANCH[D]. W[m]. MATHEWS. John BROWN. Geor. W. SMITH. Daniel RIDDICK James COSTON Senr. Daniel WILLIAMS. Ed. CROSS. Bush RIDDICK. James BAKER Ju[r] & James T FREEMAN.

August Court 1834

Isaac **PIPKIN** }
vs }
Exum **LEWIS** } The following /Jury/ Jason **SAUNDERS**. Henry **HOFFLER** Asa **HILL**. Peter **EURE**. Demsey **PARKER**. Drew **SAUNDERS**. Tim°. **HAYS**. Abner **EASON**. Richard **HAYS**. Zack **HAYS** Abram **BENTON**. John **SPARKMAN** being Sworn & impannell^d. find all the issues infavor the defendant. the ~~def^d~~. /Pltff/ appeard & Craved [sic] an appeal to the Sup Court. Which was Granted & he enterd into Bond with John **SAUNDERS** & Henry **GILLIAM** Secuity

Wash **SMITH** }
vs }
Isaac F **STAFFORD** &Co: } The following Jurors Miles **PARKER** Jur. Elisha **HUNTER** Demcy **PARKER**. Abso **BLANCHARD** Levi **ROGERS**. Jacob **POWELL**. Rich^d. **CROSS**. John **MORRIS**. James **BENTON** Nathan **NIXON**. Jethro **WILLY** & W^m. H **GOODMAN** being Sworn & impannell^d. find all the issues in favor of Pltff & asses his damage to $21.20 of Which 20$ is principal

Orderd that Jack **WALKER** have a licence to Sell Oysters Cakes &c.

" Orderd that W^m. L. **BOOTH**. John **RIDDICK**. Exum **LEWIS** & W^m W **COWPER** Audite & Settle the Estate of Ebon **BRISCO** with Ab. W. **PARKER** admr & make report.

[110] Tuesday 19th. Augt. 1834

issd. Orderd that the County Trustee pay Richard **HAYS** Twelve Dolls & 50/100 for wheels furnish^d. the poor house.

" Orderd that Willie **RIDDICK** be appointed Overseer of the road leading from the run of **BENNETT**s Creek to the fork of the road at Geor [sic] **COSTON**s quarter in the room of James. M. **RIDDICK**

The Sheriff having returned the inquisition which he had been orderd to hold over Mary **TAYLOR** Touching her being a Lunatic or Idiot by Virtue of an order made at May Term 1834. which Said inquisition having the said Mary **TAYLOR** to be an Idiot. It is therefore Orderd adjudged & decreed by the Court that the inquisition of the Jury & the report therof finding ~~of the Jury~~ Said Mary to be an Idiot. be confirm^d. And on Motion Orderd. that Whitmil [sic] **STALLINS** be appointed Guardian of Said Mary **TAYLOR** that he give Bond in the Sum of $2000. with Nathan **RIDDICK** & J. H **RIDDICK** securities

A Deed in Trust from Will **KING** to Jesse **HOBBS** was proved in Open Court by the Oath of Whit **STALLINS** & orderd to be registered

Court adjourned untill Wednesday Morning
Wednesday Court met according to adjournment.
Present. Joseph **RIDDICK** Thomas **SAUNDERS** & Abraham. W. **PARKER**

issd. Orderd that W^m. G. **DAUGHTRY** Obtain a licence to retail Spiritous Liquors for one year at his Tavern.

A Inventory of the Estate of James **PHELEPS** dec^d. was returnd by Geor **COSTON** Exor & orderd to be recorded.

A Deed of Sale from James R **RIDDICK** to John A **ANDERSON** was proved in Open Court by the Oath of Jesse **WILSON** & orderd to be registed

Orderd that the Clk Examine the List of Taxes & put into the Jury Box the names of those liable to Serve as Jurors.

Demsey **PARKER** Came into Court. relinquish^d. the Guardianship of Louisa **JONES** orphan of Henry **JONES**. dec^d. whereupon it was orderd that Henery **GILLIAM** be appointed that he enter into Bound

August Court 1834

[sic] with James R. **RIDDICK** & James **BOOTH** Securities in the sum $3000.

Orderd that admistration upon the Estate of Lawrenc [sic] **SAUNDERS** dec^d. with the will annexed be Granted unto Drew. M. **SAUNDERS** that he give Bond with Jason **SAUNDERS** & Gilbert **SAUNDERS** in $1000.

[111] Wednesday 20th. Augt 1834

Jeptha **FAWLKS** }
    vs }
Peter B. **MINTON** } The following Jurors. Lem^l. **RIDDICK** Elisha **HUNTER**. Abner **EASON**. Lem^l. **CLEAVES**, Asa **HILL**. Willis J. **RIDDICK**, Elijah **HARRELL** Exum **LEWIS**. W^m. **BENTON** W^m. **ARNOLD** Henry **BOND** & Tim^o. **WALTON**. being imp^d. & Sworn find all the issues infavor of the pltff & asses his damage to $222.31.

Jeptha **FAWLKS** }
    vs }
Abraham. W. **PARKER** } The following Jurors. Lem^l.. **RIDDICK**. Elisha **HUNTER**. John. S. **ROBERTS**. Abner **EASON** Lem^l. **CLEAVES**. Abel **ROGERSON**. Elijah **HARRELL**. Exum **LEWIS**. W^m. **BENTON**. W^m. **ARNOLD** Sol. **ROUNTREE** & Willis J. **RIDDICK** being duly Sworn & impannelld. By the Court (Non. Suite) the pltff prayed for & Obtained an appeal to the Sup. Court & enterd into Bonds with. Henry **GILLIAM** & David **PARKER** Securities.

The following Insolvent Taxables was allowd Lass [sic] **RIDDICK** D Shff in his different Captaincys. (to wit) Francis. **BUCHANY** 1. poll Leven **CUFF**. 1. Willis **EVANS** 1. James **EVANS** 1. Wm **GOODWIN**. 1. Wm **MORSE** 1. Stewart **MORSE** 1. Isaac F **STAFFORD**. 5. Jesse **WYATT**. 1. Willowby **MANNING** 2 [?] Whitmil **MATHEWS**. 1. Willey **CARTER**. 1. Nathan **HARELL** Ju^r 1. Nathan. **HARRELL** Senr. 1. Jethro **HARRELL** Ju^r. 1. Thomas **EVANS**. 1. Thomas **JOHNSON**. 1. Robert **LEE**. 1. Nathan **SMITH**. 1. James **BOYT**. 1. W^m. **HUMPHLET**. 1. John D **MATHEWS**. 1. Will **TAYLOR**. 1. Demsey **BOYT**. 1. Richard **CARNELIOUS**. 1. Lewis **CARTER**. 1. Ira **CARTER** 1. Samuel **COPELAND**. 1. Whitmil **GOODMAN**. 1. Timothy **HOWELL** 1. John **JONES**. 1. John **LANG**. 1. Willie **PARKER**. 1. Riddick **ARNOLD** 1. Charles **BAKER**. 1. W^m. **BENTON** Ju^r. 1. Willie **CROSS**. 1. Nathaniel **DOUGHTY**. 1. Moses D. **HARE**. 1. Henry **HARE**. 1. Charles **JONES**. 1. Isaac. H. **JINKINS**. 1. Bryant **MATHEWS**. 1. Auston **MORGAN** 1. W^m. W. **PARKER** 1. Law S. **DAUGHTRY**. 5. in all 55 & that Jethro. H. **RIDDICK** in his Districts be alle^d. 11: (to Wit. Jethro **BRINKLEY**. 1. Westly **KNIGHT**. 1. Riddick **PEAL** [?] 1. Wynns **BAKER** 1. Benj B. **BALLARD**. 1. Jesse L **HARE**. 1. Benj **KNIGHT** Jur 1. Fre^d. **BLANCH**^{D}. 1. Robert **PARKER** 1. Noah **ROBINS**. 1. Daniel. S. **WARD** 1.

The audited acct. of the Estate of Thomas **ROUNTREE** dec^d was Exhibited into Open Court. as also a division of Said Estate & ordered to be recorded

[112] It is orderd by a Majority of the Court of pleas & qr Sessions that the order made at last Term in relation to the building of a Court House be hereby resinded, in part, so fare as it relates to the lenght [sic] of the building. that it Shall be 40 feet Square Only & the porch & portico. taken off from the building & that the Court room be below Thos **SAUNDERS**. W^m L **BOOTH**. Henry **COSTON**. Ab. W **PARKER**. R. **GATLING** Simon **WALTERS**. Whit **STALLINS**. W^m **LEE**. Jos **RIDDICK** W^m. W. **COWPER** Henry **WILLEY** Barnes **GOODMAN**. Hardy D. **PARKER**.

The Shff having returnd. the inquisition which he had been orderd to hold over the body Mary **TAYLOR** touching her being a Lunatice or Idiot. by Virtue of an order made at May Term 1834. Which Said inquisition having found the said Mary **TAYLOR** to be an Idiot. It is therefore orderd that. & adjudged & decreed by the Court. that the inquisition of the Jury & the report therof finding the said Mary to be an Idiot. be Confirm^d. And On Motion Orderd that Whitmil **STALLINS**. be appointed Guardian of Said Mary **TAYLOR** he giving Bond in the Sum of $2000. N. **RIDDICK** & J. H. **RIDDICK** /Secties/ [sic] [Remainder of page is blank.]

November Court 1834

[113] State of North Carolina } November Court 1834
    Gates County   }

    At a Court of pleas & qr Sessions began & held for the County of Gates in Gatesville. 3rd Monday in November 1834. & 17th day. Present. Thomas **SAUNDERS** Hardey. D. **PARKER** & Abraham W **PARKER** Esqr.

The Last will & Testament of Jesse **SAVAGE** decd. was Exhibited into Open Court & proved by the Oaths [sic] Caleb **SAVAGE** and Oliver **HARRELL** the two Subscribing witnesses thereto & at the Same time John **SAVAGE** the Exor therin Named appeard & qualified & he enterd into Bond & Security. as the Law requires.

A Bill of Sale from David **OUTLAW** to James **BAKER** was proved in Open Court & orderd to be registerd.

A Bill of Sale from Joel B. **HURDLE** to James **BAKER** was proved in Open Court & orded to be registerd

A Deed of Sale from Samuel **FELTON** to Elbert. K. **RIDDICK** was proved in Open Court & orderd to be registerd.

A Deed of Sale from John **GRIFFITH** to Abraham **RIDDICK** was proved in Open Court & orderd to be registerd.

A Deed of Sale from Hiram **LOOMIS** to John **GRIFFITH** was proved in Open Court & orderd to be registerd.

A Deed of Sale from James R **RIDDICK** Shff to Edwin **CROSS** was ackgd. in Open Court & orderd to be registerd.

A Deed of Sale from Jason **ROUNTREE** & wife to Thomas **HOGGARD** was proved in Open Court & orderd to be registerd.

A Relinquishment from Law. S. **DAUGHTRY** to Wm. G. **DAUGHTRY** was proved in Open Court & orderd to be registerd.

A Deed of Sale from Abner **LASSITER** to Molly. **JOHNSON** was proved in Open Court & orderd to be registerd.

A Deed of Sale from Jacob **MATHEWS** to Elbert. H. **RIDDICK** was proved in Open Court & orderd to be registerd.

A Deed of Sale from James. R. **RIDDICK** Shff to Edwin **CROSS** was ackgd. in Open Court & orderd to be registerd.

A Deed of Sale from Daniel **FIELDS** to Allen **SMITH** was proved in Open Court & orderd to be registerd.

    Court adjourned untill Tuesday.

[114] Tuesday Morning 18th. Nov 1834 Court Met.
Present {Thomas **SAUNDERS** Joseph **RIDDICK** John C **GORDON**} Esquires

The following persons was drawn & Sworn as Grand Jurors (to Wit) John **MITCHEL** (Foreman) Benj **FRANKLIN**. Elbert H **RIDDICK** Demcy **HOBBS**. Wm **KING**. Rubin **EASON**. Robert **ROGERS**. John **LANGSTON**. James **BOICE**. Jethro **HARRELL**. Kedar **TAYLOR**. James **BOOTH**. Archd. **JONES**. Samel. **HARRELL**. Fred. **JONES**. Charles **JONES** Will **HOBBS** & Miles **PARKER** Jur.

November Court 1834

The following petty [sic] Jurors was Sworn. Jesse. M. SAVAGE. Benj. EURE Will. MILLER Fred. ROOKS. Elijah HARRELL. Benj BROWN. Simon KING & Jos HURDLE.

State }
    vs (A&.B) }
Mills. ROBERTS et als } The following Jurors. James BENTON. Benj EURE. W^m. MILLER. Fred. ROOKS. Elijah HARRELL Benj BROWN. Simon KING. Jos HURDLE W^m A [?] MATHEWS. John SPEIGHT. Jethro GOODMAN & Edwin CROSS being duly Sworn & imp^d. find the defendants Guilty as Charged.

State }
    vs. (A&.B) }
Jeptha FAULKS } The following Jurors Henry G. WILLIAMS Simon KING Sol ROUNTREE. Bray PARKER Docton HAYS. Jos HURDLE. Elijah HARRELL. Benj BROWN. Kedar HINTON Mills SPARKMAN. Demcy PARKER & James SMITH. being duly Sworn & impanell^d. Say the def^d. is Guilty as Chaged. By the Court Let Jep FAULKS pay a fine of $20. &Cost [sic]

A Deed of Sale from Benj WILLIAMS to allen WILLIAMS was ackg^d. in Open Court & orderd to be registerd.

A Deed of Sale from Jesse MATHIAS to Kedar ELLIS was proved in Open Court & orderd to be registerd

A Deed of Sale from Simon WALTERS Gu^d to John C. JINKINS was ackg^d. in Open Court & orderd to be registerd.

A Deed of Sale from John LASSITER et als to Willis HOFFLER was proved in Open Court & orderd to be registerd.

A Deed of Sale from Abraham PRUDEN to Mary HARRELL was proved in Open Court & orderd to be registerd.

A Deed of Sale from George HARRELL to Mary HARRELL was proved in Open Court & orderd to be registerd.

A Deed of Sale from John GATLING to Nathan PIERCE was proved in Open Court & orderd to be registerd.

[115] Tuesday 18th Nov 1834

The Last will & Testament. of Isaac PIERCE was proved in Open Court by the Oath of John ALPHIN at the Same time Joseph GORDON the Exor thrin [sic] named appeared & qualified

The Last will & Testament of William HARRELL dec^d. was Exhibited into Open Court & proved by the Oath of Marmaduke NORFLEET One of the Subscribing Witnesses & at the Same time William H HARRELL one of the Exors therin named appeard & qualified

A Deed of Sale from Robert RIDDICK to James WOODWARD was proved in Open Court & orderd to be registerd.

A Deed of Sale from Calvin BRINKLY to Edwin MATHIAS was proved in Open Court & orderd to be registed.

A Deed of Sale from Demcy BOND to Susanah LASSITER was proved in Open Court & orderd to be registerd

A Deed of Sale from Benbury WALTON to David PARKER was ackg^d. in Open Court & orderd to be

November Court 1834

registerd

A Deed of Sale from Wills COWPER to Rachel YATES was proved in Open Court & orderd to be registerd.

A Deed of Gift from Humph^ry. PARKER to James. A. BALLARD was provd in Open Court & orderd to be registerd.

A Deed of Sale from Elisha H BOND to Rid GATLING was proved in Open Court & orderd to be registerd.

A Mortgage from Rachel YATES to Noah HARRELL was proved in Opn Court & orderd to be recorded.

A Deed of Sale from Will WALTON to Abel ROGERSON was proved in Open Court & orderd to be registerd.

Same to Same was proved in Open Court & orderd to be registed

A Deed of Sale from Jesse WIGGINS to Wills COWPER was proved in Open Court & orderd to be registerd.

A Deed of Sale from Jno EURE to W^m. H. SAVAGE was proved in Open Court & orderd to be registerd.

A Deed of ~~Sale~~ /Gift/ from Jason ROUNTREE & wife to Nancy HARRELL was proved in Open Court & orderd to be registerd.

A Deed of Sale from Benbury WALTON to Wm PETTY was proved in Open Court & orderd to be registerd.

A Deed of Sale from James R RIDDICK Shff to Jesse WIGGINS was proved in Open Court & orded to be regis^d.

A Deed in Trust from Abel ROGERSON to Henry GILLIAM & J. H. RIDDICK was proved in Open Court & orderd to be registd

[116] Wednesday. 19th. Nov

Court met. Present {John C. GORDON Henry WILLEY Jos. RIDDICK} Esquires

A Deed of Sale from Ab PRUDEN & wife to Thomas HOGGARD was proved in Open Court & orderd to be registerd.

A Deed of Sale from Briant BEST to [sic] Wife to David PARKER was proved in Open Court & orderd to be registerd.

Account Sales of one Negro belonging to Geor KITTRELL dec^d. by Daniel WILLIAMS Exor was returnd & orderd to be recorded.

Account Sale of Estate Solomon EASON was returnd by the Exor & orderd to be recorded.

An Inventory of the Estate of Solomon EASON was returnd by the Exor & orderd to be recorded.

Acc^t. Sales of the Estate of Law SAUNDERS dec^d. was returnd by the adm^r & orderd to be recorded.

An Inventory of the Estate of Lawrence SAUNDERS dec^d. was returnd by the adm^r. & orderd to be recorded.

November Court 1834

The ~~audited~~ acc^t. of Sales of the Estate of John **HARE** dec^d. was returnd by the adm^r & orderd to be recorded

The audited acc^t of John **WALTON** admr of John **HARE** dec^d. was returnd to Court & orded to be recorded.

The audited acc^t. of the Exor of Ab **BEEMAN** dec^d. was returnd to Court & orderd to be recorded

The audited acc^t of William **BYRUM** Exor of Luke **HOLLOWEL**_ was returnd to Court & orded to be recorded

The audited acc^t of Ab **RIDDICK** adm^r of Barshaba **FRANKLIN** dec^d. was returnd to Court & orded to be ~~registerd~~ recorded

The audited acc^t. & division of the Estate of Peter **HARRELL** dec^d. was returnd to Court by H **GILLIAM** adm^r & orderd to be recorded

The Guardian acc^t of John **JONES** Gu^d to James **CROSS** was returnd into Court & orded to be recorded.

Orderd that Francis **DUKE** be appointed overseer of the Road in the room of Jethro **GOODMAN**.

Orderd that John **GAREY** [?] be appointd ad$\underline{m}$ on the Estate of Eliza. [?] **SUMNER** Dec^d. that he enter into Bond with Simon **WALTERS** & Jesse **WIGGINS** his Securities in the Sum of $2000.

Orded that Thos. E **RIDDICK** renew his Constable Bond with Securites

[117] Wednesday 19th Novr 1834

John **SPEIGHT** }
    vs (Appl. }
Nathl **EURE** Gu^d. } The following Jurors. Noah **ROUNTREE** Pryor **SAVAGE**. John **SAUNDERS** Sol. **ROUNTREE**. Eli **WORRELL**. Benj **EURE** Simon **KING**. Fre^d. **ROOKS** Elijah **HARRELL**. William **MILLER**. Benj **BROWN**. & Jethro **BLANCHARD** being duly Sworn & impanell^d. find all the issues in favor of the pltff & asses his damage to $35.60 &Costs.

Same }
  vs }
Same } Same Jurey being impane^d & Sworn find all the issues infavor pltff & asses his damage to $35.60—from which two Judgts the defendant prayed for & obtained an appeal to the Sup Court. & he enterd into Bonds & Security agreeable to Law.

Britton **SMITH** }
    vs Appl }
Bray **PARKER** } Same Jury being Sworn & impannel^d find all the issues infavor of the defendant.

W^m & Henrey **PUGH** }
    vs }
Jos. J. **BARNES** } Henry **GILLIAM** the bail in this Case Surrenderd the body of Jos. J. **BARNES** orderd that Said Bail be dischg^d.

W^m & Henry **PUGH** }
    vs Case}
Jos. J. **BARNES** } The following Jurors Noah **ROUNTREE** Solomon **ROUNTREE**. Simon **KING** Eli **WORRELL**. Jason **SAUNDERS** Jos **HURDLE**. Fre^d. **ROOKS** Benj **EURE**. Elijah **HARRELL**. John **SAUNDERS**. William **MILLER**. & Benj **BROWN**. being Sworn to try this issue (to wit) to say whiether the def^d Jos. J. **BARNES** does fraudulenty Conceal any money Goods or Effects to avoid the

November Court 1834

pay^t. of his debts say that they find that Jos. J. **BARNES** does fraudulenty Conceal Goods money & Effects ordered that he be in Custody untill he dischage the Claim

Orderd that Mills **EURE** W^m. L. **BOOTH** Henry **GILLIAM** & Ethel^d **CROSS** or any three audite the acct of John **EURE** adm^r of John **EURE** dec^d & make report.

[118] " Ordered that Blake **BRADDY** be appointed Over Seer of the road in the room of Jno. **SPEIGHT**.

Ordered that Jno. C. **GORDON** be appointed adm^r. on the Estate of Lucretia **BEEMAN** dec^d. that he enter into bond with H. **GILLIAM** & Jos. **GORDON** his Securities in the Sum of $5,000

Ordered that Jno. C. **GORDON** be appointed Guardian to Israel **BEEMAN** & William **BEEMAN** orphants of Jno. **BEEMAN** that he enter into bond with Timothy **WALTON** & Bembury **WALTON** Securities in the sum of $8.000 Each.

" Ordered that Jno. C. **GORDON** James **MORGAN** Jno. O. **HUNTER** Wiley **RIDDICK** & Jesse **WIGGINS** or any [sic] them audite the accts. of Abram & James **BENTON** Exor^s. of Seth **BENTON** dec^d. & make report

Ordered that letters of administration issue to Mills **PILAND** on the Estates of James & Isaac **PILAND** dec^d. and that he enter into bond with Seth **PILAND** Jesse **PILAND** Reuben **PILAND** and Asa **PILAN** [sic] & that he enter into bond of $1.500 Each.

Ordered that Henry **GILLIAM** Mills **ROBERTS** W^m. G. **DAUGHTERY** an [sic] Jno. C. **GORDON** or any three of them audite the acct. of W^m.. E. **PUGH** the Exo^r. of Henry **PUGH** & that the s^d. Exo^r be allowed 5 p^r. Ct and make report.

Ordered that Asa **HUNTER** of Couler [sic] & Luke **BAGLEY** Son of Jacob **BAGLEY** Dec^d. be Brought to Feb. Term 1835 to be Bound out by a presentment of the Grand Jury of this term 1834.

Ordered that Miles **KNIGHT** orphan of Ja^s. **KNIGHT** Dec^d. be bound unto Edwin **KNIGHT** S^d. boy is to learn the trade of Black Smith & to be furnished as the law requires

Ordered that letters of Adm^r. be Granted to Thos.. **SAUNDERS** on the Estate of Barshaba **SEARS** dec^d. that he enter into bond with H. **GILLIAM** & Jo^s: **FREEMAN** his Securities in the Sum of $2.500

Ordered that H **GILLIAM** Thos. **SAUNDERS** an W^m. G. **DAUGHTERY** audite the acts. of David **CROSS** Exo^r.. of David **LEWIS** and that the S^d. Exo^r. be allowed 5 p^r.. Ct. upon his receipt.

Ordered that letters of Adm^r. be granted to Joseph **FREEMAN** on the Estate of Jno. **FREEMAN** Dec^d. and that he enter into bond with Thos **SAUNDERS** Nathaniel **EURE** his Securities in the Sum of $3.000

[119] " Ordered that Edwrd. **BRIGGS** be appointed Over seer of the road in the room of Col. I. R. **HUNTER**.

" Ordered that a writ of dower Issue to the Shff of this County to Summons a Jury to lay of [sic] the dower of Walton **FREEMAN** dec^d. Widow.

Ordered that Hance **HOFFLER** be appointed Guardian to Caroline **HAYS** orphan of Benjn. **HAYS** & enter into bond with Ja^s T. **FREEMAN** /& Noah **ROUNTREE**/ in the Sum of $2,000

" Ordered that Riddick **GATLING** Henry **GILLIAM** David **PARKER** be appointed to make a division of the negroes belonging to the Estate of Barshaba **SEARS** dec^d. between the legal heirs.

Ordered that the Commissioners of Publick Buildings cause such repair to be put on the **HACKLEY** Swamp Bridge as the publick Convenience may require.

November Court 1834

Ordered that Adm^r. de boni [sic] non upon the estate of James **CROSS** be Commited to Edward **CROSS** & enter into bond with Jethro & Henry **WILLEY** Securities in the Sum of $600.

" Ordered that Henry **GILLIAM** Jesse **WIGGINS** & Wiley **RIDDICK** audite the acct. of Ja^s. **MORGAN** adm^r of Abram **BENTON** dec^d. and that the S^d. adm^r. be allowed 5 pr. Ct.

Ordered that Jno. **SAVAGE** of Nansmond & State of Virginia Exor to the last will & testament of Jesse **SAVAGE** dec^d. & he enter into bond with Henry **GILLIAM** & Jno. **MATTHEWS** in the Sum of $20,000

Ordered that Ja^s. **SAVAGE** be appointed Guardian to Mary **SAVAGE** & Benjamin **SAVAGE** orphants of Jesse **SAVAGE** & enter into bond with Henry **GILLIAM** Jno. **MATTHEWS** & Jesse M. **SAVAGE** in the Sum of $6,000 Each

Ordered that W. F. **RIDDICK** renew his Guardian Bond as Guardian for I. B. **HUNTER** & enter into bond with Isaac R. **HUNTER** & Ja^s. M. **RIDDICK** as securities

issued Ordered that Barns **GOODMAN** Hillery **WILLEY** Simon **WATERS** William **MOORE** & Henry **GILLIAM** be appointed Connmissioners or any three of them to divide the negroes belonging to the Estate of Jesse **SAVAGE** Dec^d. agreeable to the will of S^d Dec^d.

Ordered that Timothy **WALTON** be appointed Gua^d. to Nathl. **JONES** orphan of Nathl. **JONES** & enter into bond with Jno. **WALTON** & Bembery [sic] **WALTON** in the Sum of $3,000.

[120] " Ordered that the County Trustee pay to W^m.. **PARKER** the Sum of $1.08 State vs W^m.. & Henry **BENTON**.

" Ordered that letters of administration be granted to Allen **SMITH** on the estate of Lemuel **CLEVES** & he enter into bond with Henry **WILLEY** & W^m.. **CLEVES** in the Sum of $3000

" Ordered that the County trustee pay W^m.. S. **DAUGHTERY** Six Dollars for bringing Elijah **READ** from the Frying pan

Ordered that the County trustee pay unto Simons **ROUNTREE** for Sevices up to this term $13.60

issued Ordered that Barns **GOODMAN** Jno. C. **GORDON** Jno. V. **SUMNER** Jno. P. **BENTON** Demsey **KNIGHT** with the County Surveyor lay off & Set apart to James **MORGAN** & Miles **PARKER** Such part of the land that Henry **HARE** is entitled to out of the lands of Jno.. **HARE** dec^d. then make report to the next Court

" Ordered that Jo^s. **GORDON**, Jno. C. **GORDON**, Tilly W. **CARR** Hardy D. **PARKER**, & Barnes **GOODMAN** be appointed Connmissioners to divide the negroes & other personal estate of Jethro **SUMNER** Dec^d. agreeable to the Will

Ordered that Benjn. **SUMNER** Exo^r. of Jethro **SUMNER** Dec^d. sell at publick sale on a credit of Six months all the perishable property belonging to the estate of S^d. Dec^d. which was left by the will of the dec^d. to his widow during her life & after her death to be divided &c in order that a division may be made according to the directions of S^d. Will. & likewise all the other perishable property of Said Dec^d.

" Ordered that Bembry **WALTON**, Timothy **WALTON** and Ja^s. T. **FREEMAN** be appointed to audite the accounts of Cader **FELTON** Adm^r. of Frederick **HINTON** it is further ordered that the above named auditers, place a valuation upon one negro to the end that a distribution of the proceeds of Said negro may be made among the heirs. It is further ordered that Said administrator be allowed 5 p^r. Ct. Connmissions on the receipts of Said Estate.

November Court 1834

" Ordered that H GILLIAM Isaac PIPKIN Demsey GOODMAN & Henry WILLEY or any three of them be appointed to audite the accounts of Daniel WILLIAMS the Exor of George KITTREL [sic] dec^d. and that he be allowed Conmission of 5 p^r. Ct. on his receipts as such It is further ordered that the S^d. auditors or any three of them be appointed to allot to & set apart to Jno. ODOM in right of his wife, Mary ODOM the proportionable /Part/ of the said Mary of the personal estate of the said George according to the provisions of his will

[121] State of No. Carolina }
Gates County. } At a Court of pleas & qr Sessions begun & held for the County of Gates at the Court House in Gatesville 3r^d Monday in February 1835
Present {Thomas SAUNDERS Jos RIDDICK Whit STALLINS & W^m. W. COWPER} Esquires

William H. GOODMAN returned his Guardian accts with Henery GOODMAN Peninah GOODMAN Mariah GOODMAN John GOODMAN & Richard GOODMAN which was orderd to be recorded.

Hardy. D. PARKER return^d. his Guardian accts with Jesse WIGGINS Martha & Eliz^a. WIGGINS which was orderd to be recorded

A deed of Sale from James R. RIDDICK to Harrison ELLIS was duly ack^g in in [sic] Open Court & orderd to be registerd

Allen SMITH returnd an Inventory of the Estate of Lemel [sic] CLEAVES dec^d. into Open Court Which was orderd to be recorded

A Deed in Trust from Willis CASEY to Simon STALLINS was proved in Open Court by T. W. STALLINS & orderd to be recorded.

Exum JINKINS return^d. his Guardian acct with Sarah. E. ODAM which was orded to be recorded.

W^m. W. COWPER Gu^d to Uriah BABB & Celia LEWIS returned his Guardian accts. which was orderd to be recorded.

A Deed of Sale from Thomas GOOMER & others to Geor. W. SMITH was proverd in Open Court by the Oath of Caleb SAVAGE & orderd to be regis^{td}

An Inventory of the Estate of Jesse SAVAGE was return^d. by John SAVAGE Exor & orderd to be recorded.

An acct Sales of the Estate of Lem^l. CLEAVES dec^d. was returnd to Court by A. SMITH adm^r & orderd to be recorded.

Orderd that John RIDDICK Give Jos RIDDICK & James R RIDDICK Securties to his Constable Bond.

issd Orderd that Whit STALLINS. John MITCHEL. Nathan RIDDICK & Jethro H RIDDICK or any three audite the accts of Jesse HOBBS Exor of of [sic] W^m. KING dec^d & make report to Next Court & divid [sic] same

Orderd that John W. ODAM renew his Guardian Bond with Simon WALTERS & Henery WILLIEY [sic] secuities

Orded that Jos GORDON be appointed Gu^d to Isaac Solomon Whitmil & Eletia EASONs orphans of Hardy EASON with John R NORFLEET & Marmaduke NORFLEET Securities

[122] Monday 16th Feb^{ry}.

Orderd that Letters of adm^r on the Estate of Jacob POWELL dec^d be Granted unto David PARKER that

February Court 1835

he enter into Bond with Rubin **HINTON** & James **PARKER** Securites in the Sum of $400

Henry G **WILLIAMS** Gu^d. to Jos **SPEIGHT** Exhibited into Open Court his acct which was orderd to be recorded.

Acc^t. Sales of the Estate of Eliz^a. **SUMNER** was Exhibited into Open Court by the adm^r & orderd to be recorded.

A Deed of Sale from Nathan **RIDDICK** to Lem^l. **CLEAVES** was proved in Open Court by the Oath Levi **BEEMAN** & ord [sic] to be regist$\underline{ed}$

A Division of the Negros belonging to the Estate of Jesse **SAVAGE** dec^d. was returnd into Open court & orderd to be filed

Mills **EURE** Gu^d to the orphans of Stephen **LEE** dec^d. was returnd to Court & orderd to be recorded.

A division of the Estate of Geor **KITTRELL** agreeable to his [sic] was returnd to Court & orderd to be filed.

Jethro **HARRELL** Gu^d to the orphans of Ebon **BRISCO** dec^d. returnd his acct^s which was orderd to be recorded.

A Division of the Lands of John **HARE** d$\underline{e}^d$ was returnd to Court & orderd to be registerd

Joseph **FREEMAN** Gu^d to David **FREEMAN** returnd his accts into Open Court which was orderd to be recorded.

A Marriage Contract between Simon **STALLINS** & Fru$\underline{i}$zy **TAYLOR** was proved in Open Court by John **MITCHEL** & orderd to be regist$\underline{ed}$

" Orderd that Seth /W./ **ROUNTRE** be appointed overseer of the road in room of Riddick **TROTMON**.

A Deed of Sale from Hardy H. C. **JONES** to Zachariah **BOON** was ack^d. in Open Court & orderd to be registerd.

Miles **HOWELL** Gu^d. to the orphans of Elisha **CROSS** dec^d. returnd his accts into Open Court which was orderd to be recorded

Whitmil **STALLINS** Gu^d to the orphans of Henry **WALTON** de^d returnd his accot. into Open Court which was oreder [sic] to be recodd [sic]

Eli **WORRELL** Gu^d to W^m. J. **HUDGINS** return^d. his Guardian acct into Open Court which was orderd to be recorded

A Deed of Sale from John **EVERIT** & wife was ack^d. in open Court & orderd to be registerd. to David **DUNFORD** Ju^r.

a Bill [sic] Sale from James **GRIFFIN** & others to Jethro **SUMNER** was proved in the State of Vi^a. & ord$\underline{ed}$ to be recorded in Gates

" Orderd that Thomas **SAUNDERS** have a retail licence to retail Spirits in his house

[123] Monday 16th Feb^{ry}. 1835

Orderd that letters of adm^r upon the Estate of Edwin **MATHEWS** dec^d be Granted to John O. **HUNTER** that he ~~rinto~~ [?] enter into Bonds for $1000 with Isaac R. **HUNTER** & Ed R **HUNTER** Securities.

Orderd that Simmons **ROUNTREE** give Bonds as Constable with John R **NORFLEET** & Eli **WOR-**

February Court 1835

RELL Securities.

Orderd that John **WILLEY** be appointed Gu^d to Mary **WILLIAMS** orphan of Jonathan that he enter into Bond for $3000 with Riddick **GATLING** & Henry **WILLEY** Securities.

A Deed of Sale from Thomas **SAUNDERS** to Robert **SIMONS** was prooved in Open Court by the Oath of David **PARKER** & orderd to be registed

David **PARKER** Exhibited his Gu^d. acct into Open Court with John **FELTON** orphan which was orderd to be recorded.

A Deed of Sale from Tim^o. **WALTON** to Andrew **BAKER** was proved in Open Court by the Oath [sic] Ja^s **BAKER** & orderd to be registerd.

A Deed of Sale from Thos. R. **COSTON** to Tim^o. **TROTMON** was ackg^d. in Open Court & orderd to be registerd.

Willis **BUNCH** Gua^d. to Nancy **HURDLE** Exhibited his acct. into Open Court which was orderd to be recorded.

A Deed of Sale from Jacob **EASON** to Willis **BUNCH** was proved in Open Court by the Oath of Jno. T **BENTON** & orderd to be registerd

A Deed of Sale from Ed R **HUNTER** to Andrew **EASON** was ackg^d. in Open Court & orderd to be registerd.

Exum **JINKINS** Gu^d. to Sophia /A/ **ODAM** returnd his acct into Open Court which was orderd to be recorded.

Edwin **SMITH** Gu^d. to Henaretta [sic] **COPELAND** returnd his acct. into Open Court which was orderd to be recorded.

John C **GORDON** Gu^d. to Thomas. A. **SMALL** Exhibited his acct into Open Court which was orderd to be recorded.

Orderd that W^m W **POWELL** enter into Bond as Constable with Jno. P. **BENTON** Benj **FRANKLIN** & Riddick **JONES** Securities

Orderd that letters of adm^r /de bonas non/ upon the Estate Nancy **GAREY** be Granted to Thomas. G. **BENTON** that he enter into Bond for $500 with Jesse **WIGGINS** & Barnes **GOODMAN** Securities

Orderd that Jesse **EASON** be allow^d. to Streighten the main road leading from Sandy Cross to Jos **GORDON** on his own land

John W. **ODAM** Gu^d. to Prissilla **ODAM** Exhibited into Open Court his acct which was orderd to be recorded.

A Deed of Sale from Sarah **SAVAGE** to James **SAVAGE** was proved in Open Court by Jesse. M. & John **SAVAGE** & orderd to be registerd.

[124] Monday 16th. Feb^{ry}. 1835

John. C. **GORDON** Gu^d. to Sarah M **LASSITER** Exhibited his accts. into Open Court which was orderd to be recorded.

A Deed of Sale from W^m. W. **COWPER** to Exum **LEWIS** was ackg^d. in Open Court & orderd to be registerd.

February Court 1835

A Division of the Negros belonging to Estate [sic] Lewis **EURE** de^d. was returnd into Open Court & orderd to be filed.

Orderd that Edwin **SMITH** renew his Guardian Bond with Henaretta **COPELAND** in $2000 H. D. **PARKER** Allen **SMITH** Securities

Willis. F **RIDDICK**. Gu^d. to Jacob B **HUNTER** returnd into Open Court his acct which was orderd to be recorded

A Deed of Sale from H. H. C. **JONES** to Hening. T. **SMITH** was ackg^d. in Open Court & orderd to be recorded.

A Deed of Sale from James **BOYSE** to Thomas **JONES** was proved in Open Court by Burwell **GRIFFITH** & orded to be registerd

James **SMITH** Gu^d to Edward **HARE** returned into Open Court his acct. which was orderd to be recorded.

John C **GORDON** Guardian to Tim°. **LASSITER** Exhibited into Open Court his acct. which was orderd to be recorded.

Orderd that Joseph **HURDLE** Ju^r be appointed oveseer of the road in room of Guy **HOBBS**

An Inventory of the Estate of Eliz^a. **SUMNER** dec^d. was returnd into Open Court by the adm^r & orderd to be recorded.

Daniel **WILLIAMS** Gu^d. to Lem^l. ~~CLEAVES~~ /FIELDS/ returnd his acct. into Open Court Which was orderd to be recorded.

Ab. W. **PARKER** Gu^d. to Will **JOHNSON** returned his acct. into Open Court which was orderd to be recorded.

Seth W **ROUNTREE** Gu^d. to the orphans of Trotmon **BAGLEY** returnd his accts. into Open Court & orderd to be recorded

Orderd that four of Jesse **WIGGINS** hands & two of Allen **DAUGHTRY** work upon the road leading from **DUKE**s fork to John **MATHIAS**

A Deed of Sale from Nathaniel **TAYLOR** et als to Thos. W. **STALLINS** was proved in Open Court by W^m. **SPIVEY** & orderd to be registerd.

An acct ~~Sales~~ /Currenet/ of the Estate James **GORDON** dec^d was returnd into Open Court by the adm [sic] Jn° C **GORDON** & orderd to be recorded

An acct Sales of Estate James **GORDON** dec^d was retu^d orded to be recorded

Arthur **WILLIAMS** Gu^d to Mary **WILLIAMS** return^d his acct into Open Court which was orderd to be recorded

Isaac R. **HUNTER** Gu^d to orphans Benj **BRIGGS** returnd his accts into Open Court & orderd to be recorded.

[125] Monday. 16th Feb^ry 1835

Nathan **NIXON** Gu^d. to Marey & Jos. G. **WALTERS** returnd into Open Court his acct^s which was orderd to be recorded

February Court 1835

James **PRUDEN** Gu^d. to Harriet B **GATLING** return^d into Open Court his acct. which was orderd to be recorded

A Deed of Sale from Louisa **BARNES** et als to James **WILLIAMS** was proved in open Court as to H **GILLIAM**s Signature & orderd to be rg^t [sic]

[Three illegible words crossed out and overwritten.] John H **HASLETT** Gu^d to Lewis & Sophia **HURDLE** returned into Open Court his accots which was orderd to be recorded.

" Orderd that James **COSTON** /Jur/ be appointed Over__ of the road in room of Abram [?] **SPIVEY**

Andrew **MATHEWS** Gu^d. to Kedar & Hollody **JONES** ~~Audi~~ returnd into Open Court his acct which was orderd to be recorded

   The Court adjournd until Tuesday 10 Oclock
Tuesday Morning Court Met according to dgment [sic]
   ~~The Sh~~ Present: Hardy. D. **PARKER** Joseph **RIDDICK** Thomas **SAUNDERS**. Simon **WALTERS** & Whit **STALLINS** Esquires

The Shff returnd the following persons to Serve at this Court as Jurors (to Wit) Tinson **EURE**. Daniel **FIELDS** W^m. **BENTON** Senr. Calvin **BRINKLEY**. Moses **WILKINS** Solomon **SMALL**. Aron **PIERCE**. Wm **PILAND** James **PARKER**. Isaac **BRINKLEY** John **BARNES**. James **BENTON**. Jos **RIDDICK** Ju^r. Demcy **VANN** Isaac **PIERCE**. Edward **BRIGGS**. W^m. H. **GOODMAN**. James. C. **RIDDICK** David **PARKER**. Peter **EURE**. Miles **PARKER** Ju^r. Allen **SMITH** Tim^o. **ROGERS**. Willis **BUNCH**. Jesse R **KEY**. Gilbert **SAUNDERS** Isaac **SPEIGHT**. Miles **BROWN**. John **RIDDICK**. John **ROUNTREE** Charles **EASON**. James **COSTON** Ju^r. W^m A **MATHEWS**. Rubin **MILLER** W^m.. **HARRELL**. Ju^r. & Jacob **POWELL**.

The following persons was drawn & Sworn as Grand Jurors. David **PARKER** forman. Chas. **EASON**. Daniel **FIELDS**. Wm A. **MATHEWS** James **BENTON**. Tim^o. **ROGERS**. Aron **PIERCE**. Calvin **BRINKLY**. Peter **EURE**. W^m. H. **GOODMAN**. Jesse R **KEE**. Miles **BROWN** W^m. **BENTON** Senr. Tinson **EURE**. Gilbert **SAUNDERS**. Willis **BUNCH** Ed **BRIGGS**. & James **PARKER**.

Orderd that letters of adm^r be Granted to Henry **COSTON** upon the Estate of Fre^d. **LASSITER** dec^d that he give bonds of $400. with Ja^s. **COSTON** & H **GILLIAM** Secuty

Orderd that H **GILLIAM** be allow^d one Dollar for Blank Book

Orderd Miles **BRIGGS** enter into Bond as Constable with Joseph **GORDON** & Jno. O. **HUNTER** Security.

[126] Tuesday. 17th. Febry 1835.

Orderd that **REDMON** (a free boy of Colour) be bound as an apprentice to W^m. W. **COWPER** to Learn the trade of farmer.

Orderd that Willis. J. **RIDDICK** renew his Guardian Bonds with Sally **JAMES** & Noah **HINTON** with Ja^s R. **RIDDICK** & Ja^s. T. **FREEMAN** S^ty.

" Orderd that the County trustee pay Wills **COWPER** Three Dolls 20/100 an Error in his Tax.

Orderd that John **SAUNDERS** enter into Bonds with. John **GATLING** Robert **ROGERS**. Pryor **SAVAGE** & Miles **PARKER**, as Constable.

Orderd that Jethro **REED** (a free boy of Colour) be bound. as an apprentice to Wm **HANCY** [?] to learn the trade of farmer

February Court 1835

Orderd that. Augustus **REED** (a free boy of Colour) be bound as an apprentice to Henry **COSTON** to learn the trade of farmer

Orderd that William **GREEN** a bastard be bound as an apprtice [sic] to Henry **PRICE** to learn the trade of farmer

Orderd that John **WALTON** renew his Guardian Bond to Leah **HINTON** in the sum of $2000. with Tim^o. & Benbury **WALTON** Secuity [sic]

Orderd that Rubin **LASSITER** enter into Bond as Constable with Jos **RIDDICK** Ju^r. & Jas. T. **FREEMAN** Security.

A Division of the Negros belonging to the Estate of Barshaba **SEARS** was return^d. to Court & orderd to be filed.

An Inventory & acct. Sales of the Estate of Barshaba **SEARS** was returned to Court & orderd to be recorded.

Catharine **GREGORY** Gu^d to the orphans of Jos [?] **GREGORY** returned her accts into open Court & was orderd to be recorded

A Deed of Sale from Nancy **RIDDICK** to W^m. **GATLING** was proved in Open Court by Riddick **GATLING** & orderd to be registerd

Charles **EASON** Gu^d. to Eliz^a. & Senah **EASON** returnd returned [sic] into Open Court his accts which was orderd to be recorded.

The audited acct of Kedar **FELTON** adm^r of Fre^d. **HINTON** dec^d. was returnd into Open Court & orderd to be recorded

A Deed of Sale from Wright **HAYS** to Henry L. **BLOUNT** was ackg^d. in Open Court & orderd to be registerd.

A Bill of Sale from Charles **CARTER** to W^m. **SEARS** was proved in Open Court by the Oath of Jas **SIMPSON** & orderd to be registerd

Whit **STALLINS** Gu^d. to Mary **TAYLOR** returnd into Open Court his Acct. which was orderd to be recorded.

A Deed of Sale from **DAUGHTRY** & **FAULKS** trustees was proved & ackg^d. in Open Court to B. **WALTON** & orded to be registerd.

[127] Tuesday. 17th. Feb^{ry}. 1835

A Deed of Sale from ~~James~~ Simmons **JONES** to James **JONES** was proved in Open Court by John F **PARKER** & orderd to be registerd.

A Deed of Sale from James **BAKER** to Calwine [sic] **BRINKLEY** was proved in Open Court by Levey **SUMNER** & orderd to be registerd

Willis J. **RIDDICK** Gu^d. to the orphans of James **HINTON** returnd into Open Court his acct. which was orderd to be recorded

A Bond from Exum **JINKINS** to Thomas **SAUNDERS** & Wm W. **COWPER** was proved in Open Court by H. **GILLIAM** & orderd to be regis^{ted}

A Deed of Sale from Jonathan **WILLIAMS** to Demcy **PARKER** was proved in Open Court by W^m.

February Court 1835

SEARS & orderd to be registerd.

A Deed of Gift from Nathan RIDDICK to Jesse. R. KEE was ackg^d. in Open Court & orderd to be registerd.

An acct Sales of Estate Fre^d HINTON was returnd to Court by Kedar FELTON adm^r & orderd to be recorded.

Riddick GATLING Gu^d. to Chas SUMNERs orphans returnd his acct. into Open Court which was orderd to be recorded

A Power of attorney from James FREEMAN & Martha MOORE of Tenesscee [sic] was proved in Open Court by the Oathes of Demcy SPARKMAN & Levi BEEMAN & orderd to be registerd.

Nathan RIDDICK returnd his Guardian accts with William BROWN Sarah BROWN. Martha WALTON Drew TROTMON & & [sic] Henry WALTON which was orderd to be recorded.

An inventory of the Estate of W^m. HARRELL was returnd into Open Court & orderd to be recorded

A Deed of Sale from Ezekiel TROTMON to Nathan RIDDICK was proved in Open Court by Jesse R KEE & orderd to be registerd.

An acct Sales of the Estate of Barshaba SEARS de^d. was returnd to Court by the adm^r & orderd to be recorded.

A Deed in Trust from John. O. HUNTER to Tille. [sic] W. CARR was ackg^d. in Open Court & orderd to be registerd.

A Deed of Sale from Richard CROSS to Richad HINTON was proved in Open Court by James COSTON & orderd to be registerd

William E. PUGH Gu^d to the orphans of Henry PUGH returnd into Open Court his accts which was orderd to be recorded.

A Division of the Estate of Wm HARRELL dec^d was returnd into open Court & orderd to be filed.

An acct Current of the Estate of Wm HARRELL dec^d was returnd into Open Court & orderd to be recorded.

[128] Tuesday. 17th. Feb^{ry} 1835.

A Deed of Sale from Richard HINTON to Nathan PIERCE was ackg^d. in Open Court & orderd to be registerd.

Eliz^a. GRANBERY retur^d. her Gu^d acct with Geor. W. GRANBERY which was orderd to be recorded.

A Deed of Sale from Willie RIDDICK Trustee to Jesse WIGGINS was ackg^d in Open Court & orderd to be registerd.

A Deed of Sale from W^m. L. BOOTH to W^m W COWPER was proved in Open Court by John RIDDICK & orderd to be registerd.

A Bill of Sale from W^m. W. STEDMAN to Noah HARRELL was proved in Open Court by Saml. HARRELL & orderd to be registerd

Nathaniel EURE returnd his Guardian accts into Open Court with Susan A. SPEIGHT Sophia SPEIGHT & Wm BABB & ord to record [sic]

February Court 1835

Also with Corda & /May/ **WILLIAMS** which was ~~ree~~ Ord<u>ed</u> to be recorded

A Deed of Sale from John B **GATLING** to Richd **ODAM** was proved in Open Court by James **PRUDEN** & orderd to be registerd

James **COSTON** returnd into Open Court his Gu^d. acct. with James K **COSTON** & orderd to be recorded.

Nathl **EURE** returnd into Open Court his Gu^d. acct with the orphans of Lewis **EURE** & orderd to be recorded.

Thos **HOGARD** retur^d his Gu^d acct with Zac **SMITH** & recorded [sic]

A Deed of Sale from Nathan **RIDDICK** to **RIDDICK** & **STALLINS** was proved in Open Court by Jesse R **KEE** & orderd to be registerd.

A Deed of Sale from Jno **BROTHERS** to James **MATHIAS** was proved in Open Court by W^m. **ARNOLD** & orderd to be registerd.

George **COSTON** returnd into Open Court his Gu^d. accts with Mary **RIDDICK** & Isaac **HUNTER** & orderd to be recorded.

An audited acct of James **MORGAN** with Estate of A. **BENTON** & division [sic] Same was returnd into Open Court & orderd to be recorded.

An Inventory & acct. Sales of the Estate of John **JORDAN** was returnd into Open Court by the adm^r & orded to be recorded

A Deed of Sale from Jas R **RIDDICK** to W^m W **HARRELL** was ackg^d. in Open Court & orderd to be registerd.

An Inventory & acct Sales of the Estate of John **FREEMAN** dec^d. was returnd to Court by the adm^r & orderd to be recorded.

An Inventory of the Estate of Lucreatia **BEEMAN** dec^d. was returnd by the adm^r. & orderd to be recorded.

A Deed of Sale from Gilbert. G. **SAUNDERS** to Exum **JINKINS** was proved in Open Court by Jno. B. **JINKINS** & orderd to be registerd

[129] Tuesday. 17th. Feb^{ry}. 1835

John **WALTON** returnd into Open Court his Gu^d. ac<u>ot</u>. with Leah **HINTON** which was orderd to be recorded

James T. **FREEMAN** returnd into Open Court his Gu^d. acot. with the orphans of Robert **TAYLOR** & orderd to be recorded

A Deed of Sale from James R **RIDDICK** to Seth R. **MORGAN** was <u>akg</u>^d. in Open Court & orderd to be registerd.

A Deed of Sale from Jesse **EASON** to Jos **EASON** was prove<u>e</u>d in Open Court by Jethro. H. **RIDDICK** & orderd to be registerd.

An Inventory & acot Sales of the Estate of W^m. **BLANCHARD** dec^d. was returnd to Court by admr & orderd to be recorded.

February Court 1835

Joseph **HURDLE** returnd his Gu^d acct with Mary & Caroline **SUTTON** which was orderd to be recorded.

A Deed of Sale from Jas. R. **RIDDICK** to Elbert **RIDDICK** was ackg^d. in Open Court & orderd to be registerd.

Thomas **SAUNDERS** returnd into Open Court his Gu^d. acot. with Asa **ODAM**. & orderd to be recorded.

James **BOOTH** returnd into Open Court his Guardian accts with Sarah **HINTON** & John **HARE**s orphans & orderd to be recorded

State }
vs } F & A. D [or &C]
John **CUFF** } The following Jurors Jos **HURDLE**. Briant **BROTHERS**. Allen **SMITH**. Sol **SMALL** W^m. **HARRELL** John **BARNES**. Jno. P. **BENTON** Prior **SAVAGE** James **COSTON** Ju^r Sol **ROUNTREE**. Demcy **PARKER**. & Miles **PARKER** Jur being imp^d. & Sworn Say def^d. is Guilty as chg^d after which the def^d. was dischg^d.

John. C. **GORDON** Exor of John **SMALL** & others
vs
Ann **SMALL** widow of Jno **SMALL**. Rubin **SMALL** Jacob **POWELL** & wife Eliz^a. Burwell **BROTHERS** & wife Martha John **SMALL** & James A **SMALL** Christian **SMALL**. & Charity **SMALL** infants without any Guardian orderd that. W^m. W. **STEDMAN** Clk of this Court be appointed Gu^d. ad. litum to the infant heirs herin before named to wit. James. A. **SMALL** Christian **SMALL**. Charity **SMALL**. Jo **SMALL** [sic] & by Virtues of Notin [?] is hereby accepted by all the parties. & the Gu^d. ad litem Whereupon the following issue was made up for the Jury Is the paper Writing now offerd for probate by John. C. **GORDON** as the last will & Testament of

[130] John **SMALL** dec^d.
Rep & issue. The following Jurors (to wit) Abel **ROGERSON**. Jethro **WILLEY**. Levi **ROGERS**. John **BROWN**. Nathl **EURE**. Ab **SPIVEY**. Marmaduke **NORFLEET** John **SAUNDERS**. Rubin **HINTON**. Leven **HOFFLUR**. Jesse **PILAND** & Miles **PARKER** Ju^r being duly impanell^d & sworn find the paper writing offerd by Jno C **GORDON** for probate as the last will & Testament of John **SMALL** is not the will of John **SMALL**.

An acct. Current of Daniel **WILLIAMS** Exor of George **KITTRELL** dec^d was return^d & orderd to be recorded

The Court adjournd untill Wednesday.
Wednesday 18th Feb^{ry}. Court met according to adjourment
Present.. Jos **RIDDICK**. Thomas **SAUNDERS** & Whit **STALLINS** Esqr^s.

Jeptha **FAULKS**. Mills **ROBERTS**. W^m. E. **PUGH**. Abel **ROGERSON**. William M **DORSEY**. & John S. **ROBERTS**. Surrended the body of Will **PETTY** in a Suite at the instance of Thomas **WHITE** ag^t. him & orderd that they be discharged from his bail & he was orderd into the Custody of the Shff. It was orderd at the Same time that the Said Bail be dischard [sic] in an other Case of Same vs. Same & Jon. H. **HAUGHTON**

Joseph **FREEMAN** } appl [sic]
vs }
John. P. **SAVAGE** } The following Jurors. (to wit) Isaac **PIERCE**. John **BARNES**. Allen **SMITH** W^m. H. **HARRELL**. Thomas **SMITH**. Sol **ROUNTREE**. Levi **ROGERS** Sol **SMALL**. Benjn **WYNNS**. Demsey **PARKER**. James **COSTON** Ju^r & Miles **PARKER** being duly Sworn. & imp^d. find all the issues infavor Dfn^d

The last will & Testament of Richard **SMITH** dec^d. was Exhibited into Open Court by Thomas **SMITH**

February Court 1835

& was duly proved by the Oath of William **HUDGINS** one of the Subscribing witnesses thereto the Exor Noah **HARRELL** therein named refused to qualify. It was orderd therefore that letters ~~Testam~~ of admistration with the will annexed be Granted unto Thomas **SMITH** at Same time he appeard & give Bond & Security & qualified agreeable to Law. orderd that Said will be recorded.

Orderd that letters of admistration be Granted upon the Estate of John **SMALL** dec^d. unto John C. **GORDON** that he enter into Bonds for $2000. with Joseph **GORDON** & Burwell **BROTHERS** Security.

[131] Wednesday. 18th. Feb^{ry}. [sic]

Orderd that Henry **PHELPS** a free boy of Colour aged 14 years be bound an apprentice to James **WILLIAMS** to be a farmer

" It was orderd that the Commissioners appointed to Superintend the building the Court House at Gatesville be authorized to make such additions to the building as they may deem proper & adviseable provided it Can be perform^d. for a faire [sic] Compensation

" Orderd that Lassiter **RIDDICK** Coroner be allow^d. Twenty Dolls for holding inquest upon the bodies of Cheaton [?] **DANIEL** & a negro Girl belonging to Benbury **WALTON**. that the County trustee pay the same.

" Orderd that Henry **GILLIAM**. John. C. **GORDON**. W^m. G. **DAUGHTRY** & Mills **ROBERTS** or any three of them divide the Suplus [sic] Estate of Henry **PUGH** dec^d. in the hands of Wm E. **PUGH** Exor agreeable to the last will & Testament of Said Henry **PUGH** dec^d.

" Orderd that the following persons be appointed Inspectors to hold an Election for the Convention. (to wit)
" at Gatesville. Henry R. **PUGH** & John R **NORFLEET**.
" at. Mintonsville. Jesse. R. **KEE** & John **MITCHEL**.
" at. **HUNTER**s Mill. W^m. H. **HARRELL** & Thomas **RIDDICK**.
" at. **GOODMAN**s. Jasons **SAUNDERS** Cap. William **LEE** & W^m. **GOODMAN** Esqr.
" In William L **BOOTH**s Cap^{cy}. W^m. L. **BOOTH** & Nathl. **HARRELL**
" at the folley. Henry **RIDDICK** & James **MORGAN**.
" at **HASLIP**s [sic] Simon **WALTERS**. &. James **SAVAGE**

Orderd that the Clk of the Court Erase from the docket a Judgement entered up in a Suite at the instance of W^m. W. **COWPER** vs Thomas **SAUNDERS** adm^r. of Barshaba **SEARS** dec^d.

" Orderd that Henry **GILLIAM**. John **WALTON**. James R. **RIDDICK** & Thomas **SAUNDERS** or any three audite & State the acts. of Levi **ROGERS** adm^r. of Eanas [sic] **SCARBOROUGH** dec^d. & divide the Same.

" Orderd that James **BOOTH**. Overseer of the New road leading through the White pot pocoson appear at the next Court to Shew Cause why James R **RIDDICK**s hands should not be taken off his road & put upon the Road under Lassiter **RIDDICK** overseer.

" Orderd that Simmons **ROUNTREE** take Charge as overseer of the road, that part of the road formerly work^d. by Jno D. **PIPKIN** Say from Mrs Ann **HARVEY**s to **WIGGINS** Hill.

Orderd that Andrew **BAKER** be permitted to with draw from

[132] the County Court office a Case at his instance against Quinton H. **TROTMON** & that the Clk retain in S^d office a Copy of the Same

Orderd that Redman **WALKER** a free boy of Colour be bound an apprentice to W^m. W. **COWPER** to be

February Court 1835

a farmer.

Orderd that. John /S./ **ROBERTS** be allow^d the Sum of Forty four Dolls for Sundry bed Steads Cotts &c. Test W^m. W **STEDMAN** Clk By H. **GILLIAM**. D. C

State of No. Carolina }
    Gates County} SS [?]
At a Court of pleas & qr Sessions begun & held for the County of Gates at the Court House in Gatesville on the. 3rd. monday in May 1835. 18th. day.
    Present. Willis. F. **RIDDICK**. Jos **RIDDICK**. Henry **COSTEN** & B **BALLAD**

The Shff returnd the following persons to Serve this Term as Jurors to wit. James **BOOTH**. John **KING**. Saml. **HARRELL**. Wm **MILLER** Ju^r Robert **HILL** Ju^r. Lewis **GREEN**. Blake **BRADY**. James **SUMNER** Noah **HINTON**. Benj. **FRANKLIN**. Am$\underline{as}$ **HOBBS**. Wm **MILLER** Senr. Belver **SEARS**. Eph **BUNCH**. James **BRINKLY**. W^m. **HOBBS**. James **ARLINE**. &. Benj. **SAUNDERS**. Absalom **BLANCHARD**. Robt. **WILSON** John **POWELL**. Fras **SMITH**. John W. **BARR**. Miles **HOWELL**. Jesse **BENTON**. Ervan **HARRELL**. ~~Lewis G~~ James **BROWN** of Ja^s. John **TAYLOR** W^m. **JONES**. John **SAUNDERS** John **HINTON** Senr. & Leven **HOFFLER**.
The following persons were drawn & Charged as Grand Jurors James **BOOTH** (foreman) John **KING**. Saml **HARRELL**. W^m. **MILLER** Jur Robt. **HILL** Ju^r. Lewis **GREEN**. Blake **BRADY**. James **SUMNER**. Noah **HINTON**. Benj. **FRANKLIN**. Amas **HOBBS** Wm **MILLER** Senr. James **ARLINE** & Benj **SAUNDERS**.

A Bill [sic] Sale from Charles **CARTER** & Lewis **CARTER** to W^m. **SEARS** was proved in Open Court by the Oath of John **ALLEN** & orderd to be regis^d.

A $\underline{deed}$ in Trust from Harrison **ELLIS** to James **MORGAN** was proved in open Court by the Oath of John **BARNES** & was orderd to be registerd

A Deed in Trust from John **ARNOLD** to Alfred **BALLARD** was proved in Open Court by the Oath of John **WIGGINS** & orderd to be regist$\underline{ed}$

The Guardian of Parthenia **PARKER** returnd his acot into Open Court which was orderd to be recorded.

[133] Tuesday Morning. 19th May 18345

The Court Met according to adjour$\underline{n}$ment.
Present. John **WILLEY** Joseph **RIDDICK**. W^m. **HUDGINS** W^m. W. **COWPER** & Demcy **KNIGHT** Esqrs.

An acct. Current of the Estate of W^m. **KING** dec^d. was returned by Jesse **HOBBS** the Exo^r & orderd to be recorded

A Deed of Sale from Levi **CREECY** to James **ARLINE** was ack^d. in Open Court by Levi **CREECY** & orderd to be registerd.

A Bill of Sale from Cyntha **BRINKLY** & Calvin **BRINKLEY** /to Leah **ROUNTREE**/ was proved in Open Court by the Oath of Henry **SPIVEY** & orderd to be registed

A Bill of Sale from David **OUTLAW** to James **COSTON** was proved in Open Court by the Oath R. **RAWLS** & orderd to be registerd.

An Inventory of the Estate of John **SMALL** dec^d. was returnd into Open Court & orderd to be recorded.

David **MELTEARE** returnd into Open Court his acct as Gu^d. to Christian **PARKER** which was orderd to be recorded. An Inventory of the Estate of Edwin **MATHIAS** was returnd into Court & orderd to be

May Court 1835

recorded.

A Release from Jethro **WILLEY** to Levi **CREECY** was proved in Open Court by the Oath of Henry **WILLEY** & ord^{ed} to be registerd

A Deed of Sale from Henry **STALLINS** to Edward **HOBBS** was proved in Open Court by the Oath of J^{no}. **MITCHEL** & orderd to be registerd

A Deed of Sale from Timothy **ROGERS** to Eliz^a. **LEE** was proved in Open Court by the Oath of Isaac **WILLIAMS** & orderd to be registerd

A Deed of Sale from W^m. **BROWN** to John **BROWN** was proved in Open Court by the Oath of Briant **BROTHERS** & orderd to be registerd

A Deed of Sale from James **ARLINE** to Joshua **LIVESAY** was proved in Open Court by the Oath of James **CARTER** & orderd to be regis^d

A Deed of Sale from Jacob **POWELL** to Willie. P. **JONES** was proved in Open Court by the Oath of Jos **GORDON** & orderd to be registerd.

John **MATTHEWS** Gu^d. to Margaret. & Eliz^a. **BENTON** Exhibited into Open Court his accts which was orderd to be recorded.

The Last will & Testament of W^m. **PARKER** dec^d. was offerd for probate & thereis [?] being no Executor appointed thereto. the Execution of the will was proved in due form of Law by John **BENTON** a Subscribing Witness thereto Martha **PARKER** widow of the said W^m. **PARKER** appearing in Open Court & refusing to administer. Whereupon adm$_in$stration with the will annexed was Co$_m$itted to Jesse **WIGGINS** he giving bond in $2000 with James **MORGAN** & Barnes **GOODMAN** Security.

[134] 19th. May 18.35 [sic]

A Deed of Sale from James **FIGG** to John **FIGG** was proved in Open Court by the Oath of John **MATHWS** [sic] & ored [sic] to be regis^d.

An acct. Sales & inventory of the Estate of Jacob **POWELL** was returnd into Open Court by David **PARKER** adm^r. & orderd to be recorded.

An acct. Sales of the Estate of Henry **GREEN** dec^d. was returnd into Open Court by Jos **GORDON** the adm^r. & orderd to be recorded.

An acct. Sales & inventory of the Estate of Isaac **PIERCE** dec^d. was returnd into Open Court by Jos **GORDON** adm^r. &. Orderd to be recorded.

An Inventory /& acct Sales/ of the Estate of Seth **BENTON** dec^d. was returnd into Open Court by James & Ab **BENTON** Executors & orderd to be recorded

A division of the Negros belonging to the heirs of Geor [sic] **SUTTON** dec^d. was returnd into Open Court & orderd to be filed

A relinquishment from Henry **GILLIAM** to John D **PIPKIN** was proved in Open Court by the Oath of John **WILLY** & orderd to be regis^d.

An acct. of the hire Negros & rent lands belonging to the Estate of Solomon **EASON** was returnd by the Executor & orderd to be recorded

A deed of Sale from W^m. E **PUGH** Clk &. M. to Fredrick **JONES** was ackg^d. in Open Court & orderd to be registerd.

May Court 1835

A Deed of Sale from Hardy H. C JONES to Miles HOWELL. was proveed in Open Court by the Oath of Myles PARKER & orded to be registerd

A deed of Sale from John LEWIS to Nathl. CULLINS was proved in Open Court by the Oath of W^m. L. BOOTH & orderd to be registered

A Deed of Sale from John RIDDICK to W^m. W. COWPER was ackg^d. in Open Court & orderd to be registerd.

A deed of Sale from David ROOKS to W^m. SEARS was proved in open Court by the Oath of John WILLY & orderd to be ~~recorded~~ registerd

A deed of Sale from Levi ROGERS Exor to Timothy HAYS was proved in Open Court by the Oath of Jethro WILLEY & orded to be registerd

A Deed of Sale from John D. PIPKIN to Isaac PIPKIN was proved in Open Court by the Oath of John SAUNDERS & orderd to be regist^d.

A Gu^d. acct. of Demcy PARKER to Henry JONES. was returnd into Open Court & orderd to be recorded.

A deed of Sale from W^m. E. PUGH Clk. & M. to Isaac PIPKIN was ackg^d. in Open Court & orderd to be registerd.

An act. Current of the Estate of James BRINKLY dec^d. with Archibald ELLIS adm^r was returnd into Open Court & orderd to be record [sic]

A deed of Sale from James BOYCE to Richard ODAM was proved in Open Court by the Oath of Etth^d. CROSS & orderd to be registerd

[135] 19th. May 1835

An acct. Current of the Estate Robt. SMITH was returnd into Open Court by the Executrix & orderd to be recorded.

A deed of Sale from Saml. S. BOND to James COSTON was proved in Open Court by the Oath of B. B. BALLARD & orderd to be register [sic]

A deed in Trust from Quinton. H. TROTMON to Jesse R. KEE was proved in Open Court by the Oath of Nathan RIDDICK & orded to be regis^d.

A deed of Sale from Robt P HAYS to Geor POLSON was proved in Open Court by the Oath of Lassiter RIDDICK & orderd to be registerd.

A deed of Sale from. Elisha UMPHLET to Ab PRUDEN was proved in Open Court by the Oath of Wm H. SAVAGE & orderd to be registerd

A deed of Sale from Jesse WIGGINS & Rizup [sic] RAWLS to Allen DAUGHTY was ackg^d. in Open Court & orded to be registerd

A deed of Sale from Jesse MATHIAS. to Joseph MATHIAS was proved in Open Court by Demsey VANN & orderd to be registerd.

An acct. Current of the Estate of Ab PIERCE with the Executor was returnd into Open Court & orderd to be recorded.

An acct. of the Sales of Fre^d. LASSITER dec^d. was returnd into Open Court & orderd to be recorded.

May Court 1835

An acct. Current of the Estate of Willie **JINKINS** dec^d. with the admr. was returnd into Open Court & orderd to be recorded.

issd. Orderd that the County Trustee pay Henry **GILLIAM** Clk Sup Court sundry bills Cost to amt. . Twenty three Dolls & 78/100.

issd. Orderd that the County Trustee pay W^m. W. **STEDMAN** Clk this Court Sundry bills Cost to the amt one hundred & Six Dolls & 85/100.

issd. Orderd that the County Trustee pay W^m W **STEDMAN** Fifty Dollars for extra Services as Clk this Court.

Orderd that Henry **GILLIAM** be all^d. Thirty five Dollars for Stationary for one year. & Some Extra Services.

issd. Orderd that Lassiter **RIDDICK** be all^d. two Dolls & 76/100 for a deduction James **GOODMAN**s. Tax also Twenty Dollars for holding two inquest [sic] upon. John. D. **MATHEWS**. & Ngro [sic] **TIBE** [?] property Jno **GATLING**

Orderd that Jesse **WIGGINS** adm^r of W^m. **PARKER** dec^d. Sell what of the Negros of Said ~~Estate~~ **PARKER**s may remain after the trustee in the deed of Trust. from S^d. **PARKER** for the Security of David **BENTO_** has Sold a Sufficiency to Satisfy Said Trust.

issd. Orderd that. Mills **EURE**. W^m. L. **BOOTH** & Demcy **SPARKMAN** audite & Settle the accts. of Isaac & James **PILAND** dec^d. with Mills **PILAND** Amrd. [sic] & report to Next Court & divi$\underline{d}$ the Same

[136] 19th. May 1835.

issd.. Orderd that. the county Trustee refund unto Robert. **BLANCHARD** one Dollar & 20/100 Error in Tax.

Orderd that Ab **SMITH** be app^d. Gu^d. to Jos **LANDING** orphan W^m. **LANDING** & enter into Bonds for $200. Rich^d. **ODAM** & Thos **HOGARD**

" Orderd that John **MITCHEL** Nathan **RIDDICK**. Jethro. H. **RIDDICK** & Isaac **HARRELL** or any three audite & Settle the Estate of Wm. **BLANCHARD** dec^d. & divide the Same among the heirs & make report.

Orderd that. W^m. W. **COWPER** Gu^d. to Celia **LEWIS** pay Mary **CULLINS**. Sixty Dollars for Keeping s^d. Celia one year from Feb^{ry}. 1835 to Feb^{ry}. 1836.

Orderd that. James **HUNTER** & Asa **HUNTER** two free boys of Colour be bound as apprentices to Abel **ROGERSON**.

issd. Orderd that. Riddick **MATHEWS** be permited to have a retail Licenc to retail Spirits at one place in Gatesville.

issd Orderd that a Notic [sic] issue to Kinchen **NORFLEET**. to appear at next Court. to Shew Cause why James **BOOTH** Should not have his hands & Work the part of road which **NORFLEET** now Works

issd. Orderd that. James R **RIDDICK**^{s} hands Work on Lassiter **RIDDICK**s road leading from the hone$\underline{e}$y pots to. Jno. B **BAKER**s lane instead of Working on Jas **BOOTH**s road.

Orderd that the County Tax & Court House Tax be the Same as that Collected for the year 1833. & that in addition to the parish Tax of 1833. the Sum of 5/100 on Each poll & 5/100 on Each 100$ Valuation Lands be laid & Collected.

May Court 1835

Orderd that Notic. to the overseer of the road leading from John. B. BAKERs. to Ab. W. PARKEs [sic] to Shew Cause why Some of his hands Shall not Work on the road under W^m.. HARVEY [?]

issd. Orderd that. the County trustee pay Seth BENTON one Doll & 20/100 for an Error in listing one poll.

Orderd that Allan SMITH. be appointed County. Surveyor with the present. Surveyor.

issd Orderd that Joseph EASON. be appointed overseer on the road leading from Josiah BRIGGS to archibald ELLIS in room of Chas. EASON.

issd Orderd that John KING be appointed overseer in Stead Ezekiel LASSITER leading from Ab W PARKERs to Gatesville.

issd Orderd that. Abraham PRUDEN be appointed overseer on the road from WOODs old field to Winton Cosway [sic] in room Ab. SMITH.

[137] 19th. May 1835

issd. Orderd that. Henry BOND be appt^d overseer. of the road. leading from the fork of the road at Thomas WALTONs place to the MINGO path Neare. James W RIDDICKs plantation in room of Walton FREMAN decd.

issd. Orderd that John LOVET be permitted to have a retail Licenc to retail Spiritious Liquors at one place in Gatesville

issd. Orderd that the following persons be appointed inspectors at the different Elections in Gates County. at the ensuing Elections in Gates County. (to wit.)
at. the Folley. Miles BRIGGS Henry RIDDICK. James MORGAN
" " "   Demsey KNIGHT. & W^m. S. COWPER
" HUNTERs Mill, Robert HILL Senr. Joseph GORDON. Jethro RIDDICK
" " " " John G. LILES. & George COSTON
at Mintonsville. John MITCHEL. James BRINKLEY. Henry
" " "   SPIVEY. Ja^s. T FREEMAN & James BOYCE
at Gatesville. Jos RIDDICK Prior SAVAGE. Sim^{ns}. ROUNTREE
" "   Rubin HINTON & James BOOTH.
at Demsey PARKERs. Levi EURE. Demsey SPARKMAN. Elisha PARKER
" " ". Mills SPARKMAN & Mills EURE.
at W^m.. H. GOODMAN. Jos FREEMAN. W^m. LEE W^m. GATLING
" " " Wm GOODMAN Esqr. & John LANGSTON
at John HALETTs [sic] Barnes GOODMAN. Simon WALTERS Geor SMITH
" " " " James SAVAGE & W^m. K. MOORE

issd. Orderd that Mills ROBERTS be appointed overseer of the road leading from POWELLs Shop to the fork road neare Rubin HINTONs in room Nathan NIXON.

issd Orded that Jethro WILLY be allow^d. Seven Dollars &. 80/100 for Sundry Services in State Cases.

issd Orderd that Rubin PILAND be appointed overseer of the road leading from Saram Creek landing to the White Oak branch in room W^m. H. SAVAGE.

issd Orderd that Thomas LASSITER be appt^d. overseer of the road leading from the Watrey Swamp to HUNTERs Mill in room E. JONES

issd Orderd that George COSTONs hands at his HUDGINS plantation Work on the road leading from the honey pot road ~~to~~ a Cross DUKEs Creek also Marmaduke NORFLEETs hands at his HARRIS plantation Work on Same

103

May Court 1835

issd. Orderd that W^m. **HARVEY** be app^d overseer road. from **HARVEY**s Mill to the x road in room Simmons **ROUNTREE**.

[138] 19th. May 1835

issd. Orderd that Ab W **PARKER** have a licenc to retail Spirits at his Store for one yeare.

issd. Orderd that John **WALKER** a free man of Colour from V^a. have a licenc to Sell Cakes & oysters in S^d County one yeare

issd Orderd that the following Justices be appointed to take the list of Taxes this yeare. to wit.
John. C. **GORDON** in Folly district. **HUNTER**s Mill. Jos **RIDDICK**
Whit **STALLINGS. MINTON**s. do. Gatesville. W^m. G. **DAUGHTRY**.
Ab W **PARKER**s. **BOOTH**s.   do. **DOUGHTRY**s. Barnes **GOODMAN**
Richard **ODAIM** [sic] in Jason **SAUNDERS** district.

issd. Orderd that the County trustee pay Jethro H **RIDDICK** twenty three Dollars & 25/100 a mistake in Solomon **EASON**s Taxes

issd. Orderd that the Shff be allow^d Fifty Dollars for Extra Services

issd. Orderd that W^m. E. **PUGH** County att^ny. be all^d. Fifty Dollas for Extra Services

issd Orderd that the County trustee pay Mary **HUDGINS** two Dolls 40/100 for two polls too much Charged in Taxes

An acct. Current of the Estate of Seth **BENTON** dec^d. with the Exors was returnd into open Cout & orderd to be recorded

State   } A. & B.
 vs   }
Ab **SPIVEY**} The following Jurors. (to Wit) Miles **HOWELL**. W^m. **SEARS**. John **BRADY**. Hardy **CROSS**. Ja^s. **BROWN** of Ja^s. John **HINTON**. Senr. Leven **HOFFLER**. Whit **HILL** James **WILLIAMS** Demcy **PARKER**. Jethro **WILLEY**. & Miles **PARKER** Jur. being duly Sworn & impanell^d. say that the def^d. is Guilty by the Court find [sic] 2$.

State   }
 vs   } Nusame. [?]
John **BENTON** } The Same Jury except Rubin **HINTON** in room of James **BROWN**. being Sworn & impanel^d. Say def^d is not Guilty.

State   }
 vs   } A. &. B.
Rubin **HINTON** } The Same Jury exept [sic] Rubin **HINTON** in his room James **BROWN**. Say def^d. is not Guilty.

Sarah **SMITH** widow of Richard **SMITH** dec^d. Came into Court & enterd her desent from her said husbands will.

John A **ROBERTS** }
     vs   }
Benj **WYNNS**.   } The following Jury (to Wit) John **BRADY**. Abel **ROGERSON**. Jethro **WILLY**. James **WILLIAMS**. Miles **PARKER**. Absalom **BLANCHARD**. James **BROWN**. Levin **HOFFLER**. Whit **HILL**. John **HINTON**. Hardy **CROSS** & Miles **HOWELL**. being duly Sworn & impaell^d find all the issues infavour of the defendant.

May Court 1835

[139] 219th. May 1835
Simmonds **ROUNTREE** }
    vs   }
Nusum **CUFF**   } The following Jurors (to Wit) John **BRADY** Fisher **FELTON**. Abel **ROGERSON**. Briant **BROTHERS**. Whitmil **HILL**. Ab. **SPIVEY**. John **FIGG**. James **BROWN** Leven **HOFFLER**. Miles **HOWELL**. John **HINTON**. & Absalom **BLANCHARD** being duly Sworn & inpanell^d. find all the issues infavour of the def^d. from which said Verdict the plaintiff prayed for & obtained an appeal to the next Sup Court of Law to be held for the County of Gates. & enterd into bond with Henry **GILLIAM** & Jethro **WILLEY**. Securities.

Abraham W. **PARKER** } Case
    vs   }
Law. S. **DAUGHTRY** } It appearing to the Court that Lawrence S. **DAUGHTRY**. has given Notice to his Creditors that he intended to take the benefit of the act of assembley pass^d in 1822 for the relief of Insolvent debtors. & whereas None of his Creditors made opposition. thereto. he was permitted to take the Same in due form & it was orderd that his Bonds be discharged from Such in all the Cases in which he has Notified his Creditors.

Will W. **COWPER** } Debt
    vs   }
Thomas **SAUNDERS** admr} The following Jurors (to Wit) John **BRADY**. Fisher **FELTON** Abel **ROGERSON**. Briant **BROTHERS**. Whit **HILL**. Ab **SPIVEY** John **FIGG**. James **BROWN**. Leven **HOFFLER**. Miles **HOWELL**. John **HINTON** & Absalom **BLANCHARD**. being duly Sworn & inpanll^d find all the issues infavour of the Pltff & asses his damage to $80. with intes [sic] from 15th March 1834.

      Court adjournd untill Wednesday morning
    Wednesday Morning Court met.
Present. Thomas **SAUNDERS**. John **WALTON** & W^m.. G. **DAUGHTRY** Esq^{rs}.

Nathan **RIDDICK** Exhibited his acct as County Trustee which was rec^d. by the Court & orderd to be filed.

Allen **SMITH** was appointed one of the County Surveyors he appeard in Open Court enterd into Bond & was qualified [Remainder of page is blank.]

[140] John. C. **GORDON** Gu^d. to Israel & W^m. **BEEMAN**.
John C **GORDON** admr of Lucreatia **BEEMAN** & Eliz^a **BEEMAN**
    vs
Levi **BEEMAN** & Demsy **SPARKMAN** as Exors of John **BEEMAN** dec^d. report made & Confirmd. orderd that H **GILLIAM** be ale^d. $20 for report This Cause Coming on to be heard upon the pleadings the report of the refferee & the Evidence. it. is orderd adjudged & decreed that the petitiones recover of the defendants. the Sum of Two thousand One hundred & ninty Six Dollars & 76.½.^{Cts}. It is further orderd that. the Sum of . 20$ allow^d. for report togeather with all the legal Tax Cost be paid Out of the said fund of two thousand one hundred & Ninty Six Dolls & 76.½.

At a County Court of pleas & qr Sessions held for the County of Gates at the Court House in Gatesville on 3rd. monday in August 1835.. 17th. day.
    Present Demsy **KNIGHT** Jos **RIDDICK**. Henry **WILLEY** & Richard **ODAM** Esqr.

A Deed of Sale from W^m. G. **DAUGHTRY** to John **LOVET** was ack^g in Open Court & orderd to be registerd.

An audited acct of the Estate of James & Isaac **PILAND** & division of the Same was Exhibited into Open Court & ordered to be recorded.

105

August Court 1835

An Inventory of the Estate of Richard **SMITH** dec^d. was Exhibited into Open Court by the adm^r. & orderd to be recorded

The last will & Testament of Jacob **ODAM** dec^d. was Exhibited into Open Court. & proven by the Oath of Thomas **HOGARD** & Ethel^d **CROSS**. two of the Subscribing witnesses thereto & at Same time Rich^d. **ODAM** the Exor therin name^d Came into Court & qualified agreeable to Law orderd that the Same be recorded.

An audited acct. & division of the Estate of Jesse **SAVAGE** was Exhibited into Court & orderd to be recorded.

A Deed of Sale from W^m. **GATLING** to James **WILLIAMS** was proved in Open Court by the Oath of Rich^d. **ODAM** & orderd to be registerd.

A Deed of Sale from Lem^l. **BENTON** to Jno **BENTON** was proved in Open Court by Oath of Henry H. **BENTON** & orderd to be registerd.

[141] August. 1835.

A Deed of Sale from Cyphan [sic] **CROSS** to James **WILLIAMS** was proved in Open Court by the Oath of Rich^d. **ODAM** a Witness & orderd to be registerd

An audited acc^t. & division of the Estate of Lucreatia **BEEMAN** infant and [sic] was Exhibited into Open Court by the admr. & orderd to be recorded.

An acct. of Pedlers & retail Licenc iss^d. by the Shff James R **RIDDICK** was Exhbited into Court Sworn to & orderd to be filed.

A Division of the Estate of Henry **PUGH** dec^d. was Exhibited into Open Court & orderd to be recorded.

Demsy **PARKER** former Gu^d. to Louisa **JONES** [sic] was Exhibited into Open Court & orderd to be recorded.

The last will. & Testament of Henry **BRIGGS** dec^d. was proved in Open Court by the Oath of John C. **GORDON** & at the same time the Executors Edward **BRIGGS** & Miles **BRIGGS**. Came into Open Court & qualified as the Law requires orded that the same. be recorded.

The Court. adjourned untill Tuesday Morning
    Tuesday Morning Court Met according to [End of entry.]
Present. Jno. C. **GORDON**. Jos **RIDDICK**. Henry **COSTON**. Rid **GATLING**.

The following Grand Jurors was drawn & sworn. (to wit) Humphry **PARKER**. Fre^d. **ROOKS**. Jos **GATLING**. W^m. A. **MATHEWS**. Marmk. [sic] **BAKER**. Edwin **CROSS** Levi **SUMNER**. Daniel **WILLIAMS**. Jno. **ALPHIN** Guy **HOBBS**. James **JONES** Senr. Jonas **HINTON**. Jos **HURDLE**. James **BRIN**. Tim^o. **SPIVEY** & Simonds **ROUNTREE**.

Eliz^a. **BRIGGS** Came into Open Court & enterd her di<u>sen</u>t to the will of her husband Henry **BRIGGS** dec^d.

State   }
 vs   }
Jethro **WILLEY** } The following Jurors. (to wit) Peter **EURE**. Nathl **EURE** W^m.. **MILLER** Jur. W^m. F. **BENNETT** James. M. **RIDDICK** James A. **HARRELL**. Demsey **PARKER**. Jas. T. **FREEMAN** Tinson **EURE**. Sol **ROUNTREE**. Mills **SPARKMAN**. Miles **PARKER** Jur being imp^d. & sworn (withdrawn).

August Court 1835

A Deed of Sale from Ab **HURDLE** to Jesse **EASON** was proved in Open Court by the Oath of Jethro H **RIDDICK** & orderd to be registerd.

A Deed of Sale from Saml. **HARRELL** to Michael **WILLIAMS** was ~~proved~~ ackg^d. in Open Court & orderd to be registerd.

The Last will & Testament of James **LASSITER** dec^d. was Exhibited into Open Court & proved by the Oath of John **GATLING** one of the Subscribing witnesses thereto. at the Same [sic] George **COSTON** & Thomas **COSTON** two of the Exors therein named appeard & qualified agreeable to Law orderd that the Same be recorded.

[142] Tusday.. 18th Augt. 1835.

The following insolvents was allow^d. the Shff of Gates County in the Settlement of his Taxes (to wit) to Jethro. H. **RIDDICK** the number of 30. to Lassiter **RIDDICK**. Forty.

A Deed of Sale from John **HINTON** Sen to W^m. **HINTON** was ackg^d: in Open Court & orderd to be registerd.

A Deed of Sale from Saml. **BROWN** ~~was~~ to Henry **GILLIAM** was proved in Open Court by Benj **BROWN** & orderd to be registerd.

A Lease from James **BENTON** to Jacob **SPEIGHT** & wife was proved in Open Court. by W^m. **HUDGINS** & orderd to be registerd.

An acct Sales of the Estate of Jesse **SAVAGE** dec^d. was Exhibited into Open Court & orderd to be recorded.

A Deed of Sale from Jos **EASON** to Jesse **EASON** was Exhibited into Open Court proved by Jethro H **RIDDICK** & orderd to be registerd

Orderd that the following persons be appointed patroll Comittes [sic] for Honey pot District.   Jos **RIDDICK** Lassiter **RIDDICK** Jos R **RIDDICK**
Cap Wm **BOOTH**s district.   John **RIDDICK** W^m. L. **BOOTH** & Demsy **SPARKMAN**
~~HUNTERs Mill~~ /Bush **RIDDICK**/   " Abel **ROGERSON** Timo **WALTON**. & Isaac S **HARRELL**
HUNTERs Mill   " Jethro H **RIDDICK** Thos. **RIDDICK** & Henry **COSTON**
Nathl **DAUGHTEY**s   " Elbert. H. **RIDDICK** Barnes **GOODMAN** Simon **WALTERS**
Cap **SAUNDES**   " Wm **GOODMAN** Isaac **PIPKIN** & Rid **GATLING**
Folley District   " Jno C **GORDON**. Ed R **HUNTER** & Willis. F. **RIDDICK**

Orderd that Wm. **MORGAN** orphan of Seth be bound as an apprentice to John **LOVET**.

" Orderd that Allen **SMITH** be appointed overseer of the road leading from **KITTRELL**s Meeting house to the Honey pot road in room of James **BOOTH** resigned. the hands are. James **PARKER**s Miles **PARKER**s. Leven **CUFF** Daniel **CUFF** Malachia **CUFF**. Thos **PEEL** Wm. **CLEAVES** hands. EASONs. & James **BOOTH**s hands at his plantation & Jack **CUFF**

Letters of admr on the Estate of Mary **FIELDS** was granted to James **WILLIAMS** & he ent$\underline{ed}$ into Bond with John **FIGG** Security

Orderd that John **HUDGINS** orphan of Leven **HUDGINS** be bound an apprentice to Wm **HUDGINS**.

Letters of admr on the Estate of Susan E **PUGH** was granted to Wm E. **PUGH**. & he give bond in the sum of $1500. Jno O **HUNTER** Lass. **RIDDICK**

" Orderd that Jethro H **RIDDICK** be all^d Twenty Dolls & 80/100 for Services as Constable &c

August Court 1835

James. R. **RIDDICK** Shff renewed his Shff Bonds which was approved of & orderd to be filed.

[143] Tusday 18th Augt. 1835

Letters of admr upon the Estate of Thos **SMITH** ded with the will annexed was granted to John **SMITH** & he enter into Bond & Secuity

" Orderd that Henry **GILLIAM** be allowd Sixty five Dollas & 70/100 for repaires on Creek Bridge & the Court House.

" Orderd that Mormaduke **BAKER** be appointed overseer of the road leading from the Va. line to Blake **BAKER**s hill in room Nathl **DOUGHTY** resigned

letters of admr upon Estate Martha J. **MATHEWS** was granted to E. **MATHEWS** & he ented into Bond & Security.

" Orderd that Jethro H **RIDDICK** be alld ~~5~~6$ mistake in Taxes

" Orderd that Nathan **HARRELL** Jur be appointed overseer of the road leading from the fork road Neare Richd. **ODAM**s. to **WYNN**s ferry in room Saml **HARRELL** resigned.

Orderd that Thos **COSTON** be apptd overseer of the road in room & Stead of Noah **HARRELL** resigned.

" Orderd that Hillory **WILLEY**. Daniel **WILLIAMS** Henry **WILLEY**. Jon **WILLIAMS** & Simon **WALTERS** or any three of them audite the accot of Levi **ROGERS** admr of Eanos **SCARBOUGH** [sic] decd. & James **WILLIAMS** acct as admr of Marey **FIELDS** & that they make report.

" Orderd that Elbert H **RIDDICK**s hands David F **FELTON**s hands. John **WILLIAMS**. Wm A. **MATHEWS** & Anthoney **MATHEWS**. Work on the New road. leading from Mddler [sic] Swamp to road Neare **HASLETT**s.

Isaac **FRYER** }
    vs }
STAFFORD. DAUGHTRY &c } The following Jurors. Briant **BROTHERS** Kind. **PARKER**. Asa **HILL**. Miles **BRIGGS**. Henry L. **BLOUNT**. Wm **MILLER** Jur. Benbury **WALTON**. Archd. **JONES** John **LOVET**. Sol **ROUNTREE**. Joshua **ALLEN**. & Miles **PARKER**. being duly Sworn & impd. find all the issues infavour pltff & asses his damage to $1002.50. ints upon the different Charges as they fell due

" Orderd that the Clk give Notice at the Court House door in Gates County of the filing a Certain petition by Kinchen **NORFLEET** & John **NORFLEET**.

Joshua **ALLEN** }
    vs }
James **WILLIAMS**} The following. Jurors. Miles **BRIGS** Benbury **WALTON**. Asa **HILL**. Tinson **EURE**. Wm **MILLER** Jur Henry L **BLOUNT**. John **LOVET**. Kindred **PARKER** Briant **BROTHERS**. Sol **ROUNTREE**. Miles **PARKER** Jur. Archd. **JONES** being duly Sworn & inpd. find all the issues infavour pltff & asses his damage to $33.4½ from which Judgt. the defd. prayd. an appeal. which was Granted & he enterd into Bonds with Jno **FIGG** & Danl. **WILLIAMS** Security.

[144] Wednesday 19th. Augt. 1835

" Orderd that John A **ANDERSON** be permitted to withdraw from the Clks office one Judgt. agt. John **HUMPHLET** & one agt. Eli **HUMPHLET**. that he file a Copy in Said office.

Orderd that. Wm. L **BOOTH** be permitted to withdraw a Judgt. agt. Etthel. **MATHEWS** from the Clks

August Court 1835

office & file a Copy Same
    Test W^m. W. STEDMAN Clk By H. GILLIAM D. Cl

State of N°. Carolina }
    Gates County} At a County Court of pleas & qr Sessions begun & held for the County of Gates at the Court House in Gatesville. 3rd monday in November 16th. day .
Present { Barnes GOODMAN Ab. W. PARKER John WILLEY Jos RIDDICK Hardy. D. PARKER Willis. F. RIDDICK} Esquires

A deed of Sale from Andrew P MATHEWS to Jn° C GORDON was ack^g. in Open Court & orderd to be registered.

A Deed of Sale from Tim°. HAYS to Riddick HAYS was proved in Open Court by Jas R HAYS a Subscribing Wits [sic] & orderd to be registerd

A Deed of Sale from W^m L BOOTH to W^m. W. COWPER was proved in Open Court by Jn°. RIDDICK a subscribing Wits & orderd to be registerd

A Deed of Sale from Wm FAULKS & others to Elijah HARE was proved in Open Court by Barnet MAUCH [Bernard MARCH³] a Subscribing Wits & orderd to be regist^d.

A Deed of Sale from W. E. PUGH to D. M. SAUNDERS was ackg^d. in Open Court & orderd to be registerd.

A Deed of Sale from W^m. L. BOOTH to W^m. W. COWPER was proved in Open Court by Jn°. RIDDICK a subs. wits & orderd to be registerd

A Deed of Sale from Edward HOWELL to David HOWELL was ack^d. in Open Court & orderd to be registerd.

A deed of Sale from Chas. JONES to James JONES was proved in Open Court & orderd to be registerd. by James MORGAN.

A deed of Sale from James WOODWARD to Thomas RICE was proved in Open Court by the Oath of Jos GORDON & orderd to be registerd.

A deed of Sale from Nancy RIDDICK to Riddick GATLING was proved in Open Court by the Oath of W^m. GATLING & orderd to be registerd.

[145] Tuesday Morning Court Set [sic] according to adjournment.
Present. {Tho^s. SAUNDERS Jn°. C GORDON Henry COSTON & W^m. G. DAUGHTRY} Esquires.

The Shff returned the following persons to Serve as Jurors to this Court. (to Wit) Isaac PARKER. Rob PARKER of Ja^s. Boon EURE. John BLANCH^D. Thos. LASSITER. Rubin PARKER Barnet MARCH. James BARNES. Jos SPEIGHT. Theo^s PARKER. Tim°. TROTMON. W^m. WHITE. James WOODWARD. Jn° BENTON Ju^r Job BLANCHARD. Jn°. P. BENTON. W^m. PERRY. Jn°. JONES. Moses HILL. Will BEASLEY. Richard CURL. Starkey EURE. Kedar RIDDICK. Ja^s. EURE Jn°. H. HOFFLER Michael WILLIAMS. Thos EASON. Danl. RIDDICK. Jno POWELL. Seth PILAND Thos. W. STALLINS. Jn°. WIGGINS. Milton EASON Britton SMITH. Henry RIDDICK of Ro & Jethro TEABOUT.

    At Same time the following persons was drawn & Chaged as Grand Jurors. Henry RIDDICK of Ro. Foreman. Seth PILAND Jno. H. HOFFLER. Danl.. RIDDICK Jas EURE. John POWELL. Ju^r. Richard CURL. Jn°. BENTON Ju^r. Thos. W. STALLINS. Theo^s PARKER. Tim°. TROTMON Jn°.

---

³ Microfilm Reel C.041.40007, Gates County Real Estate Conveyances 1829-1836, Vol: 14,15, 15:294-295

November Court 1835

JONES. Thos **LASSITER**. Isaac **PARKER**. Michael **WILLIAMS**. Kedar **RIDDICK**. Boon **EURE**. Thos **EASON**.

A. deed of Sale from Jesse **WIGGINS** to Allen **DAUGHTRY** was ack^d. in Open Court & orderd to be registerd.

A. deed of Sale from Allen **DAUGHTRY** to Jesse **WIGGINS** was ak^d. in Open Court & orderd to be registerd.

A. Deed of Sale from James **JONES** & wife to Andrew **MATHEWS** was ack^d. in Open Court & orderd to be registerd.

A. deed of Sale from Jno R **NORFLEET** to Thos R **COSTON** was proved in Open Court by Rich^d. H **PARKER** & orderd to be registerd.

A deed of Gift from Peggy **MATHEWS** to Margate [sic] E **MATHEWS** was proved in Open Court by Pleasant **MATHEWS** & orderd to be registerd.

A deed of Sale from ~~Gree~~ Lewis **GREEN** to Margaret **GREEN** was ack^d. in Open Court & orderd to be registerd.

A. deed of Sale from W^m. E. **PUGH** to Thomas **HINTON** was ack^d. in Open Court & orderd to be registerd.

A. deed of Sale from Easton **BLANCHARD** to Henry **BOND** was proved in Open Court by Jno W **BOND** & orderd to be registerd.

[146] Tuesday. 17th. Nov

A deed of Trust from Asa **HILL** to H **GILLIAM** was proved in Open Court by the Oath Lassiter **RIDDICK** & orded to be registed

A. deed of Sale from Rob **ROGERS** to Blake **BRADY** was ack^d. in Open Court & orderd to be registerd.

A. Deed of Sale from Edward **PARKER** to Jordan **PARKER** was proved in Open Court by James **MORGAN** & orderd to be registerd.

A Deed of Sale from Britton **SMITH** to Charny **UMPHLET** was ack^d. in Open Court & orderd to be registerd.

An acct Sales of the Estate of Richard **SMITH** dec^d was return [sic] into Open Court & orderd to be recorded.

A division of the Lands Mills R **FIELDS** dec^d. was returnd into Open Court & orderd to be registerd.

An audited acct. of the Estate of Ebon **BRISCO** was returnd into Open Court & orderd to be recorded.

An acct. Sales & inventory of the Estate of Hardy **WILLIAMS** de^d. was returnd into Open Court & orderd to be recorded

An acct. Current of Levi **ROGERS** adm^r of Enos **SCARBOROUGH** de^d. With a division of Sale [sic] was returnd into Open Court & ord recde [sic]

An acct. Current of Geor **COSTON** Exor of James **PHELPS** dec^d. was returnd into Open Court & orderd to be recorded.

A. Division of Estate Mary **FIELDS** with an acct. Curent. by J. **WILLIAMS** admr was returnd into Open

November Court 1835

Court & orderd to be recorded.

Acct. Sales of a Negro Girl /& Lands/ Sold by Levi **ROGERS** Exor of M. R **FIELDS** dec^d was returnd to Court & orderd to be recorded.

An audited acct. of Estate of Mills. R. **FIELDS** with a division bal [?] was returnd by the Exor Levi **ROGERS** & orderd to be recorded.

The Last will & Testament of David **COSTON** dec^d. was retu Exhibited into Open Court by H. **GILLIAM** the Exor & proved by the Oath of W^m. G. **DAUGHTRY** the Subscribing Witness thereto & at Same time the Exor therin named was duly qualified. Orderd. that Letters Testamentry be Granted Said Exor.

An Inventory of the Estate of Jos **LASSITER** dec^d was Exhibited into Open Court & orderd to be recorded.

An acct. Sales of the Estate of Jacob **ODAM** dec^d. was returnd into Open Court & orderd to be recorded.

A deed of Sale from Benbury **WALTON** to G. W **REED** was proved in Open Court by R. K. **SPEED** & orderd to be registerd.

A deed Bill Sale from B. **WALTON** to Ja^s **PACKER** [sic] was proved in Open Court by Oath Ja^s. T. **FREEMAN** & orderd to be registerd.

[147] Tuesday. 17th. Nov

N° 1. State }
      vs }
John **UMPHLET** } Anthony **MATHEWS**. Peter **EURE**. Barnet **MARCH**. Sol **ROUNTREE**. Thos. R. **COSTON**. Jos **GATLING**. A. **SPIVEY**. Noah **ROUNTREE**. Nathan **NIXON**. Ja^s **BAKER** Ju^r. Jas **BROWN** of Ja^s. Henry G. **WILLIAMS** a Jury being Sworn & imp^d. Say def^d. is Guilty. by the Court Let def^d be fin_d $1.

State }
    vs } Same Jury No. 1. Say def^d. is not Guilty.
Marm^k. **JONES** }

issd. Orderd that Willis. F. **RIDDICK**. W^m. H. **HARRELL**. Ja^s A **HARRELL** & Ed R. **HUNTER** audite & Settle the accts. of Jos **GORDON** admr Exor Isaac **PIERE** [sic] & report

issd. Orderd that. David **UMPHLET** be appointed overseer in Stead of Rich^d. **CURL** from the White Oak to Ethel^d. **CROSS**es.

issd. Orderd that Kinchen **NORFLEET** Keep in Good repair or be appointed overseer of the road leading from his Mill to 2.¼ miles of the road leading to **KITTRELL**s Meeting house.

issd. Orderd that Barnes **GOODMAN** & W^m.. L. **BOOTH** Esqr be appointed to take the private Examination of Absila **JONES** wife of James **JONES** touching her Signature to a deed of Sale.

issd. Orderd that John H **HASLET**. W^m. **BABB** Bryant. **MATHEWS** & Aron **PRICE**s hands Work on the road leading from Ja^s M **RIDDICK**s to Jno H **HASLETT**s also James M **RIDDICK**s Jacob **MATHEWS** Work on Same road

Orderd that admin_stration upon the Estate of Isaac. R. **HUNTER** dec^d. be Granted unto Ed R. **HUNTER** that he enter into Bond with W^m. F. **BENNET**. John. O. **HUNTER**. Richard. H. **PARKER** & Willis F **RIDDICK** for $.<u>8000</u>

November Court 1835

Orderd that adminstration upon the Estate of W^m. **RIDDICK** dec^d. be Granted unto. Isaiah **RIDDICK** that [sic] enter into Bonds with Jethro. H. **RIDDICK** & Abel **ROGERSON** Security in the Sum of $400.

Orderd that adm^r upon the Estate of Hasety [?] **WILLIAMS** dec^d be Granted unto Jon **WILLIAMS** that he give bond & Security Say Levi **ROGERS** & Simmonds **ROUNTREE** in the Sum of $1200.

Orderd that adm^r. on the Estate of Saml. **BROWN** dec^d. be Granted unto Henry **HOFFLER** that he enter into Bond with. Kinchen **NORFLEET** & James **COSTON** Security in the Sum of $1.000.

issd. Orderd that W^m. **HAYS** be appointed overseer of the road leading from **BENNETT**s Creek Bridge to **MINGO** path in room Wills. J. **RIDDICK**

Orderd that John C **GORDON** adm^r. upon Estate [sic] Will **MILLER** that he give Bond with Jos. **GORDON** & Thos **TWINE** Securty in the sum $600.

[148] Tuesday. 17th. Nov

Orderd that admistration on the Estate of John **EURE** Jur. dec^d. be Granted unto John **KING**. that he enter into Bond with Tinson **EURE** & Charny **UMPLET** [sic] in the Sum of $200.

Orderd that Mary **BENTON** be appt^d. Gu^d. to India [?] **BENTON** that She enter into Bonds with Ja^s **MORGAN** & Whit **JONES** Sety [sic] for $400.

Orderd that adm^r upon Estate. John **GOODMAN** & Rich^d. **GOODMAN** orphans Lem^l. **GOODMAN** that he enter into Bonds with John **WILLY** & W^m. H **GOODMAN** Secuity in the Sum of $10.000 Each.

Orderd that the Shff enter [?] Single tax from Walton **FREEMAN**s adm^r.

Orded that Guy **HOBBS** be appt^d. Gu^d. to Mary **KING** orphan Wm. **KING** & Give bond with Nathan **RIDDICK** & Abel **ROGERSON** for $3000

issd. Orderd that Prior **SAVAGE** be appt^d overseer of the road from Cross roads neare L. **HOWELL** to Gatesvill [sic] in room John **BROWN** resig^d.

issd. Orderd that Saml. **FELTON** be appointed overseer of the road in Stead Henry **BOND** resigned.

issd. Orderd that Geor **REED** be appointed Overseer of the road leading by his house to the Old Indian Neck road in room B. **WALTON**

issd. Orded that Riezup **RAWLS** be appointed overseer of the road from the fork Neare Ed. R. **HUNTER**s to **HARRELL**s Creek in Stead of John **RAWLS** resigned.

Orderd that Nathan **NIXON** renew his Guardian Bonds for Tim°. **WALTON**s orphans. with Nathan **RIDDICK** & Abel **ROGERSON** Security

Orderd that James **PRUDEN** be appointed Gu^d. to Richd B. **GATLING** orphan E. B. **GATLING** in room Jn° D. **PIPKIN** that he enter into Bonds with Henry **GILLIAM** & Rich^d. **ODAM** Secuity in Sum $3.000.

Orderd that Mills **ROBERTS** be app^d. Gu^d. to John & Emaley **RIDDICK** orphans of J. W. **RIDDICK** & into [sic] Bonds for $3000 Each with James R **RIDDICK** & Riddick **GATLING** Security.

Orderd that Jacob **DILDAY** a free boy of Colour be bound an apprentice to John **WILLY** to lean the trade of husbandy

issd. Orded that John **SAUNDERS** be allow^d. one Dollar 25/100 for a poll tax paid by mistake in List.

issd. Ordered that the County Trustee pay Jn°. **RIDDICK** one Dollar 60/100 for Cost on Serch [?] warrant of Anthony **GREEN**.

November Court 1835

Orderd that an order pass^d at last Term imposing double Tax on Sundry persons be & is herafter recinded.

issd. Orderd that Henry & John BOND adm^r of W^m. HINTON dec^d. sell on a Credit of Six Months ISAAC & CLARISA Slaves belonging to Said Estate to pay bals [sic] debts.

[149] Wednesday Court met. 18th Novr

issd. Orderd that Lassiter RIDDICK Coroner be allow^d. Thirty Dollars to be paid by the County. Trustee for holding three Inquests over the bodies John ROUNTREE. Nancy PARKER & Celea EURE.

issd. Orderd that the County Trustee pay unto Henry GILLIAM Clk of Gates Sup. Court the Sum of Ninty five Dolls & 58/100 for Sundry bills Costs in Said Court.

issd. Orderd that the County Trustee pay Jno. B. BAKER & Ja^s. R. RIDDICK undertakers to build the Court House four hundred Dollars for Extra Work upon the Same.

issd. Orderd that Henry GILLIAM. John WALTON. Tim^o. WALTON & Burwell BROTHERS or any three audite & Settle the acct^s of Henry & John BOND Adm^r. of W^m. HINTON dec^d. & make report.

issued. Orderd that John. B. BAKERs hands James PEEL & Peter TRAVIS Work on the road under W^m. HARVEY overseer from Mrs HARVEYs Mill to the Cross roads neare Lem^l. HOWELLs.

Orderd that. James PARKER orphan of W^m. PARKER dec^d. be bound as an apprentice to John H HASLETT.

Orderd that John PARKER orphan of Same be bound to Jesse WIGGINS

issd. Ordered that Henry GILLIAM Thomas SAUNDERS. W^m. G. DAUGHTRY Jesse BROWN & Rubin HINTON Lay off & Set a part to Eliz^a. BEEMAN Wife of John BEEMAN her part the Negros belonging to S^d Estate agreeable to the Will

issd. Orderd that John C. GORDON adm^r. of John SMALL Senr dec^d. Sell Negros HANAH MINGO & LEWIS belonging to S^d Estate at. 6. mos to make a division

No 1. M. A. SANTOS }
    vs }
W^m. D. SIMONS } The following Jurors-to Wit. Asa HILL. Miles PARKER. Ja^s. T. FREEMAN. John KING. Lewis GREEN Willis. R. HAYS. Kindred PARKER. Richard HAYS. W^m. BENTON. Nathan NIXON. Jos BROOKS. & Henry BOND being duly imp^d. & Sworn find all the issues infavour Pltff. & asses his damage to $148.38 of which the Sum of $8.38 is inters^t.

Gov to use John BOYT }
    vs }
John. D. PIPKIN et als. } The Same Jury No. 1 Except. Asa HILL & Henry BOND in their room Levi ROGERS & Sol ROUNTREE being duly Sworn & impd. find all the issues infavor Pltff & asses his damage to $45.56.¼ for Conditions broken.. Value Obligation $2000. Judg^t. for $2000 to be disch^d. by pay^t. Judg^t. Orderd Clk be allow^d. $10. for report one half to be paid by Each party.

[150] Wednesday 18th Nov

Thomas BAGLEY } Appl.
    vs }
James COSTON Senr.} The following Jurors to wit. Levi ROGERS Willis. R. HAYS Lewis GREEN. Rob PARKER John. KING. W^m. BENTON. Richard HAYS. Sol ROUNTREE. Miles PARKER. John SPARKMAN. Nathan NIXON. & Ja^s. T. FREEMAN being duly Sworn & impanell^d. (Jury withdrawn)

An acc^t. Current of the Estate of W^m. BLANCHARD & division of the balance in hands adm^r. was re-

November Court 1835

turnd to Court & orderd to be recorded

W^m. W. **STEDMAN** Clk of this Court renewed his official Bond with Henry **GILLIAM**. Jos **GORDON** & Abel **ROGERSON** which was rec^d. by the Court & orderd to be registerd.
    Test W^m. W **STEDMAN** Clk By H. **GILLIAM** D. C

State of N°. Carolina }
    Gates County.} At a Court of pleas & qr Sessions begun & held for the County of Gates at the Court House in Gatesville on the. 3rd. Monday in Feb^{ry}. 1836 being 15th said Month. pr_sent_ W^m. L. **BOOTH**. Henry **WILLEY**. John **WILLEY**. Riddick **GATLING**. W^m. **LEE** Ab. W. **PARKER**. Wm **HUDGINS**. Benj B **BALLARD**. W^m. **GOODMAN**. Thos **SAUNDERS**. Henry **COSTON**. Whit **STALLINS**. Hardy. D. **PARKER**. Lem^l. **RIDDICK**. Simon **WALTERS**. Richard **ODAM**. Barnes **GOODMAN** Joseph **RIDDICK** David **PARKER**. John. C. **GORDON** W^m. W. **COWPER** & Jesse. R. **KEYS**. Esquirs.

Lem^l. **RIDDICK**. David **PARKER** & Jesse R **KEYS**. appeared in Open Court & took the Several Oaths prescribed by Law as Justices of the peace for the County of Gates.

W^m. G.. **DAUGHTRY** was duly Elected as Clk of this Court to fill the Vacancy Occasion_d_ by the death of W^m. W **STEDMAN** former Clk for the unexpired. Time Say untill _augt_. 1837 & he enterd into Bond & Security agreeable to Law & & said Bond was orderd to be registerd.

A Deed of Sale from Bray & Uriah **EURE** to Rubin **PILAND** was pro_ov_ed in Open Court by the Oath of Thomas **HOGGARD** a Subscribing witness & orderd to be registerd.

[151] Feb^{ry}. Court. 1836

A Deed of Sale from Kedar **ELLIS** to Benj **FRANKLIN** was proved in Open Court by Ab **MILTEARE** & orderd to be registerd.

A Deed of Sale from Demsy **PARKER** to W^m. R **BOOTH** was ack^d. in Open Court & orderd to be registerd.

A Deed of Sale from Britton. O. **BAR** [sic] to Wright **BARR** was prooved in Open Court by Ab **BENTON** & orderd to be registerd.

A Deed of Sale from Jesse **ARLINE** to Richard **OSTIN** was proved in Open Court by the Oath of John. W. **ODAM** & orderd to be regist_ed_

A Deed of Gift from Nathan **RIDDICK** to Easter **RIDDICK** was proved in Open Court by Jesse R **KEYS** & orderd to be registerd

A Deed of Sale from John B. **GRIFFIN** to Jos **RIDDICK** was ack^d. in Open Court & orderd to be registerd.

A deed of Sale from Jesse & John **BENTON** to Willey **RIDDICK** was ackg^d. in Open Court & orderd to be registerd.

A Deed of Sale from Marmaduke **NORFLEET** to Willis F **RIDDI__** was prooved in Open Court by W^m. F **BENNET** & orderd to be registed

A Deed of Sale from Jason **SAUNDERS** to Sarah **ROOKS** was proved in Open Court by the Oath of John **SAUNDERS** & orded to be registed

a [sic] Deed in Trust from Thos **EASON** to Jos **GORDON** was ackg in Open Court & orderd to be registerd.

February Court 1836

A Deed of Sale from Thos **EASON** & Jos **GORDON** to Jesse **EASON** was ack^d. in Open Court & orderd to be registerd.

A Mortgage Deed from Nathan **WARD** to **HATTON** & **COOK** was ackg^d. in Open Court & orderd to be registerd.

A deed of Sale from Andrew **EASON** to Abner **EASON** was prooved in Open Court by the Oath of Jos **GORDON** & orderd to be registerd

A deed of Sale from John **GRANBERY** to Jesse **WIGGINS** was ack.g^d. in Open Court & orderd to be registerd.

A deed of Sale from H. H. **JONES** to Miles **HOWELL** was prooved in Open Court by the Oath of Enoch **BRITT** & orord [sic] to be registerd

A deed of Sale from Jas R **RIDDICK** to Jason **SAUNDERS** was ackg^d. in Open Court & orderd to be registerd.

A Marriage Contract between Frances **COTTER** & Hillery H **EURE** was proved in Open Court by the Oath of B. F **WELCH** & orderd to be registerd.

The Gu^d acct of Edwin **SMITH** with Heneritta [sic] **COPELAND** was Exhibited into Open Court & oreed [sic] to be recorded

The Gu^d acct of An^d. **MATHEWS** with Kedar & Hollody **JONES** was returnd into Open Court & orderd to be recorded.

[152] Feb^{ry}. 15th

The Gu^d. acct of Henry G **WILLIAMS** With. Jos **SPEIGHT** orp was returnd to Court & orderd to be recorded.

A deed of Sale from Geor W **GRANBERY** to John **GRANBERY** was ack^d. in Open Court & orderd to be registerd.

The Guardian acct of Exum **JINKINS**. with Sopha a **ODAM** was returnd to Court & orderd to be recorded.

a division of the Lands of John **GRANBEY** dec^d was returnd into Open Court & orderd to be registerd

a Gu^d. acct of Eli **WORRELL** With W^m. J. **HUDGINS** was returnd into Open Court & orderd to be recorded.

A Guardian acct of Daniel **WILLIAMS** with Lem^l **FIELDS** orp was returnd into Open Court & orderd to be recorded

A Guardian acct of Jesse **SAVAGE** with Benj **SAVAGE** orphan was returnd to Court & orderd to be recorded.

A Gu^d. acct of John W **ODAM** with Prissilla **ODAM** orphan was returnd into Open Court & orderd to be recorded.

a Gu^d. acct of Geor. **COSTON** with Isaac R **HUNTER** orphan was returd into Open Court orderd to be recorded.

a Gu^d acct. of Geor. **COSTON** with Mary A **RIDDICK** was returnd into Open Court. & orderd to be recorded.

February Court 1836

A Guardian acct of John H **HASLETT** with Sophia **HURDLE** was returnd into Open Court & orderd to be recorded.

A Guardian acct of Hardy D **PARKER** with James **WIGGINS** heirs was returnd into Open Court & orderd to be recorded.

A Guardian acct. of Exum **JINKINS** with Sarah E **BLOUNT**. was returnd into Open Court & orderd to be recorded.

Mills **EURE**s Gu^d. acct. with W^m **LEE** orphan was returnd into Open Court & orderd to be recorded.

A deed of Sale from Martha **HORTON** & John W **ODAM** to James. C. **SMITH** was proved in Open Court by Ja^s **ARLINE** & ord$\underline{ed}$ to regs^d.

Joseph **FREEMAN**s. Gu^d. acct with David **FREMAN** was returnd into Open Court & orderd to be recorded.

James **SMITH** Gu^d acct. with Edward **HARE**. orphan was returnd into Open Court & orderd to be recorded.

Eliz^a. **GRANBERY** Gu^d. acct with G$\underline{er}$ W **GRANBERY** was returnd into Open Court & orderd to be recorded.

A division of the Negros of James W **RIDDICK** dec^d was returnd into Open Court & orderd to be recorded.

[153] Monday. 15th. Feb^{ry}.

A division of the Lands of Thos **BOND** dec^d was returnd to Court & orderd to be registerd.

A division of the negros of Jethro **SUMNER** was returnd into Court. & orderd to be recorded.

A division of the personal Estate of Eliz^a. **SUMNER** dec^d was returnd to Court & orderd to be recorded.

A division of the Negros belonging to the Estate Lem^l **GOODMAN** dec^d. was returnd to Court & orderd to be recorded.

$\underline{a}$n acct Sales of Estate John **EURE** Junr de$\underline{d}$ was returnd to Court & orderd to be recorded.

A division of the Negros belonging to Estate Jno **BEEMAN** dec^d. was returnd to Court & orderd to be recorded.

Jethro **HARRELL**.s [sic] Gud. acct with E. **BRISCOE**es heirs was returnd into Court & orderd to be recorded.

A division of the Negros belonging to the Estate W^m. **HINTON** dec^d. was returnd into Court & orderd to be recorded.

Orderd that Henry L **BLOUNT** be appointed Gu^d to Sarah E **ODAM** (als. Sarah E **BLOUNT** his Wife.

Mary **BENTON**s Gu^d. acct with Jordan **BENTON** orphan was returnd into Court & orderd to be recorded.

Nathan **RIDDICK** Gu^d. to Mary **WALTON**. Henry **WALTON** Sarah **BROWN** & Wm **BROWN** orphans was retur^d & orderd to be recorded

Guy **HOBBS** Gu^d. acct with. Mary **KING** orphan was returnd & orderd to be recorded.

February Court 1836

A. division of the Negros of John. &. Richard **GOODMAN**. was returnd & orderd to be recorded.

An Inventory of the Estate Saml. **BROWN** dec^d. was returnd. & orderd to be recorded.

A. division of the Estate of Sol **EASON** was returnd into Court & orderd to be recorded.

Josiah **BRIGGS** Gu^d acct. with Daniel **HURDLE** orphan was returnd into Court & orderd to be recorded.

It was orderd that Ab W **PARKER** administer upon the Estate of William **HARRELL** dec^d. a (minor) that he enter into Bonds with Nathl **EURE** & Demsy **PARKER** Security in $200.

Miles **HOWELL** Gu^d. to the orphans of Elisha **CROSS** dec^d. returnd his accts into Open Court & orderd to be recorded

David. L. **MELTEARE** Gu^d to Christian & Parthenia **PARKER** returnd his accts into Open Court. & was orderd to be recorded

[154] Tuesday Morning Court met at 10 OClock

Present. John **WILLEY**. Jos **RIDDICK** John **WALTON**. & W^m W **COWPER**} Esques. [sic]

The Shff returnd. the following persons to Serve at this Term as Jurors (to wit.)
Jos **RIDDICK** Ju^r. David F. **FELTON** Seth **BENTON** Mk **NORFLEET**. Henry **CARTER**. Thos R **COSTON** Edwin **MATHIAS**. James **MATHIAS**. Nathl. **JONES**. Jason **ROUNTREE**. Jethro **GOODMAN**. Demcy **PARKER** (of Miles) Levi **ROGERS**. Kedar **POWELL** Henry **HOFFLER**. Norman **KING**. Fr^a. **JONES**. Geor W **REED**. Mills **SPARKMAN** James **COSTON** Senr. Arch^d. **JONES**. Kedar **HINTON**. Henry **KING**. Benj **EURE**. Wm **CROSS**. Moses **SPIVEY**. Thomas **SMITH**. Riddick **JONES**. Nathl **HARRELL**. Abs. **SPIVEY**. Ab **PIERCE**. Shadrick **PILAND**. Ja^s **ROGERS** Burwell **BROTHERS**. Ab **SMITH** & Leml **HOWELL**.
  The following persons. was drawn & Charged as Grand Jurors—(to wit).
James **COSTON** (forman) Moses **SPIVEY**. Lem^l **HOWELL** Shadrick **PILAND** Ab **SMITH**. Mills **SPARKMAN** Benj **EURE**. Geor. W. **REED**. James **ROGERS**. Jason **ROUNTREE**. Levi **ROGERS**. David F **FELTON** Thos. **COSTON** Marmaduke **NORFLEET**. Kedear **POWELL**. W^m. **CROSS**. Nathl. **HARRELL**. & Burwell **BROTHERS**.

It was orderd that in Each County /Court/ herafter to be held for Gates County. that the State docket be taken up. on Wednesdays.

The Grand Jury Came into Court & reported the absence of the forman from some Cause, wherupon Thos R **COSTON** was aptd. forman & he took the Oath as such.

A deed of Sale from Lavinia **WILLIAMS** to Jos R. **RIDDICK** was proved in Open Court by Arch^d. **JONES** & orderd to be registerd

A deed of Sale from Demsy **SPARKMAN** & wife to Mills **SPARKMAN** was proved in Open Court by W^m L **BOOTH** & orderd to be registerd

A. deed of Sale from Nancy **WILLIAMS** et als to Jas R **RIDDICK** was proved in Open Court by Allen **SMITH** & orderd to be registerd

A deed of Sale from W. E. **PUGH** to Lassiter **RIDDICK** was pro ack^d. in Open Court & orderd to be registerd.

[155] Tuesday 16th Feb^{ry}. 1836

A deed of Sale from Feletia **FREEMAN** to Mills **SPARKMAN** was proved in Open Court by W^m. L. **BOOTH** & orderd to be regist^d.

February Court 1836

A deed of Sale from Jesse **BROWN** & wife to Mills **SPARKMAN** was proved in Open Court by W^m. L. **BOOTH** & orderd to be registerd

A deed of Sale from. Eliz^a. **PARKER** to Mills **SPARKMAN** was proved in Open Court by Kind. **PARKER** & orderd to be registerd

A. deed of Sale from W^m. G **DAUGHTRY** to John **BROWN** was ack^d. in Open Court & orderd to be registerd.

A deed of Sale from **HARRELL & COSTON** to Rubin **LASSITER** was prooved in Open Court by Jethro. H. **RIDDICK** & orderd to be registrd

A deed in Trust Executed by Richd. H **FIELDS** Henry **WILLEY** & Dani^l. **WILLIAMS** was proved in Open Court by Jet **WILLY** & oreded [sic] to be reg^d.

A deed of Sale from Elisha H **BOND** to Nathl **EURE** was prooved in Open Court by W^m W **COWPER** & orderd to be registed

A Mortgage deed from Riddick **MATHEWS** to John **MATHEWS** was proved in Open Court by H **GILLIAM** & orded to be registerd

A. Bill Sale from Burwell **GRIFFITH** to Thos **SAUNDERS** was proved in Open Court by Richd **ODAM** & orderd to be registerd.

A. deed of Sale from Rob. P. **HAYS** to Zach **HAYS** was proved in Open Court by Tim^o. **HAYS** & orderd to be registerd.

A deed of Sale from Job R **HALL** to John. S. **ROBERTS** was prooved in Open Court by Ja^s R **RIDDICK** & orderd to be registrd

A deed of Sale from Ja^s R **RIDDICK** to Zac **HAYS** was proved in Open Court by Tim^o. **HAYS** & orded to be regist^d.

A deed of Sale from Margaret A **BALLARD** to Jordan **PARKER** was proved in Open Court. by Kedar **TAYLOR** & orderd to be regs^d.

A deed of Sale from Thos **HOGGARD** to Ab. W. **PARKER** was proved in Open Court by W^m L **BOOTH** & orderd to be registerd.

A deed of Sale from Margaret. A. **BALLARD** to Kedar **TAYLOR** was proved in Open Court by Jordan **PARKER** & orderd to be reg^d.

A deed of Sale from John **WALTON** to Kedar **HINTON** was ack^d.. in Open Court & orderd to be registerd.

A deed of Sale from John **MATHEWS** to Rid **MATHEWS** was prooved in Open Court by H **GILLIAM** & orderd to be registr^d..

A deed of Sale from Malacha **CUFF** to Henry **WILLY** was proved in Open Court by Henry. G. **WILLEY** & ored to be regs^d.

A deed of Sale from Martha S **BAGLEY** & Thomas **BAGLEY** to Easton **BLANCHARD** was prooved in open Court by Jethero H **RIDDICK** and ordered to be registered.

[156] Tuesday 16th. February 1836

A Bill of Sale from Ro R **SMITH** agent. to Josiah **PERRY** was prooved in open Court by Caleb **PERRY**

February Court 1836

and ordered to be registered.

A deed of Sale from Samuel **EURE** to Abm W **PARKER** was prooved in open Court by John **WILLEY** and ordered to be registered.

A deed of Sale from Elisha **UMPHLET** to Dempsey **PARKER** was prooved in open Court by A. W. **PARKER** and ordered to be registered.

Ordered that Thomas **SAUNDERS** have licence to retail Spiritous Liquors by the small measure

A deed of Sale from Thomas **RICE** to Richard H. **PARKER** was prooved in open Court by Willis F **RIDDICK** and ordered to be registered.

A deed of Sale from Ann E **LASSITER** & John **LASSITER** to George **BROOKS** was prooved in open Court and ordered to be registered, prooved by Henry **HOFFLER**

A deed of Sale from Britten **SMITH** to Dempsey **PARKER** was prooved in open Court by Elisha **PARKER** and ordered to be registered.

A deed of sale from Randol **SHERRAD** agent for Levi W **PARKER** to Abram **PARKER** was prooved in open Court and ordered to be registerd; prooved by Kindred **PARKER**.

Abram **PARKER**'s guardian account with William **BLADES** was returned to Court and ordered to be recorded

James **COSTEN**'s guardian account with James R **COSTEN** was returned to Court and ordered to be recorded

James **PRUDEN**'s guardian account with Harriet B. **GATLING** was returned to Court and ordered to be recorded

John C **GORDEN**'s guardian act with Sarah M **LASSITER** was returned to Court and ordered to be recorded

John C **GORDEN**'s guardian act. with Timothy **LASSITER** was returned to Court and ordered to be recorded

Willis J **RIDDICK**s guardian accounts with Sally **HINTON** James **HINTON** & Noah **HINTON** was returned to Court and ordered to be recorded.

John C. **GORDEN**'s guardian accounts with Israel **BEEMAN** & William **BEEMAN** was returned to Court and ordered to be recorded.

Willis **BUNCH**'s guardian account with Nancy **HURDLE** was returned to Court and ordered to be recorded.

Nathan **NIXON**'s guardian act. with Mary Ann **WALTON** was returned in open Court and ordered to be recorded.

Joseph **HURDLE**'s guardian act with Caroline M **SUTTON** was returned Court [sic] and ordered to be recorded.

Nathan **NIXON**'s guardian act. with Joseph G **WALTON** was returned to Court and ordered to be recorded.

[157] Tuesday February 16th. 1836

February Court 1836

Nathaniel EURE's guardian acts. with Henry, Mary & Mills EURE and [sic] ordered to be recorded

Nath'. EURE's guardian acts with Corda & Mary WILLIAMS was returned to Court and ordered to be recorded.

W^m.. W. COWPER's guardian act. with Celea LEWIS was returned to Court and ordered to be recorded.

Whitmel STALLING's guardian acts with Asa & Daniel WALTON was returned to Court and ordered to be recorded.

Nathaniel EUREs guardian acts. with Susan & Sophia SPEIGHT & W^m.. BABB was returned to Court & ordered to be recored.

James T. FREEMANs guardian acts. with Robert, Edward & David TAYLOR was returned to Court and orderd to be recorded.

Seth W. ROUNTREEs guardian acts with Malinda & Matilda BAGLEY was returned to Court and orderd to be recorded

W^m. W. COWPERs guardian act. with Uriah BABB was returned to Court and orderd to be recorded

A deed of Sale from Riddick B EURE & Nancy EURE was prooved in open Court by W^m. L BOOTH & orderd to be registered.

Willis F RIDDICKs guardian act with Jacob Benjamin HUNTER was returned to Court and ordered to be recorded.

Thos SAUNDERS guardian act with Asa ODAM was returned to Court & ordered to be recorded.

John WALTON's guardian act. with Leah HINTON was returned to Court and ordered to be recorded.

John WILLEYs guardian act with Mary WILLIAMS was returnd to Court & orderd to be registered. [sic]

Ordered that Willis F. RIDDICK, W^m. H HARRELL, Edward R HUNTER & Thos TWINE be appointed to settle & audite the accounts of Joseph GORDEN executor of Isaac PRICE dec^d. and make report.

Ordered that Willis F. RIDDICK, W^m. H HARRELL, Edward R HUNTER & Thos TWINE be appointed to settle & audite the accounts of Joseph GORDEN admr. of James GRANBERRY dec^d. & make report to next Court.

It was ordered that the County trustee pay Abel ROGERSON the sum of Twenty five dollars for a bed &c burnt, which was used by W^m. BRIGGS who died at his house.

[158] Tuesday February 16th. 1836

Ordered that the County Trustee pay John R GILLIAM Twenty four dollars for his attendance on Wm BRIGGS at Abel ROGERSONs

Ordered that the County Trustee pay Allen SMITH admr. of Lemuel CLEAVES dec^d. Two dollars & forty Cents for attendance 3 days on Grand Jury.

Ordered that the County Trustee pay Guy HOBBS One dollar & Twenty five Cents for mistake in listing & paying for 1 Blk Poll

Ordered that the County Trustee pay Rufus K SPEED Twenty dollars for attendance on W^m.. BRIGGS.

February Court 1836

Ordered that letters of administration be granted to John ROBERTS Sr on the estate of Sarah JONES dec^d. & that he enter into bond for five hundred dollars with Henery GILLIAM & W. G. DAUGHTRY his securities.

Ordered that ~~that~~ Thos TWINE be appointed Guardian to Sally Ann HUNTER with George COSTEN & Thos COSTEN securities in the sum of three thousand dollars

Ordered that John FELTON be appointed guardian to his Grand Daughter Sarah HINTON by giving bond for Seven thousand dollars with Noah HINTON & Abel ROGERSON securities.

Ordered that Simmonds ROUNTREE renew his Constable Bond by Giving Lassiter RIDDICK & Henry GILLIAM securities.

Ordered that Henry GILLIAM be appointed guardian to Mary, Harriett, Elizabeth & Martha PARKER orphans of Abm. PARKER dec^d. that he enter into bonds in the sum of One thousand dollars with W^m.. G. DAUGHTRY & Marmaduke NORFLEET securities.

Ordered that letters of administration be granted to Willis [?] WALTON on the estate of Asa WALTON dec^d. and that he enter into bonds of five hundred dollars with James BRINKLEY and Calvin BRINKLEY securities.

Ordered that Jethro H RIDDICK renew his constable bond by giving Nathan RIDDICK & Whitmel STALLINGS securities.

Ordered that James JENKINS orphan of Arthur JENKINS dec^d. be bound to W^m.. GATLING to learn the trade of a Farmer.

Ordered that Washington CROSS orphan of James CROSS dec^d. be bound apprentice to James COSTEN Sen. to learn the trade of a Farmer

Ordered that Alfred REED (of Colour) be bound to Jacob HAYS to learn the trade of a farmer.

[159] Tuesday February 16th. 1836

Ordered that Miles BRIGGS renew his Constable Bond by giving Whitmel STALLINGS & Jas R RIDDICK securities.

Ordered that Abram BONNER orphan of John BONNER be bound apprentice to Marmaduke NORFLEET to learn the arts & misteries [sic] of Gig making.

Ordered that Jordan PARKER be permited to take out letters of administration on the estate of Afred BALLARD by giving John C GORDON & Henry GILLIAM securities in the sum of Two Hundred dollars.

Ordered that John WILLY have letters of administration upon the estate of Charles VANN dec^d. with Henery GILLIAM & Jethero WILLY securities in the sum of One Hundred dollars.

Ordered that James C RIDDICK renew his Constable Bond by giving Lassiter RIDDICK & Jas R RIDDICK securities.

Ordered that Allen SMITH admr. of Lemuel CLEAVES dec^d. sell a negro man by the name of MILLS on a credit of six months to pay the debts of said dec^d.

Ordered that W^m.. PHELPS orphan of __[blank]__ be bound to John LOVETT to learn the trade of Shoe-maker.

Ordered that Anaca CORBAL daughter of Charlotte CORBAL a free girl of colour be bound to Willis R.

February Court 1836

HAYS.

Ordered that Ainah [?] **CORBELL** [sic] a girl of Colour be bound out to John S **ROBERTS** until she arrives at Twenty one years of age.

Ordered that Riddick **GATLING**, John C **GORDEN** & John **WALTON** be appointed as a committe with orthority [sic] to examine the Books & Papers of the County Court Clerk's office and report the same to the next County Court.

Ordered that Wright **JONES** a boy of Colour be bound to Jordan **PARKER** to learn the misteries of a workman.

Ordered that John **PARKER** be appointed overseer of the Road heretofore kept by Capt. John **SPEIGHT**.

Ordered that Isaac **PIPKIN** W^m.. **GOODMAN** & Richard **ODAM** be appointed processioners to procession the lands of Elisha H **BOND** and report accordingly.

Ordered that John **MITCHEL**, Henry **GILLIAM** Burwell **BROTHERS** & Joseph **RIDDICK** be apponted to settle the Current accounts of Whitmel **STALLINGS** administrator of Nathan **CULLINS** dec^d.

[160] Tuesday February 16th. 1836

Ordered that the County Trustee pay W^m.. W **STEDMAN** Twenty five dollars for ½ years extra services rendered.

Ordered that W^m.. L **BOOTHE**, John **WILLEY** Riddick **GATLING** Jno. **SAUNDERS** & Kindred **PARKER** settle & state the accounts of W^m.. W. **COWPER** admr. of James **JONES** dec^d. & that they report to the next County Court their proceedings.

Ordered that Thos **HURDLE** be appointed overseer of the road leading from Warrick Swamp to the snake Branch in liew of James **COSTEN** former overseer and that he may be intilled [sic] to same hands worked by **COSTEN**.

Ordered that Isaac **S/P/EIGHT** be appointed overseer of the Road. Called by the name of the "WYNNs Ferry Road"

Ordered that John C **GORDEN** one of the Commissioners of the buildind [sic] of the Court House pay to order of W^m. B **SHEPHERD** Forty dolls for extra work done to sd. house.

Ordered that the county Trustee pay Lassiter **RIDDICK** Ten dollars for holding inquest over the body of Alfred **BALLAD**.

Ordered that Joseph **GORDEN** be appointed guardian to George **GRANBERRY**'s heir, James **GRANBERRY** Thos **GRANBERRY** Bathsheba **GRANBERRY** & Elizabeth **GRANBERRY** and offerd security Henry **GILLIAM** [One half of line has been left blank.] in a bond of Four thousand Dollars, O___ __

Ordered that Thos **SAUNDERS** renew his guardian [sic] for Asa **ODOM** in the Sum of Five thousand dollars by giving Henry **GILLIAM** & Riddick **GATLING** securities.

Ordered that Peter **EURE** be appointed guardian to Oliver & Sarah **GRANT** with Henry **CARTER** & Nathaniel **EURE** as securities in the sum of Five hundred dollars.

" Ordered that the County Trustee pay to W^m. T. **WATHAN** [?] One dollar & thirty three Cents for witness Ticket State vs Reuben **HINTON**.

17th. Ordered that letters of administration on the estate of Daniel **PARKER** dec^d. be granted to Hardy D.

February Court 1836

PARKER & that he enter into Bond & security in the sum of Fifteen thousand dollars, his securities Henry GILLIAM & Wm G. DAUGHTRY Also ordered that the said admr. sell the perishable estate of said dec^d. on a credit of six months.

Ordered that Thos SAUNDERS have licence to retail Siritous [sic] Liquors by the small measure.

[161] Tuesday February 16th. 1836

Ordered that letters of administration be granted to A. W. PARKER upon the estate of William HARRELL dec^d. orphan of Mary HARRELL dec^d. by giving Nathaniel EURE & Dempsey PARKER security in the sum of Two hundred dollars.

Ordered that Henry L BLOUNT be appointed guardian to his wife (Sarah ODOM formerly) now Sarah E BLOUNT

Ordered that the county Trustee pay to David PARKER Sixty eight cents for W^m. T WATHANs witness ticket, State vs Reuben HINTON

The Guardian acct Riddick GATLING with Eliza. & Mary SUMNER orphans was returnd & orderd to be recorded.

The guardian Act of W^m.. E PUGH with Rebeca C. Josiah [?] Mills. & Nathaniel T PUGH was returned to court and orderd to be recorded. Test W G DAUGHTRY Clerk

State of North Carolina }
     Gates County } At a court of Pleas & qr Sessions began and held for the County of Gates at the Court house in Gatesville the 3rd. monday in May 1836
Present. {John C. GORDEN Riddick GATLING Joseph RIDDICK John WILLY} Esqrs

A deed of Sale from John KNIGHT to John WIGGINS was prooved in open Court by M R HARRELL a subscribing witness and ordered to be registered.

A deed of Sale from Joseph GORDEN To Robert HILL was prooved in open Court by the oath of Jacob J HARVEY a subscribing witness & ordered to be registered

A deed of sale was prooved in open Court by the oath of John H HASLET a subscribing witness from John MATTHEWS to Fletcher HASLET and ordered to be registered

A deed from Jas R RIDDICK to Benjamin SAUNDERS was prooved in open Court by the oath of D M SAUNDERS and ordered to be registered.

[162] M A SANTOS
    vs
W D SIMMS
    James R RIDDICK as bail for the defendant surrendered him in open Court in discharge of himself & the person praying him into custody it is ordered that he be discharged

A Deed of sale from Joseph SPEIGHT to Robert HILL was prooved in open Court by the Oath of R RAWLS a subscribing witness & ordered to be registered.

A Deed of sale from Levi BEEMAN to George COSTEN was prooved in open Court by Oath of T COSTEN and ordered to be registered

A deed of sale of [sic] from John ARNOLD to John P BENTON was prooved in open Court by John WIGGINS & orderd to be registered.

May Court 1836

A Deed of Sale from John **COPELAND** to James **RUSSEL** was prooved in open Court by Oath of Miles **HOWELL** & ordered to be registered.

A deed of Sale from Thos **HOGGARD** to Bray **EURE** was prooved in open Court by oath of Boon **EURE** & ordered to be registerd.

A deed of sale from Moses R **HARRELL** to John **WIGGINS** was prooved in open Court by oath of M **HARRELL** & ordered to be registered.

A Deed of sale from Daniel S **HOBBS** to Abm **SPIVEY** was prooved in open Court by oath of James **BOICE** & ordered to be registered.

A deed of sale from James **POWELL** to Joseph **SPEIGHT** was prooved in open Court by the oath of John C **GORDEN** & ordered to be registered.

A deed of sale from Willis R **HAYS** to James **EVANS** was exibited [?] and prooved in open Court by oath of Lassiter **RIDDICK** & ordered to be registered

A bill of Sale from Jethero **BRINKLEY** to Josiah **RIDDICK** was prooved in open Court by Oath of John O **HUNTER** & ordered to be registered

A Deed of sale from Jethro **LASSITER** to Jas T **FREEMAN** was prooved in open Court by Oath of W. **BAKER** and ordered. to be registered

A deed of Mortgage from Daniel S **HOBBS** to Burwell **BROTHES** was prooved in open Court by John B. **SHEPHERD** on oath & orderd to be registered

A deed of Sale from Andrew & Barshaba **DAUGHTRY** to Miles **BROWN** was prooved in open Court by Oath of John **WALTON** & ordered to be registered.

A deed of Sale from Benbury **WALTON** to John **WALTON** was acknowledged in open Court & ordered to be registered.

A deed of sale from Jesse **MATTHIAS** to Riddick **JONES** was prooved in open Court by oath of Dempsey **VAN** [sic] & ordered to be registered

[163] A deed of Sale from Isaac **PIPKIN** to W^m.. B. **WYNNS** was acknowledged in open Court & ordered to be registered.

A deed of Sale from Moses **HILL** to Joseph **HURDLE** was proved in open court by the oath of Jacob **NIXON** & ordered to be registerd.

A Deed of Sale from Easton **BLANCHARD** to Joseph **BROOKS** was prooved in open Court by oath of Jethero **BLANCHARD** & ordered to be registerd

A Deed in Trust from Westley W **SPIGHT** to Miles **BROWN** was prooved in open Court by the oath of Henry **HOFFLER** & ordered to be registerd

A deed of Sale from Burwell **GRIFFITH** to Richard **ODAM** was prooved in open Court by the oath of Thos **SAUNDERS** & ordered to be registered

A deed of Sale from George **BROOKS** to Jethero **BLANCHARD** was prooved in open Court by oath of Joseph **BROOKS** & ordered to be registered

A deed of Sale from Henry S **SPIVEY** to Peter B **MINTON** was prooved in open Court by oath of A **BLANCHARD** & ordered to be registered

May Court 1836

A deed of Sale from Marmaduke ELLIS, Joseph R BILUPS, Mary R BILUPS & Robert NEWSOME to John BENTON Jn'. was prooved in open Court by oath of Humphry PARKER & ordered to be registerd.

A deed of Sale from Willis F RIDDICK to Thos R COSTEN was ~~prooved~~ /ackn^d/ in open Court and ordered to be registerd.

A deed of Sale from Jethero & Ann SUMNER to James RUSSEL was proooved [sic] in open Court by oath of Miles HOWELL & ordered to be registerd.

A deed of Sale from James MATTHIAS to James MORGAN was prooved in open Court by oath of Jordan PARKER & ordered to be registerd

A deed of Sale from John HINTON to hance HOFFLER was prooved in open Court by oath of H. GILLIAM & ordered to be registered.

A deed of sale from Jamimay THORENTON [sic] to Jesse EASON was prooved in open court by oath of Joseph RIDDICK & ordered to be registered

A deed of sale from Benj: SAUNDERS. to James SAUNDERS was prooved in open Court by oath of D. M. SAUNDERS and ordered to be registered

A deed of sale from Abram PRUDEN to J Riddick EURE was acknowledged in open Court & ordered to be registered.

A deed of sale. from William TAYLOR to Starkey EURE was prooved in open Court by oath of Simon STALLINGS & ordered to be registerd

A ~~de~~ Bill of Sale from Ira, Charles & Ludy CARTER was prooved in open Court & ordered to be registered, proved by Bray EURE

A Bill of Sale from Thos SMITH & others to Kedar POWELL was prooved in open Court by oath Saml. HARRELL & orderd to be registerd

A deed of Sale from Ann BOND to Samuel S BOND was proved

[164] in open Court by oath of Ezekiel T JONES & ordered to be registered

A deed of Sale from John O HUNTER & Wm ARNOLD to James MATTHIAS was acknowledged in open Court & orderd to be registerd.

    Tuesday Morning Court met at 10 Oclock A M
Present {John WALTON W^m. W. COWPER John GORDEN Riddick GATLING} Esq^rs

The Sfff [sic] returned the following persons to serve as Jurors at this Term To Wit. John SPARKMAN William PILAND, William MILLER, Timothy ROGERS, James WOODORD John P BENTON James COSTEN Isaac SPEIGHT, John WIGGINS Moses HILL James SAUNDERS John MORRIS Westly PHELPS, Joshua JONES Dempsey VANN Richard AUSTIN Abram DAVIS Fed^k. ROOKS Thos W. STALLINGS, John BRADDY John LEE Archie JONES Joseph BENTON John TAYLOR Thos RICE Jason RIDDICK Solomon SMALL Kedar TAYLOR Barnet MARCH, W^m. SEARS Moses TROTMAN Seth SPIVEY Isaac HYOTT Wm JONES & John SMITH.
    The following persons were drawn & charged & Sworn as Grand Jurors to wit. Dempsey VANN (foreman) Thomas RICE Joshua JONES, James SAUNDERS, John LEE, Seth SPIVEY, Isaac SPEIGHT Thos W STALLINGS, Westley PHELPS, John WIGGINS Archibald JONES, Isaac HIOTT, Moses TROTMAN William MILLER John SPARKMAN Fed^k. ROOKS John BRADDY & James WOODARD.

Ordered that Nathan RIDDICK Guardian be allowed to correct any & all mistakes which he may have

May Court 1836

made in his Guardian Returns.

x Ordered that the County Trustee pay to Lassiter **RIDDICK** Two dollars & 70 cents for land improperly listed by James **GOODMAN**.

x Ordered that John **SAUNDERS**, William **GOODMAN** Esqr Isaac **PIPKIN** & Nathaniel **EURE** audite and state the Act of Riddick **GATLING** admr. on the estates of John & Richard **GOODMAN** dec^d. with the_r_ Estates of dec^d. at ther [sic] the same make a division of said estates amongst the heirs at Law. & report their proceedings to this Court.

[165] x Ordered that Edward R **HUNTER** Thomas **RIDDICK** Whit^l. **STALLINGS** Thomas **SAUNDERS** Dempsy **SPARKMAN** William W **COWPER** & Barnes **GOODMAN** be appointed Wardens of the Poor.

x Ordered that The County Trustee pay to John **BAKER** Sixteen Hundred & Seventy Three dollars it being for Second pay_mt_ for building the Court House

Ordered that William **SWEAT** of Henry be bound to Bray **PARKER** to learn the trade of a farmer.

Ordered that Sally **SWEAT** of Henry be bound to John **SPARKMAN** & that he enter into bonds for same

x Ordered that John **WILLEY** Esqr. Henry **WILLIAM** [sic] Levi **ROGERS**, Henry **WILLEY** & Daniel **WILLIAMS** or any three of them audite & settle /state/ the acts of Jonathan **WILLIAMS** admr. of Hardy **WILLIAMS** dec^d. & report to next Court.

x Ordered that the County Trustee pay to W^m. E **PUGH** Fifty dollars for Extra services rendered as County attory. for the year ending this day.

x Order [sic] that the Committe_e_ heretofore appointed to examine into the Condition of the Clerks office proceed to make a thorough examination & make report to next Court.

x Ordered that John C **GORDEN** Reubin **HINTON** & Timothy **WALTON** each be allowed for their services in superintending the building the Court House the sum of Twenty five dollars & that the County Trustee pay it.

x Ordered that the County Trustee pay to John C **GORDEN** Two dollars 81 Cents for advertising the /building of the/ Court House in the Edenton Gazette.

Ordered that A W **PARKER** be allowed a licenc [sic] to retail spiritous liquors by the small measure for one year

x Ordered that Riddick **MATTHEWS** be allowed a licence to retail spiritous liquors for one year by the small measure

Ordered that Martha **EURE** a girl of Colour be bound to John **BRINKLEY** & that s^d. **BRINKLEY** enter into Bonds

Ordered the County Trustee pay to Lassiter **RIDDICK** Forty dollars for holding four inquests as Coroner.

[166] Ordered that Lassiter **SMITH** be allowed one dollar & thirty Cents for Tax on one poll improperly listed & that the County Trustee pay the same.

Ordered that the following persons (Justices) be appointed to take the list of Taxable & Taxables in their respective Captain_ce_s for the year 1836 To Wit
Dempsey **KNIGHT** of the Folly district
Henry **COSTEN** of **HUNTER**s Mill district

May Court 1836

Jesse R **KEY** of **MINTON**s District
Thomas **SAUNDERS** of the Court House district
William L **BOOTHE** of Scr_ac_h Hall district
William **GOODMAN** of Piney Woods district
Henry **WILLEY** of **HASLET** Shop District.

Ordered that William **CORBIN** a boy of Colour be bound out to John **RIDDICK**. Ordered that Asa **PHELPS** a boy of Colour be bound out to John **RID_DI_K** & that he enter into bonds.

x Ordered that John C **GORDON** Joseph **GORDEN** & John **WALTON** be appointed be [sic] appointed a committe [sic] of Finance to discharge the duties imposed by an act of assembly passed in 1827

x Ordered that the Shff be allowed Fifty dollars for extra services & that the County Trustee pay the same.

Willis **WALTON** returned an inventary of amt he rec^d. as admr. /of Asa **WALTON**/ of Whitmel **STALLINGS** guardian of Asa **WALTON** the amt of $161.40.

Ordered that a licence be granted to John **LONT** [?] to Retail spirtous liquors by the small measure for one year

Ordered that W G **DAUGHTRY** be allowed to retail spiritous Liquoars by the small measure for one year.

Ordered that John **WALKER** be allowed to retail Oysters Cakes & fruits in the County of Gates for one year agreeable to an act of assembly

Ordered that Asa **HUNTER** a boy of Colour be bound out to Whitmel **STALLINGS** and that he enter into bonds

Ordered that John O **HUNTER** admr. of Edwin **MATTHIAS** dec^d. sell a negro man by the name of **NED** belonging to said estate.

x Ordered that the County Trustee pay to James R **RIDDICK** five dollars 65 cents for cost (of suit) Offices of Court to Henry **GILLIAM**

[167] Ordered that Levi **BEEMAN** as admr. of Walton **FREEMAN** dec^d. sell old woman **SALLY** the property of said estate.

Ordered that Henry **GILLIAM**, Thomas **SAUNDERS** & Marmaduke **NORFLEET** audite an [sic] settle the accounts of Levi **BEEMAN** as admr. of Walton **FREEMAN**

Ordered that the County Trustee pay to John **RIDDICK** thirteen dollars & 60 Cents for services rendered, attending on the Grand Jury Seventeen days.

  Court adjorned
Wednesday morning Court met at 10 Oclock
  Present {David **PARKER** John **WILLEY** W^m. W. **COWPER** John **WALTON**} Esq^{rs}.

x Ordered that John C **GORDEN**, Humphy **PARKER**, Jordan **PARKER** & Dempsey **KNIGHT** with the County surveyor make a division of the desert Land of David **BRINKLEY** among his heirs agreeable to his will & report &&c [sic]

Ordered that Thomas **GOMER** [?] be bound To Francis **DUKES** to learn farming &c.

x Ordered that the County Trustee pay to Jethero H **RIDDICK** Thirteen dollars for Old warden Claim p^d. by s^d. **RID_DI_CK**

May Court 1836

x Ordered that County Trustee pay Jethero H **RIDDICK** Seventeen dollars 80 Cents for act renderd for services attending Pety Jury &c &c.

x Ordered that the County Trustee pay Rich^d. **CURL** 94 Cents for witness Ticket vs. Bray **PARKER**

x Ordered that the County Trustee pay to W^m. H. **SAVAGE** ni/n/ety Cents for State witness Ticket vs Bray **PARKER**

x Ordered that the County Trustee pay To Henry **GILLIAM** Thirty Two /52/100/ dollars for act rendered

x Ordered that Willis F **RIDDICK**, Edward R **HUNTER** James **COSTEN** Senr. Rich^d H **PARKER** or any three of them state the acts of John C **GORDEN** admr. on the estate of Charles **BRIGGS** dec^d. & report to next Court & make a division of said Estate. Also ordered that the same persons or any three of them audite & State the acts of John C **GORDEN** admr on the estate of John **SMALL** dec^d. & report

[168] to next Court & make a division of said estate among the legal heirs.

Ordered that W H **GOODMAN** renew his guardian Bond & that he enter into Bonds for Peny, Maria & Henry **GOODMAN** in the sum of Ten Thousand dollars by giving Riddick **GATLING** & W G **DAUGHTRY** securities

Ordered that Riddick **GATLING** renew his guardian bond of Mary & Elizabeth **SUMNER** & be bound in the sum of Twenty thousand dollars with Whitmel **STALLINGS** & W H **GOODMAN** securities.

Ordered that the County Trustee pay to the Clerk thirty Three dollars 14 cents for costs of four State causes vs John **JONES**, Bray **PARKER** Henry **COSTEN** & John **KING**

Ordered that John **WALTON** renew his bond as Register for this County agreeable to Law & give for security Henery **BOND** & Timothy **WALTON**.

A deed of Gift & release thereon from James **TREVATHAN** to Henry **TREVATHAN** was prooved in open Court by oath of John **WALTON** a subscribing witness and ordered to be registered.

Ordered that the County Trustee pay to Jas. R **RIDDICK** one hundred & sixteen dollars & 83 Cents for furnishing materials and painting the Brick work of the Court House.

Ordered that the County Trustee pay to Jesse **BROWN** Ten dollars & 70 Cents for boarding Prisoners in Jail & 4 Blankets.

Ordered that Joseph **GORDEN** be appointed Guardian to Sophia & David **BRINKLEY** orphans of Miles **BRINKLEY** and that he enter into bond in the sum of Two thousand dollars with Marmaduke **NORFLEET** & Henry **GILLIAM** securities.

Ordered that John C **GORDEN** renew his Guardian Bond for Timothy & Sarah M **LASSITER** orphans of Henry **LASSITER** by giving bond for Fifteen thousand dollars each with Noah **HARRELL** & George **COSTEN** his securities.

Ordered that W. G. **DAUGHTRY** be appointed to take

[169] Charge of the New Court House, to have it cleaned and the windows to be open when necessary with a resonable Compensation for his services. Also ordered that that [sic] in future all persons who shall abuse the Court House, shall be fined as follows; for chewing tobacco & sipiting [sic] on any part of the House or floor fifty Cents for writing or marking with eather ink or Pencil on any part of the wall /or window facings/ above or below fifty Cents for cuting any part of the house or bar or otherwise defacing the same above or below one dollar and that the Clerk make this order publick by keeping a notice constantly posted on one of the Pillows [sic] below & above stairs and on each of the doors of the Offices & jury Rooms.

May Court 1836

Ordered the Charman of the County Court of Pleas & qr Sessions be requested to have benches & Tables provided for the several Jurry Rooms. Also the necessary Tables & benches for the Court Rooms and each of the Offices & alo [sic] 3 doz spit boxes for the use of the above named rooms and report the amt to next Court.

Ordered that Thomas SAUNDERS advertise for 30 days and sell on a credit of Six months at publick sale the Old Court House & take bond & securty for the amt of sale

A bill of Sale from George M MULLEN to Richard ODAM was proved in open Court by the oath of Isaac PIPKIN & ordered to be registered.

Ordered that John SAUNDERS (a Colourd Man) renew his bond of indentures for Washington SMITH and offers security Whitmel STALLINGS & Fedrick ROOKS which was rec^d by the Court.

A deed of Sale from Christian Moses HURDLE to Christian TWINE was prooved in open Court by the Oath of Joseph R EASON and ordered to be registered.

A deed of Sale from J R RIDDICK to Pryor SAVAGE was prooved in open Court by Oath of J R RIDDICK & orderd to be registerd.

A deed of Sale from Jas R RIDDICK Shff to William

[170] HUDGINS was acknowledged in open Court and ordered to be registered.

A deed of sale from James FIGG to Nancy BOND was prooved in open Court by the oath of John FIGG & ordered to be registered

A deed of sale from Bryant BROTHERS & Mary BROTHERS to Ezekiel T JONES & Elizabeth G JONES was proved in open Court by the Oath of Pryor SAVAGE & ordered to be recorded.

A deed of Sale from John LEWIS & Rachel LEWIS to Mills SPARKMAN was prooved in open Court by the oath of William L BOOTHE and ordered to be registered.

A deed of Sale from Lewis BRINKLEY Henry BRINKLEY Isaac BRINKLEY Jerry BRINKLEY, Louisa PARKER Ammon BRINKLEY & Timothy BRINKLEY to John O HUNTER was prooved in open Court & ordered to be registerd.

A deed of Release from Nathan RIDDICK Trustee to Peter B. MINTON was acknowledged in open Court & ordered to be registerd.

The last Will & Testament of Abram HURDLE was prooved in open Court by the Oat [sic] of Jesse EASON a subscribing witness & ordered to be recorded

A Deed of Sale from Ezekiel T JONES & Elizabeth G JONES to Thomas SAUNDERS was prooved in open Court by the oath of Pryor SAVAGE & ordered to be registerd

Ordered that the following Tax be laid for 1835 to wit.
Publick Tax   6 cents each on $100 valuation of Land & 20 cents each on the Pole
County Tax   6 "   "   ditto "   "   " do. & 15 do do " " do
Court House 20 "   "   ditto "   "   "   & 50 do do ---- do
Parish do   13 "   "   ditto "   "   "   & 38 " do ---- do.

The division of the lands of Benjamin HAYS dec^d was returned to Court and orderd to be recorded

The following Persons were appointed inspectors at the polls at the different elections to be held in august next. To Wit
James MORGAN Henry RIDDICK Dempsy KNIGHT Humphry PARKER, James COSTEN Senr.

May Court 1836

Risop **RAWLS** & Willis F **RIDDICK** } Folly District
Jethro H **RIDDICK** William H. **HARRELL** Isaac **HARRELL**, Burwell **BROTHERS**, Thomas **RIDDICK** Henry **COSTEN** & Thomas **TWINE**} **HUNTER**s Mill do

[171] James T. **FREEMAN**, John **MITCHEL** Guy **HOBBS**,
Bushrod **RIDDICK**, Jesse R **KEY** Joseph **HURDLE** & James **BOICE**} **MINTON**s district
Pryor **SAVAGE**, Joseph **RIDDICK** of Thos, Jesse **BROWN**, Marmaduke **NORFLEET** Asa **HILL** Simonds **ROUNTREE** & Solomon **ROUNTREE**} Gatesville district
Dempsy **SPARKMAN**, Mills **EURE**, Mills **SPARKMAN** William **SAVAGE** A. W. **PARKER** Etheldred **CROSS**, & Nathaniel **HARRELL**} Scrach Hall "
W^m. **GOODMAN** Esqr. Joseph **FREEMAN** William **LEE**, Francis **DUKES**, Nathaniel **EURE** James **SAUNDERS** & John **SAUNDERS** Senr.} Piney Woods "
Simon **WALTERS** William **MOORE** James **SAVAGE**,
George **SMITH**, John **ODAM** Samuel **CROSS** & Henery G **WILLIAMS**} **HASLET** Shop do

a Division of the real estate of William **MILLER** dec^d. returned to Court and ordered to be registered

Elizabeth **BROTHERS** Guardian act. with Robert **BROTHERS**, James **BROTHERS**, & Richard **BROTHERS** for the year 1833 returned to Court & orderd to be recorded

Elizabeth **BROTHERS** Guardian act with Robert **BROTHERS** James **BROTHERS** & Richard **BROTHERS** for the year 1834 returnd to Court & ordered to be recorded.

Elizabeth **BROTHERS** Guardian act with Robert **BROTHERS** James **BROTHERS** & Richard **BROTHERS** for 1835 returned to Court & and [sic] orderd to be recorded.

Elizabeth **BROTHERS** Guardian act with James **BROTHERS** & Richard **BROTHERS** for the year 1836 (May Ct.) was returned to Court &ordered to be recorded

Edward **BRIGGS**' Guardian acts. with Ann E **MANSARD** & Jannet M **MANSARD** for the years 1834 & 1835 up to Feby Ct. were returned to Court and ordered to be recorded

Nathan **RIDDICK** Trustee of Gates County presented his Current [sic] with said county and ordered it filed

Mills **PILAND**'s Guardian act. with Susan **PILAND** John **PILAND** & Mildred **PILAND** orpans of Elisha **PILAND** returned to Court & ordered to be recorded

John **MATTHEWS** Guardian act with Eliza **BENTON** was returned to Court and ordered to be recorded

[172] Dempsy **PARKER**s Guardian act with Henry **JONES** orphan of Henry **JONES** dec^d. returned to court & ordered to be recorded

Ordered that James H **PARKER** be appointed overseer of the Road leading from **NORFLEET**s Mill to John **WALTON**s & Robert **SIMONS** Joseph **SIMONS** & Jacob **HINTON** work on said Road.

Ordered that Richard **ODAM** be appointed to work /overseer/ on the Road leading from **WOOD**s Old field to **WYNNS** Cross way

Ordered that W^m H **SAVAGE** be appointed overseer of the Road leading from W^m L **BOOTHE**s to the Cow pen Swamp

DAUGHTRY & **FOWLKES** } Tuesday May Ct. County Ct. 1836
    vs   } Appeal.
Henry **BOND**   } The following Jurors to wit. Kedar **TAYLOR** Timothy **ROGERS** Barnet **MARCH** Joseph **BENTON** Solomon **SMALL** John **SMITH** Willis **WALTON** James **CARTER**

May Court 1836

Dempsy **PARKER** of John Dempsy **PARKER** of Miles Henry **HAYS** John **SAVAGE** William **HOFFLER** & James **BRIGGS** being duly sworn & impanelled find all the Issues infavour of the plantiffs and acess their damages to $15

Thomas **BAGLEY** & wife }
    vs   appeal }
James **COSTEN** Senr } The following Jurors to wit Timothy **ROGERS** Kedar **TAYLOR** Barnet **MARCH** Joseph **BENTON** Solomon **SMALL** John **SMITH** Willis **WALTON** Exum **LEWIS** Jesse **SAVAGE** Mills **SPARKMAN** W^m. **HOFFLER** & Dempsy **PARER** [sic] being duly Sworn & impl^d. find all the Issues in favor of the plffs and acess their damages to $15.45

Jethero **EURE** }
    vs }
Abram W **PARKER** } Case The following Jurors to wit Timothy **ROGERS** Kedar **TAYLOR** Barnet **MARCH** Joseph **BENTON** Solomon **SMALL** Willis **WALTON** James **CARTER** Mills **SPARKMAN** Exum **LEWIS** Leven [?] **HOFFLER** Abm **SPIVEY** & John **SMITH** being duly Sworn & impl^d find all the issues in favour of the defendant.

W^m. W. **POWELL** }
    vs }
Jesse **MATTHIAS** et als } Appeal. William **POWELL** being Solmly [sic] Called & failing to appear is nonsuited.

Henry **HAYS** }
    vs }
W^m B **HARVEY** } Appeal. The following Jurors to wit Timothy **ROGERS** Kedar **TAEELOR** [sic] Barnet **MARCH** Joseph **BENTON** Solomon **SMALL** John **SMITH** Willis **WALTON** James **CARTER**. Mills **SPARKMAN**

[173] Jethero **WILLEY** Exum **LEWIS** & Thomas **COSTEN** being duly sworn & impanelled say they canot agree Mistrial

State } Wenesday morning 10 Oclock Court met
    vs   } A & B. Jury Impld. & Sworn find the
Jesse **WIGGINS** Junr. } Verdict not not [sic] Guilty.

State }
    vs   } A & B. Jury Impanelled & Sworn find a Verdict not Guilty. Ordered by the
Jesse **WIGGINS** Jur. } Court that the Prosecutor W^m. **BENTON** /Sen/ pay all Costs.

State }
    vs   } A & B.
Jethero H **RIDDICK** et als } Daniel S **WARD** submits the following Jury to wit Timothy **ROGERS** Kedar **TAYLOR** Barnet **MARCH** Joseph **BENTON** Solomon **SMALL** Willis **WALTON** James **CARTER** Mills **SPARKMAN** Exum **LEWIS** Leven **HOFFLER** & Abm **SPIVEY** being duly Sworn & impanelled Say that the defendant Jethero H **RIDDICK** is not Guilty

State }
    vs }
Isaac **HOFFLER** } Recognizance Ordered by the Court that Isaac **HOFFLER** be discharged from the payment of his forfeited recognizance upon his paying Cost of Court

State }
    vs }
FOWLKES & UMPHLET } F & A The following being duly Sworn & impanelled to wit. Anthony **MATTHEWS** John **POWELL**, Simon **STALLINGS**. Riddick **TROTMAN** James **BOICE** Wiley

May Court 1836

RIDDICK Dempsy PARKER of Miles William KING. Isaac HOFFLER, Nathan NIXON Dempsy PARKER of John & James BAKER, say the defendants are guilty as charged in the bill of Indictment

State }
    vs }
Riddick TROTMAN et als } Affray. Jury Impanelled & Sworn find the verdict Guilty in manner & form as charged in the bill of indictment. Ordered by the Court that that [sic] the said defendants Riddick TROTMAN & Thomas W STALLINGS be fined $1. each

[174] State }
    vs }
Simon STALLINGS et als } A & B Simon STALLINGS submits. TROTMAN pleads not Guilty. The following Jury to wit, Timothy ROGERS Kedar TAYLOR Barnet MARCH Joseph BENTON Solomon SMALL John SMITH Willis WALTON James CARTER Jesse SAVAGE Mills SPARK-MAN & Exum LEWIS being duly sworn & impanelled say that TROTMAN is not Guilty. Ordered by the Court that Simon STALLINGS be fined $1.

State }
    vs }
Abel UMPHLET } It appearing to the Court that the defendant Abel UMPHLET is the father of a Bastard Child begotten of him on the body of one Mary FAWLK which child has been sworn by the said Mary FOWLKES [sic] to the said UMPHLET for said child is by the Court afff affiliated & Judgment rendered vs the said UMPHLET for the sum of fifteen dollars for the 1st. years maintainance of said Child & $10. per year for six years thereafter.

State }
    vs }
Abel UMPHLET } It appearing to the Court that the defendant Abel UMPHLET is the father of a Bastard child begotten of him on the body of one Nancy EURE which child has been sworn by the said Nancy EURE to the said Able UMPHLET Said child is by the Court affiliated & Judgment rendered vs the said UMPHLET for the sum of fifteen dollars for the 1st. years maintainance of said child & $10 per year for six years thereafter

A Division of the lands of Benjamin HAYS decd. returned to Court and ordered to be registered.
    Test W. G. DAUGHTRY Clk [Remainder of page is blank.]

[175] State of North Carolina }
    Gates County } At a Court of pleas & qr. Sessions begun and held for the County of Gates at the Court House in Gatesville the 3rd. Monday of /in/ August 1836
Present {Hardy D PARKER Jesse R KEY David PARKER Wm. W COWPER Barnes GOODMAN} Esqrs

Jas R RIDDICK being duly elected Sherriff for the ensuing Two years, Offered three Bonds for five thousand pounds each, with, Henry GILLIAM, Joseph RIDDICK, Lassiter RIDDICK & Jethero H RIDDICK his securities, for the faithful performance of the duties of said Office which was recd. by the Court.

Ordered that the petition filed by the Court of Elizabeth EURE, report of Commissioners and order of Confirmation made, be set aside.

Ordered that James T FREEMAN be appointed admr. of the estate of Fedrick MORRIS Decd. by giving Bond for One thousand dollars with Hance HOFFLER, & Seth W ROUNTREE his securities.

x Ordered that Etheldred CROSS be appointed Overseer of the Road leading from winton Crost-way [sic] to WOODs old mill Field & that the following hands work on said Road Viz Richard ODAM's, Etheldred CROSS's John SPARKMAN's John LEEs, Jno POWELL Riddick GATLINGs (at his gaite) Bray PARKER, Abm PRUDEN Willis CROSS's Abm CROFFORD [sic] & Abm SMITH.

August Court 1836

x Ordered that James M **RIDDICK**'s hands work upon the Publick Road over which Willis **RIDDICK** is overseer.

[176] *x* Ordered that Risup **RAWLS** Henry **COSTEN** & Henry **RIDDICK** be appointed to audite and state the accounts of James **COSTEN** admr of John **JORDAN** dec^d.

x Ordered that John C **GORDEN** Willis F **RIDDICK** Joseph **RIDDICK** & Nathan **RIDDICK** audite and state the accounts of Jacob J **HARVEY** admr. of Mary A S **HARVEY** dec^d., & also to make a division her [sic] estate among the Heirs and Report to next Court.

x Ordered that Joseph **BENTON** be appointed overseer of the Road from the Virginia line to the Flat branch in the room of W^m W **POWELL**.

x Ordered that Drew M **SAUNDERS** be appointed overseer of the Road leading [sic] James **SAUNDERS**' to **MANEY**'s Ferry in room of James **SAUNDES** resigned.

Ordered that Tim **HUNTER** be appointed overseer of the Road leading from Jesse **EASON**s to George **COSTEN**s old place in stead of Thos **RIDDICK** resigned.

x Ordered that the Shff pay to John **MATTHEWS** Two dollars & 63/100 for error in listing Slaves

x Ordered that Joseph **RIDDICK**, Timothy **WALTON** Nathan **RIDDICK**, Thomas **RIDDICK** & William **HARRELL** be appointed commissioners to divide the lands of Hardy **EASON** dec^d. among the Heirs according to Law and take with them Allen **SMITH** County surveyor.

Ordered that Asa **HILL** be allowed to sell spiritous Liquors by the small measure for one year in Gatesville

x Ordered that James R **RIDDICK** Lemuel **RIDDICK** Henry **WILLEY** & Lassiter **RIDDICK** be appointed to audite and state the accounts of Allen **SMITH** admr of Lemuel **CLEAVES** dec^d. & make a division of said estate among the Heirs & report to next Court.

x Ordered that Henry **HAYS** be appointed overseer of the Road from **HARVEY**'s mill to the + Roads in room of W^m. B **HARVEY** resigned.

x Ordered that the Shff pay to James **IREDELL** One Hundred dollars for defending the Justices of County of Gates in the Supreme Court of N. C. at the instance of Zachariah **HITE**.

[177] *x* Ordered that the Shff pay to # Asa **HOFFLER** Seven dollars 24/100 to # Allen **BROWN** Six dollars 87/100 & to Henry **BOOTHE** Six dollars 87/100 for services rendered standing Guard during the prevalence of the Small pox of Gates County.

Ordered that Burwell **BROTHERS** be granted letters of administration on the estate of James **BAKER** dec^d. by giving Bond for fifteen thousand dollars with Whitmel **STALLINGS** & Jet H **RIDDICK** his securities.

Ordered that Isaac S **HARRELL** be appointed admr to the estate of Richard **HINTON** dec^d. and that he enter into bond for Six thousand dollars with Henry **BOND** & W^m. **HARRELL** his security.

Ordered that Jacob N **HARVEY** administer on the estate of Mary **HARVEY** dec^d. giving a bond for Six thousand dollars, with Joseph **GORDEN** & Marmaduke **NORFLEET** his securities

Ordered that Isaac S **HARRELL** be appointed Guardian to Sarah, Louisa & Deannah **HINTON** Orphans of Wm **HINTON** dec^d. & that he give bond of Five thousand dollars each, with Henry **BOND** Thos R **COSTEN** & Wm **HARRELL** his securities.

A bill of Sale was proved in open Court by the oath of Elizabeth **DUKES** a subscribing witness from

August Court 1836

Kedar **ELLIS** to Benjamin **FRANKLIN** orderd to be registerd

A bill of sale from Kedar **ELLIS** to Benjamin **FRANKLIN** was prooved in open Court by the Oath of Elizabeth **DUKES** a subscribing witness and ordr [sic] to be registered

A deed of Sale from Thos **HOGGARD** & Abm **PRUDEN** to James **WILLIAMS** was proved in open Court by the oath of John **SPAKMAN** a subscibing witness and ordered to be registered.

A deed of Sale from Jobe **BLANCHARD** to Hardy **JONES** was prooved in open court by the oath of Benj: **BROWN** a subscribing witnss and ordered to be registered

[178] A deed of Sale from Charlotte **GREEN** was acknowledged in open Court and ordered to be registered.

A deed of Sale from Willis F **RIDDICK** to Marmaduke **NORFLEET** was prooved in open Court by the Oath of W^m F **BENNETT** a subscribing witness and orderd to be registered.

A deed of Sale from Paul **JONES** to Job R **HALL** was prooved in open Court by the oath of Jethero H **RIDDICK** a subscribing winess and ordered to be registered

An inventary & account of sales of the property of Abram **HURDLE** dec^d. returned to Court and ordered to be recorded

x Ordered that the Shff pay Rufus K. **SPEED** Three Hundred & thirty six dollars 36/100 for services renderd attending persons afflicted with small Pox

The Last will & Testament of James **JONES** dec^d. was prooved in open Court by the Oath of Andrew P **MATTHEWS** a subscribing witness and ordered to be recorded

The last will & Testament of Nancy **GRANBURY** dec^d. was exibited in open Court, prooved by the Oath of Joseph **GORDEN** & ordered to be recorded

James **MORGAN** brought into Court the last will & Testament of James **JONES** which was prooved in due form of law by the oaths of the subscribing witnsses and quallified as execuetor of the said James **JONES** and upon motion ordered that letters Testamentory Issue and at the same time appeared in open Court Absilla **JONES** the widow of said James **JONES** and signified her dissatfaction with her husbands will and caused her disent from said James **JONES** will to be entered upon the Records of the Court which dissent was accordingly recorded.

A deed of Sale from Wm **HUDGINS** was acknowledged in open Court to Thos **EASON** & ordered to be recorded.

A Deed of Sale from James **JOHNSON** & Margaret **JOHNSON** his wife to Miles **PARKER** was acknowledged in open Court & ordered to be registered

[179] A Deed of sale from David **DUNFORD** to John **DUNFORD** was acknowledged in open Court and ordered to be registered

A Deed of Sale from Jonothan **WILLIAMS** to Miles **PARKER** was prooved in open Court by the oath of W^m W **COWPER** a subscribing witness and ordered to be recorded.

A Deed of Sale from William **GOODMAN** to Jethero D. **GOODMAN** was prooved in open Court by the Oath of Hardy **CROSS** a subscribing witness and ordered to be recorded.

A deed of Sale from Thos R **COSTEN** to Samuel R **HARRELL** was prooved in open Court by the ~~Oath of~~ acknowledgment of Thos R **COSTEN**

August Court 1836

A Deed of Sale from Nathaniel to Miles **CULLINS** was prooved in open Court by the oath of W^m L **BOOTHE** a subscribing witness and ordered to be registered.

A deed of Sale from John **GRIFFITH** to Dempsey **GRIFFITH** Pleasant **GATLING** Nancy **SAUNDERS** & Martha **GRIFFITH** was acknowledged in open Court and ordered to be recorded

A deed of Sale from Burwell **GRIFFITH** to Dempsey **GRIFFITH** Pleasant **GATLING** Nancy **SAUNDERS** & Martha **GRIFFITH** was acknowledged in open Court & ordered to be recorded.

A Deed of gift from Burwell **GRIFFITH** to Dempsey **GRIFFITH** Pleasant **GATLING** (wife of James **GATLING**) Nancy (wife of Jason) **SAUNDERS** & Martha **GRIFFITH** was acknowledged in open Court & ordered to be registered

A Deed of Sale from David **BENTON** to Joseph **BENTON** was prooved in open court by the oath of Abraham **BENTON** & ordered to be registered.

Jonothan **WILLIAMS** returned his act current with the estate of Hardy **WILLIAMS**. orderd that it be recorded

    Court adjorned until Tuesday 10 OClock

[180] Tuesday morning 10 Oclock Court met
Present {John C **GORDON** Joseph **RIDDICK** Thos **SAUNDERS** Jesse R **KEY**} Esqrs

The Shff returned the following list of Jurors to serve at this Term, to wit: Andrew **MATTHEWS** James **MORGAN**, Seth **BENTON**, Boon **EURE**, Calvin **BRINKLEY** Seth R **MORGAN** Abner **EASON** William **CROSS**, Riddick **JONES** Adam **RAIBY**, Nathan **PEARCE** Samuel **HARRELL** Henry **HAYS**, Abm. **PRUDEN** James T. **FREEMAN** Joshua **ALLEN** James **CARTER** John **ALPHIN** John **LANGSTON** Whitmel **HILL** Robert **HILL** W^m.. **GATLING** Bryant **HARE** & Miles **PARKER**. Out of whom the following were drawn, sworn & Charged for the Grand Jury to wit James **MORGAN** (foreman) Andrew **MATTHEWS** Seth **BENTON** Boon **EURE** Calvin **BRINKLEY** Seth R **MORGAN** Abner **EASON** William **CROSS**, Riddick **JONES**, Adam **RAIBY** Nathan **PEARCE** Samuel R **HARRELL** Henry **HAYS** Abm **PRUDEN** James T **FREEMAN** Joshua **ALLEN** James **CARTER** & John **ALPHIN**

Ordered that the Shff pay the County Court Clerk thirty dollars & 46 cents for /Cost of/ 4 Indictments tried at May Term in which the state failed to Convict.

" Ordered that the shff pay to John S **ROBERTS** Thirty four dollars 22½/100 for makin [sic] Spit Boxes Benches & Tables for the Court House

" Ordered that the shff pay to John C **GORDEN** & John **WALTON** Two dollars per day each for eight days & Riddick **GATLING** the same for five days for services rendered on committee of Finance.

" Ordered that John **WALTON** be allowed & the shff pay the same five dollars & 13/100 for a Record Book

Ordered that William **HARRELL** & Thos W **STALLINGS**'s hands work on the Road from Worrick Swamp to snake Branch under Thos **HURDLE** overseer

[181] Tuesday 16th. 1836

" Ordered that ~~James~~ /Joseph/ **BENTON** be appointed overseer of the Road in room of Wm **POWELL**

Ordered that Henry **GILLIAM** be appointed Guardian to William **HARE** orphan of John **HARE** & give a bond $500. with Jethero H **RIDDICK** & James R **RIDDICK** securities

" Ordered that Jordan **PARKER** be appointed overseer in room of James **MORGAN** resigned.

August Court 1836

A deed of Sale from Abel **ROGERSON** to Jesse **HOBBS** was acknowledged in open Court and ordered to be registered.

A deed of Sale from Burwell **BROTHERS** to Daniel S **HOBBS** was prooved in open Court by the oath of John **SHEPHERD** a subscribing witness and ordered to be registered

A division of the lands of John J **ODOM** returned to court and ordered to be registered

A deed of sale from Robert to Joseph **HILL** was acknowledged in open Court and ordered to be registered.

A deed of Mortgage from W^m.. **DANIEL** To Henry **GILLIAM** was prooved in open Court by the Oath of Jas C **RIDDICK** a subscribing witness and ordered to be registered.

A deed of Sale from Jas R **RIDDICK** Shff to Amos **HOBBS** was acknowledged in open Court and ordered to be registered

A deed of Sale from Jesse **MATHIAS** & Joseph **MATHIAS** to Abm **RIDDICK** was pro_ved_ in open Court by the oath of Dempsey **KNIGHT** a subscribing witness & ordered to be registered.

A deed of sale from Elisha H. **BOND** to Henry **BOND** was prooved in open Court by the oath of Jno. W **BOND** a subscribing witness and ordered to be registered

A deed of sale from Elisha H **BOND** & Mills **ROBERTS** to Nathl. **EURE** was prooved in open Court by the Oath of Henry **GILLIAM** a subscribing witness and order_d_ to be registered

A deed of Sale from Jesse **PORTER**, Sabra **PORTER** Amos **PARKER**, William **PARKER** & Humphrey **PARKER** to Miles **PARKER** & Abm **PARKER** was prooved in open Court by the Oath of Henry **BRINKLEY** a subscribing witness and ordered to be registered

[182] Tuesday 16th.. 1836

A deed of Sale from George **FREEMAN** & Henry **GILLIAM** to Archibald **JONES** was prooved in open Court by the oath of Jno W. **BOND** subscribing witness and ordered to be registered

A bill of Sale from Riddick **SMITH** to Henry **COSTEN** was prooved in open Court and ordered to be registered prooved by Oath of William **JONES**

A. W. **PARKER** executor of Reuben **PARKER** dec^d. returned an_d_ Inventory and an account of Sales of the property of said Dec^d. ordered that they be recorded.

Benjamin **FRANKLIN** admr of John **BRINKLY** dec^d. returned his act. current and ordered that it be recorded

Henry **HAYS** }
    vs }
W^m.. B. **HARVEY** } John **LANGSTON** Whitmel **HILL** Robert **HILL** William **GATLING** Bryant **HARE** Miles **PARKER** Wm **JONES** Reuben **PILAND** Nathaniel **HARRELL**, Daniel **HOBBS** Wm **BOOTHE** & Edward **BRIGGS** being Sworn & Impanelled find all the Issues infavour of the plff and assess his damage $8.34

Ordered by the Court that W^m. **POWELL** be permitted to draw his note from the Office of County Court Clerk against Jesse **MATHIAS** & others.

David **PARKER** }
    vs }
Jethero **HARRELL**} Nonsuit

August Court 1836

Exum **JENKINS** }
    vs }
Henry L **BLOUNT**} Jury, Whitmel **HILL** Robert **HILL** Bryant **HARE** Miles **PARKER**, Reuben **PILAND** Nathaniel **HARRELL**, Daniel S **HOBBS** Edward **BRIGGS**, Edwin **CROSS**, Marmaduke **NORFLEET**, Miles **BRIGGS** & Solomon **ROUNTREE** being Sworn & Impanelled find that the defendant does detain the Negro Girl **MARTILLA** declared for and that she had been bailed to the defendant and that he the defendant had destroyed the bailment and that the statute of limitation was no bar and they find the value of the slave to be

[183] Tuesday 16th. 1836

Six hundred dollars and assess the plffs damages to five Cents.
    The defendant Henry L **BLOUNT** for the Said Judgment prayed an appeal to the Superior Court which was granted & he entered into Bonds with Henry **GILLIAM** Marmaduke **NORFLEET** & Thos A. **JORDAN** securities

    Court adjorned until Wednesday 10 O clock
    Wednesday Court met according to adjorment [sic]
  Present {Joseph **RIDDICK** Henry **COSTEN** John **WILLY** Thos **SAUNDERS** } Esqrs.

State }
vs }
John **LOVET** et als } John **LANGSTON** Whitmel **HILL** Robert **HILL**, W^m. **GATLING** Bryant **HARE** James **BOICE** Solomon **ROUNTREE** W^m.. **KING** Drew **TROTMAN** Joseph **HURDLE**, Simon **KING** & Thomas R **COSTEN** (Jury) being Sworn & Impaneld find both Guilty as charged in the bill of indictment.
    Ordered by the Court that John **LOVETT** be fined fifteen dollars & that Matthew **JORDAN** be fined five dollars.
    The defendant Matthias [sic] **JORDAN** for the said Judgment prayed for an appeal to the superior Court, which was granted & His recognsance [sic] with John **WILLEY** security was taken for One Hundred dollars each

State }
vs }
Ira **CARTER** et als} Ira **CARTER** & Samuel **EURE** being called out and failing to appear forfeited their recognisance

State }
vs }
Roden **PARKER** } Roden **PARKER** & William **LEE** being solemnly called and failing to appear, their recognisance is forfeited & William **LEE** failing to appear

[184] Wednesday 17th.. 1836

and bringing before the Court the body of Roden **PARKER** his recognisance is forfeited. Issue alias for Roden **PARKER** and Fi Fa against Roden **PARKER** & W^m.. **LEE**.

State }
  vs }
Richard M **HARVEY** } R M **HARVEY** Submits. Ordered that he be fined 6^d.

State }
  vs }
Reuben **BROTHERS** et als } R **BROTHERS** pleads not guily [sic]. Jury Imp^d. & sworn find not Guilty

August Court 1836

Thos **COSTEN** et als }
    vs }
Henry **COSTEN** } John **LANGSTON** Whitmel **HILL** Robert **HILL** W^m. **GATLING** Bryant **HARE**, James **BOICE** Solomon **ROUNTREE** W^m.. **KING** Joseph **HURDLE** Simon **KING** Bray **PARKER** & Guy **HOBB** [sic] (Jury) being sworn & Impanelled Find all the Issues in favour of the Plffs and assess their damage $201.13¼ and by consent of parties the plffs pay all costs except the defendant attornys fee

A. W. **PARKER** }
    vs }
Ervin **HARRELL** } Submited to the Court On motion offered /and/ upon hearing the evidence it is ordered by the Court that the petition and all proceedings ___[blank]___ be dismissed.

Ordered that Miles **TAYLOR** a coloured boy son of Betsey **TAYLOR** as a fit subject to be bound out and that he be bound to John **RIDDICK** and that henter [sic] into bonds &c

x Ordered that the Shff pay Mills **ROBERTS** Seventeen dollars & ninety four Cents it being amt paid by said **ROBERTS** to James **BROWN**, Thos **BLANCHARD** & Charles **DELANY** for keeping Guard.

x Ordered that the Shff pay Lassiter **RIDDICK** Coroner Twenty /$20./ dollars for holding inquest over the bodies of Asa **WIGGINS** & Andrew **BAKER**

x Ordered that Mills **EURE** be requested to let out and superintend the Repairs of **COLE**s Creek Bridge, to the lowest undertaker and that the Timber be of good Heart Pine

[185] Wednesday 17th. 1836

Ordered that John **WALTON** Henry **GILLIAM** W^m.. G **DAUGHTRY** Reuben **HINTON** or any three of them audite and state the accounts of Thos **SAUNDERS** admr. of Bathsheba **SEARS** dec^d. with the estate of said dec^d. and that the said perons [sic] make a division of the parishable estate of said dec^d. among the distributees agreeable to Law.

Ordered that Joseph **HURDLE** administer on the estate of Andrew **BAKER** dec^d. and that he enter into bonds for One thousand dollars with Drew **TROTMAN** & Calvin **BRINKLEY** securities

Ordered that Miles **BRIGGS** be granted the administration of on the estate of Asa **WIGGINS** dec^d. and give Bond for five Hundred dollars with John **WIGGINS** & Dempsey **PEAL** securities.

Ordered that William **PRICE** a coloured boy about 10 yeas of age and Abram **REED** a coloured boy about six yeas of age be bound out to Joseph **RIDDICK** and that he enter into Bonds &c.

The following is a list of Insolvents returned by the shff for the year 1835 & sworn to in open Court Matthew **HOBBS** Isaac **JENKINS** Paul **JONES** Briant **MATTHEWS** Elisha **WALTON** W^m.. D **SIMMS** Abraham **MORGAN** Junr. Jesse **WIATT** Robert **PARKER**

A deed of Sale from Riddick B **EURE** to Elisha **PARKER** was prooved in open Court by the Oath of Levi **EURE** a subscribing witness and ordered to be registered
                  Test W G **DAUGHTRY** Clk

[186] State of North Carolina}
        Gates County} At a Court of pleas & quater Sessions begun & held for the County of Gates at the Court house in Gatesville the 3rd. Monday of November A D 1836
Present Hardy **PARKER** Lemuel **RIDDICK** Richd **ODAM**} Esq^rs.

x Ordered that the Shff pay to Henry **GILLIAM** D. Clerk under **STEDMAN** Thirty Two dollars 90/100 for costs of sundry indictments in which the State failed to convict

November Court 1836

Ordered that the Shff pay to Henry **GILLIAM** Eight dollars on act of **REYNOLDS** Bill for painting Blinds to the Court House

Ordered that Pryer **SAVAGE** be granted Letters of administration on the estate of Lemuel **HOWELL** dec^d. and that he enter into bonds for Five hundred dollars with He<u>ny</u> **GILLIAM** security.

Ordered that Letters of administration be granted to Burwell **BROTHERS** on the Estate James **BROTHERS** dec^d. that he give bond for Two Thousand dollars with Isaac S **HARRELL** & James T **FREEMAN** securities

Ordered that letters of administration on the estate of Isaac **SPEIGHT** dec^d. be granted to Willis **CROSS** & that he give Bond for One thousand dollars with Richard **ODAM** & Nathaniel **EURE** securities.

Ordered that letters of administration upon the estate of Henry **JONES** be granted to Dempsy **PARKER** and that he enter into bond in the sum of Three thousand dollars with Dempsey **SPARKMAN** & Nat<u>a</u>niel **EURE** securities for the same

Ordered that letters of administration on the Estate of Jethero **RIDDICK** dec^d. be granted to David **RIDDICK** and that he enter in to bond with Elbert **RIDDICK** & Jonothan **WILLIAMS** securities in the sum of four hundred dollars.

Ordered that John **WILLEY** be appointed Administrator on the Estate of Eff **LEWIS** dec^d. and that he give Bond in the sum of One thousand dollars with Henry **GILLIAM** & William **LEE** securities.

[187] Ordered that John C **GORDON** be appointed administrator on the estate of James **MILLER** dec^d. infant and that he give bond in the sum of One Hundred dollars with Timothy **WALTON** security.

Ordered that Thomas **SAUNDERS** be appointed administrator on the Estate of Asa **ODAM** dec^d. infant that he give bond for the sum of Fifteen thousand dollars with Richard **ODAM** & Abraham W **PARKER** securities.

Ordered that Abram W **PARKER** be appointed administrator on the estate of Elisha **HARRELL** dec^d. and that he enter into bond for One hundred dollars with Nathl **EURE** & Dempsey **SPARKMAN** securities.

Ordered that Abram W **PARKER** be appointed administrator on the estate of Mary **JOHNSON** dec^d. and that he give bond for one hundred dollars with Dempsey **SPARKMAN** & Nathaniel **EURE** securities.

Ordered that Abm. **RIDDICK** of <u>h</u>ertford County be appointed administrator on the Estate of Timothy **HOWELL** and that he give bond for One hundred dollars & Riddick **GATLING** security

Ordered that Richard **ODAM** be appointed administrator on the Estate of George **HARRELL** dec^d. and that he give Bond for Two thousand dollars with Willis **CROSS** & Thomas **SAUNDERS** his securities

x Ordered that John **HAYS** be appointed overseer of the Road from the fork near Thos **HINTON**s to **HUNTER**s Mill in stead of Thos **HINTON** Resigned

x Ordered that the Hands of Moore **SAVAGE** and Marmaduke **BAKER** work ~~un~~ on the Road leading from James M **RIDDICK**'s to Jno **HASLET**s under Elbert **RIDDICK** Overseer

x Ordered that W^m H **MC GUIRE** [?] be appointed Overseer of the Road leading from the middle of **POWELL**s mill run or race to the Virginia line.

x Ordered that Robert **BROTHERS** be appointed Overseer of the Road leading from Josiah **BRIGGS**' to M^r. A **ELLIS**' whereof Jos **EASON** was former overseer

x Ordered that John **FELTON** be appointed Overseer of the Road leading from **BENNET**s Creek Bridge to the **MINGO** Path in room of W^m. **HAYS** Resigned

November Court 1836

[188] x Ordered that James M **RIDDICK**s Hands work on the Road leading from Jas M **RIDDICK**'s to Jno **HASLETT**s. E **RIDDICK** Overseer

Ordered that Whitmel **EURE** infant be bound to Riddick **EURE** until he arrives to the age of 21 years and that said Riddick **EURE** be bound to learn him the trade of House Carpenter and give the said Whitmel one years education

Ordered that Starkey **LAWRENCE** be bound to W^m.. B. **HARVEY** until he arrives at 21 yeas of age and that the said **HARVEY** be bound to learn him the trade of a Blacksmith.

Ordered that Richard **CROSS** son of Wiley **CROSS** be bound to James **ROGERS** until he becomes of age

x Ordered that the shff pay back to Henry **CROFFORD** one dollar & Twenty five cents for Error in Tax of 1834

Ordered that Lassiter **RIDDICK** be appointed guardian to Harriet B **GATLING** and that he enter into Bond in the sum of Six Thousand dollars with James R **RIDDICK** and Joseph **RIDDICK** his securities for the same.

Ordered that Allen **SMITH** be appointed Guardian to Thomas **MATTHEWS** orphan of John **MATTHEWS** dec^d. and that he give Bond in the sum of Five thousand dollars with Lassiter **RIDDICK** & James R **RIDDICK** his securities.

x Ordered that Riddick **GATLING** John **WILLEY**, Robert **ROGERS** James **ROGERS** & Francis **DUKES** be appointed to audite and state the accounts of Joseph **FREEMAN** adm^r. of John **FREEMAN** dec^d.

Ordered that Henry **GILLIAM** W G **DAUGHTRY**, James **PARKER** & Joseph **RIDDICK** Junr. audite and state the accounts of David **PARKER** adm^r. of Jacob **POWELL** dec^d.

Ordered that Burwell **BROTHERS** adm^r. on the Estate of James **BROTHERS** dec^d. sell one Negro on a Credit six months for a division between the lawfull heirs.

Ordered that John **WILLEY** adm^r. on the estate of Eff **LEWIS** dec^d. Sell a negro man named **JACK** on a credit of six months to make a division among the Heirs

The last Will & Testament of Isaac **GREEN** dec^d. was exibited in open Court by Joseph **GORDEN** Executor and prooved by the Oath of Luke **GREEN** one of the subscribing witnesses

[189] The last Will and testament of John **SAUNDERS** dec^d. was exibited into open Court and duly prooved according to law by the Oaths of Samuel **CROSS** & William H. **GOODMAN** the two subscribing witnesses thereunto whereuppon Nancy **SAUNDERS** quallified as executrix in due form of law.

The last will and testament of John **HAYS** dec^d. was exibited in open Court by Docton **HAYS** & James **SMITH** and prooved by the Oath of James **HARE** one of the subscribing witnesses, whereupon Docton **HAYS** & James **SMITH** quallified as executors in due form of law.

The last will & Testament of John **MATTHEWS** dec^d. was exibited in open Court by James **SAVAGE** and duely prooved by the Oaths of Levi **BEEMAN** & Andrew **JOHNSON** the subscribing witnesses whereupon James **SAVAGE** quallified as executor.

The last Will and testament of Charity **MILLER** dec^d. was exibited into open Court by John C **GORDEN** and duly prooved by the Oath of Reuben **SMALL** one of the subscribing witnesses, whereupon John C **GORDEN** qualified as executor.

Ordered that Thomas **SAUNDERS** Henry **GILLIAM** William G **DAUGHTRY** & John **WALTON** be

November Court 1836

appointed Comissioners to ~~divide~~ audite the accounts of John ROBERTS adm^r. of Sarah JONES dec^d. and divide the personal property of said estate among the heirs according to Law.

Ordered that Willis F RIDDICK Edward R HUNTER Thomas TWINE & Samuel R HARRELL be appointed to audite and settle the ~~accounts~~ Estate of James GRANBURY dec^d. Jos GORDEN adm^r. Also to make a division of the personal property & negroes of said dec^d. among the Heirs of said dec^d.

Ordered that the same men be appointed Commissioners to audite and settle the accounts of John B BAKER Ex^r. of Richard B GREGORY dec^d.

Ordered also that the same men be appointed Commissioners to audite and settle the Estate of Isaac PEARCE dec^d. with Joseph GORDEN adm^r.

[190] Ordered that Dempsey SPARKMAN be appointed administrator on the estate of John SPARKMAN dec^d. and give bond for Six thousand dollars with A. W. PARKER & Mills SPARKMAN securities.

Ordered that James T FREEMAN be appointed adm^r. On the Estate of David TAYLOR dec^d. Orphan of Robert TAYLOR dec^d. and that he give bond for One thousand dollars with John HINTON & Abel ROGERSON.

Ordered that Jane SWEAT and Elizabeth SWEAT be bound to Ann N HARVEY until they be come [sic] of ~~age~~ lawful age and that she enter into Bonds &c

x Ordered that the Sheff pay to John ROBERTS the amount of Sixteen dollars & fifty Cents for provisions furnised Guard.

x Ordered that the Shff pay W. G. DAUGHTRY Clerk Seven dollars & 95/100 on act of State vs Reuben BROTHERS County Expense

x Ordered that the Shff pay to Jonothan WILLIAMS One dollar & Twenty three Cents for Tax overpaid.

Ordered that Leah HOFFLER widow of Garrot HOFFLER be appointed Guardian to her four Children, Penelope, James Robert, Emily & Leah HOFFLER and give bond for One thousand dollars each with Mills ROBERTS & James T FREEMAN securities.

Ordered that James BRIGGS be appointed Guardian to Henrietta BRIGGS orphan of Henry BRIGGS dec^d. and give Bond for Three thousand dollars with Miles BRIGGS & Edward BRIGGS securities.

Ordered that Jonas HINTON be appointed Guardian to Richard BLANCHARD & Give Bond for One thousand dollars with Willis S RIDDICK & Absolam [sic] BLANCHARD securities.

Ordered that infuture [sic] that the State docket will be taken up on Tuesday and that the Clerk advertise the same at the Court House door

Ordered that Isaac PARKER be apointed Overseer of the Road leading from BONDs Landing to the fork near Mills ROBERTS's and that the following hands work on same to wit: James EURE /J^r./ John MORRISS J^r. Robert PARKER, Nathan PARKER Garrison HALL, Elisha BOND Isaac PARKER & Henry B LASSITER.

Ordered that Jethero D GOODMAN be appointed Overseer/of the Road/ in room of Blake BRADDY resigned

[191] x Ordered that Allen DAUGHTREY be appointed overseer of the Road in room of Eli WORRELL resigned & that Thos R COSTENs hands work on said Road

A deed of Sale from Asa WALTON, Millicent POWELL & William WALTON was prooved in open Court by the oath of Jesse WHITE One of the subscribing witnessess and ordered to be registered

November Court 1836

A deed of Sale from James **COSTEN** Junior to Peter B **MINTON** was acknowl dged [sic] in Open Court and ordered to be registered

A deed of Sale from Abraham **PRUDEN** to Bray **EURE** was prooved in open Court by the Oath of Thos: **HOGGARD** a subscribing witness and ordered to be registered.

A deed of Sale from John B **BAKER** to John **WORRELL** was prooved in open Court by the Oath of William **BAKER** a subscribing witness and ordered to be registered

A deed of Sale from Andrew R **HARRELL** to William R **BROTHERS** was acknowledged in open Court and ordered to be registered

A deed of sale from Andrew R **HARRELL** & Julia **HARRELL** to William R **BROTHERS** was acknowledged in open Court by Andrew R **HARRELL** and ordered to be registered

A deed of sale from Shadrack **STALLINGS** and Nancey **STALLINGS** to Fredrick **JONES** was exibited in open Court and acknowledged by the said Shadrack & Nancey **STALLINGS** and ordered to be registered

A deed of sale from William **ARNOLD** to James A **BALLAD** was prooved in open Court by the oath of James **MORGAN** a subscribing witness and ordered to be registered

A deed of sale from Richard John K **FIELD** to Daniel **WILLIAMS** was prooved in open Court by the oath of Henry **WILLEY** a subscribing witness and ordered to be registered.

A deed of sale from James **GOODMAN** to Charles **JONES** was prooved in open Court by the oath of Jethero **WILLEY** a subscribing witness and ordered to be ~~recorded~~ registered

A deed of sale from Riddick **TROTMAN** to John **WHITE** was prooved in open Court by the oath of Nathan **NIXON** a subscribing witness and ordered to be registered.

A deed of sale from Nathan **NIXON** to Zachariah **NIXON** was acknowledged in open Court and ordered to be registered.

[192] A deed of Sale from Timothy **WALTON** to Nathan **NIXON** was acknowledged in open Court and ordered to be registered

A release from T. W. **CARR** Trustee to John O **HUNTER** was prooved in open Court by John C **GORDEN** and orderd to be registered

A deed of sale from John B **BAKER** to Lassiter **RIDDICK** was prooved in open Court by the Oath of William J **BAKER** a subscribing witness and ordered to be registered.

A deed of sale from Wm H **GOODMAN** to Lemuel **SMITH** was acknowledged in open Court and ordered to be registered.

A deed of Sale from Nathan **WARD** to Burwell **BROTHERS** was prooved in open Court by the Oath of Abner **EASON** a subscribing witness and ordered to be registered.

A deed of sale from Bray **PARKER** to Hannah **HUMPHLET** was acknowledged in open Court and ordered to be registered

A deed of Sale from Abraham **PRUDEN** & Martha **PRUDEN** to Jason **ROUNTREE** was acknowledged in open Court and ordered to be registered.

A deed of ~~sale~~ Gift from Jethero **EURE** Senr: to Jethero **EURE** Junr was prooved in open Court ~~and~~ by the Oath of William **CARTER** and ordered to be registered

November Court 1836

A deed of sale from John C GORDEN to James POWELL was acknowledged in open Court and ordered to be registered.

A deed of sale from Joseph GORDEN to Isaac S HARRELL was acknowledged in open Court and orderedered [sic] to be registered.

A deed in Trust from James COPELAND to Miles BRIGGS was prooved in open Court by the Oath of Robert H BALLAD a subscribing witness and ordered to be registered

A deed of sale from Julia LAWRENCE to Lassiter RIDDICK was prooved in open Court by the oath of Lemuel RIDDICK a subscribing witness and ordered to be registered.

A deed of sale from Samuel FELTON to David F. FELTON was acknowledged in open Court and ordered to be registered

A deed of sale from Jethero BLANCHARD to Courrie [?] BLANCHARD was prooved in open Court by the oath of Robert BLANCHARD a subscribing witness and ordered to be registered

A division of the lands of James BOOTHE dec^d. returned to Court and ordered to be registered

[193] A division of the lands of John WIGGINS Miles PARKER and Garret KNIGHT returned to Court and ordered to be registered

A deed of Sale from Robert ROGERS to William LEE was prooved in open Court by the Oath of Hardy CROSS a subscribing witness and ordered to be registered

A deed of Sale from John WIGGINS to Dempsey PEAL was acknowledged in open Court and ordered to be registered.

The Shff returned in open Court the report of a Jury summoned by him agreeable to an order of august County Court to lay off a publick Road begining at the Middle-Swam [sic] Road near James M RIDDICKs thence runing to the piney Woods Road near John H HASLETs in the most suitable direction for the publick convenience, which report was received by the Court and ordered to be filed in the Clerks Office.

The following Justices to wit. J R KEY, Henry COSTEN Willis F RIDDICK Jno C GORDEN, Jos RIDDICK Jno WILLEY Lemuel RIDDICK Richard ODAM, Riddick GATLING Hardy PARKER, Abm W PARKER W^m.. L BOOTHE & Henry WILLEY, Elected Thomas F JONES Solicitor for the County of Gates to fill the vacancy caused by the removal of W^m. E. PUGH Esqr.
    Court adjorned.

    Tuesday Court met
    Present {Thomas SAUNDERS, John WALTON, John C GORDEN} Esqrs

The Shff returned the following list of Jurors to serve at this term to wit. Aaron PEARCE, Elijah HARRELL Guy HOBBS, John WILLIAMS, Lewis GREEN, Leven HOFFLER, Benjamin SAUNDERS Willis R HAYS Kedar HINTON Jethero HOWELL Dempsey PARKER Robert HAYS Eli WORRELL, Thomas SMITH, William BABB, Edwin CROSS, Riddick MATTHEWS, Elisha SMALL, Isaac

[194] PARKER, Thos EASON George W SMITH, Henry HOFFLER James BROWN of James & Edward JONES, Out of whom the following were drawn, sworn & Charged for the Grand Jury to wit: William BABB (Foreman), Aaron PEARCE Elijah HARRELL Guy HOBBS John WILLIAMS Lewis GREEN Levin HOFFLER Benjn. SAUNDERS Willis R HAYS Kedar HINTON Jethero HOWELL Dempsey PARKER Robert HAYS Eli WORRELL Thomas SMITH Edwin CROSS Riddick MATTHEWS and Elisha SMALL

November Court 1836

Mary **ROBERTS** }
   vs }
W^m F **BENNET** et als } Debt } The following Jury to wit Isaac **PARKER** Thomas **EASON**, George W **SMITH** Henry **HOFFLER** James **BROWN** of James Edward **JONES** Abel **ROGERSON** Nathan **WARD** Dempsey **PARKER** Jas T **FREEMAN** Nathaniel **EURE** & Jas **COSTEN** Junr. being sworn & Impanelled find all the Issues in favour of the plff and assess her damages $37.34/100 Value of the obligation Seven Hundred dollars.

State }
   vs }
Mills **ROBERTS** } Same Jury as above being sworn and Impanelled find the defendant Not Guilty as Charged in the bill of Indictment.
                      Teste
                        W G **DAUGHTRY** Clk

END

DECEDENT INDEX

BABB
 Christoper 9
 Christopher 10, 11,12
BAGLEY
 Jacob 118
 Trotmon 99,124
BAKER
 Andrew 184,185
 James 177
BALLAD
 Alfred 160
BALLARD
 Afred 159
BEEMAN
 A. 105
 Ab. 116
 Abraham 4,18
 Eliza 140
 Israel 11
 Jno. 93,96,118, 153
 John 39,49,53, 55,140,149
 Lucreatia 128, 140,141
 Lucretia 118
BENTON
 A. 128
 Abraham 44,62
 Abram 119
 Elisha 29
 Jethro 29,68
 Seth 18,118, 134,138
BLANCHARD
 Will. 34
 Wm. 109,129, 136,150
BOGE
 Jonathan 11
BOGURE
 Charles 78
BOND
 Richard 14
 Richd. 11,12,17, 48,103
 Thos. 153
 William 52,69
BONNER
 John 159
BOOTHE
 James 192

BOYCE
 Jonathan 49
 William 56,62
BRIGGS
 Ailsey 99
 Benj. 99,124
 Benja. 55
 Benjamin 15
 Charles 167
 Chas. 107
 Henry 141,190
 Wm. 157
BRINKLEY
 David 167
 James 60,76
 John 61,72,80
 Miles 35,168
BRINKLY
 Elisha 12
 James 67,134
 Jno. 92
 John 77,182
 Miles 9,10,51
BRISCO
 E. 153
 Ebon 106,109, 122,146
 Ebron 14
BROTHERS
 James 186,188
 William 27
BROWN
 Saml. 147,153
CLEAVES
 Lemel 121
 Leml. 121
 Lemuel 158, 159,176
CLEVES
 Lemuel 120
COPELAND
 Henry 3,6
 Heny 49
COSTEN
 Isaac 11
 James 67
 Jas. 5
COSTON
 David 146
CROSS
 A. 85
 Ab. 85,86
 Abm. 12,49

CROSS
 Abraham 14,84
 Abram 14,84,85
 Christain 9
 Elisha 6,47,49, 122,153
 James 21,119,158
 Jno. 6
 Taylor 5
CULLINS
 Nathan 79,91,159
DANIEL
 Cheaton 131
DILDY
 Mary 95
EASON
 Hardy 2,3,12,51, 53,73,121,176
 Sol. 153
 Solomon 108,116, 134
 Wm. 34
EURE
 Celea 149
 John 81,117
 John, Jr. 148,153
 John, Sr. 78
 Lewis 8,48,124, 128
FIELDS
 M. R. 146
 Marey 143
 Mary 142,146
 Mills R. 91,93,98, 100,146
FRANKLIN
 Barshaba 99,116
 Barsheba 9,31
 Jonas 10,20,28
FREEMAN
 Jno. 118
 John 128,188
 Walton 104,105, 107,108,119,148, 167
FREMAN
 Walton 137
GATLING
 E. B. 51,148
 Etheldred B. 5,6
 James 3
GOODMAN
 John 148,153,164

GOODMAN
 Leml. 6,49,148, 153
 Lemuel 5
 Richard 153,164
 Richd. 148
GORDON
 James 78,90,124
GRANBERRY
 James 9,10,157
 John 20
 Thomas 6,7
GRANBERY
 James 35,51
GRANBEY
 John 152
GRANBURY
 James 189
 Nancy 178
GREEN
 Aaron 12
 Henry 94,95,134
 Isaac 188
GREGORY
 Jos. 126
 Richard B. 189
 Richd. B. 51
HARE
 Jno. 120
 John 12,16,32,42, 43,48,57,105,116, 122,129,181
HARRELL
 Abm. 68
 Abram 67
 Elisha 9,187
 George 187
 Judith 47
 Mary 88,101,161
 Peter 24,26,44,48, 116
 Theos. 95
 William 115,153, 161
 Wm. 127
HARVEY
 Mary 177
 Mary A. S. 176
HAYS
 Benj. 79,105
 Benjamin 61,170, 174

HAYS
Benjn. 119
John 189
HAYSE
Benjamin 66
HINTON
Fred. 95,126,127
Frederick 46,47,120
Frederick, Jr. 46
Fredk., Jr. 52
James 12,56,96,127
Reuben 66
Reuben, Jr. 24,26,35,43
Richard 177
Rubin 103,107
Will 90
Wm. 78,148,149,153,177
HOBBS
David 106
Thomas 3,27
HOFFLER
Garret 90,102
Garrot 98,190
James 60
HOFLER
James 12,46
HOLLOWEL
Luke 31
HOLLOWEL_
Luke 116
HOLLOWELL
Luke 18,107
HOWELL
Lemuel 186
Lottey 75
Timothy 187
HUDGINS
Leven 142
HUNTER
Elisha 13
Isaac 5,9,15,66
Isaac R. 147
Sophia 62
Sophia C. 62
HURDLE
Abram 170,178
Henry 29,48
Kedar 6
JENKINS
Arthur 158

JENKINS
Willey 77
JINKINS
Willie 135
Willis 101
JOHNSON
Mary 187
Thomas 88
JONES
Henry 2,12,21,26,51,70,96,110,172,186
James 78,89,90,98,160,178
Jas. 78
Nathl. 119
Sarah 158,189
JORDAN
John 128,176
JORDON
Armstead 12
KING
Mary 72,80
William 18,31,63
Wm. 121,133,148
KITTREL
George 120
Geor 116,122
George 40,42,52,54,62,86,98,130
KNIGHT
Jas. 118
LANDING
James 78
Wm. 136
LASSITER
Absolom 95
Fred. 125,135
Henry 5,30,55,168
James 141
Jos. 146
LEE
Step. 30
Stephen 56,122
LEWIS
David 72,77,118
Eff 186,188
John 66
Salley 81
Sally 27
Sarah 2,46
MATHEWS
Edwin 123

MATHEWS
John D. 135
John W. 77,88
Martha J. 143
MATHIAS
Edwin 133
MATTHEWS
John 188,189
John W. 60,61
MATTHIAS
Edwin 166
MELVIN
Frederick H. 30
MILLER
Charity 189
James 187
Will 147
William 171
MORGAN
Mathias 4
Seth 14,142
MORRIS
Fedrick 175
MUPHREY
Wm. 94
MURFREE
Nathaniel 47
MURPHEY
Nathaniel 42
NEGROES
SAM 95
TIBE 135
WEAVER
Hillery 102
ODAM
Asa 187
Jacob 146
ODOM
Asa 5,52
Ben 48
Benja. 5
Benjamin 2
Ira 5,48
Monica 38,47
OVERMAN
Josiah 32
PARKER
Abm. 158
Abraham 43
Abram 38,42,44,69
Daniel 160
David 6,56
Jos. 5

PARKER
Nancy 149
Reuben 182
Sophia 38,47
Wm. 133,135,149
PEARCE
Abner 32,34,48
Daniel 27
Isaac 189
PHELEPS
James 110
PHELPS
James 74,104,146
PIERCE
Ab 92,135
Abraham 91
Isaac 115,134
PIERE
Isaac 147
PILAND
Elisha 3,13,58,171
Isaac 118,135,140
James 118,135,140
Jas. 5
Milley 5
POWELL
Jacob 122,134,188
PRICE
Isaac 157
PRUDEN
Nathaniel 5
PUGH
Henry 2,10,27,57,58,68,118,127,131,141
Susan E. 142
RAWLS
Richard 79
RIDDICK
J. W. 148
James 38,44,52,55,99
James W. 39,43,152
Jethero 186
Jno. 6
Micajah 6,18,35
Wm. 147
ROGERS
Elizabeth 2,3,6,39
James 49

ROGERS
 Jonathan 3,39
ROUNTREE
 John 149
 Thomas 31,40,47,111
 Thos. 99
SAUNDERS
 Elizbeth 67
 Gilbert 110
 John 189
 Law. 116
 Lawrenc 110
 Lawrence 116
SAVAGE
 Jesse 113,119,121,122,140,142
SCARBOROUGH
 Eanas 131
 Enos 46,101,146
SCARBOUGH
 Eanos 143
SEARS
 Barshaba 118,119,126,127,131
 Bathsheba 185
SMALL
 Jno. 129
 John 129,130,133,167
 John, Sr. 149
 Jos. 94
 M. H. 55
 Moses H. 2,6
SMITH
 Joseph 16,86
 Richard 130,138,140,146
 Robert 6,48
 Robt. 4
 Thos. 143
SPARKMAN
 John 190
SPEIGHT
 Isaac 186
SPEIGHTS
 Charity 46,62
 Henry 3,11,13,49
 Thomas 13
STEDMAN
 Wm. W. 150
SUMNER
 Charles E. 6,15,57

SUMNER
 Chs. E. 11,55
 Eliza. 116,122,124,153
 Jethro 87,91,120,153
SUTTON
 Geo. 72
 Geor. 134
TAYLOR
 David 190
 Robert 4,18,107,129,190
TROTMAN
 Elisha 51
 Riddick 12
VANN
 Charles 159
WALTERS
 Lewis 39,47
WALTON
 Asa 158,166
 Henry 3,27,55,122
 Jesse 24,52,54,92
 Timo. 148
 Timothy 11
 Timothy, Sr. 43
WIGGINS
 Asa 184,185
 James 5,48,152
 Prisscilla 46
WILLIAMS
 Halon 5,49
 Hardy 146,165,179
 Hasety 147
 James 7
 Jonathan 12,123
WOOD
 Edward 11

NOTES

FEMALE INDEX

Absila
JONES 147
Absilla
JONES 178
Ailsey
BRIGGS 99
Ainah
CORBELL [C] 159
AMY [C] 70
Anaca
CORBAL [C] 159
Ann
BOND 92,163
GRANBERRY 10
GRANT 19
HARVEY 131
PARKER 76
SMALL 129
SUMNER 163
Ann E.
LASSITER 20, 156
MANSARD 104, 171
Ann N.
HARVEY 190
Balinda
BAGLEY 99
Barshaba
DAUGHTRY 162
FRANKLIN 99, 116
SEARS 118,119, 126,127,131
Barsheba
FRANKLIN 9,28, 31
Bathsheba
GRANBERRY 160
SEARS 185
Betsey
LANG [C] 75
PRICE [C] 75
TAYLOR [C] 184
Caroline
HAYS 71,79,105, 119
SUTTON 72,129
Caroline M.
SUTTON 156
Catharine

Catharine
GREGORY 126
Celea
EURE 149
LEWIS 157
Celia (See also Selah)
LEWIS 11,56, 94,95,121,136
Charity
MILLER 189
Charity
SMALL 129
SPEIGHTS 46,62
WILLIAMS 50
Charlott
EASON 108
GREEN 94
Charlotte
CORBAL [C] 159
GREEN 178
Chitty
JONES 2
PARKER 70
Christain
CROSS 9
SMALL 2,55
Christian
GWINN 21
PARKER 133, 153
SMALL 129
TWINE 169
Christian E.
SMALL 90
CLARISA [C] 148
Cyntha
BRINKLY 133
Deannah
HINTON 177
Easter
RIDDICK 151
Easther
MITCHEL 73
Eletia
EASON 121
Eliza
BEEMAN 140, 149
BENTON 104, 133,171
BOND 92,103
BRIGGS 141
EASON 126

Eliza
FRANKLIN 28
GRANBERY 91, 128,152
HAYS 71,73,79
LEE 133
PARKER 155
POWELL 129
ROGERS 73
SUMNER 96,116, 122,124,153,161
TAYLOR [C] 72, 95
WIGGINS 121
Eliza. H.
RIDDICK 13
Elizabeth
BOND 17
BRISCO 3
BROTHERS 63, 171
COFFIELD 101
DUKES 177
EASON 55
GRANBERRY 20,63,160
HARRELL 49,63
JONES [C] 57
LEE 33,88
LEWIS 66
MATTHEWS 60
PARKER 158
RIDDICK 6
ROGERS 2,3,6, 39,58,73
SAUNDERS 67
SMITH 53
SUMNER 57,168
SWEAT 190
WIGGINS 88
Elizabeth G.
JONES 170
Emaley
RIDDICK 148
Emeline
LANG [C] 75
Emily
HOFFLER 190
ESTHER [C] 36, 53,54
FANNY [C] 85
Feletia
FREEMAN 155

Frances
COTTER 151
SMITH 6
Fruizy
TAYLOR 122
Fruzy
TAYLOR 18,108
HANAH [C] 149
Hannah
HUMPHLET 192
Harriet B.
GATLING 6,51, 91,125,156,188
Harriett
NORFLEET 84
PARKER 158
Harriett B.
GATLING 56
Hasety
WILLIAMS 147
Helon
LEE 78
Henaretta
COPELAND 123, 124
Heneritta
COPELAND 151
Henrietta
BRIGGS 190
Henrietta
COPELAND 3, 49,88
India
BENTON 148
Jainy
WILLIAMS 75
Jamimay
THORENTON 163
Jane
FRANKLIN 28
PARKER 63
SWEAT 190
Jane R.
RIDDICK 6
Janet M.
MANSARD 104
Jannet M.
MANSARD 171
JINNY [C] 77
Judith
HARRELL 47
LEWIS 27

Julia
  HARRELL 191
  LAWRENCE 192
  ROBINS [C] 30
Kiddy
  PARKER 89
Lavina
  BRINKLY 67
  FIELDS 46,104
  SMITH 16
  WILLIAMS 35
Lavinia
  BRINKLEY 80
  BRINKLY 103
  BRISCO 106
  FIELDS 91
  SMITH 86,91
  WILLIAMS 154
Leah
  HINTON 12,55, 95,126,129,157
  HOFFLER 190
  ROUNTREE 133
Lena
  EASON 55
Levina
  BRINKLEY 60
Lottey
  HOWELL 75
Louisa
  BARNES 11,56, 83,84,125
  BRINKLEY 81
  CROSS 85,86
  HINTON 177
  JONES 2,21,51, 104,110,141
  LEE 30
  LEWIS 66
  PARKER 76,170
Louisia
  CROSS 85
Lovey
  BRADY 44
Lovonya
  FREEMAN 105
Lucreatia
  BEEMAN 128, 140,141
Lucretia
  BEEMAN 49,118
  FRANKLIN 28
Lucy
  WALTON 20

Ludy
  CARTER 163
Mairy C.
  CROSS 85
Malinda
  BAGLEY 157
Marey (See also Mary)
  FIELDS 143
  WALTERS 125
Margaret
  BENTON 104, 133
  CROSS 6
  GREEN 145
  HOSKINS 83
  JOHNSON 178
  PARKER 76,101
  RIDDICK 32
  WILLIAMS 79
Margaret A.
  BALLARD 155
  BOND 12
Margaret Ann
  LILES 57
Margaret C.
  BROOKS 20
Margaret J.
  CROSS 5
Margate E.
  MATHEWS 145
Maria
  GOODMAN 168
Mariah
  GOODMAN 5, 88,121
MARTHA [C] 36,53
Martha
  BEEMAN 7
  BROTHERS 129
  EURE [C] 165
  GRIFFITH 179
  HORTON 33,99, 152
  MOORE 127
  PARKER 44,69, 133,158
  PRUDEN 192
  TAYLOR 93
  WALTON 127
  WIGGINS 121
  WILLIAMS 35
Martha B.

Martha B.
  GATLING 5
Martha J.
  MATHEWS 143
Martha Jane
  MATTHEWS 19
Martha R.
  SUMNER 11
Martha S.
  BAGLEY 155
  MELVIN 20,30
Marthal
  WIGGINS 88
MARTILLA [C] 182
MARY [C] 85
Mary (See also Marey)
  BENTON 148, 153
  BRIGGS 92
  BRINKLY 10
  BROTHERS 170
  BUTLER 19
  BUTLER [C] 75
  CULLINS 136
  CUTLER 94
  DARDEN 108
  DILDY 95
  ELLIS 13
  EURE 93,106, 157
  FAWLK 174
  FIELDS 142,146
  FLOOD 100
  FOWLKES 174
  HARE 57,105
  HARRELL 26,41, 63,88,101,114,161
  HARVEY 177
  HINTON 26,78
  HUDGINS 7,54, 138
  HUNTER 15,55, 93
  JOHNSON 187
  KING 72,80,148, 153
  MATTHEWS 19
  ODOM 120
  PARKER 76,158
  RIDDICK 128
  ROBERTS 194
  SAVAGE 5,88,

Mary
  SAVAGE 119
  SUMNER 57,96, 161,168
  SUTTON 72,129
  TAYLOR 98,108, 110,112,126
  TAYLOR [C] 72
  WALTON 12,36, 56,93,153
  WILLIAM 12
  WILLIAMS 5,49, 58,90,95,123,124, 157
Mary A.
  EURE 95
  RIDDICK 95,152
Mary A. S.
  HARVEY 176
Mary Ann
  RIDDICK 6,55
  WALTON 43,58, 96,156
Mary G.
  CROSS 12,49,83, 84,85,90
Mary J. B.
  GATLING 91
Mary Jane
  BALLARD 108
  MELVIN 30
Mary Jane Boyt
  GATLING 21
Mary M.
  CROSS 83,84
Mary R.
  BILUPS 163
Matilda
  BAGLEY 99,157
  MELTEAR 41
May
  WILLIAMS 128
Mildred
  BEEMAN 7
  KITTRELL 42
  PILAND 171
MILEY [C] 85
Milicent
  BRINKLEY 36
Milley
  KITTRELL 40
  PILAND 5,54
  TOOLEY 19
  WILLIAMS 58

Millicent
  FREEMAN 105
  POWELL 191
Milly
  GREEN 12
  PILAND 3,93
Molly
  JOHNSON 113
Monica
  CROSS 99
  ODOM 38,47
Mourning
  WILLIAMS 101
Nancey
  STALLINGS 191
Nancy
  BEEMAN 7
  BOND 17,76,95,
103,170
  EADERS 100
  EURE 157,174
  GAREY 123
  GRANBURY 178
  HARRELL 115
  HAYS 106
  HURDLE 6,55,
89,123,156
  JORDON 12
  PARKER 40,58,
149
  RIDDICK 39,126,
144
Nancy
  SAUNDERS 179,
189
  WILLIAMS 154
Partheana
  PARKER 89
Parthenia
  PARKER 132,
153
Peggy
  MATHEWS 145
  STALLINS 100
Penelope
  CARTER 7
  HOFFLER 190
Penina
  WALLACE 106
Peninah
  GOODMAN 121
PENNINAH [C]
85
Penninah

Penninah
  GOODMAN 5,88
Peny
  GOODMAN 168
Phereba
  TROTMAN 44
PLEASANT [C]
70
Pleasant
  MATHEWS 145
  GATLING 179
  TAYLOR 49
Polly
  HOWELL 106
Pricilla
  ODOM 48
Prisscilla
  WIGGINS 46
Prissila
  ODAM 93
  ODOM 2
  PARKER 58
  WIGGINS 94
Prissilla
  ODAM 123,152
Prudence
  WILLIAMS 32,
63
RACHEL [C] 85
Rachel
  BEEMAN 7
  LEWIS 170
  MORGAN 14
  YATES 115
Rebeca
  PUGH 88
Rebeca C.
  PUGH 161
Ruth
  POLSON [C] 34
Sabra
  PORTER 181
Salley
  JONES 78,89
  LEWIS 81
SALLY [C] 167
Sally
  BLANCHARD
[C] 103
  CROSS 47,89
  HINTON 126,156
  LEWIS 27
  POWELL 15,55
  SWEAT 165

Sally
  WILLIAMS 35
Sally Ann
  HUNTER 158
  MELVIN 30
Sarah
  BOND 54
  BROWN 12,56,
93,127,153
  GRANT 160
  HARRELL 25
  HINTON 52,88,
129,158,177
  JONES 158,189
  LEWIS 2,46
  ODOM 161
  PARKER 13
  POWELL 88
  ROOKS 151
  SAUNDERS 89
  SAVAGE 123
  SMITH 138
  WALLACE 106
  WALTON 99
  WATSON 67
Sarah Ann
  HUNTER 98
Sarah E.
  BLOUNT 152,
153,161
  ODAM 121,153
Sarah M.
  LASITER 92
  LASSITER 124,
156,168
Sarah Margaret
  LASSITER 30
Selah (See also
Celea, Celia)
  LEWIS 11
Senah
  EASON 108,126
Sidney
  HURDLE 29,89
Sopha A.
  ODAM 152
Sophia
  BRINKLEY 168
  DUKE 76,90
  EASON 2
  HUNTER 62
  HURDLE 48,94,
125,152
  PARKER 38,47

Sophia
  REED [C] 75
  SPEIGHT 95,128,
157
Sophia A.
  HURDLE 89
  ODAM 123
Sophia Ann
  ODAM 92
Sophia C.
  HUNTER 62
Susan
  BEEMAN 11
  HILL 92
  PILAND 3,93,171
  SPEIGHT 157
  WOLFREY 19
Susan A.
  SPEIGHT 95,128
Susan E.
  PUGH 142
Susan J.
  HILL 56
Susanah
  LASSITER 115
Susannah
  PILAND 8
Temble
  EASON 2
Thursey
  PARKER 76
Treasey
  WALTON 80
Wealthy
  RIDDICK 44
Wealty
  RIDDICK 44

NICKNAMES
Ann=Nancy
Chitty=Chester
Fanny=Francis
Margaret=Peggy
Mary=Polly
Peggy=Margaret
Penina=Penny
Penelope=Penny

Polly=Mary
Sarah=Sally
Treasey=Theresa

NAME INDEX

A

AKERMAN
Ebenezar P. 27
ALLEN
John 132
Joshua 19,59,66,
143,180
ALLSTIN (*See also*
AUSTIN)
Richard 19
ALPHIN
Jno. 141
John 2,7,17,35,59,
65,115,180
ANDERSON
John A. 74,110,
144
ARLINE
James 63,132,133
Jas. 152
Jesse 29,34,63,81,
151
ARNOLD
John 7,132,162
Riddick 111
William 107,191
Wm. 111,128,164
ASTON
Thos. 97
AUSTIN (*See also*
ALLSTIN,OSTIN)
Richard 164

B

BABB
Christoper 9
Christopher 10,
11,12
Uriah 9,12,56,95,
121,157
William 10,11,
36,38,58,59,61,63,
95,193,194
Wm. 61,128,147,
157
BAGLEY
Balinda 99
Henry 33,79
Jacob 118
Jacob D. 75

BAGLEY
John 75
Luke 75,118
Malinda 157
Martha S. 155
Matilda 99,157
Thomas 37,150,
155,172
Trotman 99,
124
BAKER
Andrew 27,29,
34,37,42,89,123,
131,184,185
Blake 36,102,
143
Charles 37,111
James 23,33,89,
95,97,102,113,
127,173,177
James, Jr. 19,59,
80,97,109
James, Sr. 19,80
Jas. 123
Jas., Jr. 147
Jno. B. 15,24,
33,90,136,149
John 165
John B. 13-15,
21,22,30,33,36,
42,58,75,77,82,
104,108,136,149,
189,191,192
Lawrence 10
Marmaduke 1,
33,81,82,187
Marmk. 141
Mormaduke 143
W. 162
William 191
William J. 192
Wynns 33,111
BALLAD
Alfred 160
B. 132
James A. 191
Robert H. 192
BALLARD
Afred 159
Alfred 37,132
B. B. 135
Benj. B. 90,111,
150

BALLARD
Benjamin 67
James 64,99
James A. 15,69,115
Kedar 108
Margaret A. 155
Mary Jane 108
Richard H. 27,44,
45,67
Richd. H. 21,32,
44,108
BAR (*See also*
BARR,OBARR)
Britton O. 151
BARNES
___ 53,86,96
J. 58,61,62
James 145
Jethro 32,35,38,
44,59,63,64
John 125,129,130,
132
Jos. I. 83
Jos. J. 75,82,84,
85,86,102,117
Joseph J. 57
Joseph P. 65
Louisa 11,56,83,
84,125
BARR
Britton O. 74
John W. 132
Wright 151
BEASLEY
Will 145
BEEMAN
A. 105
Ab. 116
Abraham 4,7,18
Eliza. 140,149
Israel 11,118,140,
156
Jno. 76,93,96,118,
153
John 9,11,14,18,
39,47,49,53,55,72,
106,140,149
Levi 11,18,34,39,
49,55,70,73,74,99,
104,105,107,122,
127,140,162,167,
189
Lucreatia 128,

BEEMAN
Lucreatia 140,141
Lucretia 49,118
Martha 7
Mildred 7
Nancy 7
Rachel 7
Susan 11
William 118,156
Wm. 140
BENNET
___ 187
Wm. F. 147,151,
194
BENNETT
___ 28,110,147
Wm. F. 141,178
BENTO_
David 135
BENTON
___ 53,94
A. 128
Ab. 134,151
Abraham 44,62,
179
Abram 109,118,
119
David 7,15,36,
179
Elisha 29
Eliza. 104,133,
171
Henry 120
Henry H. 37,140
India 148
James 7,29,109,
114,118,125,134,
142
James, Jr. 7
James, Sr. 53
Jesse 81,132,151
Jet 15
Jethro 29,68
Jno. 140
Jno., Jr. 145
Jno. P. 120,123,
129,145
Jno. T. 79,123
John 50,81,133,
138,151
John, Jr. 71,163
John P. 7,162,164
Jordan 153

BENTON
Joseph 164,172,
173,174,176,179,181
Leml. 140
Margaret 104,133
Mary 148,153
Seth 7,18,53,59,
118,134,136,138,
154,180
Seth, Jr. 7
Thomas G. 123
William 29
Wm. 111,120,149,
150
Wm., Jr. 111
Wm., Sr. 125,173
BEST
Briant 116
BILLUPS
Joseph R. 66
BILUPS
Joseph R. 163
Mary R. 163
BIRAM (See also **BYRUM**)
Wm. 107
BLACHARD
Easton 92
BLADES
William 156
BLANCHAD
Benj. 76
BLANCHARD
A. 20,163
Absalom 101,132,
138,139
Abso. 109
Absalam 190
B. 27
Ben. 7,8
Benja. 54
Benja., Jr. 33
Courrie 192
Demsey 37
Easton 145,155,
163
Fredk. 37
Isaac 60,82,83
Jethero 163,192
Jethro 37,42,102,
117
Job 145
Jobe 177
Josiah 34

BLANCHARD
Richard 60,190
Riddick 27
Robert 136,192
Thos. 184
Will. 34
William, Sr. 29,37
Wm. 101,109,
129,136,150
Wm., Sr. 34
BLANCHD.
Fred. 111
Jetho 109
John 145
BLANHD
Jethro 103
BLOUNT
Henry L. 126,
143,153,161,182,
183
Sarah E. 152,153,
161
BOGE
Jonathan 11
BOGER
James 11,36
BOGURE
Charles 78
BOICE (See also **BOYCE**)
James 114,162,
171,173,183,184
BOND
____ 190
Ann 92,163
Demcy 115
Demsey 71
Elisha 190
Elisha H. 33,44,
74,83,115,155,159,
181
Eliza. 92,103
Elizabeth 17
Henery 168
Henry 11,19,31,
33,34,37,42,48,57,
67,75,78,80,100,
106,111,137,145,
148,149,172,177,
181
J. 68
James 11,48,57,
108
Jno. W. 145,181,

BOND
Jno. W. 182
John 57,76,78,
148,149
Margaret A. 12
Nancy 17,76,95,
103,170
Noah 17,103
Richard 14,19
Richd. 11,12,17,
48,103
Saml. S. 135
Samuel S. 163
Sarah 54
Steward 54
Thos. 153
William 17,19,52,
69
Wm. 95
BONNER
Abram 159
John 159
BOON
Zachariah 122
BOOTH
____ 137,138
James 33,73,74,
78,80,88,96,103,
105,110,114,129,
131,132,136,142
Jas. 136
Will L. 101
William L. 131
Wm. 142
Wm. L. 71,78,
101,104,109,112,
117,128,131,134,
135,142,144,147,
150,154,155,157
Wm. R. 151
BOOTHE
Henry 177
James 5,15,37,46,
52-55,70,75,192
William 38,54
William L. 14,31,
47,57,58,69,166,
170
Wm. 182
Wm. L. 4,16,17,
24,26,34,49,56,
57,160,172,179,193
BOYCE (See also **BOICE**)

BOYCE (See also **BOICE**)
James 29,62,65,
100,101,107,134,
137
Jonathan 49
William 56,62
BOYSE
James 124
BOYT
Demsey 37,111
James 111
John 149
BRADDY
Blake 118,190
John 164
BRADY
Blake 36,44,102,
132,146
John 29,45,50,61,
82,108,138,139
Lovey 44
BRIGGS
____ 4
Ailsey 99
Andrew 91
Benj. 99,124
Benja. 55
Benjamin 15
Charles 15,59,66,
74,102,167
Chas. 102,107
Ed. 102-104,125
Edward 29,45,81,
82,125,141,171,
182,190
Edwd. 99
Edwrd. 119
Eliza. 141
Henrietta 190
Henry 80,141,190
James 172,190
Josiah 27,29,34,
52,90,136,153,187
Julian 92
Kedar 108
Mary 92
Miles 21,25,60,
64,67,70,73,107,
108,125,137,141,
143,159,182,185,
190,192
Richard 36,80
Wm. 157,158

BRIGS
Miles 143
BRIN
James 141
BRINKLEY
Ammon 170
Benj. 92
Benjn. 79
Calvin 125,133,
158,180,185
Calwine 127
David 60,167,168
Henry 170,181
Isaac 125,170
James 41,44,60,76,
137,158
Jerry 170
Jethero 162
Jethro 111
John 61,72,80,165
Lavinia 80
Levi 37
Levina 60
Lewis 170
Louisa 81
Miles 35,168
Milicent 36
Sophia 168
Timothy 170
BRINKLY
Benj. 76
Benjamin 13,93
Calvin 12,58,115,
125
Charles 69
Cyntha 133
Elisha 12
Hardy 69
James 15,21,59,67,
97,132,134
Jno. 92
John 15,77,182
Lavina 67
Lavinia 103
Mary 10
Miles 9,10,51
BRISCO
E. 153
Ebon 106,109,122,
146
Ebron 14
Elizabeth 3
John 106
Lavinia 106

BRISCO
Richard 106
BRITT
Enoch 151
BROOKS
George 20,156,
163
Jos. 149
Joseph 20,31,163
Margaret C. 20
BROTHERS
Briant 129,133,
139,143
Bryant 170
Burrell 27
Burwell 10,40,97,
103,104,129,130,
149,154,159,170,
177,181,186,188,
192
Elizabeth 63,171
James 63,171,
186,188
Jno. 128
Marmaduke 72
Martha 129
Mary 170
R. 184
Reuben 184,190
Richard 171
Richd. 63
Robert 63,171,
187
William 27
William R. 191
BROTHES
Burwell 162
BROWN
Allen 177
Benj. 114,117,
142,177
Benjamin 29,34,
45
James 59,67,105,
132,138,139,184,
194
Jas. 109,132,138,
147
Jesse 11,13,24,25,
43,44,51,56,65,67,
92,94,95,100,149,
155,168,171
John 45,50,57,
105,109,130,133,

BROWN
John 148,155
Miles 1,37,42,81,
125,162,163
Samel 108
Saml. 142,147,
153
Samuel 54
Sarah 12,56,93,
127,153
Wiley 37
William 12,56,93,
127
Willie 69
Willis 45,50
Wm. 133,153
BUCHANY
Francis 111
BUMCH
Willis 89
BUNCH
Eph. 132
Ephraim 39,81
Ephram 82,83,90
Isaac K. 41
Jacob K. 37
Willis 1,6,18,41,
53,55,123,125,156
BUSH
William 80
BUTLER
Mary 19
Mason 100
BYRUM (*See also*
BIRUM)
William 31,116

C

CALE
Tulley 37
CARNELIOUS
(*See also*
CORNELIUS)
Richard 111
CARR
T. W. 73,74,100,
107-109,192
Tille W. 127
Tilley W. 22,37,
42,64,66,67,70
Tilly W. 2,24,30,
120
CARTER

CARTER
___ 94
Charles 126,132,
163
Henry 94,154,160
Ira 74,111,163,
183
James 7,14,59,64,
133,172-174,180
Lewis
74,82,111,132
Ludy 163
Penelope 7
Wiley 5
Willey 111
William 192
Willie 88
CARTERE
James 106
CASEY
Willis 121
CLARK
William 37
CLEAVES
John 8,35
Lemel 121
Leml. 50,67,69,
99,111,121,122,
124
Lemuel 14,17,
158,159,176
William 5,23,65,
93
Wm. 48,50,78,
108,142
CLEVES
Lemuel 120
Wm. 120
COFFER
Thos. G. 37
COFFIELD
Elizabeth 101
John 101
COLE
___ 184
COOK
___ 151
COOPER (*See also*
COWPER)
Wills, Jr. 10
COPELAND
Henaretta 123,124
Heneritta 151
Henrietta 3,49,88

COPELAND
Henry 3,6
Heny 49
James 192
John 162
Samuel 111
CORNELIUS (*See also* **CARNELIOUS**)
Richd. 37
Thomas 37,49
CORNWELL
Jesse 53
COSTEN
George 5-7,13,14, 17,19,24,25,30,41, 55,59,65,66,158,162, 168,176
Henry 17,50,51,52, 57,65,66,69,92,132, 166,168,170,176, 182,183,184,193
Isaac 11
James 5,7,11,13,23,59,66, 67,156,160,164,176
James, Jr. 191
James R. 156
James, Sr. 158,167, 170,172
Jas. 5
Jas., Jr. 194
T. 162
Thomas 47,53,173
Thomas R. 19,183
Thos. 158,184
Thos. R. 163,177, 179,191
COSTON
___ 73,100,155
David 146
Geor. 74,109,110, 146,152
George 95,96,100, 103,104,128,137,141
Henry 100,101, 103,112,125,126, 141,142,145,150
James 94,102,127, 128,133,135,147,154
James, Jr. 125,129, 130
James K. 94,128
James, Sr. 109,150, 154

COSTON
Jas. 102,125
Thomas 141
Thos. 73,97,143, 154
Thos. R. 73,123, 145,147,154
COTTER
Frances 151
COWPER (*See also* **COOPER**)
W. W. 66,94
Will W. 139
Will. W. 78,94
William 56
William W. 11, 12,15,31,34,51,56, 58,66,165
Willis 64
Willis, Jr. 2
Wills 20,64,74,97, 99,100,105,115,126
Wills, Jr. 70,73
Wm. 25
Wm. L. 27
Wm. S. 137
Wm. W. 1-3,8-11, 16,21,26,31,46,47, 52,56,57,59,66,78, 89,90,93,95,101, 108,109,112,121, 124,126-128,131, 132-134,136,144, 150,154,155,157, 160,164,167,175, 179
CREECY
James R. 83
Levi 15,37,49,52, 62,64,133
CROFFORD
Abm. 175
Henry 188
CROSS
A. 85
Ab. 85,86
Ab. W. 83
Abm. 12,49
Abraham 14,84
Abram 14,84,85
Albert 89
Alfred 47
Benj. 89
Benjamin 47

CROSS
Christain 9
Cyphan 98,141
Cyprain 84
Cypran 84
Cyprian 17,83,84
Cyprian R. 20
David 61,72,118
David C. 77
E. 100
Ed. 109
Edward 119
Edwin 15,21,36, 63,67,99,113,114, 141,182,193,194
Elisha 6,47,49, 122,153
Etheld. 14,20,38, 51,88,103,107,117, 140,147
Etheldred 23,35, 47,64,71,99,171, 175
Etthd. 134
Hardy 62,64,81, 138,179,193
James 21,116, 119,158
Jno. 6
John 47,89
Louisa 85,86
Louisia 85
Mairy C. 85
Margaret 6
Margaret J. 5
Mary G. 12,49,83, 84,85,90
Mary M. 83,84
Monica 99
Richard 127,188
Richd. 109
Sally 47,89
Saml. 81
Samuel 64,77, 171,189
Taylor 5
Washington 158
Wiley 188
William 62,180
Willie 111
Willis 3,5,15,16, 21,45,61,71,73,74
Willis 82,101, 175,186,187

CROSS
Wm. 52,154
CUFF
Daniel 98,142
Jack 142
John 100,129
Leven 89,111,142
Malacha 155
Malachia 142
Nisom 62
Nusum 139
CULLINS
Christian 80
Jacob 88
Mary 136
Miles 179
Nath. 73
Nathan 20,35,36, 43,70,79,88,91,159
Nathaniel 179
Nathl. 134
CURL
Richard 34,59,66, 74,82,107,145
Richd. 29,74,99, 102,147,167
CUTLER
Mary 94

D

DANIEL
Cheaton 131
Wm. 181
DARDEN
Lemel. G. 90
Leml. G. 49,83, 85,107
Lemuel G. 12
Mary 108
Titus 49
DAUGHTERY
___ 101
Wm. G. 118
Wm. S. 120
DAUGHTEY (*See also* **DOUGHTIE**)
Nathl. 142
DAUGHTREY
Allen 191
DAUGHTRY
___ 75,126,143, 172
Allen 124,145

DAUGHTRY
Andrew 162
Barshaba 162
L. S. 68
Law. S 100,104, 107,111,113,139
Lawrence S. 49,51, 68,97,139
W. G. 158,161, 166,168,174,185, 188,190,194
William G. 29,51, 58,65,189
Wm. G. 23,44,95, 100,105,110,113, 131,138-140,145, 146,149,150,155, 158,160,185
Wm. H. 109
DAUGHTY
Allen 135
Nathl. 89
DAVIDSON
William 29,45,81
Wm. 102
DAVIS
Abraham 80
Abram 164
Miles 41
Miles M. 101
DELANY
Charles 37,184
DILDY
Mary 95
DORSEY
William M. 130
DOUGHTIE (*See also* **DAUGHTEY**)
____ 65
Nathaniel 37
Nathl. 42
DOUGHTRY
____ 138
DOUGHTY
Nathaniel 111
Nathl. 143
DUKE
____ 124,137
David O. 94
Francis 8,23,41,64, 116
Frank 4
James 76,90
Sophia 76,90

DUKES
Elizabeth 177
Francis 167,171, 188
DUNFORD
David 179
David, Jr. 122
John 179

E

EADERS
Nancy 100
EASON
____ 142
Abner 59,108, 109,111,151,180, 192
And. 29
Andrew 34,35,45, 101,123,151
Charles 29,34,55, 59,66,103,125,126
Charlott 108
Chas. 125,136
Eletia 121
Eliza. 126
Elizabeth 55
Hardy 2,3,12,50, 51,53,73,121,176
Hillory 34
Isaac 121
Jacob 123
James 69
Jesse 123,129, 141,142,151,163, 170,176
Jos. 129,142,187
Joseph 136
Joseph R. 169
Lena 55
Milton 145
Reuben 35
Rubin 81-83,114
Senah 108,126
Sol. 153
Solomon 35,53, 108,116,121,134, 138
Sophia 2
Temble 2
Thomas 194
Thos. 68,145,151, 178,194

EASON
Whitmell 64
Whitmil 121
Wm. 34
ELEY
William 23,29
ELLEN
John 80
ELLEY
William 66
ELLIS
A. 187
Archd. 74,102
Archibald 15,59, 60,66,68,134,136
Edwin 37
Harrison 121,132
Kadar 9,13,81
Kedar 76,79,90, 107,114,151,177
Marmaduke 37, 163
Marmaduke N. 13
Mary 13
EURE (*See also* **EWER**)
Benj. 81-83,114, 117,154
Benjamin 19
Boon 145,162,180
Bray 105,150, 162,163,191
Celea 149
D. 41
Dempsey 10,15
Demsey 36
Demsy 100
Elizabeth 175
Henry 37,95,157
Hillery H. 151
J. Riddick 163
James 63,93
James, Jr. 190
Jas. 145
Jethero 172
Jethero, Jr. 192
Jethero, Sr. 192
Jethro 19
Jno. 115
John 78,81,117
John, Jr. 148,153
John, Sr. 76,78
Levi 19,21,23,45, 50,137,185

EURE
Levi, Jr. 15,102
Lewis 8,48,124, 128
Mary 93,106,157
Mary A. 95
Mills 4,22,23,24, 30,38,47,49,56,59,
Mills 64,74,76,81, 88,95,96,100,117, 122,135,137,152, 157,171,184
Nancy 157,174
Nat. 74
Nataniel 186
Nathanel 33
Nathaniel 9,10,15, 45,47,48,50,51,95, 118,128,157,160, 161,164,171,186, 187,194
Nathaniel C. 21
Nathl. 11,30,49, 74,92,117,128,130, 141,153,155,157, 181,187
Peter 29,34,49,59, 109,125,141,147, 160
Riddick 188
Riddick B. 157, 185
Saml. 53,81
Samuel 19,156, 183
Starkey 41,145, 163
Tames 41
Tinson 10,125, 141,143,148
Uriah 150
Whitmel 188
EVANS
James 111,162
Thomas 111
Willis 111
EVERIT
John 122
EWER
Starkey 41

F

FAULKS

FAULKS
___ 126
Jep. 114
Jeptha 114,130
Wm. 144
FAWLK
Mary 174
FAWLKS (See also
FOWLKES,
FOWLKS)
Jeptha 111
FELTON
Cader 120
David F. 7,81,82,
107,143,154,192
Fisher 139
John 12,37,46,55,
64,80,88,123,158,
187
Kedar 46,66,72,
126,127
Saml. 148
Samuel 113,192
Shadrack 64
FIELD
Mills R. 50
Reuben 14
Richard John K.
191
FIELDS
Daniel 113,125
Lavina 46,104
Lavinia 91
Leml. 124,152
Leml. K. 100
M. R. 146
Marey 143
Mary 142,146
Mills 98
Mills R. 46,86,91,
93,98,100,146
Richd. H. 155
FIGG
James 43,96,102,
103,134,170
Jno. 143
John 23,134,139,
142,170
FLOOD
Demcy 100
Mary 100
FOWLKES (See
also **FAULKS,**
FAWLKS)

FOWLKES
___ 43,172,173
Jepha 68
Jeptha
15,38,39,47,
65-67
Mary 174
FOWLKS
Jeptha 79
FRANKLIN
Barshaba 99,116
Barsheba 9,28,31
Benj. 72,80,81,95,
114,123,132,151
Benjamin 28,69,
177,182
Benjn. 77
Burwell 28,32
Daniel 20,28
Eliza 28
Jane 28
Jonas 10,20,28
Lucretia 28
Nathan 28
Owen 28
FREEMAN
Alexander 90
David 5,63,92,
122
Feletia 155
George 54,182
Isaac P. 80
James 127
James T. 8,23,25,
27,33,54,63,65,67,
90,100,102,105,
107,109,129,157,
171,175,180,186,
190
Jas. T. 106,109,
119,120,126,137,
141,146,149,150,
162,194
Jno. 118
John 128,188
John, Jr. 41
John, Sr. 41
Jos. 82,118,137
Joseph 5,15,21,
23,37,46,63,64,92,
118,122,130,152,
171,188
Lovonya 105
Millicent 105

FREEMAN
Richard B. 105
Timo. 105
Walton 22,41,54,
59,65,89,104,105,
107,108,119,148,
167
FREMAN
David 152
Walton 137
FRYER
Isaac 143

G

GAREY
John 116
Nancy 123
GARY
Thomas S. 58
GATLING
E. B. 51,148
Etheldred B. 5,6
Harriet B. 6,91,
125,156,188
Harriett B. 51,56
James 3,179
Jno. 135
Jno. B. 90
John 9,41,57,58,
65,68,103,106,109,
114,126,141
John B. 5,55,128
Jos. 141,147
Martha B. 5
Mary J. B. 91
Mary Jane B. 6,56
Mary Jane Boyt
21
Miles 97
Pleasant 179
R. 11,40,112
Richd. B. 5,55,90,
148
Rid. 115,141,142
Riddick 2,8,9,11,
21,22,31,34,42,43,
57,59,64,68,71,75,
80,93,96,100,119,
123,126,127,144,
148,150,159,160,
161,164,168,175,
180,187,188,193
William 34,53,64,

GATLING
William 68,69,75,
182
Wm. 34,126,137,
140,144,158,180,
183,184
GATTLING
Riddick 11
GILLIAM
H. 17,30,40,42,
68,88,100,102,105,
106,107,109,116,
118,120,125,127,
132,140,144,146,
150,155,163
Henery 105,110,
158,159
Henry 1,3,9-13,
15-17,21,22,24,26,
28,30-33,35,38,40,
42,43,46,50-52,54,
56,60,61,63,65-68,
71,74,78,79,83,85,
86,87,94,95,98,100,
103,104,107-109,
111,115,117-119,
131,134,135,139,
142,143,148-150,
158-160,166-168,
175,181-183,185,
186,188,189
Heny 186
J. R. 68
John R. 10,35,65,
158
GLOVER
William 76
GOMER (See also
GOOMER)
Thomas 167
GOODMAN
___ 131
Barnes 6,23,24,
29,34,39,42,46,50,
59,60,64,71,77,87,
98,100,108,109,
112,120,123,133,
137,138,142,144,
147,150,165,175
Barns 119,120
Dempsey 10,39,
40,46,48
Dempsey S. 2,3,8,
21,62,68,70

GOODMAN
Demsey 63,64,100,120
Demsey S. 73,74
Henery 121
Henry 5,88,168
James 20,41,135,164,191
Jethero D. 179,190
Jethro 60,114,116,154
John 5,88,121,148,153,164
Leml. 6,49,148,153
Lemuel 5
Maria 168
Mariah 5,88,121
Peninah 121
Penninah 5,88
Peny 168
Richard 5,88,121,153,164
Richd. 148
W. H. 168
Whitmil 111
William H. 121
Will. 40,43,81
William 3,4,6,19,21,23,31,34,39,46,48,56,60,62,64,71,81,164,166,179
William H. 5,7,49,88,189
William, Jr. 23
William, Sr. 75
Wm. 4,10,24,28,30,42,59,61,73,100,131,137,142,150,159,171
Wm. H. 32,39,64,100,109,125,137,148,192

GOODWIN
James 37,102
Wm. 111

GOOMER (See also **GOMER**)
Thomas 121

GORDEN
Jno. C. 193
John 164
John C. 156,159,160-162,165-168,

GORDEN
John C. 176,180,189,192,193
Jos. 189
Joseph 157,160,161,166,168,177,178,188,189,192

GORDON
James 59,78,90,124
Jno. C. 21,40,71,90,92,98,99,106,
Jno. C. 118,120,124,130,141,142,144,145
John C. 3,6,15,17,21,23,24,30-32,38,43,44,55,62,64-67,77,78,90,100,105,107,114,116,123,124,129-131,138,140,141,147,149,150,159,180,187
Jos. 51,63,73,94,95,104,118,120,121,123,133,134,144,147,150,151
Joseph 2,3,7,9,12,13,22,23,27,33,35,36,41,51,52,63,67,100,115,125,130,137

GRANBERRY
Ann 10
Bathsheba 160
Elizabeth 20,63,160
George 63,160
James 9,10,157,160
John 20,41,63
John J. 64
Thomas 6,7
Thos. 160

GRANBERY
Eliza. 91,128,152
Geor. W. 128,152
George 91
Ger. W. 152
James 35,51,91
John 151,152

GRANBEY
John 152

GRANBURY

GRANBURY
James 189
Nancy 178

GRANT
Ann 19
Oliver 160
Sarah 160

GREEN
Aaron 12
Anthony 148
Charlott 94
Charlotte 178
Henry 29,34,36,94,95,134
Isaac 37,188
Kadar 33
Lewis 81,132,145,149,150,193,194
Luke 59,66,97,188
Margaret 145
Milly 12
Samuel 37
William 126

GREGORY
Catharine 126
Jos. 126
Richard B. 189
Richd. B. 51

GRIFFIN
James 108,122
John B. 151

GRIFFITH
Burrell 15,21
Burwell 124,155,163,179
Dempsey 179
John 113,179
Martha 179
Nathl. 37

GWIN
Daniel 76
Jos. 76

GWINN
Christian 21
Edward 21
James 21
John 76
Thos. 21

H

HACKLEY

HACKLEY
___ 119

HAIRE (See also **HARE**)
Moses D. 89

HALETT (See also **HASLETT**)
John 137

HALL
Garrison 190
Job R. 37,39,60,64,104,108,155,178
Wm. W. 69

HANCY
Wm. 126

HARE (See also **HAIRE**)
Briant 59,102
Bryant 1,180,182-184
Edward 12,48,89,124,152
Elijah 19,144
Harrison 92
Henry 41,108,111,120
James 189
Jesse L. 111
Jno. 120
John 12,15,16,32,42,43,48,57,105,116,122,129,181
Mary 57,105
Moses D. 111
Robert 57,105
William 105,181

HARELL
Nathan, Jr. 111

HARREL
Willis R. 104

HARRELL
___ 48,73,75,76,100,148,155
Abm. 68
Abram 67,68
Andrew 1,45,57,74,82,104
Andrew R. 104,191
Asa 15,42
Elijah 9,55,70,73,74,89,105,111,114,117,193,194

HARRELL
Elisha 9,55,89, 106,187
Elisha, Jr. 72
Elizabeth 49,63
Ervan 132
Ervin 184
George 41,114, 187
George, Jr. 37
I. S. 73,91
Isaac 47,53,70,73, 136,170
Isaac S. 63,142, 177,186,192
James 98
James A. 141
Jas. A. 147
Jasper 102
Jesse 59,66,98,102
Jethero 182
Jethro 1,45,81,102, 106,114,122,153
Jethro, Jr. 111
John 15,53
John B. 47,52
Josiah 81
Judith 47
Julia 191
M. 162
M. R. 161
Mary 26,41,63,88, 101,114,161
Mills 37
Moses R. 162
Nancy 115
Nathan 49,63
Nathan, Jr. 143
Nathan, Sr. 111
Nathaniel 10,42, 171,182
Nathl. 131,154
Noah 19,23,30,31, 51,59,61,62,105, 115,128,130,143, 168
Oliver 113
Peter 24,26,44,48, 116
Reuben 38,42
S. 29,34
Samel. 114,132
Saml. 59,81,82, 128,132,141,143,163

HARRELL
Samuel 180
Samuel R. 179,180, 189
Samuel, Sr. 100
Sarah 25
Theophilus 67,68
Theos. 95
Warren 106
William 15,21,23, 29,34,59,94,115, 153,161,176,180
William H. 115, 170
William, Jr. 51, 59,81
William, Sr. 3,45, 50,51,82
Willis 16,21,25, 37,42,102
Willis W. 104
Wm. 127,129,177
Wm. H. 130,131, 147,157
Wm., Jr. 94,125
Wm., Sr. 100
Wm. W. 128
HARRIS
____ 137
HARVEY
____ 4,104,137, 149,176
Ann 131
Ann N. 190
Jacob J. 161,176
Jacob N. 177
Mary 177
Mary A. S. 176
R. M. 184
Richard M. 184
Wm. 136,137,149
Wm. B. 172,176, 182,188
HASLET
____ 166,171
Fletcher 161
Jno. 187
John H. 107,147, 161,193
HASLETT
____ 23,143
Jno. 188
Jno. H. 147

HASLETT
John H. 29,34,36, 48,49,64,94,100, 125,149,152
HASLIP
____ 131
HATTON
____ 151
HAUGHTON
Jon. H. 130
HAYES
Wright 41
HAYS
Benj. 79,105
Benjamin 15,26, 59,61,170,174
Benjn. 119
Caroline 71,79, 105,119
Docton 47,114, 189
Elisha 103
Eliza. 71,73,79
Henry 29,36,81, 82,97,172,176,180, 182
Jacob 158
Jas. R. 144
John 73,74,187, 189
John, Sr. 68
Joseph 68
Nancy 106
Richard 39,109, 110,149,150
Riddick 82,144
Rob P. 155
Robert 104,106, 193,194
Robt. 103
Robt. P. 135
Timo. 76,109,144, 155
Timothy 5,134
Will W. 73
William W. 19
Willis 53
Willis R. 149,150, 159,162,193,194
Wm. 147,187
Wright 35,52,76, 126
Zac 103,155
Zach 104,155

HAYS
Zack 109
HAYSE
Benjamin 66
Henry 34
John 70
Wright 57,69
HERON
____ 86
HILL
Asa 70,73,74,103, 109,111,143,146, 149,171,176
Clement 45,50,54
Joseph 181
Moses 145,163, 164
Rob. 81
Robert 23,37,42, 62,161,162,180-184
Robert, Jr. 8,82, 132
Robert, Sr. 137
Robt., Jr. 83,132
Susan 92
Susan J. 56
Whit 81,83,138, 139
Whitl. 59
Whitmel 180, 182-184
Whitmell 8,29,34, 66
Whitmil 82,139
HINTON
Deannah 177
Fred. 81,95,126, 127
Frederick 7,27,46, 47,120
Frederick, Jr. 2, 15,46
Fredk., Jr. 52
Jacob 172
James 12,56,96, 126,127,156
John 14,24,33,45, 50,60,96,97,102, 138,139,163,190
John, Jr. 59,102
John, Sr. 46,66, 132,138,142
Jonas 1,37,42, 141,190

HINTON
Kedar 47,114, 154,155,193,194
Leah 12,55,95, 126,129,157
Louisa 177
Mary 26,78
Noah 2,36,46,66, 102,103,126,132, 156,158
Reuben 8,13,23, 40,46,54,66,160, 161,185
Reuben, Jr. 24,26, 35,43
Reuben, Sr. 59
Reubin 165
Richad 127
Richard 128,177
Rubin 100,102, 103,107,122,130, 137,138,149
Sally 126,156
Sarah 52,88,129, 158,177
Thomas 47,145
Thos. 71,187
Will. 24,75,90
William 12,46,60, 67
Wm. 35,52,59,78, 142,148,149,153,177

HIOTT (See also HYOTT)
Isaac 164

HITE
Zachariah 176

HOBB
Guy 184

HOBBS
Amas 132
Amos 3,18,27,31, 36,47,80,101,102, 181
Daniel 89,106,182
Daniel S. 162,181, 182
David 32,36,97, 102,103,106
Demcy 114
Demsey 70,73,74
Edward 100,133
Guy 80-82,90,98, 124,141,148,153,

HOBBS
Guy 158,171,193, 194
Jesse 15,63,81,82, 110,110,121,133, 181
Matthew 185
Moses 37
Thomas 3,27
Will 114
William 98,100
Wm. 132

HOFFLER
___ 65
Asa 177
Emily 190
Garret 90,102
Garrett 12,33,60
Garrot 98,190
Hance 24,35,119, 163,175
Hanse 103,107, 108
Henry 108,109, 147,154,156,163, 194
Isaac 173
James 60
James Robert 190
Jno. H. 145
John 82,97,103
John D. 81
John, Jr. 10,15,81
Leah 190
Levan 89
Leven 132,138, 139,172,173,193
Levin 72,138,194
Penelope 190
William 19,172
Willis 114
Wm. 108,172

HOFFLUR
Leven 130

HOFLER
Garrett 12,54
Hance 40,43
James 12,46
John 57,63
John, Jr. 53

HOGARD
Thomas 88,140
Thos. 81,86,91,
Thos. 107,128,136

HOGGARD
Thomas 5,15,16, 43,46,54,59,75, 100,113,116,150
Thos. 86,100,155, 162,177,191

HOLLAND
Luke 59

HOLLOWEL
Luke 31

HOLLOWEL_
Luke 116

HOLLOWELL
Luke 18,107

HORTON
Martha 33,99,152

HOSKINS
Margaret 83

HOWARD
James 53,73

HOWELL
David 144
Ed 92
Edward 27,75,144
Edwd. 89
Jethero 193,194
Jethro 59
Kinchen 37,102
L. 148
Leml. 149,154
Lemuel 1,59,66, 186
Lottey 75
Miles 6,17,41,47, 49,61,89,100,101, 122,132,134,138, 139,151,153,162, 163
Polly 106
Timothy 73,111,187
Wright 106

HUDGINS
___ 137
Jesse 53,103
John 142
Leven 142
Mary 7,54,138
William 37,69, 130,170
William J. 11,94
Wm. 100,133,
Wm. 142,150,178
Wm. J. 55,122,

HUDGINS
Wm. J. 152

HUMPHLET (See also UMPHLET)
Eli 144
Elisha 107
Hannah 192
John 144
Wm. 111

HUNTER
___ 23,24,65,72, 92,100,101,131, 137,138,142,166, 170,187
Benj. 93
Benjamin 79
Ed. R. 91,123, 142,147,148
Edward R. 24,32, 36,38,51,157,165, 167,189
Edwd. R. 77
Elisha 13,29,36, 109,111
I. B. 119
I. R. 15,30,40,55, 92,119
Isaac 5,9,15,55, 66,128
Isaac R. 9,14-17, 22,30-32,34,36,51, 55,62,66,67,95,99, 105,107,119,123, 124,147,152
Jacob B. 15,55, 124
Jacob Benjamin 157
Jno. O. 80,91,118, 125,142
John 12
John O. 2,15,21, 36,44,60,61,67,69,9 9,123,127,147, 162,164,166,170, 192
Mary 15,55,93
Riddick 8,59,66, 81,82
Sally Ann 158
Sarah Ann 98
Sophia 62
Sophia C. 62
Thomas B. 3,9,27,

HUNTER
 Thomas B. 55,66,80
 Thos. B. 98
 Thos. J. 98
 Tim 176
 Timo. 102,103
 Timothy 15,36
HURDLE
 Ab. 141
 Abm. 1,59
 Abram 170,178
 Daniel 52,90,153
 Henry 29,48
 Joel B. 113
 Jos. 80,114,117,129,141
 Joseph 1,59,97,102,129,156,163,171,183-185
 Joseph, Jr. 1,29,34,72,124
 Joseph T. 59,66,108
 Kedar 6
 Lewis 48,94,125
 Lewis J. 19,89
 Moses 169
 Nancy 6,55,89,123,156
 Sidney 29,89
 Sophia 48,94,125,152
 Sophia A. 89
 Thomas 30,53
 Thos. 90,160,180
 William 41
HYOTT (See also **HIOTT**)
 Isaac 164

I

IREDELL
 James 176

J

JENKINS
 Arthur 158
 Exum 5,27,48,89,92,182
 Isaac 185
 Isaac H. 37
 James 158

JENKINS
 Jethro 42
 Willey 77
 Willy 77
JERNIGAN
 ___ 74
JINKINS
 Exum 92,121,123,127,128,152
 Isaac H. 111
 John B. 128
 John C. 114
 Willie 135
 Willis 101
JNKINS
 Arthur 19
JOHNSON
 Andrew 189
 James 178
 Margaret 178
 Mary 187
 Molly 113
 Thomas 37,88,111
 Will 92,124
 William 56
 Wm. 11
JONES
 Absila 147
 Absilla 178
 Archd. 114,143,154
 Archibald 164,182
 Archie 164
 Charles 29,34,70,73,74,111,114,191
 Chas. 144
 Chitty 2
 E. 137
 Edward 72,194
 Elizabeth G. 170
 Ezekiel 81,82,103
 Ezekiel T. 164,170
 Fra. 154
 Fred. 73-75,97,114
 Frederick 70
 Fredrick 134,191
 H. 36
 H. H. 151
 H. H. C. 19,41,124

JONES
 Hardy 26,36,177
 Hardy H. C. 96,122,134
 Henry 2,12,21,26,51,70,96,104,110,134,172,186
 Heny. 26
 Hollady 88
 Holloday 6,56,69
 Hollody 125,151
 Jacob P. 90
 James 15,21,29,37,59,78,89,90,98,127,144,145,147,160,178
 James, Sr. 141
 Jas. 15,21,59,78
 Jas. S. 95
 Jno. 145
 John 6,21,26,48,58,111,116,168
 Jos. 48
 Joseph 6
 Joshua 90,164
 Kadar 6
 Kedar 56,69,88,125,151
 Louisa 2,21,51,104,110,141
 Marmaduke 6,48
 Marmk. 147
 Nathl. 119,154
 P. 34,70,74
 Parker 29
 Paul 15,37,42,178,185
 R. 73
 Riddick 9,19,38,44,60,74,81,82,103,107,123,154,162,180
 Salley 78,89
 Sarah 158,189
 Simmons 127
 Simmons H. 68
 Thomas 106,124
 Thomas F. 193
 Whit 148
 Whitl. 48
 Whitmell 6
 William 9,66,182
 William, Jr. 37
 Willie P. 133

JONES
 Wm. 132,164,182
JORDAN
 John 128,176
 Matthew 183
 Matthias 183
 Thos. A. 183
JORDON
 Armstead 12
 Nancy 12

K

KEE
 Jesse 65
 Jesse R. 125,127,
 Jesse R. 128,131,135
KEY
 J. R. 193
 Jesse R. 125,166,171,175,180
KEYS
 Jesse R. 150,151
KING
 Henry 154
 James 37
 John 95,132,136,148-150,168
 Mary 72,80,148,153
 Nehemiah 37
 Norman 154
 Simon 114,117,183,184
 Will 110
 William 18,31,63,173
 Wm. 114,121,133,148,183,184
KINNY
 C. R. 80
KITTREL
 George 120
KITTRELL
 ___ 77,142,147
 G. 30
 Geor. 116,122
 George 3,7,21,24,30,31,40,42,52,54,62,86,98,130
 John 52
 Mildred 42
 Milley 40

KNIGHT
Benj., Jr. 111
Demcy 100,133
Dempsey 6,16,23,
54,59,166,167,181
Dempsy 170
Demsey 19,64,65,
67,108,120,137
Demsy 140
Edwin 118
Garret 193
Jas. 118
John 161
Miles 118
Westly 111

L

LANDING
James 78
Jos. 136
Wm. 136
LANG
John 111
LANGSTON
Dempsey 20,46,62
Jno. 100
John 20,42,46,64,
114,137,180,182-184
LASITER
Sarah M. 92
Timothy 92
LASSITER
Abner 113
Absolom 95
Ann E. 20,156
Ezekiel 17,94,136
Fred. 125,135
Henry 5,30,35,55,
168
Henry B. 54,190
Isaac 25,37,41
James 5,7,23,24,
37,72,141
Jethro 71,162
John 20,114,156
Jonathan 104
Jos. 146
Reuben 54,63
Rubin 90,126,155
Sarah M. 124,156,
168
Sarah Margaret 30
Susanah 115

LASSITER
Thomas 137
Thos. 145
Timo. 124
Timothy 30,156,
168
LAWRENCE
Julia 192
Starkey 188
LEE
___ 4
Eliza. 133
Elizabeth 33,88
Helon 78
John 80,164,175
Louisa 30
Robert 37,111
Step. 30
Stephen 56,88,
122
William 2,4,6,8,
12,15,21,23,24,26,
33,40,46-48,59,62,
64,67,71,73,88,96,
106,131,171,183,
186,193
Wm. 12,42,43,73,
100,112,137,150,
152,184
Wm. W. 30
LEWIS
Celea 157
Celia 11,56,94,95,
121,136
David 72,77,118
Eff 75,186,188
Elizabeth 66
Exum 8,9,11,15,
26,36,94-96,108,
109,111,124,172,
173,174
John 7,11,50,64,
66,69,74,95,96,102,
103,134,170
John, Jr. 47,59
Judith 27
Louisa 66
Rachel 170
Salley 81
Sally 27
Sarah 2,46
Selah 11
LILES
Jno. G. 6

LILES
John G. 7,57,137
Margaret Ann 57
LILLEY
Jos. 80
LIVESAY
Joshua 133
LOOMIS
Hiram 113
LOVET
John 83,100,137,
140,142,143,166,
183
LOVETT
John 68,159,183
LUMIS
Hiram 107

M

M__GAN (*See also*
MORGAN)
James 107
MANEY
___ 176
MANNING
Willoughby 20
Willowby 111
MANSARD
Ann E. 104,171
Janet M. 104
Jannet M. 171
MARCH (*See also*
MAUCH)
Barnet 145,147,
164,172-174
Barnett 63
Bernard 8,144
Jno. A. 92
John A. 35,89
MATHEWS
And. 151
Andrew 88,125,
145
Andrew P. 144
Anthoney 143
Anthony 103,147
Bryant 111,147
E. 143
Edwin 123
Jacob 113,147
John 73,76,81,
100,101,103-105,
155

MATHEWS
John D. 111,135
John W. 77,88
Margate E. 145
Martha J. 143
Peggy 145
Pleasant 145
Rid. 155
Riddick 59,81,82,
100,136,155
Whitmil 111
Wm. 109
Wm. A. 114,125,
141,143
MATHIAS (*See
also* **MATTHIAS**)
Edwin 36,115,
133,154
James 128,154
Jesse 19,36,38,41,
60,74,79,82,90,92,
93,102,114,135,
181,182
John 124
Joseph 135,181
MATHWS
John 134
MATTHEWS
Andrew 6,32,56,
69,180
Andrew P. 178
Anthony 173
Briant 185
Bryant 37
Elizabeth 60
Etheldred 61,68
Etthled. 144
James 25
Jno. 119
John 2,10,13,23,
29,41,54,68,133,
161,171,176,188,
189
John W. 60,61
Martha Jane 19
Mary 19
Milliam A. 54
Riddick 13,15,29,
34,68,165,193,194
Thomas 188
William A. 16,21,
William A. 137
Wm. A. 42
MATTHIAS

MATTHIAS
  Edwin 166
  James 163,164
  Jesse 9,162,172
MAUCH (*See also* **MARCH**)
  Barnet 144
MC GUIRE
  Wm. H. 187
MC PHERSON
  Willie 36
MELTEAR (*See also* **MILTEAR**)
  David 89
  Matilda 41
MELTEARE
  David 133
  David L. 153
MELVIN
  Frederick H. 30
  Henry 30
  Martha S. 20,30
  Mary Jane 30
  Sally Ann 30
MILLER
  Charity 189
  James 187
  Rubin 125
  Will. 114,147
  William 59,66,117,164,171
  Wm. 114
  Wm., Jr. 132,141,143
  Wm., Sr. 132
MILTEAR (*See also* **MELTEAR**)
  David L. 6,56
MILTEARE
  Ab. 151
MINGO
  ___ 30,89,137,147,187
MINTON
  ___ 23,47,65,138,166,171
  P. B. 2,11,40
  Peter B. 2,3,9-11,15,21,27,30,32,35,73,74,111,163,170,191
MITCHEL
  Easther 73
  Jno. 133

MITCHEL
  John 36,100,114,121,122,131,136,137,159,171
MITCHELL
  John 23,53,65
MOORE
  Martha 127
  William 7,64,68,119,171
  William K. 63,64
  Wm. 53
  Wm. K. 90,100,137
MORGAN (*See also* **M__GAN**)
  ___ 41
  Ab. 103,107
  Abr., Sr. 81
  Abraham 13,17,35,41,59,72
  Abraham, Jr. 185
  Abraham, Sr. 4,15
  Abram 64
  Auston 11
  Danil. 14
  James 6,7,16,18,23,32,44,45,60,64,67,76,99,100,118,120,128,131-133,137,144,146,163,170,178,180,181,191
  Jas. 119,148
  Mathias 4
  Rachel 14
  Saml. 100
  Seth 14,51,64,142
  Seth R. 64,102,103,105,107,129,180
  Thomas 37
  Wm. 142
MORRIS
  Fedrick 175
  John 45,102,106,109,164
  John, Jr. 190
MORRISS
  Frederick 41
  John 50
MORSE
  Stewart 111
  Wm. 111

MULLEN
  George m. 169
MUPHREY
  Wm. 94
MURFREE
  Nathaniel 47
MURPHEY
  Nathaniel 42

N

NEAL
  Edward S. 65,83
  NEGROES
ABRAM 70
AMY 70
BUNGER 85
CLARISA 148
DAVID 70
DICK 43
ELEY 61
ESTHER 36,53,54
FANNY 85
GILES 85
HANAH 149
HARRY 10,43
ISAAC 61,85,148
JACK 188
JERRY 85
JINNY 77
LEWIS 149
MARTHA 36,53
MARTILLA 182
MARY 85
MILEY 85
MILLS 85,159
MINGO 149
MOSES 77
NED 166
PENNINAH 85
PLEASANT 70
RACHEL 85
REDMON 126
SALLY 167
SAM 95
TEMPE 85
TIBE 135
BLANCHARD
  Sally 103
BURK
  Arthur 82
BURKET
  Joseph 17
BUTLER

NEGROES
  Mary 75
  Thomas 75
CORBAL
  Anaca 159
  Charlotte 159
CORBELL
  Ainah 159
CORBIN
  William 166
DILDAY
  Jacob 148
EURE
  Martha 165
HUNTER
  Asa 118,136,166
  James 136
JONES
  Charles 43,57
  Elizabeth 57
  Matthew 50
  Wright 159
LANG
  Betsey 75
  Emeline 75
PHELPS
  Asa 166
  Henry 131
POLSON
  John 34
  Ruth 34
PRICE
  Alfred 75
  Betsey 75
  Thompson 75
  William 185
REED
  Abram 185
  Alfred 158
  Augustus 101,126
  Elisha 75,95
  Henderson 14
  Jethro 101,126
  Mills 101
  Sophia 75
ROBINS
  Henry 30
  Julia 30
SAUNDERS
  John 169
SPEIGHTS
  Timothy 50
TAYLOR
  Betsey 184

NEGROES
Eliza. 72,95
John 95
Mary 72
Miles 184
UMPHLET
Abram 69
WALKER
John 75,138
Redman 132
WEAVER
Hillery 102

ooooooooooooooooooooo

NEWSOME
Robert 163
NIXON
Jacob 163
Nathan 11,18,19,
24,43,46,58,60,65,
72,80,96,99,100,
102,103,107,109,
125,137,147-150,
156,173,191,192
Zachariah 191
NORFLEET
___ 84-86,172
Harriett 84
Jno. 84,103
Jno. R. 82,84,94,
95,145
John 69,143
John R. 9,14,25,54,
68,69,74,80,83,121,
123,131
K. 68
Kinchen 9,41,68,
70,73,74,94,95,136,
143,147
Mark 74
Marmaduke 33,70,
73,77,97,109,115,
121,130,137,151,
154,158,159,167,
168,171,177,178,
182,183
Mk. 154

O

OBARR (See also BAR, BARR)
Britton 74
ODAIM
Richard 138

ODAM
Asa 5,91,129,157,
187
Jacob 140,146
John 99,106,171
John W. 77,93,
121,123,151,152
Prissilla 93,123,
152
Richard 71,94,
134,140,150,159,
163,169,172,175,
186,187,193
Richd. 99,100,
128,136,140,141,
143,148,155,186
Sarah E. 121,153
Sopha A. 152
Sophia A. 123
Sophia Ann 92
ODOM
___ 24
Asa 5,52,55,160
Ben. 48
Benja. 5
Benjamin 2
Ira 5,48,89
Jacob 16,23,38,
45,47,81
Jno. 120
John 2,19
John J. 181
John W. 2,32,41,
42,47,48
Mary 120
Monica 38,47
Pricilla 48
Prissila 2
Richard 1,17,25,
31,33,38,64
Richd. 22,40,44,
52,59,106
Sarah 161
OSTIN (See also AUSTIN)
Richard 151
OUTLAW
David 19,27,33,
54,113,133
Jacob 29
James 41,54
OVERMAN
Josiah 32
Wm. 104

P

PACKER
Jas. 146
PARER
Dempsy 172
PARKE
Ab. W. 136
PARKER
___ 35,41
A. W. 66,76,156,
161,165,171,182,
184,190
Ab. W. 75,79,94,
98-100,102,104,
106,108,109,112,
124,136,138,144,
150,153,155
Abm. 158,181
Abm. W. 10,14,
52,156,193
Abraham 34,43,
47,48,93
Abraham W. 11,
28,41,50,51,56,82,
92,110,111,113,
139,187
Abram 15,26,38,
42,44,69,156
Abram W. 7,10,
41,53,57,59,63,65,
68,172,187
Amos 36,181
Ann 76
Bray 59,81,82,99,
114,117,165,167,
168,175,184,192
Chitty 70
Christian 133,153
D. 70,103
Daniel 38,160
David 3,6,12,29,
34,35,40,43,45,48,
51,55,56,67,88,95,
111,115,116,119,
122,123,125,134,
150,161,167,175,
182,188
Demcy 100,109,
114,127,129,134,
138,154
Dempsey 3,23,51,
53,58,59,64,66,156,
161,193,194

PARKER
Dempsy 172,173,
186
Demsey 15,33,
69,72,96,98,102,
104,109,110,130,
137,141
Demsy 102,141,
151,153
Edward 146
Elisha 137,156,
185
Eliza. 155
Elizabeth 158
H. D. 40,64,124
Hardey D. 113
Hardy 3,46,186,
193
Hardy D. 1,5,10,
22,24,31,36,38,42,
43,46-48,64,71,77,
88,98,100,112,120,
121,125,144,150,
152,160,175
Harriett 158
Hump. 93
Humphrey 2,16,
21,44,55,62,90,181
Humphrey, Sr. 45,
50
Humphry 90,93,
115,141,163,170
Humphy 167
Isaac 35,145,190,
194
Isaiah 35
James 122,125,
142,149,188
James H. 172
Jane 63
Jas. 15,59,145
Jesse 15,37,76,81,
82
Jno. F. 93
John 57,81,105,
149,159,172,173
John F. 127
Jordan 15,146,
155,159,163,
167,181
Jordon 36
Jos. 5
Kedar 34
Kiddy 89

PARKER
Kind. 74,75,102, 143,155
Kindred 20,29,34, 57,59,61,64,78,83, 93,97,143,149,156, 160
Levi W. 44,156
Louisa 76,170
Margaret 76,101
Martha 44,69,133, 158
Mary 76,158
Miles 35-37,42, 76, 80,89,93,94,102, 108,120,126,130, 138,142,143,149, 150,154,172,173, 178-182,193
Miles, Jr. 59,109, 114,125,129,130, 138,141,143
Moses 102
Myles 19,134
Nancy 40,58,149
Nathan 190
Partheana 89
Parthenia 132,153
Prissila 58
R. 81
Reuben 1,70,182
Richard 147
Richard H. 8,32, 104,156 *147*
Richd. H. 77,88, 145,167
Rob. 145,150
Robert 35,37,76, 111,185,190
Robt. 5,41,100
Roden 183,184
Rubin 73,74,145
Sarah 13
Sophia 38,47
Theos. 145
Thursey 76
William 34,45,50, 181
Willie 111
Wm. 29,42,102, 120,133,135,149
Wm. W. 111

PEAL
Dempsey 185,193

PEAL
Riddick 111

PEARCE (*See also* **PIERCE**)
Aaron 193,194
Abner 32,34,48
Daniel 27
Henry 8
Isaac 21,189
Isaac, Jr. 15,34,37, 42
Nathan 180

PEEL
James 149
Thos. 142

PERRY
Caleb 156
James 37
Josiah 156
Timothy 40
Wm. 145

PETTY
Will 130
Wm. 115

PHELEPS
James 110

PHELPS
Gideon 74
James 104,146
Wesley 37
Westly 164
Wm. 159

PIERCE (*See also* **PEARCE**)
Aaron 81
Ab. 92,135,154
Abraham 91
Aron 125
Arone 82
Isaac 102,115, 125,130,134
Nathan 114,128

PIERE
Isaac 147

PILAN
Asa 118

PILAND
Elisha 3,13,58, 171
Isaac 5,54,81, 118,135,140
James 5,118,135, 140

PILAND
James H. 81
Jas. 5
Jesse 5,15,37,42, 81,118,130
John 3,93,171
Mildred 171
Milley 5,54
Mills 3,13,58,93, 118,135,171
Milly 3,93
Peter 37,93,94
Reuben 26,44, 118,182
Rubin 81,137,150
Seth 118,145
Shad. 102
Shadrach 45
Shadrack 50
Shadrick 102,154
Susan 3,93,171
Susannah 8
William 15,59,66, 164
Wm. 125

PINTARD
____ 25

PIPKIN
Isaac 6,7,22,23, 24,29,33,34,53, 59,61,64,75,83,94, 109,120,134,142, 159,163,164,169
Jno. D. 16,101, 131,148
John D. 3,5,16,28, 39,53,55,60,64,71, 72,83,90,104,134, 149

POLSON
Geor. 135
Ruth 34

PORTER
Jesse 181
Sabra 181

POWELL
____ 102,137,187
Charles 68
Daniel 107
Eliza. 129
Jacob 37,69,102, 109,122,125,129, 133,134,188
James 37,44,107,

POWELL
James 162,192
Jno. 145,175
John 37,68,107, 132,173
John, Jr. 145
Kedar 154,163
Kedear 154
Millicent 191
Sally 15,55
Sarah 88
William 95,172
William W. 4,47, 67,69
Wm. 99,181,182
Wm. W. 7,123, 172,176

PRICE
Aron 147
Henry 126
Isaac 157

PRUDEN
Ab. 88,89,116, 135
Abm. 175,177, 180
Abraham 41,43, 100,114,136,191, 192
Abram 163
James 7,51,91, 125,128,148,156
Lewis W. 48,93
Martha 192
Nathaniel 5
William D. 19

PUGH
Henrey 117
Henry 2,10,27,57, 58,68,118,127,131, 141
Henry R. 2,41,70, 73,80,131
Josiah 88,161
Mills 161
Nathaniel 88
Nathaniel T. 161
Rebeca 88
Rebeca C. 161
Susan E. 142
W. E. 144,154
William 3
William E. 2,10, 13,25,27,57,58,65,

PUGH
William E. 68,73,82,88,109,127
Wm. 57,117
Wm. E. 41,58,65,71,73,74,79,98,118,130,131,134,138,142,145,161,165,193

R

RABEY
Adam 94
RABY
Adam 39
RAIBY
Adam 180
RAWLS
John 148
R. 133,162
Richard 79
Riezup 148
Risop 170
Risup 176
Rizeup 7,50
Rizop 19
Rizup 45,135
READ
Elijah 120
REED
G. W. 146
Geor. 148
Geor. W. 154
Jesse 35
Mills 35
RELPH
William 69
REYNOLDS
___ 186
RICE
Thomas 144,156,164
Thos. 164
RIDDI_
Willis F. 151
RIDDICK
___ 128
Ab. 99,116
Abm. 38,181,187
Abraham 9,31,38,44,55,81,113
Benja. 20
Bush. 24,65,109,

RIDDICK
Bush 142
Bushrod 22,57,65,72,101,171
Bushrod W. 59
Daniel 15,21,45,65,109
Danl. 145
David 45,59,95,186
E. 188
Easter 151
Elbert 19,129,186,187
Elbert H. 39,113,114,142,143
Elbert K. 113
Eliza H. 13
Elizabeth 6
Emaley 148
Henry 15,22,23,32,34,59,63,64,131,137,145,170,176
Isah. 15
Isaiah 4,45,108,147
J. 40
J. H. 100,110,112,115
J. R. 169
J. W. 89,148
James 38,44,52,55,99
James C. 10,25,29,39,43,45,50,67,105,125,159
James M. 28,110,141,147,175,187,188,193
James R. 7,9,15,18,19,21,24,25,27,29,31,32,35,43,49,50,54,57,58,64,66,67-69,71,72,75,79,80,87,97,101,102,105,106,110,113,
James R. 115,121,129,131,136,141,142,148,162,166,176,181,188
James W. 39,43,137,152
Jane R. 6

RIDDICK
Jas. C. 181
Jas. M. 119,147,188
Jas. R. 76,109,126,128,129,149,151,154,155,159,161,168,169,175,181
Jason 80,164
Jet. H. 29,65,92,177
Jethero 186
Jethero H. 155,167,173,175,178,181
Jethro 137
Jethro H. 3,12,17,19,21,22,24,25,27,32,43,44,52,58,59,65,74,78,80,94,99,103-105,107-109,111,121,129,136,138,141-143,147,155,158,170
Jno. 6,78,144,148
John 41,44,48,64,70,73,74,109,121,125,128,134,142,148,166,167,184
Jos. 52,66,91,92,100,101,104,106,108,112,116,121,130,132,137,138,140-142,144,151,154,193
Jos. C. 105
Jos., Jr. 125,126,154
Jos. R. 142,154
Joseph 3,4,9,15,17,21,22,27,28,30,31,34,50,57,59,60,65-68,73,77-79,94,104,110,114,125,133,150,159,161,163,171,175,176,
Joseph 180,183,185,188
Joseph, Jr. 23,188
Josiah 17,162
Kader 37
Kedar 102,145
L. 24

RIDDICK
Lass. 75,111,142
Lassiter 9,21,24,29,32,35,51,56,64,67,78,91,94,95,98,102,104-106,131,135,136,142,146,149,154,158-160,162,164,165,175,176,184,188,192
Leml. 37,111,150
Lemuel 1,176,186,192,193
Margaret 32
Mary 128
Mary A. 95,152
Mary Ann 6,55
Micajah 6,18,35
Mills 17,33,46,51,52,66,71,79
N. 112
Nancy 39,126,144
Nathan 3,12,24,27,36,44,52,54,56,58,59,65,77,82,92,93,105,107,110,121,122,127,128,135,136,139,148,151,153,158,164,170,171,176
Richard 32,37
Ro. 15,145
Robert 32,115
Robert, Sr. 63
Robt. 59,109
Tho. 68,70
Thomas 27,74,96,131,165,170,176
Thomas E. 68,77
Thos. 30,31,59,65,73,74,142,171,176
Thos. E. 116
W. 24
W. F. 6,119
Wealthy 44
Wealty 44
Wiley 15,70,118,119,173
Willey 151
William 70,73,108
William W. 4
Willie 13,22,73,

RIDDICK
Willie 74,110,128
Willis 45,175
Willis F. 7,50,51,
65,71,73,77,90,101,
124,132,142,144,
147,156,157,163,
167,170,176,178,
189,193
Willis J. 8,12,24,
29,33,34,36,48,52,
56,71,95,96,107,
111,126,127,156
Willis S. 190
Wills J. 147
Wm. 147
Wm. W. 29
RIDDIK
John 166
RIDICK
___ 167
ROBERSON
Elisha 54
ROBERTS
Jno. 24,90
John 13,14,31,37,
42,54,104,108,189,
190
John A. 103,138
John S. 76,78,111,
130,132,155,159,180
John, Sr. 158
Mary 194
Mills 2,29,59,83,
96,114,118,130,
131,137,148,181,
184,190,194
ROBINS
Julia 30
Noah 111
ROCHELL
Clement 49
ROGERON (*See also* **ROGERSON**)
Abel 3
ROGERS
Eliza. 73
Elizabeth 2,3,6,39,
58,73
Francis 73
James 49,154,188
Jas. 154
Jonathan 3,39
Leve 5

ROGERS
Levi 2,8,37,40,42,
46,49,52,62,90,93,
94,101,109,130,
131,134,143,146,
147,149,150,154,
165
Philip 75
Rob 146
Robert 2-4,6,8,46,
49,50,70,114,126,
188,193
Robt. 71,102
Timo. 125
Timothy 133,164,
172-174
ROGERSON (*See also* **ROGERON**)
Abel 27,32,41,50,
53,54,65,69,80,108,
111,115,130,136,
138,139,142,147,
148,150,157,158,
181,190,194
ROOKS
David 14,37,134
Elisha 35
Fedk. 164
Fedrick 169
Fred 102,114,117,
141
Frederick 30,40,
59
Sarah 151
William 35
ROUNTREE
Jason 53,81,96,
113,115,154,192
John 81,125,149
Leah 133
Noah 13,15,19,59,
103,109,117,119,
147
Seth W. 40,99,
103,107,122,124,
157,175
Seth Washington
31
Simmonds 57,58,
67,88,104,139,147,
158
Simmons 25,81,
88,123,131,137
Simnons 79

ROUNTREE
Simns. 137
Simonds 141,171
Simons 120
Sol. 111,114,117,
129,130,141,143,
147,149,150
Solomon 54,117,
171,182-184
Thomas 12,15,31,
40,47,111
Thos. 99
RUSSEL
James 162,163

S

SALLINGS
SALLINGS (See also **STALLINGS**)
Whitl. 59
SANDERS
John 37
SANTOS
M. A. 149,162
SAUNDERS
___ 22
Benj. 81,82,107,
132,163
Benja. 49
Benjamin 42,161,
193
Benjn. 101,194
D. M. 144,161,
163
Drew 109
Drew M. 20,110,
176
Elizabeth 67
Gilbert 61,110,
125
Gilbert G. 19,101,
128
James 61,63,
81-83,101,163,
164,171,176
Jason 20,35,57,
61,65,101,109,110,
117,138,151,179
Jasons 131
Jno. 160
John 8,13,19,23,
33,42,61,64,78,96,
100,109,117,126,

SAUNDERS
John 130,132,
134,148,151,164,
189
John, Sr. 171
Law. 116
Lawrenc 110
Lawrence 116
Nancy 179,189
Sarah 89
T. 33
Tho. 65
Thomas 1,3,5,13,
15,20-22,33,35,42,
43,44,50,51,52,54,
55,69,71,72,77,78,
88,89,92,95,104,
105,110,113,114,
121-123,125,127,
129-131,139,149,
156,165-167,169,
170,187,189,193
Thos. 24,89,91,
101,112,118,145,
150,155,157,160,
163,180,183,185
SAUNDES
___ 142
James 176
Thomas 79
SAVAGE
___ 57
Benj. 152
Benjamin 5,119
Caleb 113,121
James 39,64,89,
98,123,131,137,
171,189
James M. 77
Jas. 119
Jesse 5,23,39,49,
59,64,88,98,101,
113,119,121,122,
140,142,152,172,
SAVAGE
Jesse 174
Jesse M. 10,70,
73,98,101,114,119,
123
Jesse, Sr. 100
Jno. 119
John 113,121,123,
172
John P. 130

SAVAGE
  Mary 5,88,119
  Moore 23,187
  Prior 13,15,23,37,
42,44,65,68,96,103,
105,129,137,148
  Pryer 48,100,102,
105,186
  Pryor 73,103,117,
126,169-171
  Sarah 123
  William 89,171
  William H. 53
  Wm. H. 107,115,
135,137,167,172
SCARBOROUGH
  Eanas 131
  Enos 46,101,146
SCARBOUGH
  Eanos 143
SEARS
  Barshaba 118,119,
126,127,131
  Bathsheba 185
  Belver 132
  Will 81
  William 15,34,40,
78,82,96,104
  Wm. 44,126,127,
132,134,138,164
SHEPHERD
  John 181
  John B. 162
  Wm. B. 160
SHERARD
  Randolph 44
SHERRAD
  Randol 156
SIMMS
  W. D. 162
  Wm. D. 185
SIMONS
  Joseph 172
  Robert 123,172
  Wm. D. 149
SIMPSON
  Jas. 126
  Silas 35
SKINNER
  Henry W. 13,35,
41,76
  Joshua 12
SMALL
  Ann 129

SMALL
  Charity 129
  Christain 2,55
  Christian 129
  Christian E. 90
  Elisha 37,42,193,
194
  James A. 129
  James F. 37
  Jno. 90,129
  Jo. 129
  John 129,130,
133,167
  John, Sr. 76,149
  Jos. 94
  M. H. 55
  Moses H. 2,6
  Reuben 189
  Rubin 129
  Sol. 129,130
  Solomon 125,164,
172-174
  Thomas A. 55,
123
  Thos. 90
SMITH
  ____ 65.95
  A. 121
  Ab. 74,136,154
  Abm. 175
  Abraham 25,60
  Abram 70,73
  Allan 136
  Allen 64,79,80,
113,120,121,124,
125,129,130,139,
142,154,158,159,
176,188
  Arthur R. 64
  Britten 156
  Britton 117,145,
146
  Edwin 3,6,49,81,
88,92,123,124,151
  Elizabeth 53
  Frances 6
  Francis 48,63
  Fras. 132
  Geor. 137
  Geor. W. 100,
109,121
  George 64,171
  George W. 10,23,
59,194

SMITH
  Hening T. 124
  James 12,47,48,
59,64,71,73,88,89,
101,114,124,152,
189
  James C. 41,53,
54,152
  Jeremiah 37
  John 143,164,172,
174
  Jos. 71
  Joseph 16,86
  Lassiter 166
  Lavina 16
  Lavinia 86,91
  Lemuel 192
  Nathan 17,22,24,
47,53,86,111
  Richard 23,39,45,
50,130,138,140,146
  Richd. 47
  Riddick 71,182
  Ro. R. 156
  Robert 6,34,48
  Robert R. 42
  Robt. 4,107,135
  Sarah 138
  Thomas 23,63,
130,154,193,194
  Thos. 143,163
  Wash. 109
  Washington 169
  Zac 128
SPAIGHT (*See
also* **SPEIGHT**)
  John 20
SPAKMAN
  John 177
SPARKMAN
  D. 29
  Demcy 100,127,
135
  Dempsey 15,17,
22-24,39,44,48,49,
55,57,64,186,187,
  Dempsey 190
  Dempsy 165,171
  Demsey 30,34,36,
72,74,104,105,137
  Demsy 140,142,
154
  John 29,34,37,60,
80,82,93,102,104,

SPARKMAN
  John 109,150,164,
165,175,190
  Mills 15,20,21,45,
50,64,114,137,141,
154,155,170-174,
190
SPEED
  R. K. 146
  Rufus K. 158,178
SPEIGHT (*See
also* **SPAIGHT**)
  H. 37,70
  Henry 15,17,73
  Isaac 82,83,125,
160,164,186
  Jacob 142
  Jno. 74,118
  John 3,15,21,37,
61,70,73-75,108,
114,117,159
  Jos. 122,145,152
  Joseph 88,162
  Noah 17
  Sophia 95,128,
157
  Susan 157
  Susan A. 95,128
  Westly W. 108
SPEIGHTS
  Charity 46,62
  Henry 3,11,13,49
  John 13,53
  Joseph 48
  Thomas 13
SPIGHT
  Westley W. 163
SPIVEEY
  Henry 92
SPIVEY
  A. 147
  Ab. 109,130,
138,139
  Abm. 162,172,
173
  Abraham 45,90,
91
  Abram 1,50,125
  Abs. 154
  Henry 39,54,106,
133,137
  Henry S. 163
  Moses 45,96,97,
154

SPIVEY
Seth 45,50,53,164
Thomas 37
Thomas D. 7
Timo. 109,141
Timothy 15,37,42
Westly 98
William 74
Wm. 124
STAFFORD
___ 57,143
Isaac F. 68,109, 111
STALLING
Whitmel 157
STALLINGS (See also **SALLINGS**)
Edward 29
Nancey 191
Shadrack 191
Simon 4,163,173, 174
Thomas W. 173
Thos. W. 164,180
W. 66
Whit. 138
Whitl. 40,51,52,57, 60,165
Whitmel 2,9,158, 159,166,168,169,177
Whitmell 1-3,16, 22,31,51,53,55,57
Whitmll 27
STALLINS
___ 128
Henry 100,133
Peggy 100
Simon 121,122
T. W. 121
Thos. W. 124,145
Whit. 78,88,89,91, 93,99,107-110,112, 121,125,126,130,150
Whitmil 79,110, 112,122
STEADMAN
Wm. W. 80
STEADMON
William W. 71
STEDMAN
___ 186
Will W. 87,106
William W. 15,27, 32,44,62

STEDMAN
Wm. 98
Wm. W. 97,128, 129,132,135,144, 150,160
STOKES
Montfort 1
SUMN
James 92
SUMNER
Ann 163
Ben. 15
Benj. 71,87
Benjamin 4,15,50
Benjn. 120
Charles E. 6,15,57
Chas. 127
Chs. E. 11,55
Eliza. 96,116,122, 124,153,161
Elizabeth 57,168
James 15,45,92, 102,132
Jethero 163
Jethro 16,24,32, 56,58,68,87,91,108, 120,122,153
Jno. V. 120
John V. 35,54
Levey 127
Levi 15,37,72,141
Martha R. 11
Mary 57,96,161, 168
SUTTON
Caroline 72,129
Caroline M. 156
Geo. 72
Geor. 134
Mary 72,129
SWAIN
David S. 50
SWEAT
Elizabeth 190
Henry 165
Jane 190
Sally 165
William 165

T

TAEELOR
Kedar 172

TAYLOR
David 107,157, 190
Edward 107,157
Fruizy 122
Fruzy 18,108
John 41,132,164
Kedar 29,45,114, 155,164,172-174
Martha 93
Mary 98,108,110, 112,126
Nathaniel 124
Nathl. 53,98
Pleasant 49
Robert 4,18,107, 129,157,190
Will 111
William 163
TEABOUT
Jethro 19,145
Seth 58
TEBAULT
Jethro 47
THOMPSON
Thomas 82
THORENTON
Jamimay 163
TOOLEY
Milley 19
TRAVIS
Peter 149
TREVATHAN
Henry 168
James 168
TROTMAN
___ 174
Drew 12,56,93, 183,185
Elisha 51
Ezekiel 44
Jasper 37,107
Moses 55,95,164
Phereba 44
Riddick 5,7,12,34, 44,173,191
TROTMON
Drew 127
Ezekiel 98,127
Jasper 80
Quinton H. 132, 135
Riddick 101,122
Timo. 123,145

TWINE
Christian 169
Tho. 66
Thomas 2,5,23, 24,41,65,67,80,91, 92,170,189
Thos. 147,157, 158

U

UMPHLET (See also **HUMPHLET**)
___ 173
Abel 174
Able 174
Charney 78,83
Charny 82,146
David 37,63,81, 82,83,96,147
Elisha 59,66,78, 80,83,135,156
John 99,147
William 83,88
Wm. 83
UMPHLETT
David 20
UMPLET
Charny 148
USHER
Barnabas 10

V

VALENTINE
___ 70
VAN
Dempsey 162
VANN
___ 4
Charles 58,159
Demcey 93
Demcy 92,125
Dempsey 60,164
Demsey 13,67,74, 90,135
John 86,98

W

WADES
Nicholas 37

WALKER
Jack 109
John 28,166
WALLACE
James 106
Miles 106
Penina 106
Sarah 106
WALTERS (*See also* **WATERS**)
Charles 49
Jos. G. 125
Lewis 39,47
Marey 125
S. 61
Simon 23,29,34, 38,49,50,58,59,61, 63-65,71,77,100, 101,112,114,116, 121,125,131,137, 142,143,150,171
Sinon 49
WALTON
Asa 93,157,158, 166,191
B. 126,146,148
Bembery 119
Bembry 120
Bembury 118
Benbury 15,21,26, 30,33,46,51,57,76, 99,104,115,126,131, 143,146,162
Daniel 93,157
Elisha 13,32,33,40, 185
Henry 3,12,27,36, 55,56,93,122,127, 153
Holloday 36,44,62, 63
J. 33,40
Jesse 12,24,52,54, 56,92
Jno. 15,30,35,119
John 8,12-15,20, 22,27,30,31,33,34, 36,42,43,46,48,51, 54,55,57,60,61,69, 71,95,99,101,103, 104,105,109,116, 126,129,131,139, 149,154,155,157, 159,162,164,166,

WALTON
167,168,172,180, 185,189,193
Joseph G. 43,58, 96,156
Lucy 20
Martha 127
Mary 12,36,56,93, 153
Mary Ann 43,58, 96,156
Sarah 99
Thomas 37,89,137
Timo. 76,78,100, 111,123,126,142, 148,149
Timothy 7,11,13, 23,35,41,42,51,65, 78,118-120,165, 168,176,187,192
Timothy, Jr. 37
Timothy, Sr. 43
Treasey 80
W. 40
Will 115
William 1,10,11, 15,20,23,31,52,57, 65,191
Willis 93,158, 166,172-174
Wm. 3,9,11,52, 59,100
WARD
Daniel 52
Daniel S. 111,173
Lamuel 33
Nathan 29,33,34, 40,45,50,52,98,151, 192,194
Nathan Owen 52
Timo. 72
WATERS (*See also* **WALTERS**)
WATERS (*See also* **WALTERS**)
Simon 119
WATHAN
Henry T. 71
Wm. T. 160,161
WATKINS
Nathl. 76
WATSON
Sarah 67

WEBB
___ 75
WELCH
B. F. 151
WESTON
___ 86
WHITE
Jeremiah 1,102
Jesse 191
John 191
Jonathan 45
Thomas 130
William 59,81
Wm. 145
WIATT (*See also* **WYATT,WYOOT**)
Jesse 185
WIGGINS
___ 22,131
Asa 184,185
Eliza. 121
Elizabeth 88
James 5,48,152
Jesse 6,16,23,32, 42,64,88,100,102, 115,116,118,119, 121,123,124,128, 133,135,145,149, 151
Jesse, Jr. 173
Jno. 145
Johm 73
John 4,16,32,41, 44,46,47,70,72,74, 75,82,94,95,99,107, 132,161,162,164, 185,193
Martha 121
Marthal 88
Prisscilla 46
Prissilla 94
W. W. 94
WILKINS
Moses 125
WILLEY (*See also* **WILLIEY,WILLY**)
H. 61,62
Henry 52,62,70, 73,74,101,106,112, 116,119,120,123,
WILLEY
Henry 133,140, 143,150,155,165, 166,176,191,193

WILLEY
Henry G. 155
Hillery 119
Hillory 22,39,48, 59,60,72,143
Jethero 173,191
Jethro 17,25,42, 44,49,67,69,74,82, 83,89,99,103,109, 119,130,133,134, 138,139,141
Jno. 95,193
John 8,15,19,31, 36,44,47,53,58,65, 94,101,123,133, 144,150,154,156, 157,160,165,167, 183,186,188
WILLIAM
Henry 165
Mary 12
WILLIAMS
Allen 35,114
Arthur 12,49,90, 124
Benj. 114
Benjn. 103
C. 74
Charity 50
Charles 1,27,37, 70,79
Corda 128,157
Cordey 95
Daniel 15,21,33, 36,40,42,52,54,86, 98,100,109,116, 120,124,130,141, 143,152,165,191
Danil 155
Danl. 143
Demsey 59
Enoch 39
Halon 5,49
Hardy 15,89,146, 165,179
Hasety 147
Henery G. 171
Henry G. 33,48, 49,59,64,71,88,96, 101,114,122,147, 152
Isaac 39,68,70,73, 93,105,133
J. 146

WILLIAMS
 Jainy 75
 James 7,19,25,29, 37,59,66,82,125, 131,138,140-143, 177
 James, Jr. 37,81
 James, Sr. 58
 John 39,99,143, 193,194
 Jon. 64,143,147
 Jona. 37
 Jonathan 8,12,29, 32,37,42,52,59,62, 64,68,90,93,106, 123,127,165
 Jonothan 179,186, 190
 Lavina 35
 Lavinia 154
 M. 74
 Margaret 79
 Martha 35
 Mary 5,49,58,90, 95,123,124,157
 May 128
 Michael 141,145
 Milley 58
 Mourning 101
 Nancy 154
 Prudence 32,63
 Robert 19,35
 Sally 35
 Saml. 29
WILLIEY (See also **WILLEY**)
 Henery 121
WILLY
 Henry 17,155
 Hillory 3,6,8
 Jet 155
 Jethero 159
 Jethro 14,109,137, 138
 John 2,3,9,10,11, 19,47,134,148,159,
 John 161,183
WILSON
 Jesse 110
 Robert 1,36
 Robt. 102,132
WOLFREY
 Susan 19
WOOD

WOOD
 ___ 17,75,136, 172,175
 Edward 11
 James 11
 Wm. 11
WOODARD
 James 164
WOODORD
 James 164
WOODWARD
 James 115,144,145
WORRELL
 Eli 7,9,11,55,76,81, 94,99,117,122,123 152,191,193,194
 John 59,76,81,102, 191
WYATT (See also **WIATT,WYOOT**)
 Jesse 111
WYNN
 ___ 34,160
WYNNS
 ___ 74,100,143, 172
 Benj. 138
 Benjn. 130
 James D. 4
 William B. 83
 Wm. B. 163
WYOOT
 Jesse 37

X

None

Y

YATES
 Rachel 115

Z

None

INCOMPLETE NAMES

___
 Lewis G. 132

MISCELLANEOUS INDEX

APPRENTICES
BAGLEY
  John 75
  Luke 75,118
BLANCHARD
  Josiah 34
BONNER
  Abram 159
BROWN
  Willie 69
BUTLER
  Thomas 75
CORBAL
  Anaca 159
CORBELL
  Ainah 159
CORBIN
  William 166
CROSS
  Richard 188
  Washington 158
DILDAY
  Jacob 148
EASON
  Hillory 34
  James 69
EURE
  Martha 165
  Whitmel 188
GOMER
  Thomas 167
GREEN
  William 126
HOWELL
  Edward 75
HUDGINS
  John 142
HUNTER
  Asa 118,136,166
  James 136
JENKINS
  James 158
JONES
  Charles 57
  Holloday 69
  Kedar 69
  Matthew 50
  Wright 159
KNIGHT
  Miles 118
LANG
  Emeline 75
LAWRENCE

APPRENTICES
LAWRENCE
  Starkey 188
MORGAN
  Wm. 142
PARKER
  James 149
PHELPS
  Gideon 74
  Henry 131
  Wm. 159
POLSON
  John 34
PRICE
  Thompson 75
  William 185
REED
  Alfred 158
  Augustus 101,126
  Elisha 75,95
  Jethro 101,126
RELPH
  William 69
ROBINS
  Henry 30
SPEIGHT
  Henry 17
SPEIGHTS
  Timothy 50
SWEAT
  Elizabeth 190
  Jane 190
  Sally 165
  William 165
TAYLOR
  John 95
  Miles 184
UMPHLET
  Abram 69
WALKER
  Redman 132
WILLIAMS
  John 39

REDMON 126
ATTORNEY
(States)
  SUMNER
    Benjamin 4
CLERK & MASTER
  PUGH

CLERK & MASTER
  PUGH
    Wm. E. 98,134
CLERK OF COURT
  BAKER
    Lawrence 10
  DAUGHTRY
    W. G. 161,174,185,190,194
    Wm. G. 150
  GILLIAM
    H. (Dep.) 97,106,132,144,150,186
    Henry 135
    Henry (Dep.) 71
    Henry (Sup.) 95,98,135,149
  STEADMON
    William W. 71
  STEDMAN
    Will W. 106
    Wm. 98
    Wm. W. 97,129,132,135,144,150
  SUMNER
    Jethro 24,68
COMPANIES
  STAFFORD
    Isaac F. & 109
  WESTON, HERON & 86
    Winton Ferry 85
CONSTABLES
  BOND
    James 57
  BRIGG
    Miles 159
  BRIGGS
    Miles 25,67,125
  CLEAVES
    Leml. 67,99
    Lemuel 17
  COWPER
    Wm. 25
  FREEMAN
    James T. 25,67,102
  HOWELL
    Miles 17,61,100
  LASSITER

CONSTABLES
  LASSITER
    Rubin 126
  LEWIS
    John 95
  NORFLEET
    John R. 25
  PARKER
    David 67,95
    Jno. F. 93
    John 57
  POWELL
    William 95
    William W. 4,47
    Wm. W. 123
  RIDDICK
    James C. 25,67,105
    Jet. H. 29
    Jethro H. 17,78,99,103,142,158
    John 121
    Thomas E. 77
    Thos. E. 116
  ROUNTREE
    Simmonds 67,158
    Simmons 25,123
    Simnons 79
  SAUNDERS
    John 126
  SAVAGE
    James 39
    James M. 77
    William H. 53
  SPARKMAN
    D. 29
    Dempsey 17
  WILLEY
    Jethro 25,67,99
CORONER
  RIDDICK
    Lassiter 78,95,102,131,135,149,184
COUNTY REGISTER
  WALTON
    John 105,168
SOLICITOR
  JONES
    Thomas F. 193

COUNTY SOLICITOR
PUGH
William E. 73, 109
Wm. E. 138,165, 193
SUMNER
Benj. 71

SURVEYOR
BARNES
J. 58,61,62
Jethro 38,59
SMITH
Allan 136
Allen 139,176
WILLIAMS
Isaac 38,39,68

TRUSTEE
RIDDICK
Nathan 27,77, 105,139,171

COURT HOUSE BUILDING & MAINTENANCE
24,79,112,131,143, 149,160,165,169, 180,186
Rules 169

DISEASES
Small Pox 177,178

GOVERNOR
STOKES
Montfort 1
SWAIN
David S. 50

NEWSPAPERS
Edenton Gazette 165
Edenton Misselany 79

POOR HOUSE
22,34,66,72,110

RANGER
HUDGINS
Jesse 53

SHERIFF
RIDDICK
James R. 15,24, 31,32,35,49,72,101, 102,106,113,115, 141,142

SHERIFF
RIDDICK
Jas. R. 109,169, 175,181
Jethro H. 142
Lass. (Dep.) 111
Lassiter 98,142
SUMNER
John V. 35,54

WAR
Revolutionary 106

LOCATION INDEX

BRANCH
Flat 176
S. Hall 15
SC. Hall 45
Scrach Hall 166,171
Snake 30,90,160,180
White Oak 43,88,89, 137

BRIDGE
BENNETTs Creek 147, 187
COLEs Creek 184
Creek 143
a Cross Mrs. HARVEYs Mill Race 104
HACKLEY Swamp 119
near John WALTON's 30

CAUSEWAY/CROSS WAY
Long 92
Winton 17,25,136,175
Winton Ferrey 99
WYNNS 172

CHURCH
Lebanon 13

COMMUNITY (*See also* **TOWN**)
Mintonsville 131,137
Muddy Cross 10
Sandy Cross 123
Sunsbury 39

COUNTY
Gates 1,4,14-16,22,28,30, 31,34,36,38,39,44,46,52,58, 60-62,71,75,77,87,88,98, 106,109,113,121,132,137, 140,143,144,150,154,161, 166,175,176,186,193
Nansemond, VA 17

CREEK
BARNES 53,96
BENNETTs 28,110,147, 187
COLEs 184
DUKEs 137
HARRELLs 148
Saram 137
Sarum 43,75,89

CROSSROADS
BENTONs 53

FERRY
MANEY's 176
Winton 85,99
WYNNS 34,100,143,160

FIELD
WOODs old 17,75,136,172
WOODs old mill Field 175

FORK
DUKEs 124

FRYING PAN 120

GROVE
Piney 4

HILL
Blake BAKERs 143
WIGGINS 131

ISLAND
Fort 47

LANDING
BONDs 190
PARKER's 35
Saram Creek 137
Sarum Creek 43,89

LANE
A. W. PARKERs 76
Ab. W. PARKERs 75
Abraham PARKERs 48
Jno. B. BAKERs 136

LINE
Va./Virginia 4,143,176,187

MARSH
White 47,53

MEETING HOUSE
HARRELLs 48,75,76
KITTRELLs 77,142,147

MILL
HARVEYs 4,104,149,137, 176
HUNTERs 23,24,65,72,92, 100,101,131,137,138,142, 166,170,187
LEEs 4
NORFLEETs ___ 172
Kinchen 147
POWELLs 187

NECK
Indian 148

PATH
leading from Simon WALTERS to the main road 58
MINGO 89,137,147,187
MINGO's 30

PLACE
BRIGGS 4

PLANTATION
George COSTEN 14
HUDGINS 137

POCOSON
White Pot 131

POOR HOUSE
22,34,66,102

QUARTER
Geor. COSTONs 117

ROAD
Honey Pot 137,142
Indian Neck, old 148
Middle Swamp 193
Perquimans 25
Piney Woods 193
Robert ROGERSes 4
White Marsh 53
WYNNS Ferry 160

SHOP
HASLET 166
HASLETTs 23
POWELLs 102,137

SQUARE
Public 25

STATE
N. Carolina 44
North Carolina 1,16,30,38, 46,53,58,60-62,77,87,88,98, 113,121,132,144,150,161, 175,186
Tennessee 127
Va. 17,75,143
Via. 122
Virginia 53

STORE
GOODMANs, William, Jr. 23
MINTONs 47

SWAMP
Cow pen 106,172
Dismal 36
Folley 23-25,64,100,101, 131,137,142
Folly 137,166,170
HACKLEY 119
Honey Pot 22,77,101,142
Honey Pots 136
Honey pott 14
Juniper 76
Mddler 143
Middle 28,193
Oreapeak 68
s. H. 29

SWAMP
Somerton 33,70,73-75
Warrick 90,160
Warwick 30
Watery 72
Watrey 137
SWAMP
White Oak 107,147
Worrick 180
TAVERN
DAUGHTRY, Lawrence S. 68
TOWN
Edenton 57
Gates Court House 23
Gatesvill 148
Gatesville 1,10,16,17,25,
30,36,38,39,46,57,60,65,
68,71,77,78,88,94,98,100,
106,113,121,131,132,
136-138,140,144,150,161,
171,175,176,186

Old 47
Suffolk 75
Winton 17,25,99,136